Nico

CONFESSIONS: EROTICISM IN MEDIA

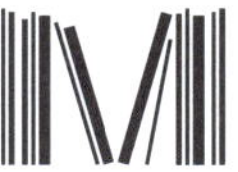

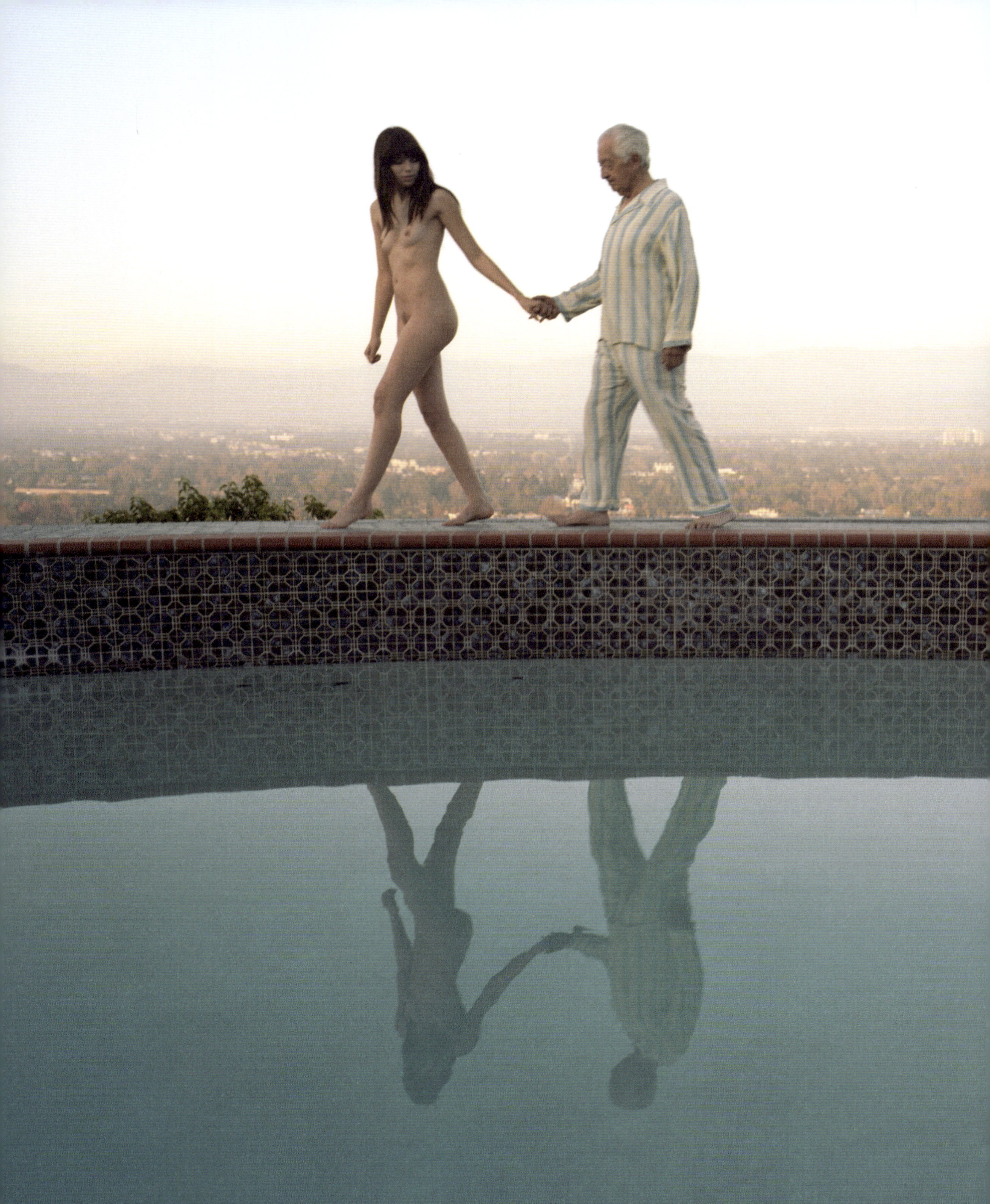

Dear readers, *Nico* is entering a new stage of maturity by shedding its magazine skin and transforming into a bookazine. The aim is to make even fewer compromises and take our dedication to marrying a beautiful object with relevant content to the next level.

In this issue entitled "Confessions", we look at the world of eroticism in media. Talking to the makers of ten erotic magazines, from Paris to New York, via Amsterdam and Copenhagen, we delve into what motivates their creative process and vision. Here the focus is not only on the content but particularly on the details that turn them into carefully crafted magazines, which range from fanzines (*Irène, Pantyhose*) to magazines that aimed at filling a gap in the market — think the now cult publications *Butt* and *GLU*.

We have also tried to set the topic against a historical canvas, talking to expert Samir "Mr. Magazine" Husni about the classic world of epic male magazines like *Playboy*.

As always, we seek new ways to titillate your senses, so we hope you will enjoy looking through our selection of ten erotic photography and illustration portfolios from talented artists that contrast different perspectives on sexuality and nudity.

The topic is vast and fascinating and we are happy to take you along for the ride.

Mike Koedinger
Editor in Chief & Creative Director

Angelina A. Rafii
Deputy Editor

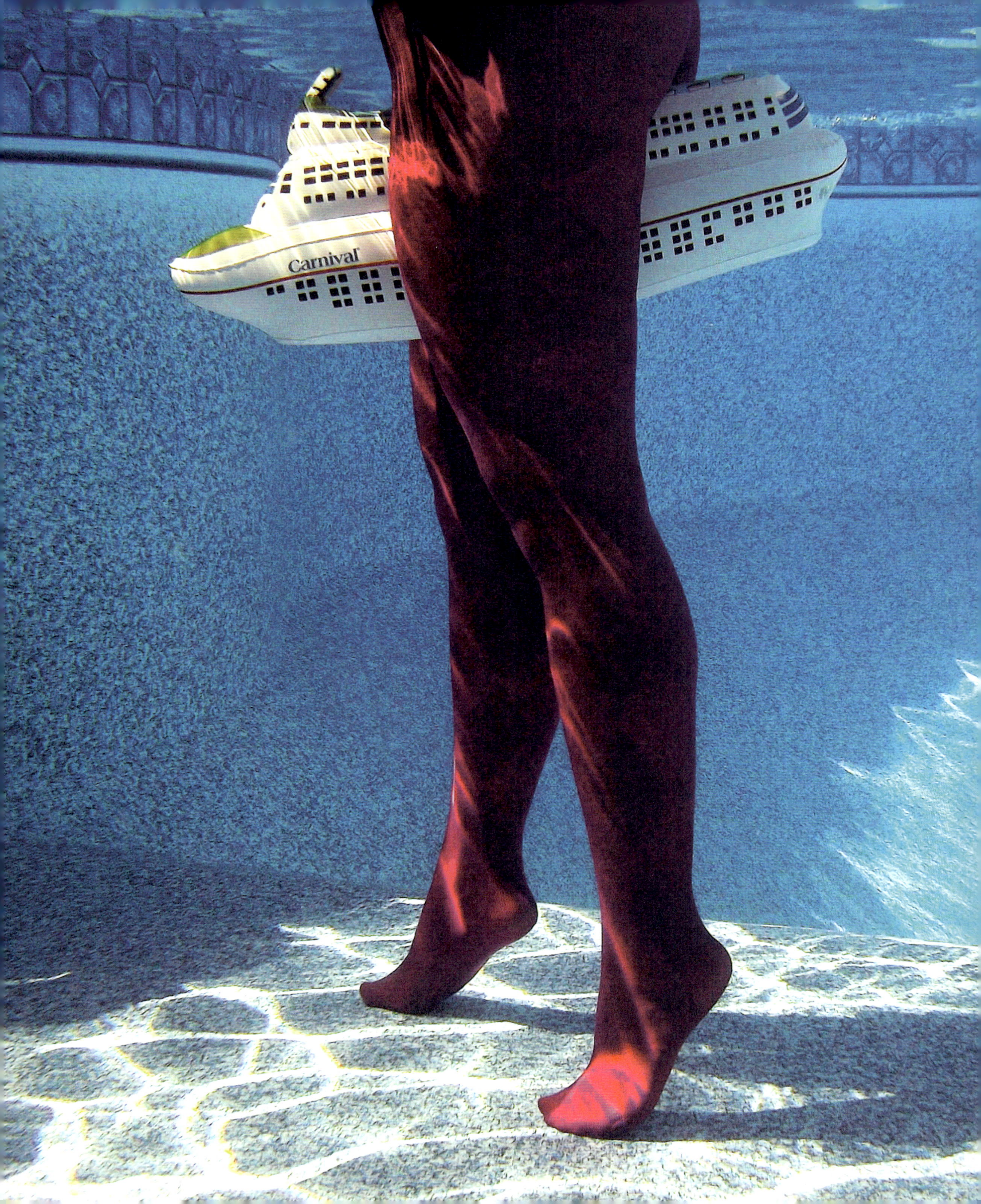
Carnival

Contents

Interviews

Pantyhose magazine by Howard Chu

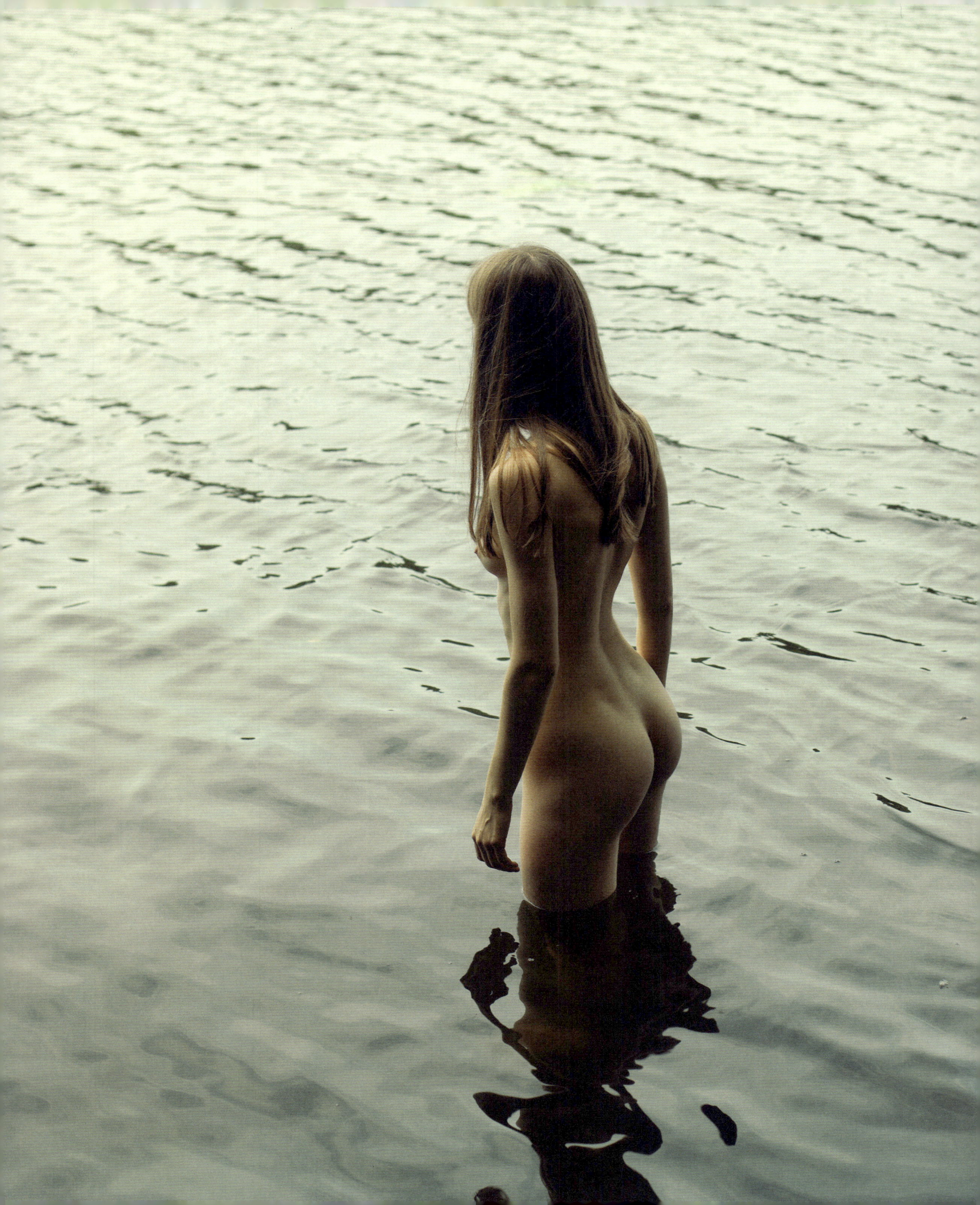

CONTENTS

Portfolios

By Angelina A. Rafii

Image by Hannes Caspar

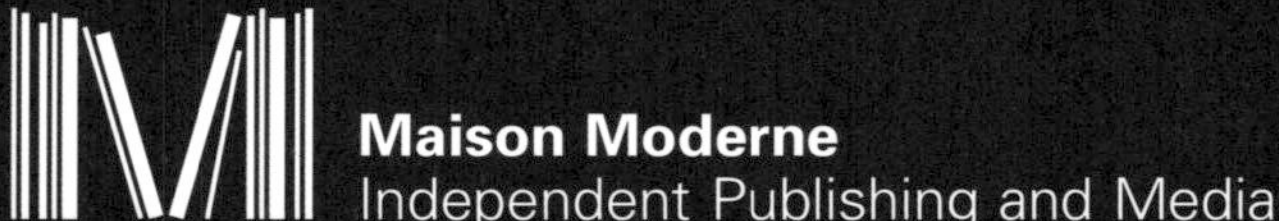

We inform, we entertain, we inspire.

We are **Maison Moderne** - Luxembourg's leading and award-winning media group.

We create magazines, books, digital content, events and broadcast TV.

We publish self-initiated projects and we create multi-channel,
branded content for clients.

Visit us on *www.maisonmoderne.lu*

We welcome submissions - please mail them to office@maisonmoderne.lu

Masthead

Founder, Editor in Chief & Creative Director:
Mike Koedinger
mike.koedinger@maisonmoderne.lu

Deputy Editor:
Angelina A. Rafii
afsi@nicomagazine.com

Art Director:
Maxime Pintadu

Interviews by
Sven Ehmann, Philippe Graff, Steven Gregor, Merel Kokhuis, Jeremy Leslie, Gintare Parluyte, Alice Pfeiffer, Angelina A. Rafii, and Victor Zabrockis.

Portrait photography by
Sébastien Agnetti, Andreas Larsson, Sandra Stein, Mads Teglers, and Tania Theodorou.

Production & editing:
Angelina A. Rafii

Layout produced by
Maison Moderne
www.maisonmoderne.lu

Published by Maison Moderne
www.maisonmoderne.lu

10, rue des Gaulois, L-1618 Luxembourg (Europe)
Phone: (+352) 29 66 28-1 | Fax: (+352) 26 18 74 77
Postal address: P.O. Box 728, L-2017 Luxembourg (Europe)

Worldwide distribution:
Gestalten.com
Pineapple Media

Worldwide subscriptions:
www.nicomagazine.com

Printed by Faber *(www.faber.lu)*
Cover paper: Planojet 300 g
Interior paper: Planojet 120 g

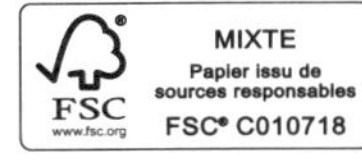

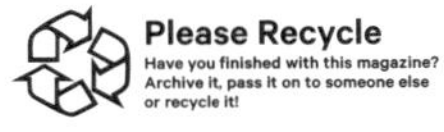

Isbn: 978-3-89955-438-0
© MM Publishing and Media S.A.
2012 Luxembourg (Europe)

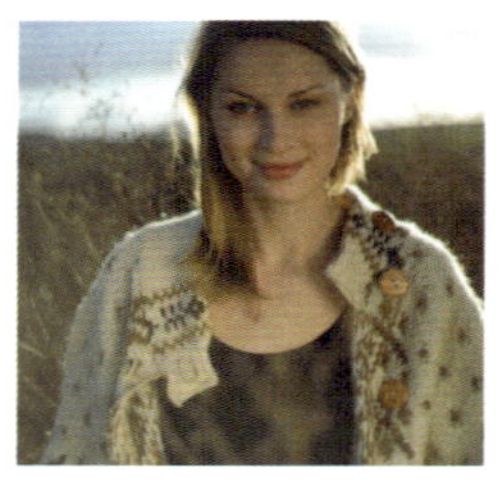

Gintare Parulyte

Living between Luxembourg and Berlin, Gintare pays her books and her expensive organic food with writing about things she loves, as well as acting in movies and plays that confront her with her ridiculous fears. Not at all an expert in pornographic matters but maybe one to be, she contributed to *Nico* by interviewing Elke Kuhlen, one of two cheerful editors of the duo *Jungsheft* and *Giddyheft*.

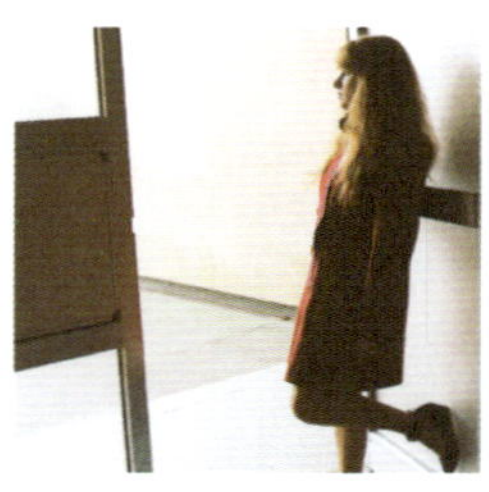

Sandra Stein

Sandra Stein is based in Brighton and Cologne as a freelance portrait photographer. With an extensive portfolio that began back in 1999 with well-known musicians; her internationally published work spans a multitude of both print and web media audiences. Work that you might recognize, and some you might not, can be viewed on : *www.sandra-stein*.de. Sandra photographed Elke Kuhlen, the creator of *Jungsheft & Giddyheft*.

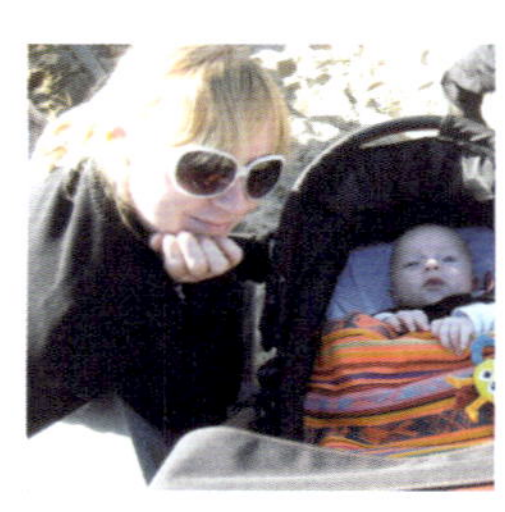

Merel Kokhuis

Merel Kokhuis is an Amsterdam-based freelance writer and editor. She works for several international (design) magazines including *Frame magazine* and many Dutch literary publishers. Her love for reading and writing is so big, she named her baby son Roman (Novel in Dutch). For *Nico* she had a chat with Jessica Gysel, the creator of *Girls like us* (*GLU*).

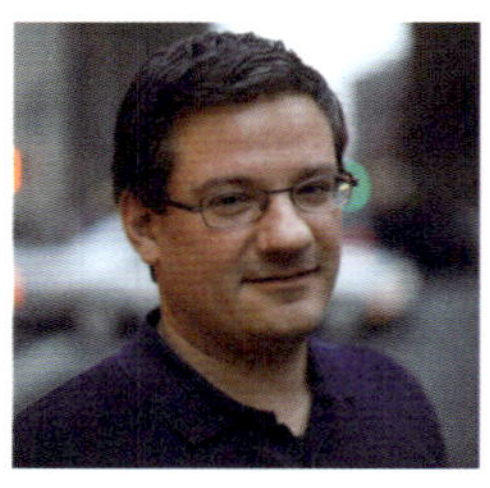

Sven Ehmann

Sven Ehmann is a creative director based in Berlin. He develops concepts and contents across all media with a focus on print, digital and environments. Since 2002 he has edited more than 30 publications for international art and design book publisher Gestalten, with a strong personal interest in editorial design, information graphics and contemporary visual culture. With the design studio Onlab he developed a redesign for Italian architectural magazine *Domus*. His personal projects include the publishing platform Etc Publications, which aims at promoting the idea of the designer as an author of serious contents. Sven lectures and gives workshops on a regular basis about innovation, concept development and visual storytelling. Beyond that he is a coffee snob and keeps dreaming about reinventing the newspaper. For *Nico*, Sven interviewed Jens Stolze editor of *S magazine*.

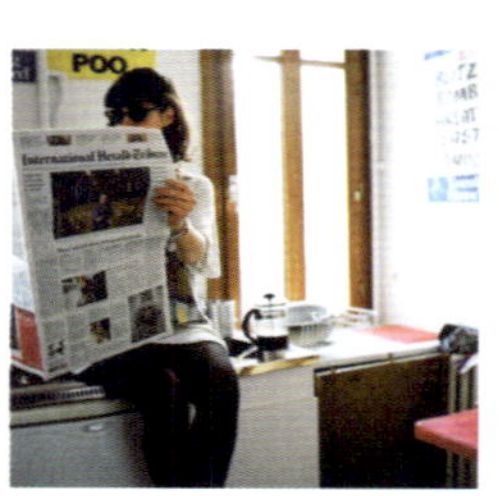

Alice Pfeiffer

Alice Pfeiffer is a Paris-based writer who contributes to a number of publications including *The New York Times*, *The International Herald Tribune*, *Dazed&Confused* and *Interview*. After completing a Masters degree in Gender Studies at the London School of Economics, and surviving a number of internships, she is now on a worldwide quest for anything slightly odd, tasteful or second-hand, which is why she is the perfect candidate to take a closer look at what Paris has to offer in terms of erotic magazines for *Nico*. Welcome to the unique worlds of *L'Imparfaite*, *Edwarda* and *Paradis*.
www.alicepfeiffer.com

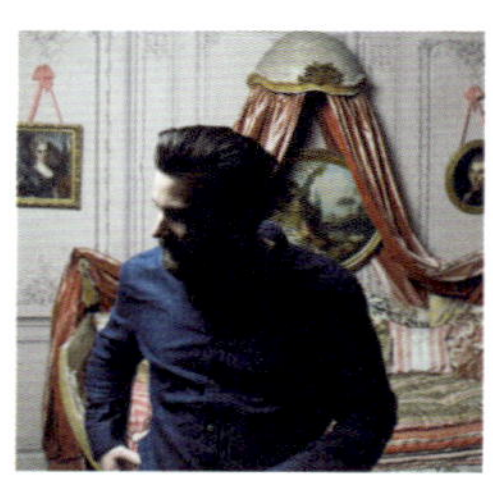

Sébastien Agnetti

Mark Ronson, Justice, Agyness Deyn, Juliette Lewis, Scarlett Johansson, John Malkovich, Serge Lutens, Riccardo Tisci, Michael Fassbender...not to be name dropping but these are just some of the faces Paris-based photographer Sébastien Agnetti has shot since he left his native Switzerland. His work can be seen in magazines such as *The Wire*, *Uomo Vogue*, *L'Officiel*, *Glamour*, *Spray*, *Exhibition*, *Lurve* and *Nico*, for which he photographed the creators of three erotic magazines. Sébastien's latest project was Yuksek's album cover.
Blog : *http://agnetti.tumblr.com*

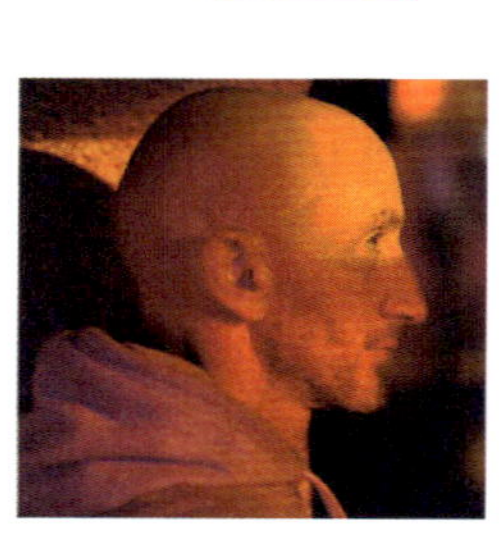

Philippe Graff

Philippe Graff was *Sportswear International*'s long-term correspondent in Paris as well as having worked as a freelance editor for many international publications in fashion, music and emerging subcultures. After being a collaborator for magazines such as German *Style* and French *Blast* he created the (then) underground lifestyle magazine *Spray*, for which he was the editor-in-chief for nearly five years before he became a regular contributor to *Nico*. Philippe currently splits his time between print and web media, while preparing a new magazine. In this edition he interviewed the girls behind *Irène* the erotic fanzine.

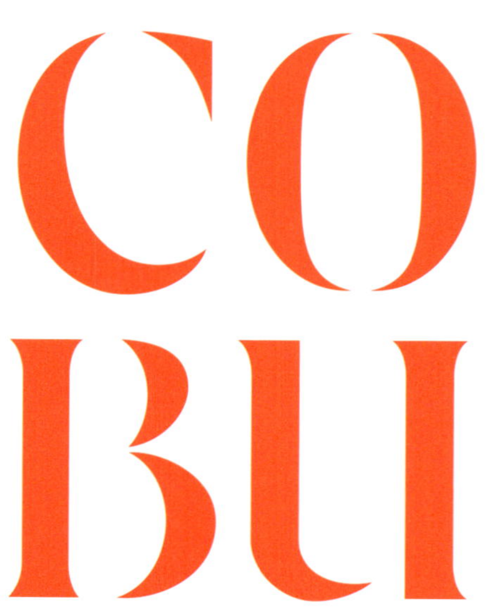

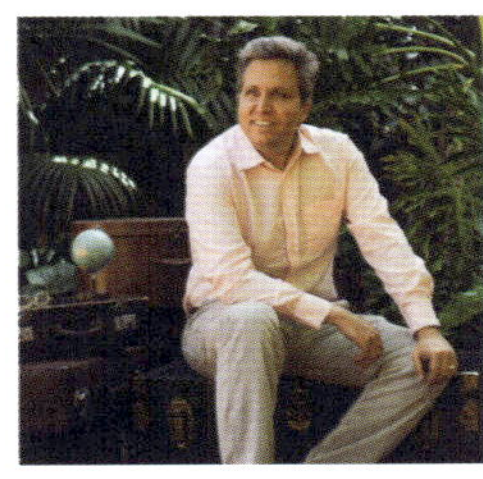

Victor Zabrockis

Greek-Brazilian Creative Director and Digital Expert Victor Zabrockis has been in love with art and sensuality since he was a precocious young man. Throughout his university years in Boston and later running a Digital Agency in Sao Paulo until 2003, he gathered enough experience and contacts to later open Barcelona´s first Pop/Street Art Collaborative work space and gallery Mercado, showcasing Gary Baseman, Megan Whitmarsh and many other European and international artists. Victor makes his living from his addiction to Digital, acting as a Strategic Internet and Technology Advisor to Corporations worldwide and running a personal project which helps talented entrepreneurs get their early stage tech Startups off the ground. Besides art and the Internet, his passions are wine, food and nature. His love is fully dedicated to both of his favorite women; his wife and daughter. For *Nico* he had a fascinating chat with *Pantyhose* creator Howard Chu.

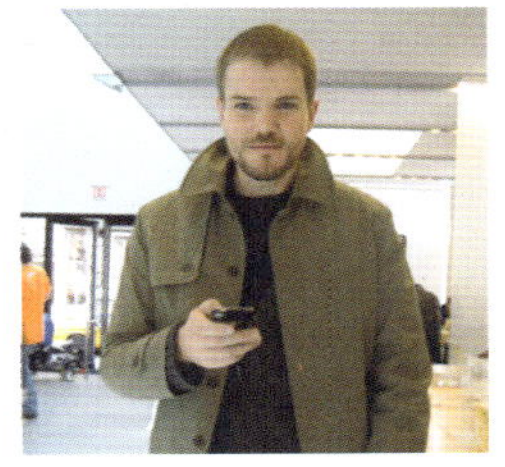

Steven Gregor

Steven is a London-based editorial designer and writer. Born in Australia, he moved to London in 2000. He currently works at Condé Nast, helping to design the award-winning iPad edition of *UK Wired*. A self-confessed mag-geek, Steven's favourite magazines are *Butt*, *Fantastic Man* and *the gentlewoman*. No surprise then, he welcomed the opportunity to speak with co-founders *Gert Jonkers* and *Jop van Bennekom* for this issue of *Nico*. *"I tried my best not to come over all fanboy during the interview,"* he says. *"Not sure I succeeded!"* Steven also publishes a regular fanzine for like-minded mag-geeks. Called *Gym Class*, the (somewhat) regular publication is available in selected European magazine and book stores… and soon as an iPad app via iTunes.

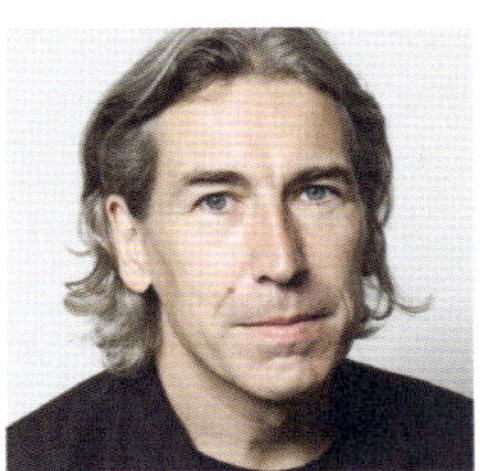

Jeremy Leslie

Jeremy is a passionate advocate for editorial design. When he's not designing magazines for print and iPad, he's writing, blogging and speaking about them. For *Nico*, he interviewed Danielle Leder, editor-in-chief of *Jacques magazine*. Read his blog at www.magCulture.com/blog.

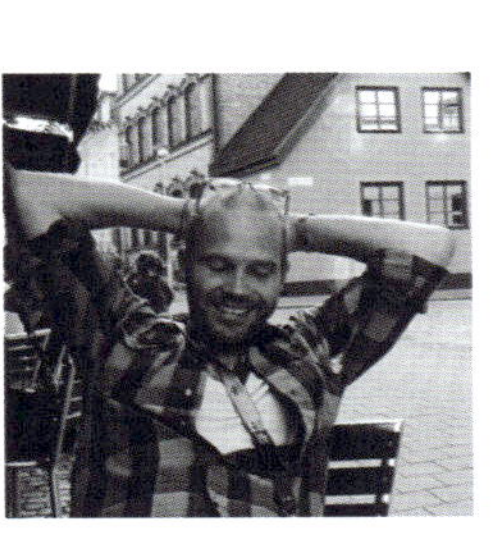

Mads teglers

Mads Teglers works have a common thematic approach, whether the images are fashion photographs, band pictures, or pure portraits. Stylistically he is close to the snapshot realism of fashion photography across the past 20 years. Glamorous, classical fashion photography with anti-realistic presentation of the model. Models are shot in everyday urban circumstances, outdoors or in private homes. The pictorial aesthetic is reminiscent of family snapshots without any ornamental light or digital post-production. Teglers' narrative is often intimate and personal. For *Nico* he shot Jens Stolze of *S magazine*. www.madsteglers.com

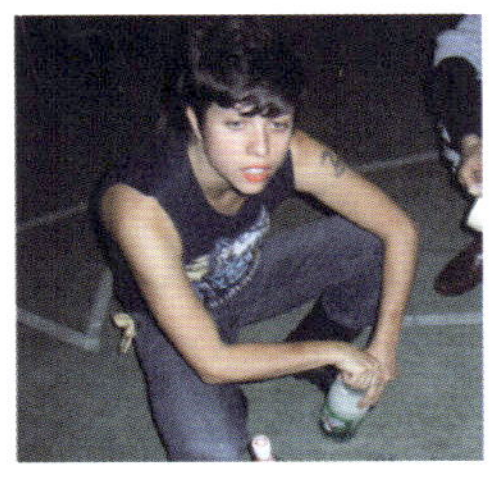

Tania Theodorou

Tania Theodorou was born in the south of Greece and studied English language and Literature in Athens. She later studied photography at The Gerrit Rietveld Academy of Arts in Amsterdam, where she currently lives and works. In this edition of *Nico* she shot Jessica Gysel, creator of *Girls Like Us* magazine. www.taniatheodorou.com

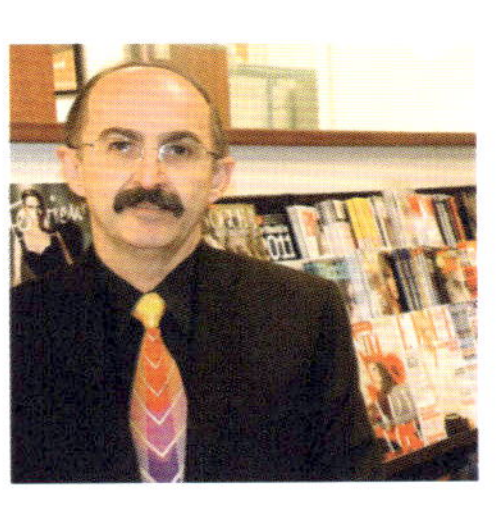

Samir Husni

Mr. Magazine™ is Samir A. Husni, Ph.D. who is the founder and director of the Magazine Innovation Center at the University of Mississippi's Meek School of Journalism and New Media. He is also Professor and Hederman Lecturer at the School of Journalism. As Mr. Magazine™ he engages in media consulting and research for the magazine media and publishing industry and edits the Mr. Magazine™ website and blog. Dr. Husni is the author of the annual *Samir Husni's Guide to New Magazines*, which is now in its 27th year. He is also the author of *Magazine Publishing in the 21st Century, Launch Your Own Magazine: A Guide for Succeeding in Today's Marketplace*, and *Selling Content: The Step-by-Step Art of Packaging Your Own Magazine*. He is also the co-author of *Design Your Own Magazine*. www.mrmagazine.com

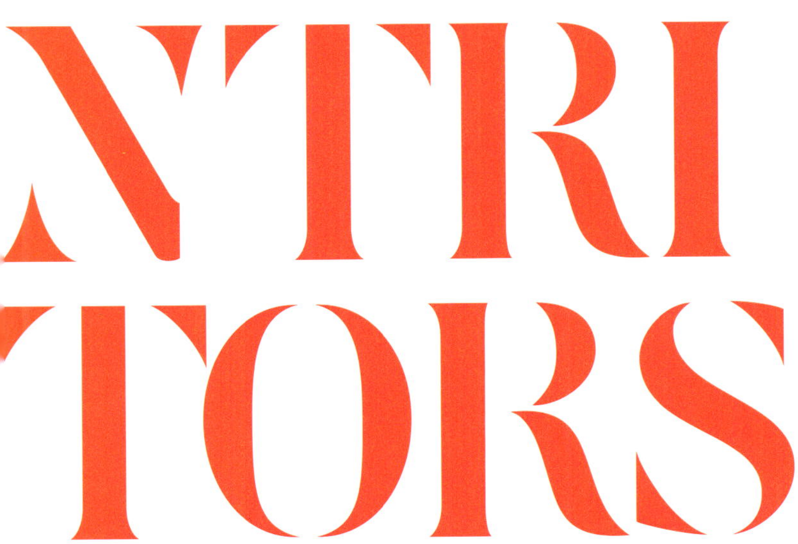

NTRI TORS

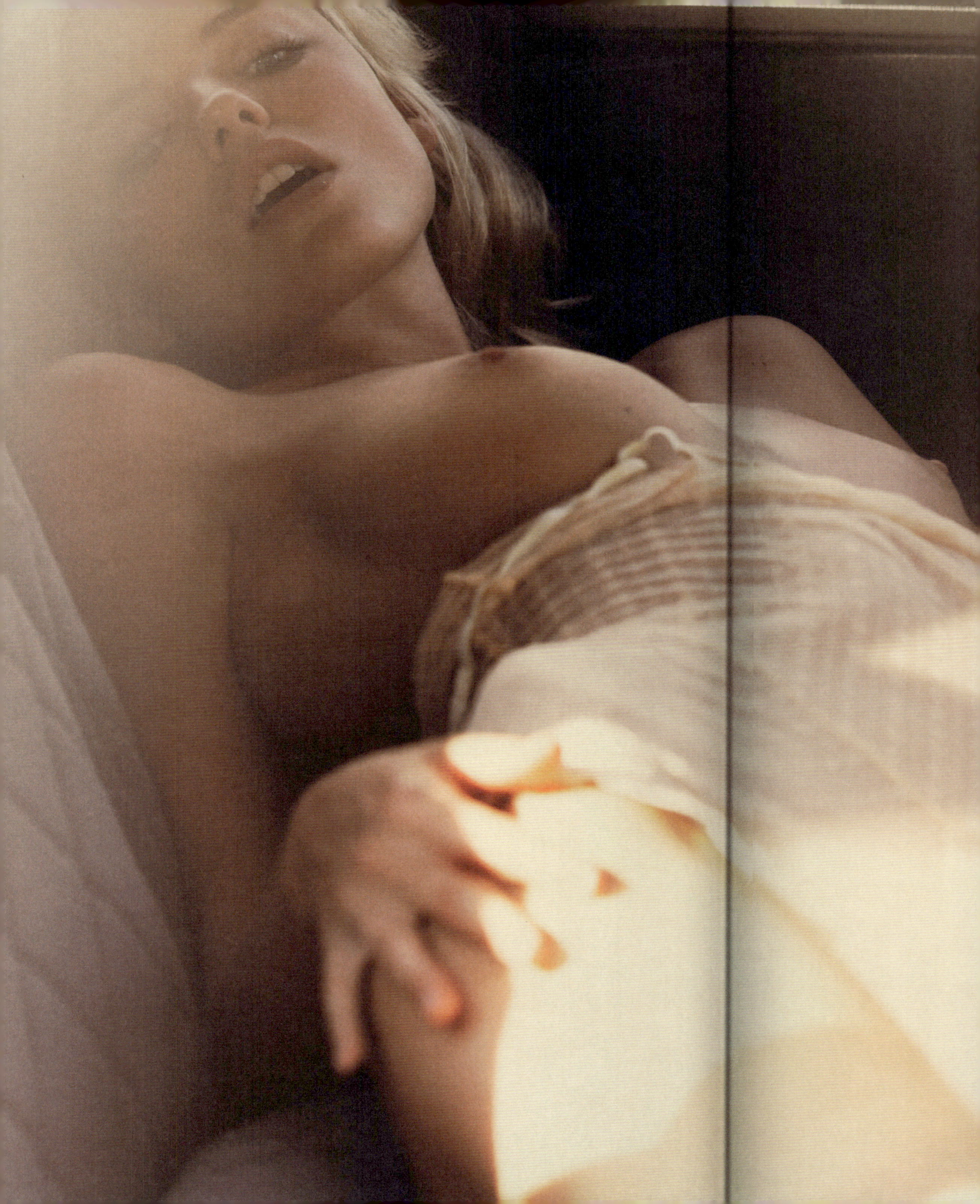

SEX, SCANDINAVIAN STYLE

The small world of well-edited, well-produced and well-printed erotic magazines is on the rise. While a major chunk of the porn industry went from the real world to the digital world and while there seem to be more naked than dressed up models in fashion and lifestyle media these days, a number of editors, designers, writers and photographers have chosen to produce a counterculture of often eclectic, mostly inspiring and always passionate erotic publications.

INTERVIEW BY SVEN EHMANN.
PORTRAIT BY MADS TEGLERS.

WWW.SMAGAZINE.COM

S magazine is one prime example.
It is special, smart, sensual, Scandinavian, ...
and all that makes it sexy. Founder and editor-
in-chief Jens Stolze - a photographer working
between Copenhagen and
New York - explains the who, how,
what and why.

"I WANTED S MAGAZINE TO BE AN OUTLET WITH CREATIVE FREEDOM FOR PHOTOGRAPHERS. A PLACE WHERE THEY COULD SHOW WHAT THEY ARE ACTUALLY CAPABLE OF DOING."

What was your favourite erotic magazine when you were a teenager? What made it special to you?

Back then there were many different magazines around. Mostly porn. My dad had a substantial collection of *Color Climax* and something called *Weekend Sex*. These magazines were hardcore. So yes, porn was influential to my youth. Later I discovered Helmut Newton and photography in general. I remember *The Face* being a great source of inspiration. The visual stimuli that erotic photography had on me since then also made it the subject for me to look for in my work as a fashion photographer later on.

When and how did you decide to start your own magazine? Did you know from the beginning that it would be what *S magazine* is now – a mix of erotic and lifestyle magazine or how did that concept idea take shape?

I wanted *S magazine* to be an outlet with creative freedom for photographers.

A place where they could show what they are actually capable of doing.

Very much inspired by directors like Larry Clark. I knew that our strength would be in visual art rather than being a traditional fashion magazine. In 2004 we started planning how and when to launch, and the first issue came out in May 2005.

You have been using terms such as sexy, styled, Scandinavian, sober, shameless, straightforward, swashbuckling, seafaring, soldering, soapy, sweaty, symbolic and storytelling to describe the character of *S magazine*. How about sensual, delicate, intimate? How did its content, profile and voice evolve over the issues?

As you can see all the words referring to us start with the letter S. This play, with the S as a symbol, came out of our first working title "Sexual" but instead of that we chose to only use the "S" as if all the S-words before belonged to us and our name as well.

The evolution came naturally. We were moving from being novices in the magazine field to creating and striving for something more meaningful to us. The features now play a big part in the magazine and they are something we work on a lot. People we feature become our friends and the editorials are still full of creative freedom. However, with digital photography also came a lack of talent. So we tend to spend a lot of time editing and we have many more people involved now.

What are the main editorial components of *S*?

Sex. Sex. Sex... I am kidding. We like to find celebrities who are fans of the magazine and to portray them.

} *p.19*

Jens Stolze shot by
Mads Teglers

}

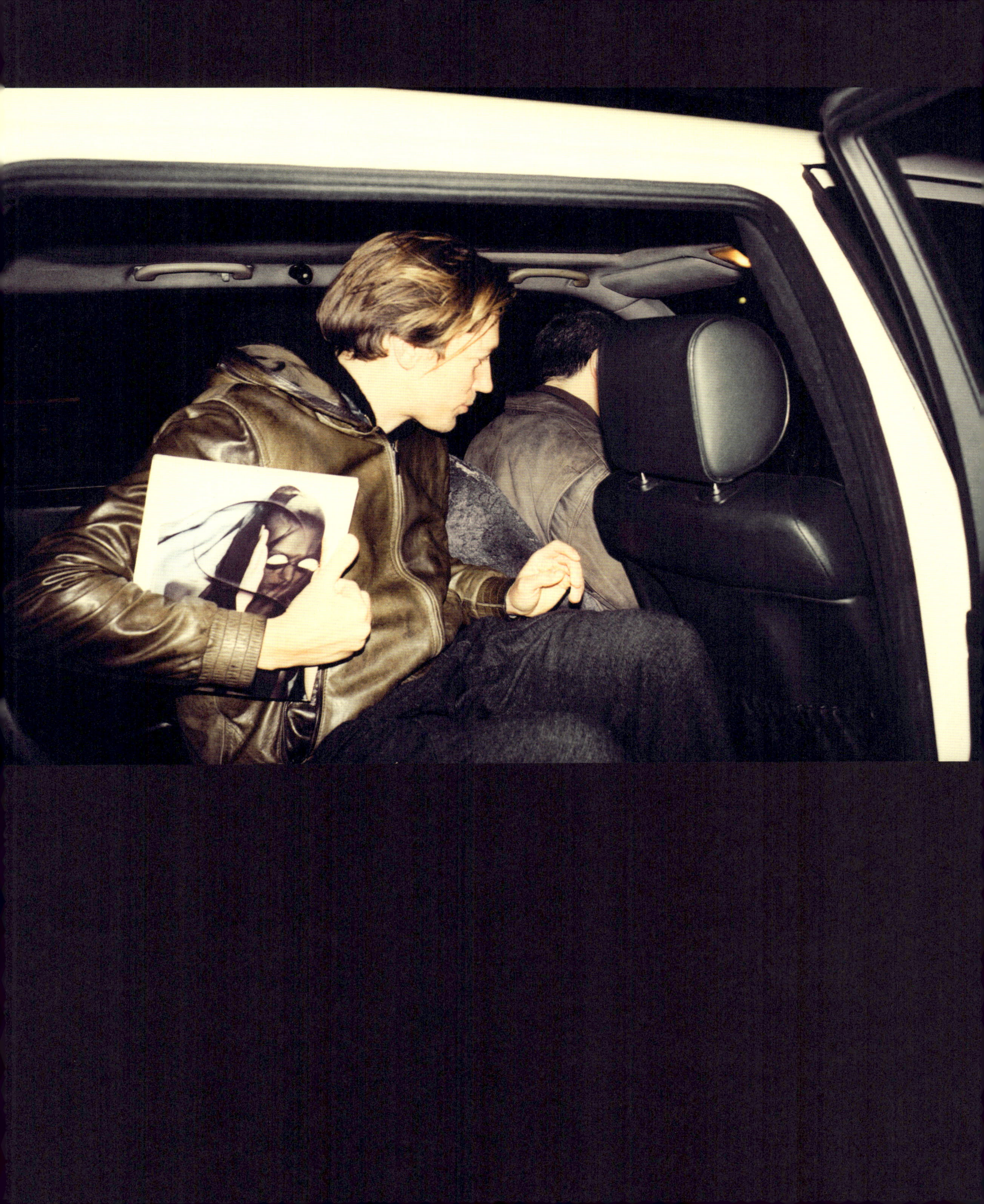

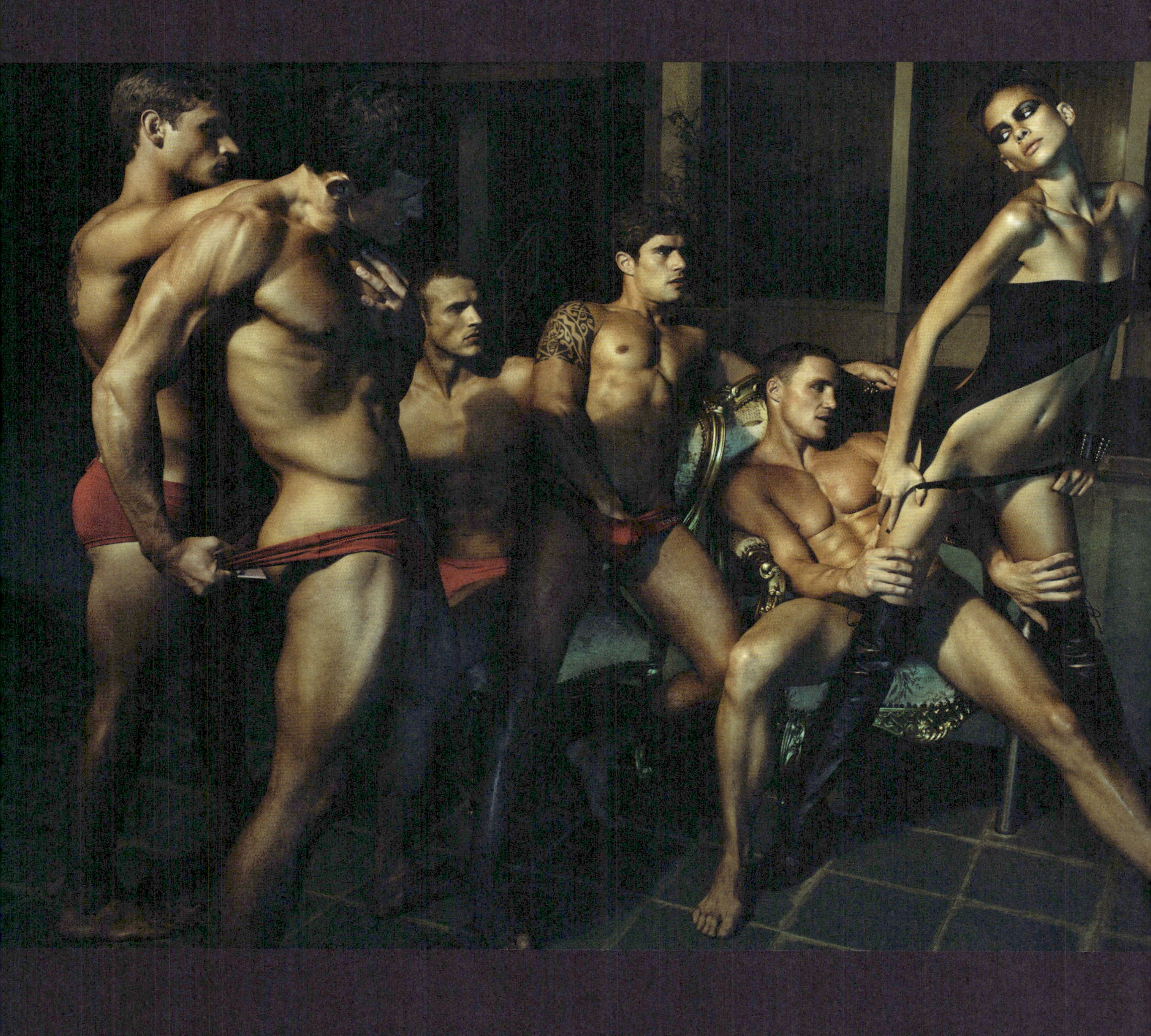

Always looking for a good mix of video artists, directors, musicians and great photography from new and established talent.

S is a very visual magazine. The style of photographers and the type of models chosen have a major impact on the profile of an erotic magazine. With these aspects in mind how would you describe the visual language of S magazine?

I think I would describe it as very saturated and colourful. S is for the visually orientated as music is for the auditory.

How are you using text?

The feature section consists of almost 100 pages of interviews, lots of text here. Else text is used for crediting the teams behind stories as well as clothes and accessories. We also play with text in the headlines.

There is a lot of sex, nakedness and erotic references in almost any popular media these days. At the same time there seems to be a new generation of highly aesthetic erotic magazines and websites, often based on personal projects. Could you describe your perspective on the development?

It's great! It takes us back to our natural state: Nudity.

How does this omnipresence of naked people, change what makes a picture truly erotic?

It is not the nudity or the part that you see straight away that makes a picture erotic, but exactly the opposite. What is left out is then left to our raw imagination and that is always better than facts of real life.

Does each issue of S have a particular subject or distinct idea? What were such ideas and how did you transfer them into the printed publication?

We have a subject that we use, but it is and will be up to the contributor to choose if they want to utilize it or not. Issue 6 for example was called "Verge" and almost any story matched this word. I think Asger Carlsen used it as an inspiration for his contribution. In issue 7 the subject was "Ajar" and we played with this word for the curator section by inviting Dactyl Foundation to present some of their artists. As if we were peeping into their gallery. We featured work by Neck Face and also Jason Dill.

You are a photographer. Please describe the relationship between your commercial work, personal projects and S.

The relation is that I get off with the stuff I have in my head by putting it into S. It is my personal outlet and I think it should also benefit others and become their personal playground as well. Many of my commercial clients have been inspired by this fact and many contributors have gained jobs after shooting for S as well.

Who else is the team behind S magazine?

The main team is Christina Chin (Creative Director), Mads Teglers (Photo Editor), Ferdinando Verderi (Art Director), Mazy Brujjerdi (Features), myself and many more bloggers and media people who we are working with.

What is your editorial meeting like? How do you discuss and decide on your content?

I decide everything. Just kidding. We talk forever about all the details. We discuss the contributors' work, whether it goes into the magazine or not, if stories fit our profile or if they do not. If we disagree we vote on it.

What are your criteria to separate a good from a bad story?

Show me a story and I will tell you. The fact is that it has to be personal, sexy and done in an aesthetic way. Professional. We are all fans of reality, not artificially, overly retouched images, but sometimes we can be deceived too.

What have been your favourite stories so far?

Bela Borsodi's contribution to issue 11. But there are so many that I love.

What are the stories you still want to do?

I have many more stories in my head, but beyond that I wish for more people to think outside the box and show the world through S what kind of art form photography is. Putting a flash on a camera is simply too easy. Storytelling is only hard when you consider yourself to be uninspired.

Are you mostly producing or reprinting (photo) stories?

We rarely reprint stuff that has been published elsewhere. It has occurred, unfortunately, but in general we are only looking for original material.

What are you and your team exploring anew about sex, eroticism, the body, fantasies, dreams, … from issue to issue?

We feel like a band on tour, I think. We all share the love for printed images and words. Regarding the sexual aspect it's about thinking from within and noticing if these pictures we are looking at are arousing somehow. It is gut feeling.

What separates erotic lifestyle from porn? Do these terms matter to you and your readers?

Porn to me is explicitness in a raw, unpolished — even dirty — universe. Penetration too. But then again if you show all this in the right context, done by the right people with skills and talent, it suddenly is aesthetic. I think this is the case because people who shoot porn are thinking from the animal perspective or from a perspective of making

} p.22

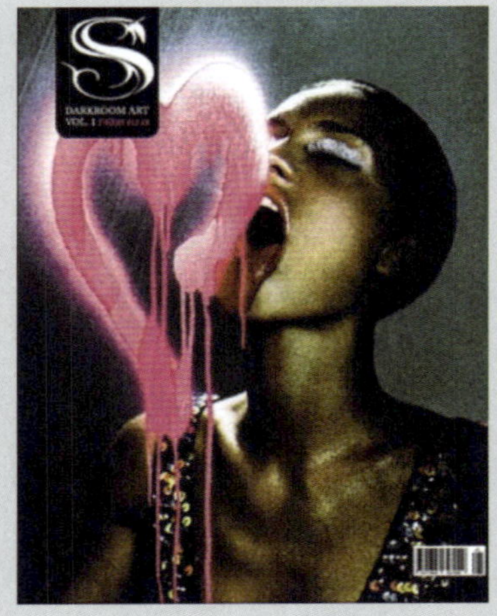

DARKROOM ART
VOL. 1

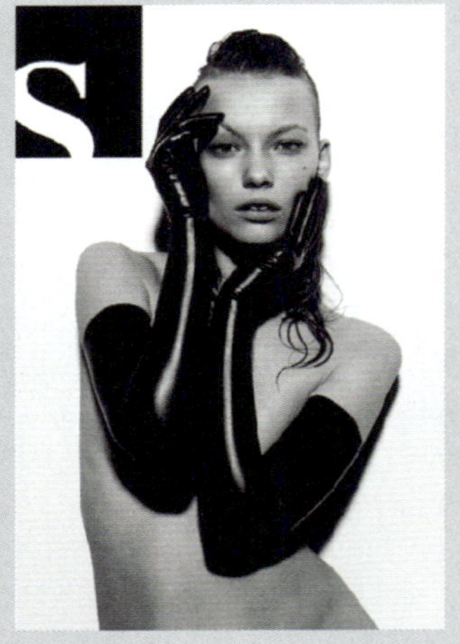

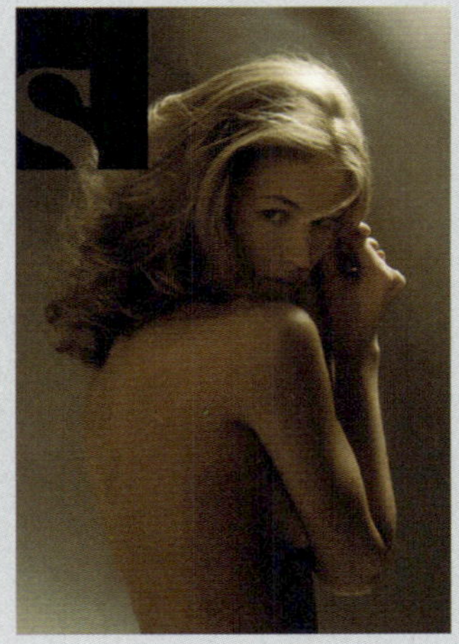

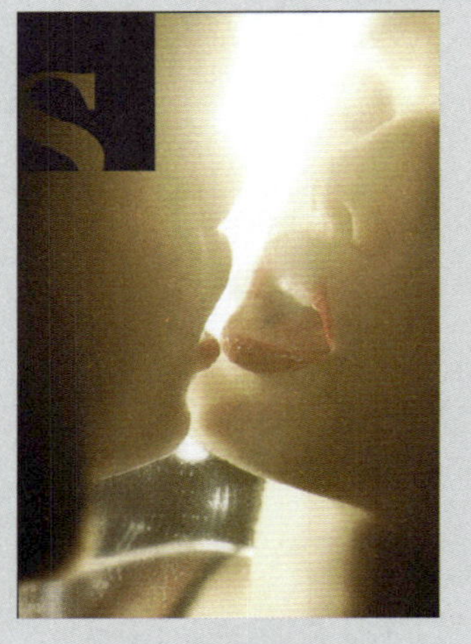

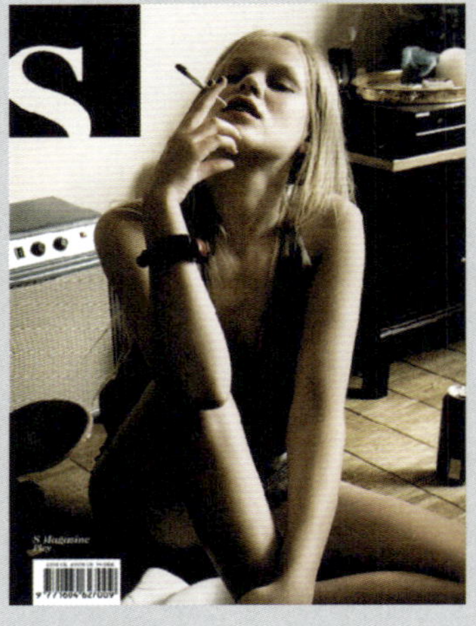

N Magazine
Sky

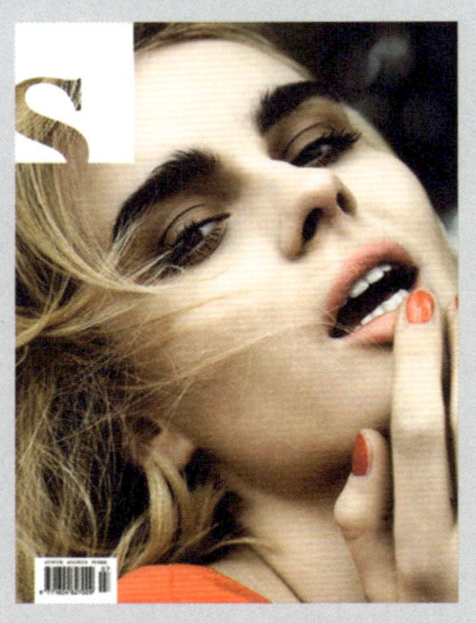

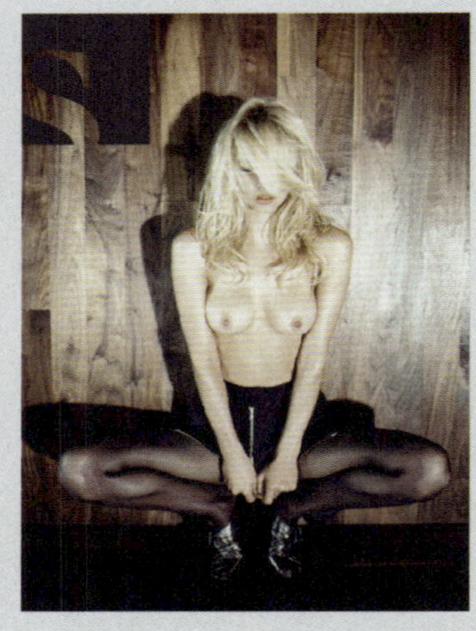

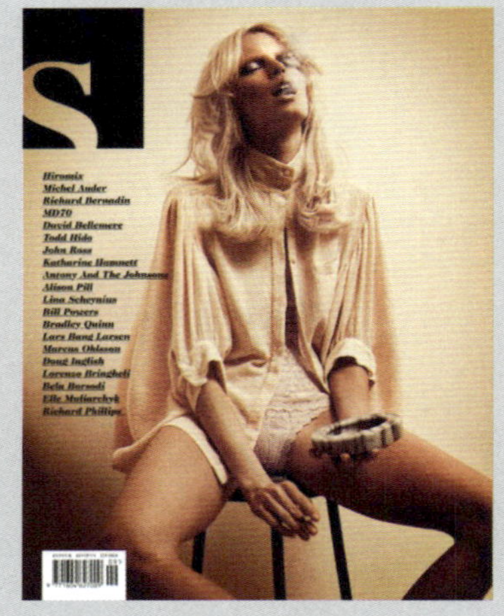

Hiromix
Michel Auder
Richard Bernadin
MD70
David Bellemere
Todd Hido
John Ross
Katharine Hamnett
Antony And The Johnsons
Alison Pill
Lina Scheynius
Bill Posers
Bradley Quinn
Lars Bang Larsen
Marcus Ohlsson
Doug Inglish
Lorenzo Bringheli
Bela Borsodi
Elle Muliarchyk
Richard Phillips

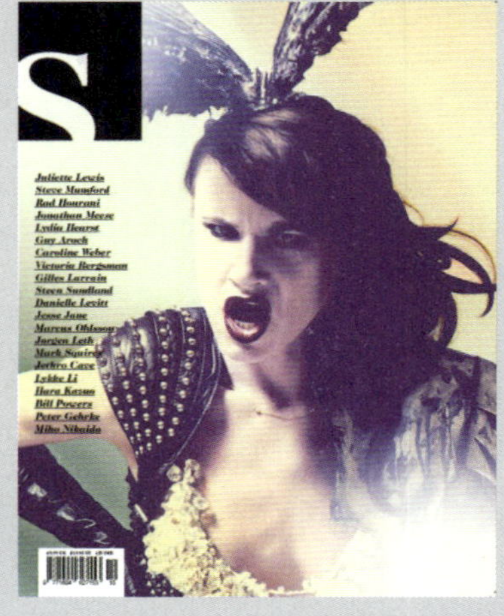

Juliette Lewis
Steve Mumford
Rad Hourani
Jonathan Meese
Lydia Hearst
Guy Aroch
Caroline Weber
Victoria Bergsman
Gilles Larrain
Steen Sundland
Danielle Levitt
Jesse Jane
Marcus Ohlsson
Jørgen Leth
Mark Squires
Jockro Cave
Lykke Li
Hara Kazuo
Bill Posers
Peter Gehrke
Miho Nikaido

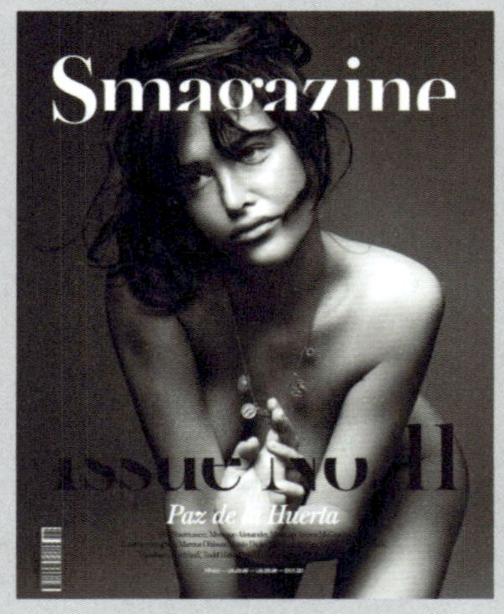

Smagazine
issue No.11
Paz de la Huerta

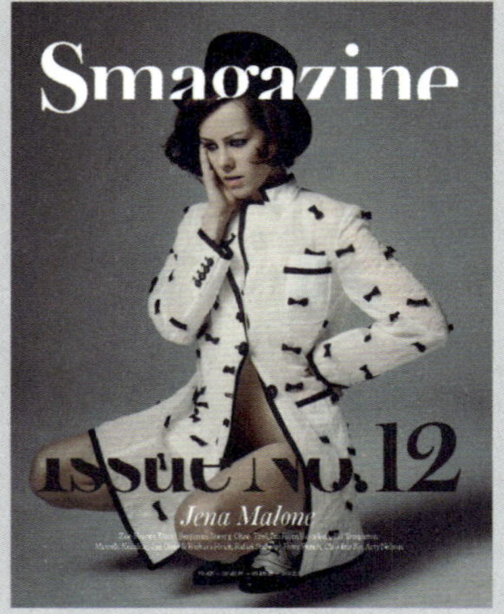

Smagazine
issue No.12
Jena Malone

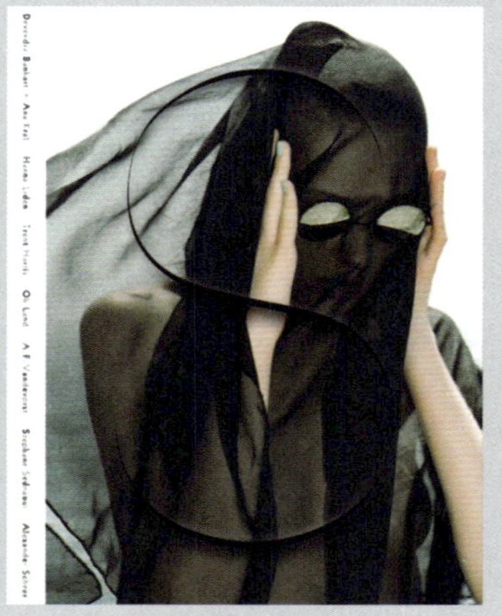

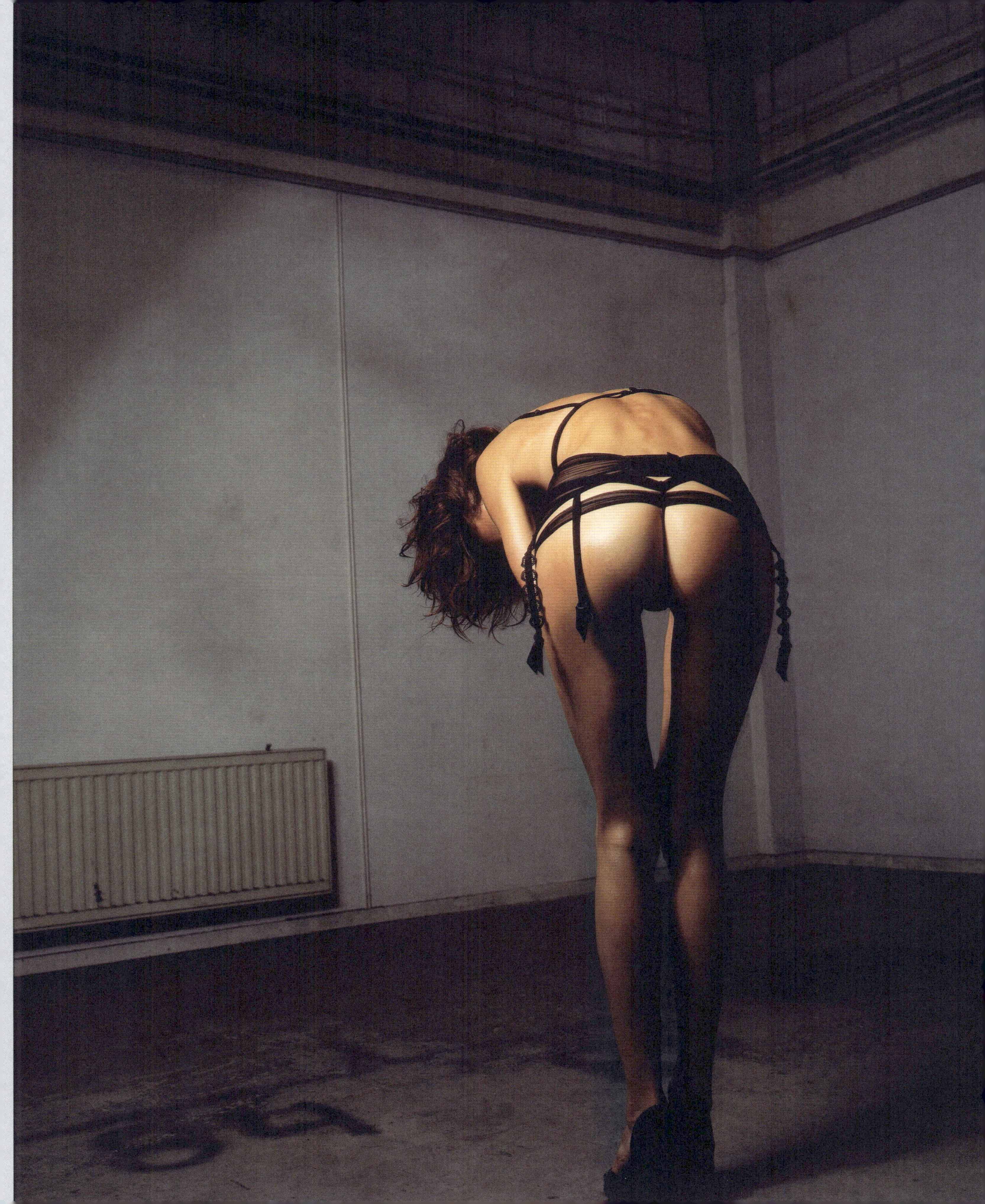

money. We are thinking more from the visual perspective and I really think this matters to our readers as well.

Who are your readers? What kind of responses are you getting?

Our audience ranges from people working in model agencies and stylists to photographers, their representatives, but also to a lot of other people. They all love it – and if they don't they are free to do their own magazine.

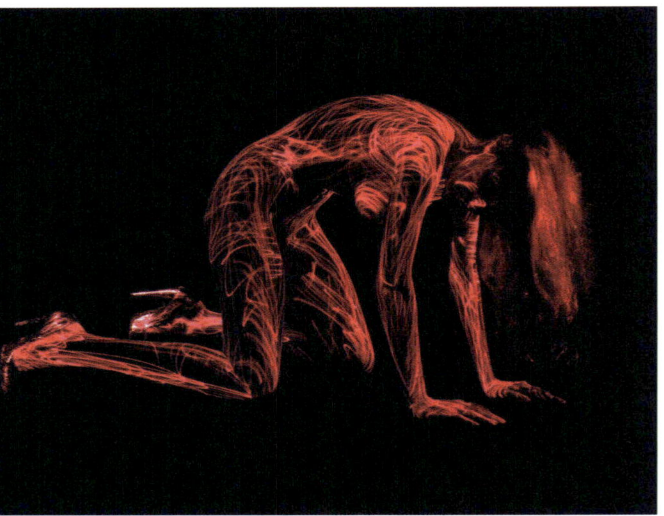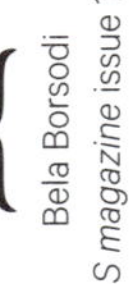

Bela Borsodi
S magazine issue 11

What is the business side of *S magazine* like? How many copies do you print, how and where do you distribute? What are your most important and successful markets?

We print around 35,000 to 40,000 copies per issue and we distribute worldwide through Export Press. Our biggest markets are New York and the US but also Australia and The Netherlands are very big sales points. London is becoming difficult unfortunately due to monopolizing from big publishing companies, like Condé Nast. We find it harder and harder to reach our readers there. It is like the commercialization of things all over the world. We feel like an independent cola brand competing against the big brands like Coca Cola.

This is very unfortunate because there are many people who would like to buy *S*, but distribution companies worldwide are simply not doing their job properly.

We have to plastic wrap the magazine even though the law of certain countries or states allows publication of nudity and even though hardcore porn can easily be found almost anywhere. But we get censored by distributors. They keep blaming the digital change, the iPad etc. Great excuse, but they are simply not true. It is easier for them to sell *Cosmopolitan* than to push erotic/lifestyle/fashion titles. It is simply easier not to do proper work. We know that we have the audience but cannot supply our demand. Issue 6 for example is a collector's item. It sold on eBay for more than 300 $. Issue 4 you cannot even find anymore. So

many people are in demand of *S* and other magazines like *S*. Hopefully we will be able to reach most of our readers with a better subscription plan shortly.

Do you experience cultural differences in what local audiences want to show and see in a magazine like *S* around the world?

Not what the audiences want to see but what the so-called democracies allow the population in their countries to view. That I do experience unfortunately. It happens in Germany in particular, in Thailand and the US too, also Singapore. But you can still buy porn in these places and vote. To me that is very weird.

How important are subscriptions? How about advertising?

We are sales dependent. So subscription is very, very important to us and we strive to be better and better in this field. Ads are also welcomed. We are creative people and simply not organized to sell ads ourselves. I do see a change in the market though and we are being approached more now. But all brands want product placement and this conflicts our freedom concept a bit.

Do you see a difference between *S* and an erotic fanzine like *Irène*, where an all female staff picks the contributions, even though they are from male and female contributors?

I am not familiar with this particular magazine, but I always find it funny when people in a group distance themselves from the rest of the world by their sex or social orientation. Guys for art, females for democracy and so on. It is really laughable because we are all humans on a round planet.

Are there other magazines on the shelves of magazine stores that you find inspirational? In what regard?

Rarely. But classic, well-crafted fashion photography always resonates with me.

What do you think about the big books of breasts, butts or penises by Taschen – now also in 3D?

I have not seen the 3D version (laughs), but I love it. An amazing collection of images. Taschen have been great at spreading the visual art worldwide.

I recently saw the Carlo Molino exhibition at Haus der Kunst in Munich and part of this design exhibition was a very simple, subtly placed display of about approximately 50 erotic Polaroïds he had taken throughout his career. Beautiful women, beautiful images. Timeless. Maybe my favourites for the time being. If you had to choose the two sexiest pictures ever – one with a male, one with a female model – which pictures would that be?

In both cases it would be Helmut Newton's work. No doubt.

"IT IS NOT THE NUDITY OR THE PART THAT YOU SEE STRAIGHT AWAY THAT MAKES A PICTURE EROTIC, BUT EXACTLY THE OPPOSITE. WHAT IS LEFT OUT IS THEN LEFT TO OUR RAW IMAGINATION AND THAT IS ALWAYS BETTER THAN FACTS OF REAL LIFE."

THREE MODERN GIRLS AND A FANZINE

When three young, London-based,
girls got together to share their interest
in eroticism, photography and the press, they
had something very rare and special in mind.
Far from all predictable visions of nudity
and sex, *Irène* was born, full of poetry
and inspiration. Shortly thereafter,
Geneviève Eliard, Esthèle Girardet
and Lucie Santamans moved back to Paris
for the pleasure of a growing audience.

INTERVIEW BY PHILIPPE GRAFF.
PORTRAIT BY SÉBASTIEN AGNETTI.

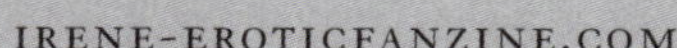

IRENE-EROTICFANZINE.COM

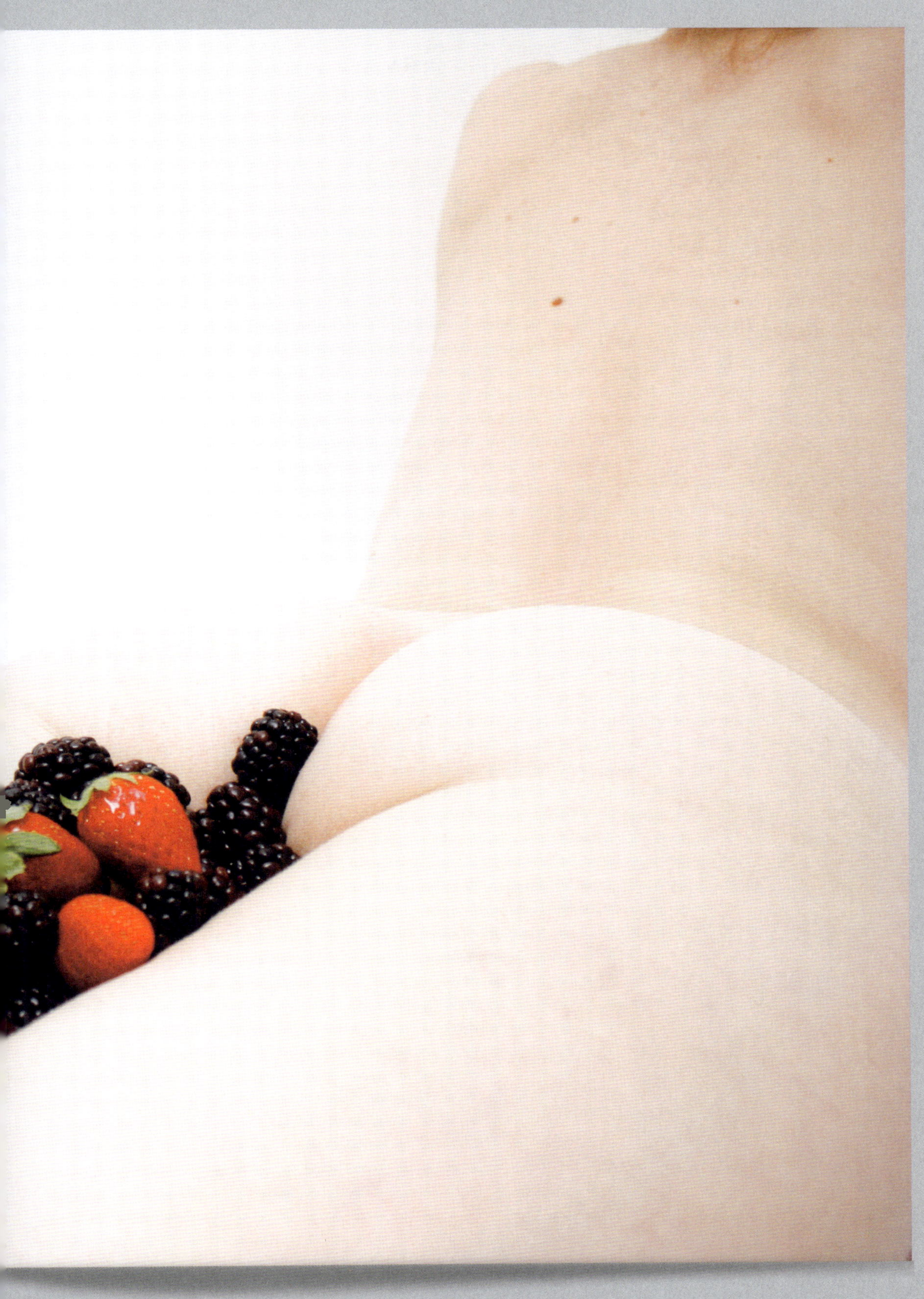

"Irène is beautiful. Irène is erotic. Irène is iconic. Irène is a new fanzine, which is proud to be all about female eroticism." explains *Irène*'s blog. Those looking for modern eroticism based on photography, collages and poetry will love *Irène* and, like it is suggested with some subtle irony, have a naked *Irène* in their homes. This kind of upscale pocket-sized magazine called fanzine clearly takes its inspiration from surrealism, which for a long time stood for high standards in troubled and sexually oriented fantasies. The move from London to Paris may be due to personal reasons, but it still corresponds to *Irène*'s taste for an unconventional yet elegant vision of eroticism that has its roots in Bataille and Nin's Paris. *Irène* also claims to be a bit naive-which makes it all the more erotic.

"WE ALSO WANT TO AVOID VINTAGE CLICHÉS- WE ARE NOT REALLY INTERESTED IN THOSE KITSCHY SNAPSHOTS OF PIN-UPS YOU CAN FIND IN THE WORLD OF BURLESQUE"

Irène is rather unique within the press today. What makes it unique in your opinion? Moreover how can one make eroticism unique, new and original when many forms of it have already been explored?

First I would say *Irène* is an independent publication, which leaves a lot of space for freedom of thought and action. Eroticism is a vast field, which has been explored in many, many ways. There are indeed many publications about eroticism. But *Irène* has a different point of view on the subject, a point of view emanating from three young women who care for their environment and the image of women in our society.

We all have great interests in photography and the beauty of images. We intended to create a publication in which the body would be seen in an artistic way, and raise the standard of thought on eroticism instead of making predictable images. *Irène* is meant to suggest and reveal more than just having images printed for free.

Irène is our feminine point of view on eroticism. Most of our photographers are indeed men, but what we look for is mostly a look that cares for women, that loves women. The point of view of the photographer about the model must be sincere. We try to explore eroticism in a way that is totally different from all those magazines, which mix it with sex. We focus on desire and sensuality in order to get back to a certain level of reflection.

We choose the photographers we work with mostly according to their artistic background. *Irène* makes it possible for them to express themselves on topics that have been demeaned quite often. It fulfills their true desires by giving them a reason as well as a structure where they can produce shootings that they had been thinking of for a long time.

This gives many of them the opportunity to engage in a field that they could not work in before, to make it personal. Maybe this is why we manage to produce very different images. Other photographers are much more used to eroticism, seasoned in it, but still, we make it then very clear that *Irène* is meant to suggest rather than show in a brutal and predictable way. This is precisely where the essence of desire lies. We created *Irène* because we had noticed that there wasn't any publication about that specific theme, neither in France nor in London. Our project takes its roots in frustration, essentially.

Why did you choose the formula of a fanzine? It seems that fanzines are in again. More generally it seems that true independent magazines are the next big thing: is this the solution for a free and creative press? What makes a fanzine different?

} *p.29*

Geneviève Eliard, Esthèle Girardet and Lucie Santamans shot by Sébastien Agnetti

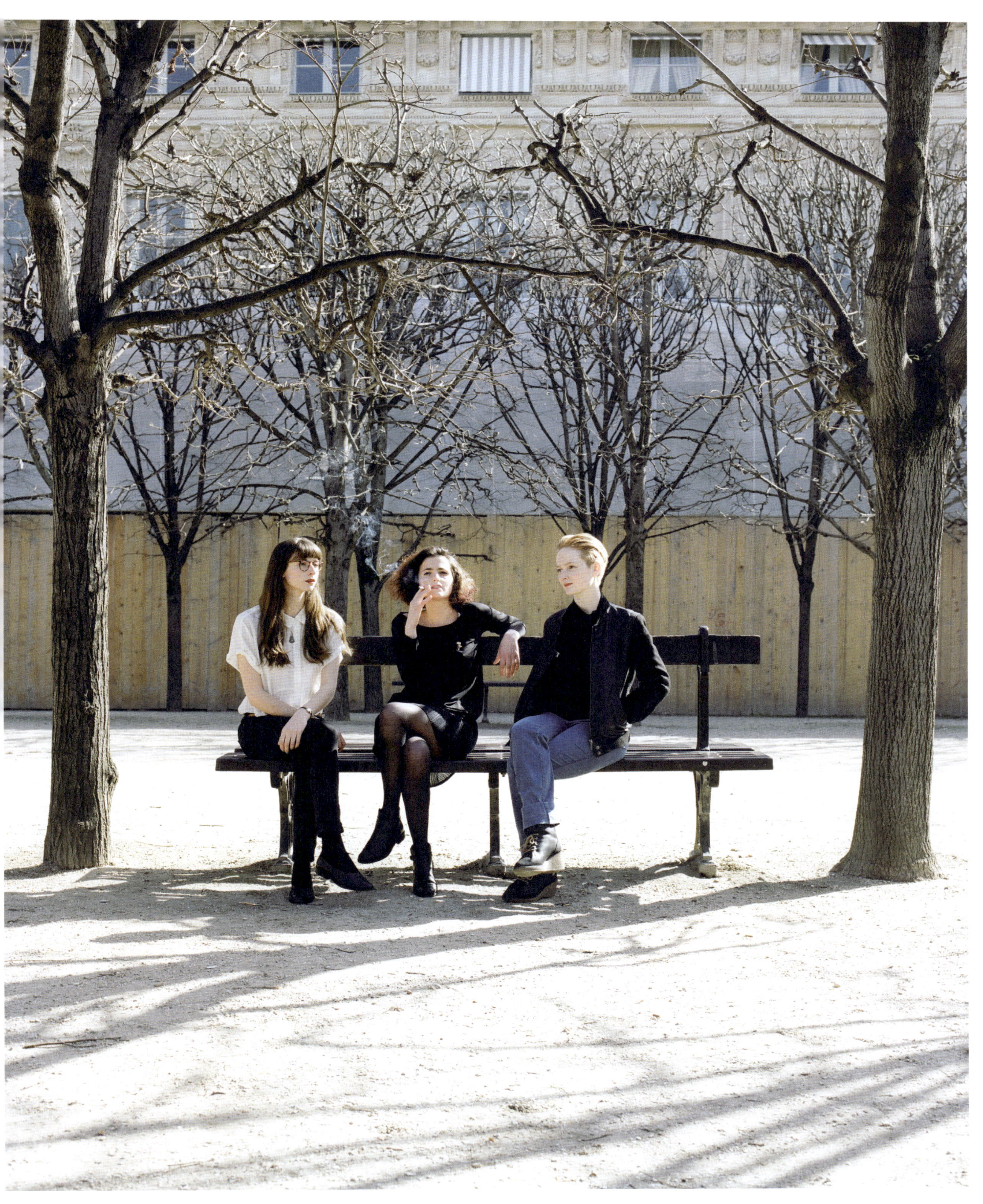

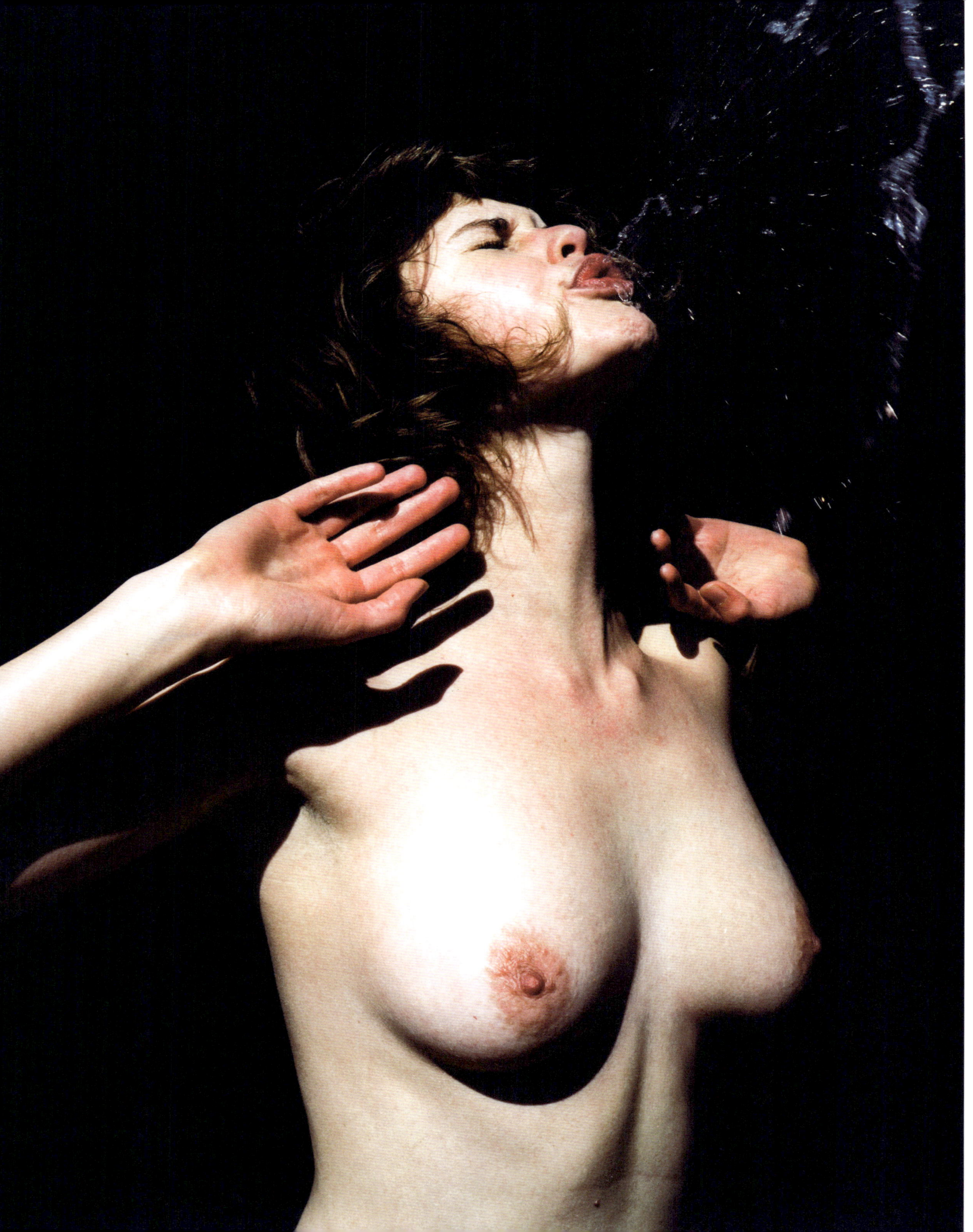

We are true fanzine lovers. We love its protest side. Basically, a fanzine is made by passionate people for other passionate people and is therefore a true exchange. We directly got rid of the idea of producing a traditional magazine. We didn't want *Irène* to be linked to any news, it is much more some kind of timeless publication, although it uses very modern methods in photography.

A fanzine leaves us much more freedom in planning the releases as well as in choosing the content. We are currently working on the third issue, which will be radically different from our first one back in December. *Irène* is in fact free to explore new ideas, new aesthetics in every issue.

There's been a new wave in the press in the last years, with quite a lot of new fanzines. We were actually in London when we launched *Irène*, where you can find lots of them in independent bookstores. This was quite an inspiration for us, with spontaneity and creativity easily expressed through this type of press. We, of course, wanted to convey a little more elegance to the formula.

You have got much more focus on upscale graphics in the new wave of fanzines. This comes from a willingness to take charge of all things, to express a specific, more radical point of view and share it with the readers. This is very much connected with the values of our generation.

The fanzine is a real good medium for us to give expression to eroticism, to deal with it in our very own way. It has in fact its own protest side. It looks like an ideal type of media, with no editorial must-dos, a free format, a focus on graphics and style. It is a real hub for creative people. Punks in the late 70s and 80s were the first ones to use this formula. They produced everything by themselves to show their collective work, their sources of inspiration, their *zeitgeist*. We are not criticizing other types of magazines. There are very creative ones indeed. We are just very much enjoying the incredible amount of independence making a fanzine gives you, especially as far as the rhythm of our releases is concerned or the evolution of the layout and the choice of images. We are now in the process of producing our third issue and we are questioning our choices everyday, because we simply want to keep our readers' attention and go on offering what they are looking for.

There have been many different variations on the theme of eroticism, whether personal or cultural… Did you take all those works into account, and how did you elaborate the theme according to *Irène*? Was it easy for you to stay away from clichés?

We try to stay far away from erotic clichés, whether past or present. We, of course, intend to avoid vulgarity, which is pretty much everywhere now. Womens' image has become commonplace, it has been spoiled with some kind of vulgarity. As a result, the way men behave towards women has been distorted. There is much less desire and seduction… only the search for satisfaction.

Irène wants to break with all that. With this idea that bends to the wishes of immediate needs and leaves no room for desire and wants to flourish. *"Everything should be gotten at once"*, seems be the slogan of our times.

We are actually looking for the human side of eroticism, and want to make readers react to real images that allow personal identification. This is some kind of universal topic but it's still under the radar. We really look for sincerity.

We were inspired by the works of photographers such as Juergen Teller and Ryan McGinley, and also from anonymous photographers, not necessarily in the erotic field.

We also want to avoid vintage clichés: we are not really interested in those kitschy snapshots of pin-ups you can find in the world of burlesque, which is some kind of hype right now- and the glittery side of seduction. We also avoid stereotyped bodies: in our last issue you can find very different types of models. Through this diversity we get closer to the true essence of people.

We spend a lot of time exploring new graphic and artistic trends, and try to get their point in order to adjust our view. This is why we also created *l'heure eXquise*, a blog, which is independent from *Irène*. It was important to be able to share our inspirations with our readers, for them to understand what this is all about, the codes and the bias.

***Irène* has very mixed contributors, both men and women, is this a conscious choice? Do you wish to bring a specific vision of eroticism as seen by women?**

Most of our photographers are men. This is not necessarily a choice, but *Irène* is indeed a very feminine perspective on eroticism since we take charge of the artistic direction and the choice of series.

The choice of the photographers is more or less our favorites. We look for sincerity in their work. We also look for trust when working with our contributors, a kind of exchange that we hope shows in our issues.

The aim of course was far from creating a feminist fanzine, which would exclude men but rather get both sexes together on the topic, and prove that the point of view of men on women can be beautiful and respectful. A female photographer won't be able to emulate this uniquely seductive link. We also would love to get men into *Irène* as models, but this is even more difficult since nude men in photography are mostly seen as gay clichés which few of them are ready to accept.

The exchange with our contributors is a real treat. *Irène* gives us the opportunity to meet photographers or illustrators we already know and whose work we appreciate. We really intend to value their work. *Irène* is some kind of platform that promotes artistic work.

In that case, is there a something specific to the female vision of eroticism? Of a woman's body?

} p.30

Our vision is a female one but it is aimed at men as well as women. Women identify themselves with the models and men admire! We think a woman's vision of another woman's body will be somehow "closer". There will probably be fewer taboos, less trouble. Women have a vision that is more detached, more sensual than sexual. Maybe women are more in control of their feelings get less overwhelmed by their desires. Women probably have a truer, more intimate view of another woman's body.

Still, since most of our photographers are men, there is a play on seduction in each of our issues.

There are relatively few texts in *Irène*… do you favor the power of images?

Irène focuses mainly on images. But every shoot comes from the idea of a poem. We do take inspiration from words. The idea is to deconstruct texts, take inspiration in their fragments and then recreate the mood of the text, in the way of some "*cadavres exquis*".

Eroticism means having a specific point of view. It is linked to cultural backgrounds, to literature, and to cinema. When you read Anaïs Nin or Georges Bataille you get very different ideas about a woman's body. Without a literary or cultural background, the discourse will lack poetry and one will be inclined to react in a more primitive way. Texts are just as essential as images, they show the direction even if within the pages of *Irène* they are less obvious than images.

There is also the blog called *Irène*. What are the specificities of both the print version and the digital one?

This is true, *Irène* consists of several mediums at the same time. We wanted to create a fanzine, first of all, because we wanted to create something material. We wanted people to go through the pages, leave it on a shelf and get back to it later.

We mostly use the blog to deliver our news, some of our inspiration. The point is to carefully select images that represent our tastes in erotic photos. It is like our mood of the day, the erotic mood of *Irène*, which very much inspires us.

The great advantage of a blog is that you get instant reactions from your followers.

Both mediums are meant to make it easier for our artists to network. A few weeks ago, we had organized a dinner with all our collaborators, to let them exchange their views on eroticism. We even had some kind of sensual menu. We would really like to plan those events more regularly. We are fond of the idea of connecting artists. We would even like to go further, to create a real community. We try to get artists to work in collaboration. For instance we have worked with German photographer Uwe Jens Bermeitinger who produces his own erotic magazine called *Tissue*, we were very happy that some of *Irène*'s photographers also worked for *Tissue*.

} p.32

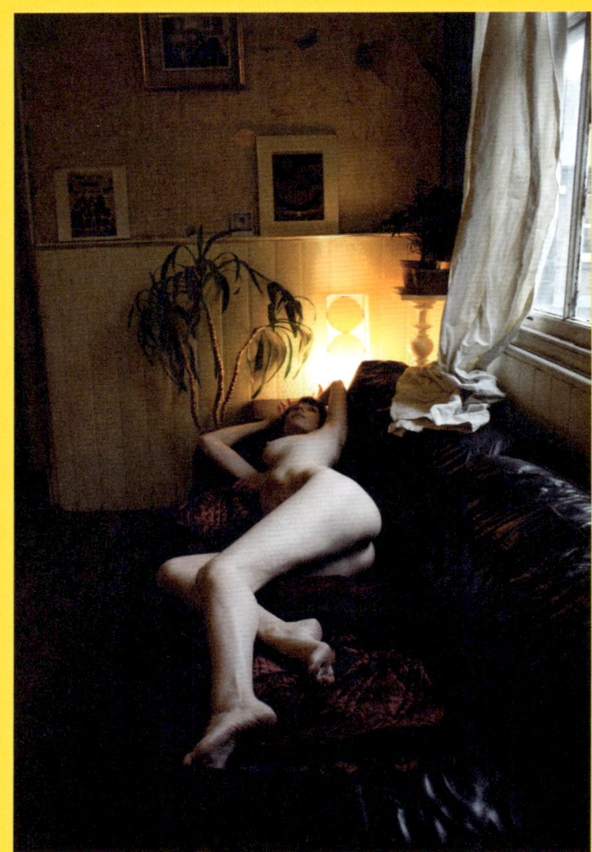

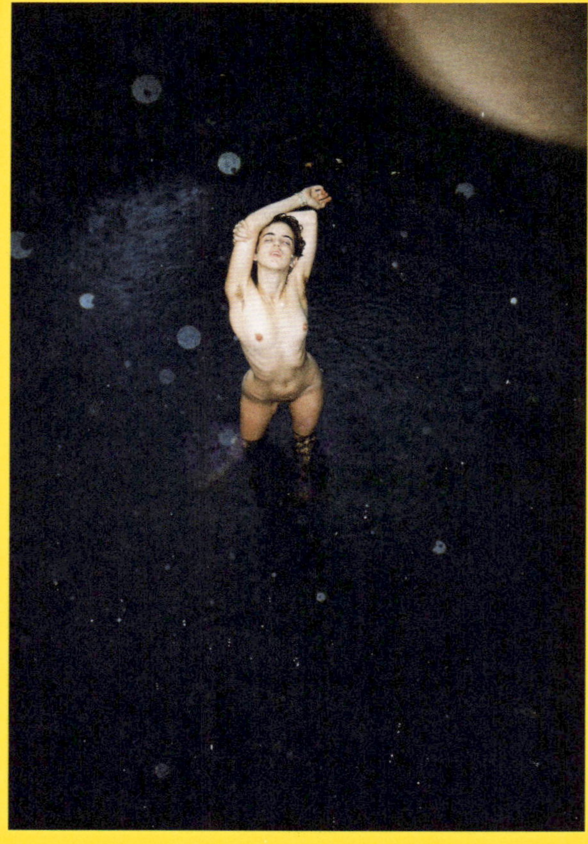

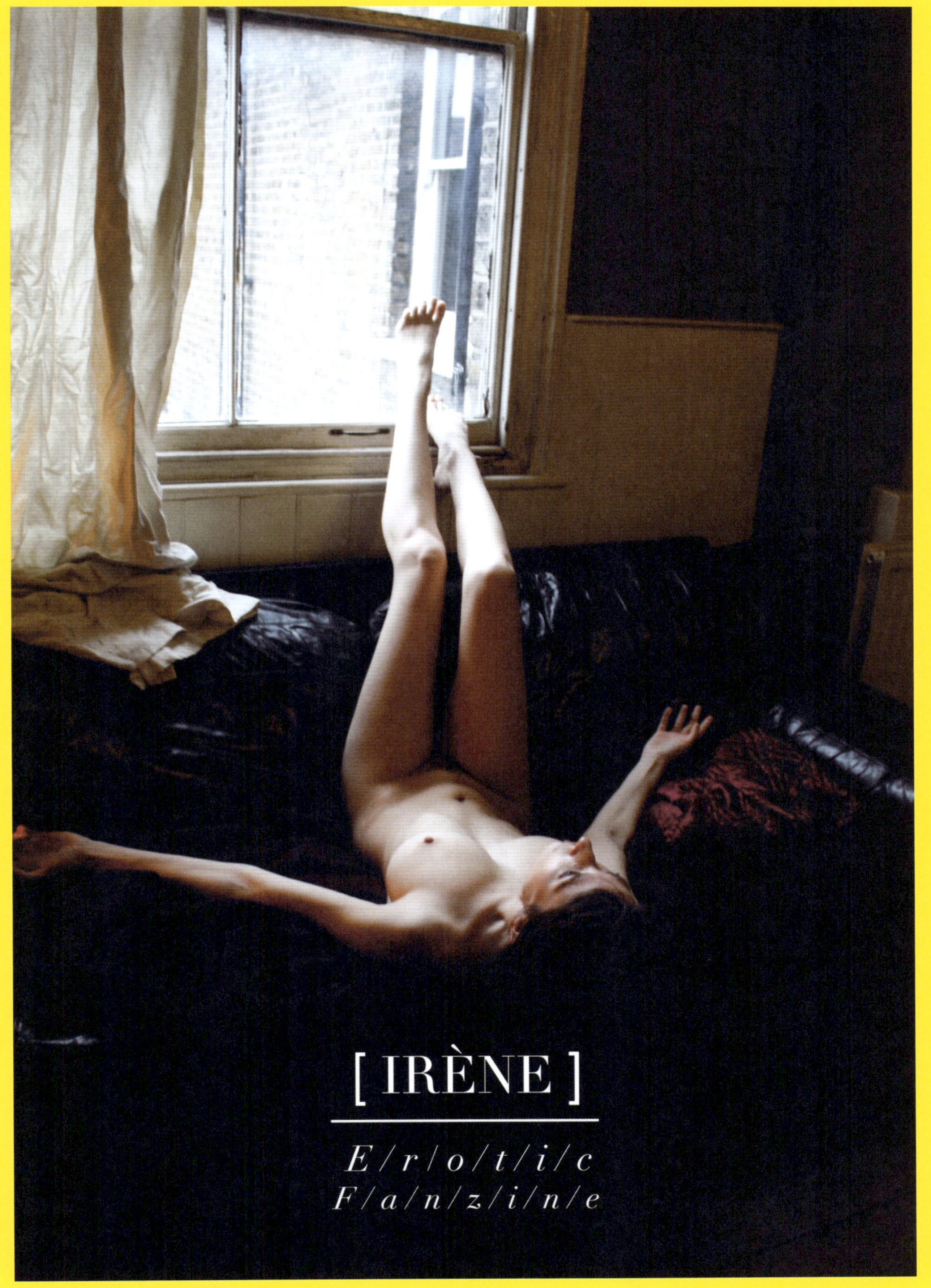
[IRÈNE]
E / r / o / t / i / c
F / a / n / z / i / n / e

Does print have a future in your opinion? Do magazines have to become beautiful objects to have a future?

Definitely! This is the big comeback of print. It is somehow paradoxical that this comes at a time when one can find everything online. People are more and more demanding when shopping. The most well-informed in the field of magazines and fanzines are truly looking for a unique object. The demand is high. To us, the ultimate success is to get a beautiful object with a strong content and at the same time, something that is really original but still has a sense to it.

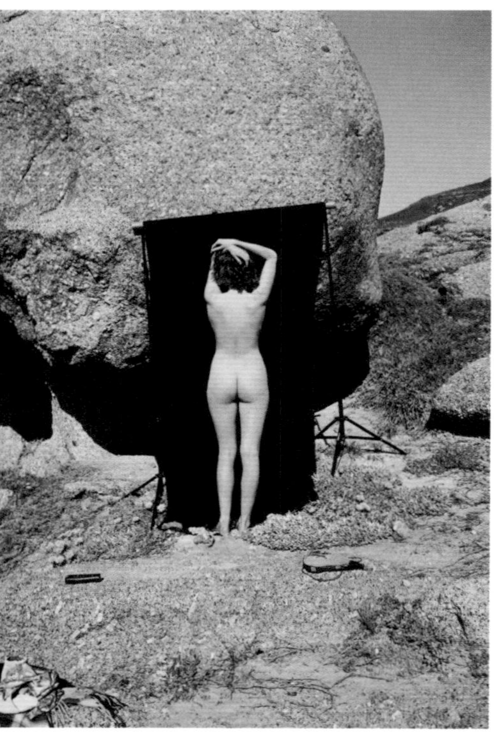

In this field where perception and fantasies have a big part, how do you manage the artistic direction and the layout? How can you use the artistic direction to raise erotic fantasies, or at least to underline them?

This is true, artistic direction has a great role in general, but at *Irène*, we want to leave a lot of space for images. The layout then uses white empty space just as a breather. Our layout is meant to be sober, to value the photography even if it has a special *Irène* touch, which you can identify easily. Our layout is light, modern and elegant. We also care for typography but we don't want to get trapped in predictable, obvious graphics.

Is *Irène* taking part in a long tradition of erotic magazines and books? Do you see any affinities with past or present trends?

We like magazines with an erotic touch such as *Purple, S,* or even magazines dedicated to eroticism like *Jacques* magazine or *Edwarda*. There are actually many influences in eroticism coming from our own cultures but the aim was to create something really new and free from any of those references. Still, we feel very close to surrealism, we do appreciate their view on eroticism, both in form and meaning.

What is your opinion about more mainstream magazines like *Playboy* and their vision of eroticism?

To be honest we aren't really interested in such magazines, at least in their contemporary version. We sometimes go through older issues in vintage bookstores but in short we think this is all outdated now. We mostly look for suggestive eroticism, there is much more power in evoking than in showing. Those are two very different visions and they target two different kinds of audiences.

Do media have an influence on the perception of the body, of eroticism? Can they renew the perception of people on the body?

We feel rather pessimistic about that. Nowadays, there are numerous stereotypes in the media. In the field of eroticism this goes through stereotyped bodies, stereotyped poses and attitudes. It would be useful to fight against that. Yes contemporary photography shows some interest in imperfections but when you consider big media, you can only find one vision of the woman's body, and one vision of the man's body. There are some changes on the way though, but they remain quite shy.

Media deals with very extreme topics, there are constantly stories about anorexia or being overweight and at the same time readers get images of perfect bodies. How can ordinary women recognize themselves in such images? Images create inhibitions and frustrations.

This is why confidential publications and independent websites give more free and edgy information. We would like our readers to identify with *Irène*, to get back to the essence of artistic imagery. We would like our readers to feel some desire for the women they see in the images even if those women do not match all the stereotypes of our times.

Are there hypes, trends in eroticism? What guides your choices of themes and photographers?

What guides us the most is our own individual desire. We do not want to follow the hype. We look for what's appealing to us. For the second issue we looked for a woman who could get rid of boundaries and would show detachment toward the stereotypes. The issue starts with a shooting by Logan White, a young LA-based photographer. His work truly goes back to the origin and essence of the body. We wanted this issue to remain spontaneous and light. Poses and attitudes were meant to be without complexity and lustful. All the photographers took a very fascinated look at those models. For our next issue we would like a man to get really involved and be an active part of it. *Irène* must not remain one unique point of view and must develop.

"THERE ARE ACTUALLY MANY INFLUENCES IN EROTICISM COMING FROM OUR OWN CULTURES BUT THE AIM WAS TO CREATE SOMETHING REALLY NEW AND FREE FROM ANY OF THOSE REFERENCES."

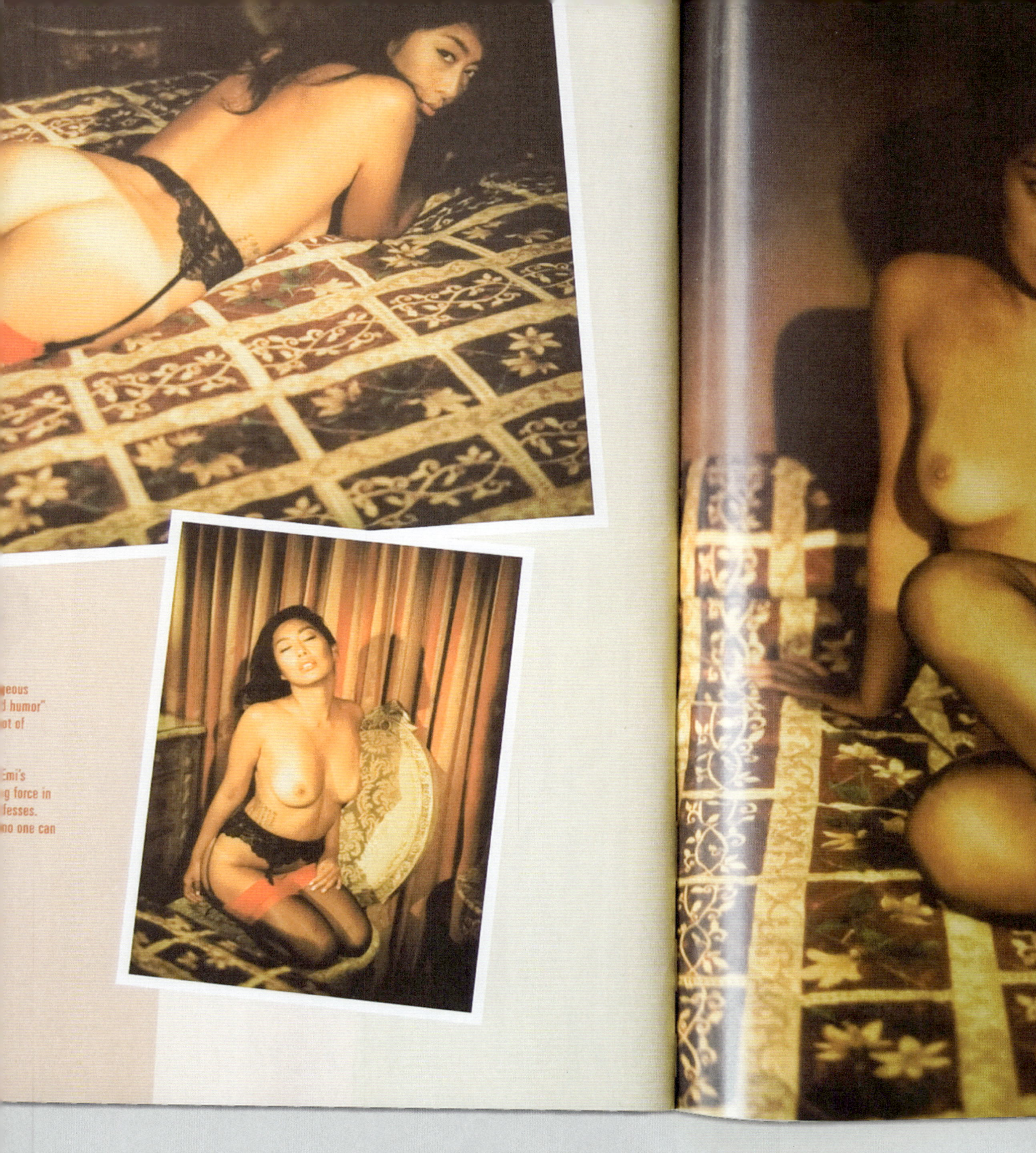

geous
d humor"
ot of

Emi's
g force in
fesses.
no one can

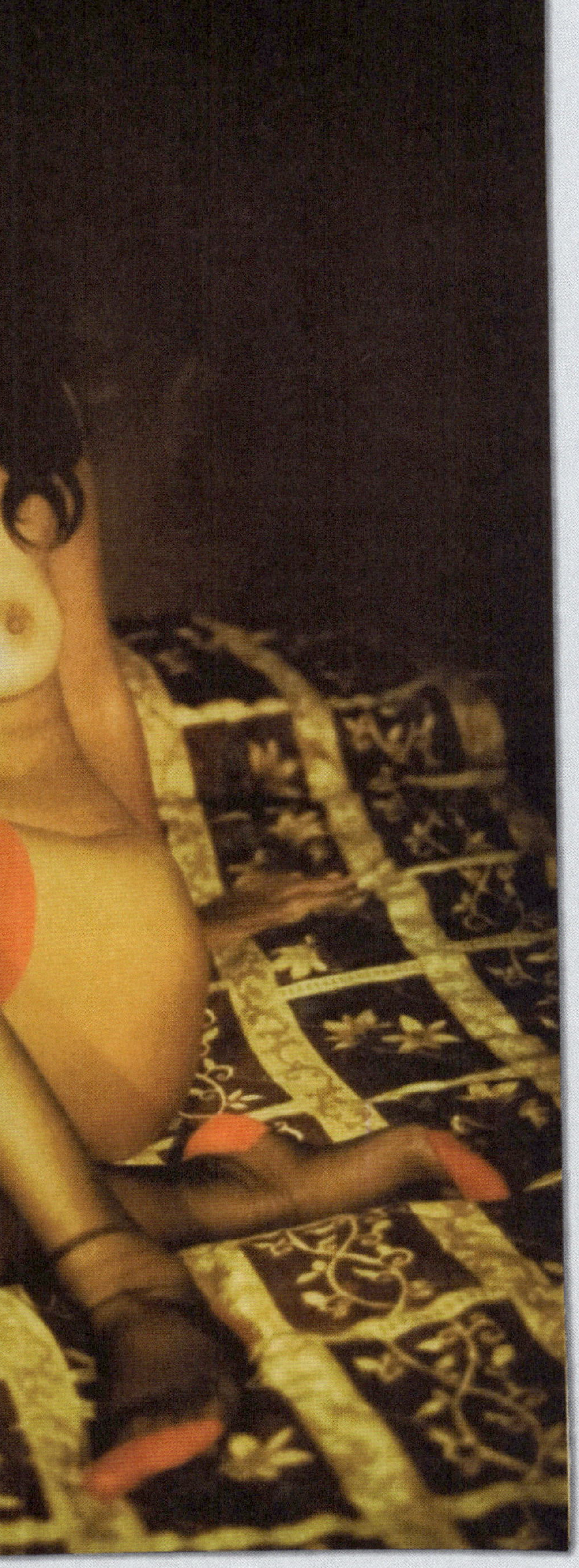

Jacques: Mixing Nostalgia With Realism

Anyone with an interest in erotic print publications has surely come across *Jacques*, a high-end erotic magazine from America. The tone is a nod to *Playboy*'s retro past while its models are girls who can take pride in their natural beauty.

Interview by Jeremy Leslie.
Portrait by Jesse Shadoan.

www.Jacques-Mag.com

Originally created by Danielle and her husband Jonathan Lederer, the two have recently split up and now Danielle Leder, a former model, herself is planning to re-launch the magazine.

"WELL JUST BECAUSE I LIKE SEX DOESN'T MEAN I DON'T LIKE OTHER THINGS. BESIDES I ENJOY HAVING SEX WHILE WATCHING MOVIES. UNLESS IT'S A STANLEY KUBRICK. YOU SHUT UP AND WATCH HIS FILMS."

Why did you launch *Jacques*?

For numerous reasons. I missed modelling, I missed working. Exploiting myself sexually, if you will. It was also a way for me to get back in touch with a world my husband forbade me to be in. He couldn't take my $10,000 a day jobs, and me working with photographers on a level he could never be. He's very controlling like that.

When I became pregnant with Jack, then after giving birth to him, I felt I became trapped. My husband trapped me, not sure why I let him, but I did. I was not allowed to do anything really that didn't focus on his career. I did hair, makeup, styling, showed his models how to pose, made them feel comfortable. Found locations, etc...

I guess, you could say he used me, but in a way I used him too.

I simply wasn't doing anything. Again, I had just given birth to my son Jack and was bed ridden for about 6 months due to massive blood loss. My husband was not working. He was struggling with his photography. He was only doing few editorials here and there. Nothing substantial, nothing to feed a family.

So I thought well, let's start a magazine, let's take our future in our own hands. Why sit around and wait for people to come knocking when I could produce something, get his name out there. With absolute creative freedom.

When I started modelling every agency told me my hips were too big, my boobs were too big. But I was comfortable with my body—I'd been a stripper for three years in Tampa, Florida and started doing burlesque when I moved to New York—and the photographers loved me. Bruce Webber loved the way I stripped.

So eventually the agencies had to give in, but I hated going on castings. It was awful seeing all these girls with no boobs, butt, body or personality. I wanted to start a mutiny and bring back the 90s supermodels.

Americans are so crazy when it comes to nudity. Too many girls are growing up feeling bad about themselves, feeling ashamed of their sexuality, their body type. We're not perfect; we all have scars, tattoos, freckles. We're black, white, Indian, Mexican, Asian. Where is that in the media today? All I see is a bunch of skinny white girls, and I can say that because I am a skinny white girl. I would like to see more of a variety in today's media.

Why produce a printed publication and not a website or other digital service?

I'm really anti-technology. I only just got a cell phone, and that was only because I was living on a mountain with two kids and no landline. I also have an obsession with

} p.39

Danielle Leder

}

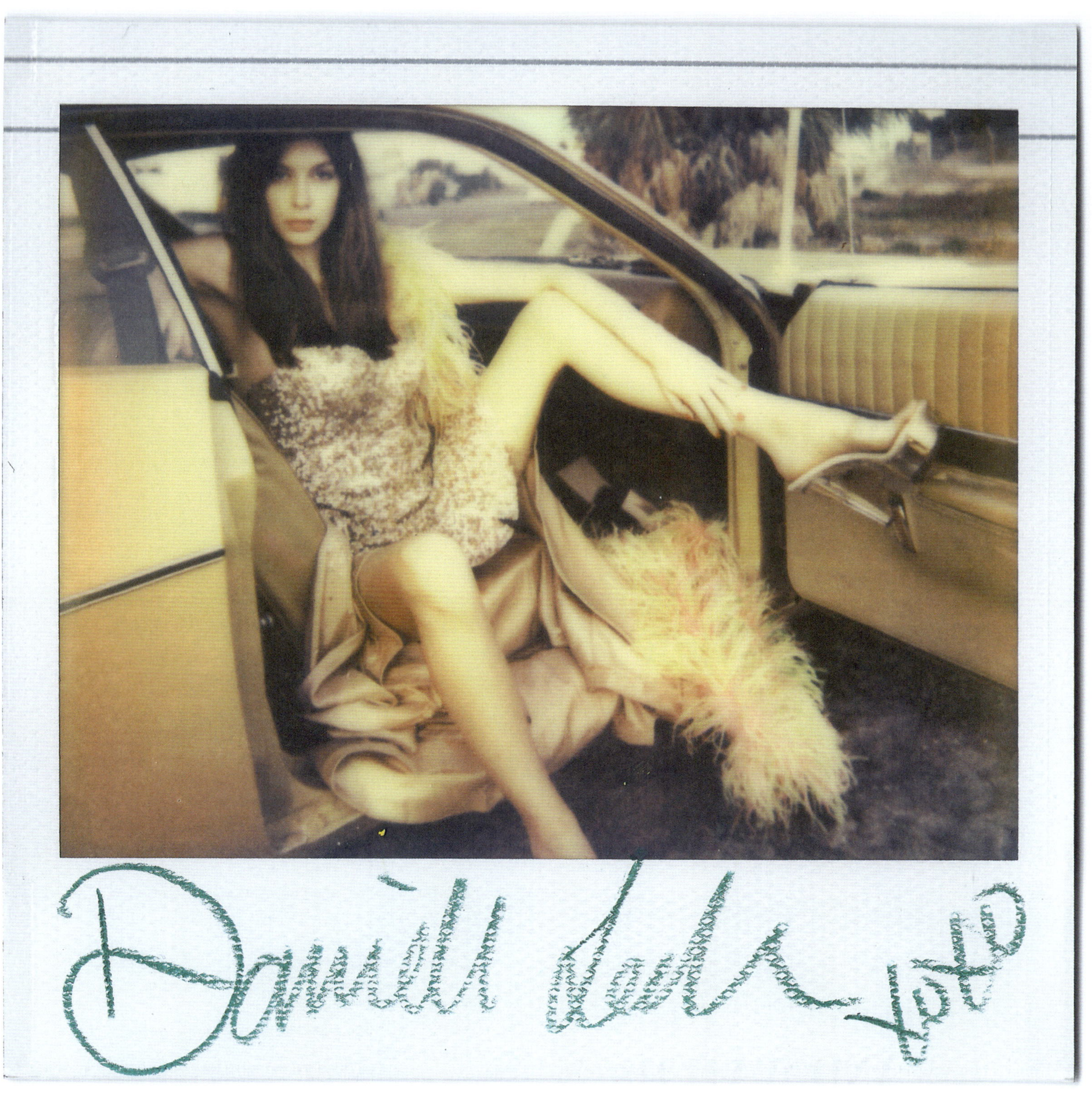

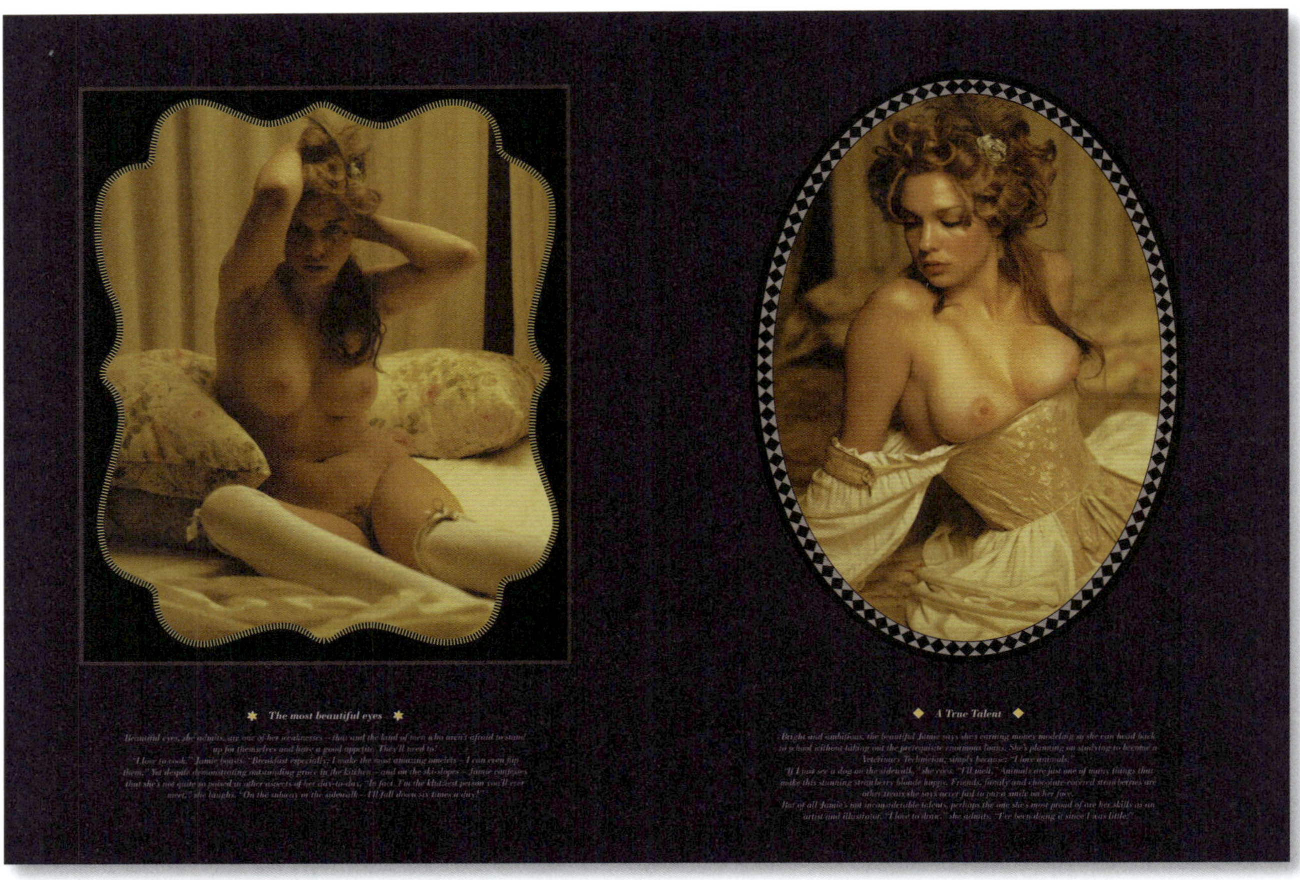

Beautiful eyes, she admits, are one of her weaknesses – that and the kind of men who aren't afraid to stand up for themselves and have a good appetite. "They'll need to."
"I love to cook," Jamie boasts. "Breakfast especially; I make the most amazing omelets – I can even flip them." Yet despite demonstrating outstanding grace in the kitchen – and on the ski-slopes – Jamie confesses that she's not quite so poised in other aspects of her day-to-day. "In fact, I'm the klutziest person you'll ever meet," she laughs. "On the subway or the sidewalk – I'll fall down six times a day!"

Bright and ambitious, the beautiful Jamie says she's earning money modeling so she can head back to school without taking out the prerequisite enormous loans. She's planning on studying to become a Veterinary Technician, simply because: "I love animals."
"If I just see a dog on the sidewalk," she coos, "I'll melt." Animals are just one of many things that make this stunning strawberry blonde happy. Friends, family and chocolate-covered strawberries are other treats she says never fail to put a smile on her face.
But of all Jamie's not inconsiderable talents, perhaps the one she's most proud of are her skills as an artist and illustrator. "I love to draw," she admits, "I've been doing it since I was little."

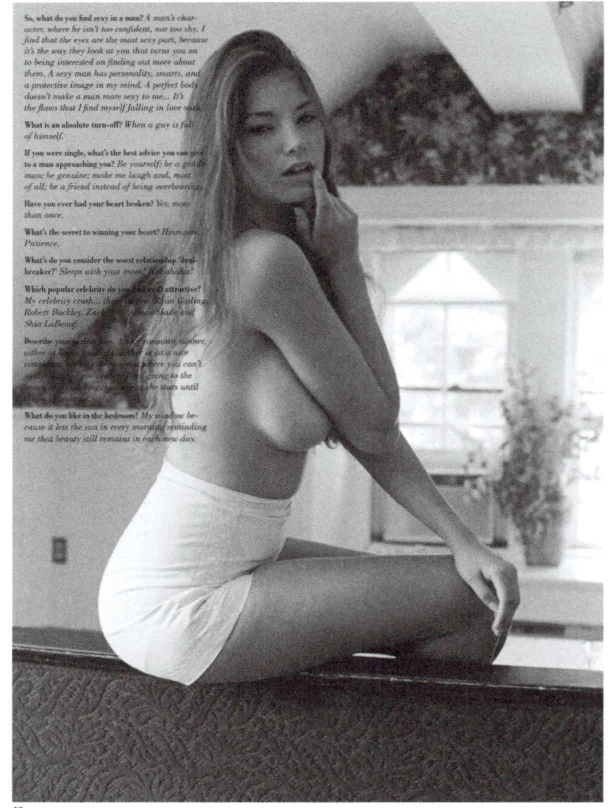

So, what do you find sexy in a man? *A man's character, where he isn't too confident, nor too shy. I find that the eyes are the most sexy part, because it's the way they look at you that turns you on to being interested on finding out more about them. A sexy man has personality, smarts, and a protective image in my mind. A perfect body doesn't make a man more sexy to me... It's the flaws that I find myself falling in love with.*

What is an absolute turn-off? *When a guy is full of himself.*

If you were single, what's the best advice you can give to a man approaching you? *Be yourself; be a gentle man; be genuine; make me laugh and, most of all; be a friend instead of being overbearing.*

Have you ever had your heart broken? *Yes, more than once.*

What's the secret to winning your heart? *Hmmmm... Patience.*

What's do you consider the worst relationship 'dealbreaker?' *Sleeps with your mom! Hahahaha!*

Which popular celebrity do you find most attractive? *My celebrity crush... there's a few. Ryan Gosling, Robert Buckley, Zac Efron, Drian Slade and Shia LaBeouf.*

Describe your perfect date. *A very romantic dinner, either at home cooked together or at a nice restaurant, having a conversation where you can't wait to reach out and kiss or hold, going to the beach or a cuddling, gazing at the stars until there's sunrise.*

What do you like in the bedroom? *My window because it lets the sun in every morning reminding me that beauty still remains in each new day.*

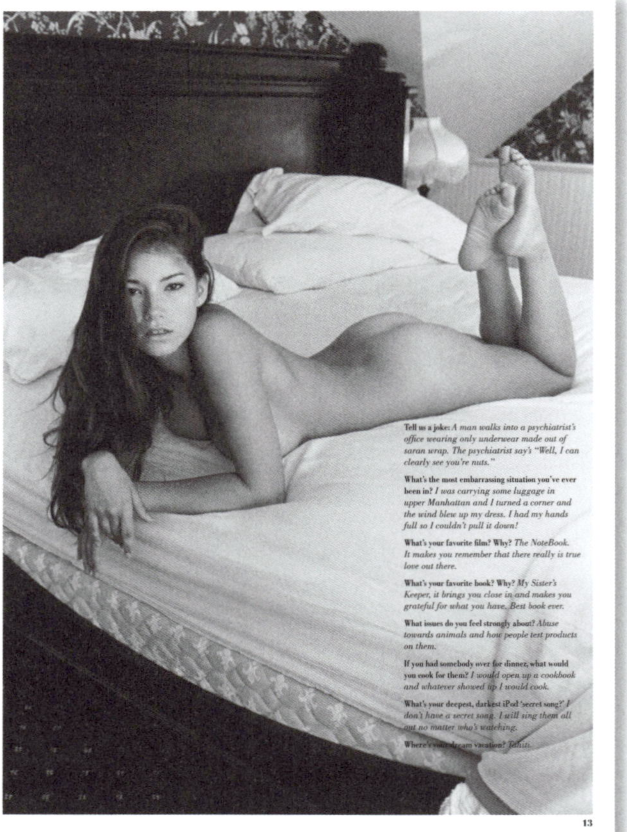

Tell us a joke: *A man walks into a psychiatrist's office wearing only underwear made out of saran wrap. The psychiatrist say's "Well, I can clearly see you're nuts."*

What's the most embarrassing situation you've ever been in? *I was carrying some luggage in upper Manhattan and I turned a corner and the wind blew up my dress. I had my hands full so I couldn't pull it down!*

What's your favorite film? Why? *The NoteBook. It makes you remember that there really is true love out there.*

What's your favorite book? Why? *My Sister's Keeper, it brings you close in and makes you grateful for what you have. Best book ever.*

What issues do you feel strongly about? *Abuse towards animals and how people test products on them.*

If you had somebody over for dinner, what would you cook for them? *I would open up a cookbook and whatever showed up I would cook.*

What's your deepest, darkest iPod 'secret song?' *I don't have a secret song. I will sing them all out no matter who's watching.*

Where's your dream vacation? *Tahiti.*

books. I love the way they feel. They're real. You can't get that personal with the Internet. But I'm coming around. I'm actually working on a website now.

What magazines inspired you to make *Jacques*?

Vintage men's magazines like *Ritz, Screw,* pre-80s *Playboy.* As I grew up I really wanted to be one of those girls in the magazines. I guess you could say I did become one. I always identified with the vixen or the over the top bombshell, I watched a lot of old Hollywood movies and musicals.

Somehow, I made a detour to be a mom. But that should never stop us. Being a mother is beautiful. I would say we're better than single, childless women. Don't get me wrong, I love my young single ladies. But we can cook, clean, do your laundry, and we have a sex drive that's out of this world! We're legal 'experienced' sex workers. I bet you I could teach a guy my age (25) a few tricks. Oh yes, and you don't need alcohol to get us in bed. We are ready and willing.

Who is *Jacques* – where did the name come from?

We wanted to name the magazine *Ritz* in the beginning, but the Ritz Carlton threatened to sue and in the end they bought our domain name and we took the cash. It took us 6 months to come up with *Jacques. Jacques* is my son, Jack.

How do you find the girls? Do you deal with the big model agencies or rely on smaller ones?

The big don't like us because we fight against them and their skinny models. We work with the smaller agencies no one knows about. They have the all-American curvy girls. But we also use girls who aren't "models", just your girl-next-door. Not saying they are any less beautiful, sometimes they really were the girl down the street from us.

Are most girls comfortable with posing topless, or do many say no? Are they surprised at castings or do they know the magazine? Do they turn you down?

Topless seems to be ok, it's the full nude with the bush that makes them stop and think. But generally after they shot topless with us, they want to do nudes. I think it's because America has them brainwashed. Funny for a country so filled and driven by sex.

Do you avoid using professional sex models/pornography stars?

We have in the past, but I think it's something I'm now interested in doing. There's nothing wrong with the sex industry. It's just the way they're portrayed that I don't like.

What criteria do you use in selecting models for the shoots?

Being able to hold a conversation is important! If you show up to meet me on your phone it's rude. I don't care how big your tits are. I'm really a stickler when it comes to manners. I may enjoy being sexual and seductive and having my girls do the same, but I like my girls to be ladies. I would never ask a girl to do something I wouldn't do myself. Not unless she really, really wanted to.

How do you describe the magazine: a magazine about sex? erotica? soft-porn? fantasy? fashion mag? Something else?

Jacques is an extension of my life. It's part of who I am. I have a million different ideas come in and out of my head every day. This gives me a chance to get some out for good.

It's really a magazine of things I like. Unfortunately because of my abusive husband (we're now getting a divorce) I really suppressed it for 5 years. I'm not going to hold it back any longer. I think *Jacques* actually suffered because I was not allowed to be who I really am. I am a really sexual person.

Why do you include non-erotic features (the issue I'm looking at has an interview with Oliver Stone)?

Well just because I like sex doesn't mean I don't like other things. Besides I enjoy having sex while watching movies. Unless it's a Stanley Kubrick. You shut up and watch his films.

Is *Jacques* an exercise in nostalgia, looking back at a more innocent time (*Playboy, Oui* etc) or is it reflecting contemporary concerns about fake bodies and retouched imagery?

Both.

Are there other magazines investigating similar themes?

There are now. I love it. I like to compare *Jacques* to Vanilla Ice. We may make fun of him now, but he did open the door for Eminem and others alike. But I think *Jacques* will have a different outcome then Vanilla Ice did.

Sex is everywhere today; music videos, mainstream magazines (Terry Richardson), advertising. Plus websites and TV. Does a magazine about sex still have a role?

Funny you mention Terry. I've always been a huge fan of his work and when I was modelling I was sent on a "go see" to meet him. I got really dressed up, made my entrance and sat down and talked to him for a bit. He knew Mons Venus (the strip club I worked in) and he asked if he could take some Polaroïds of me. Sure, I said. I showed him my boobs. He asked if he could take a picture with me (what he was really asking is if he could take a picture with my tits). He got right next to them and I saw my chance. I grabbed his head and gave him a motorboat. His face turned bright red and I told him I always wanted to do that. Who says Terry's the one you have to watch out for? He's a teddy bear compared to me.

I gave him my number and a few weeks later he wanted to hang out. Ugh, I know he does this to all the models, so

} *p.42*

Tori

Lea

Ilana

Jamie

Elize

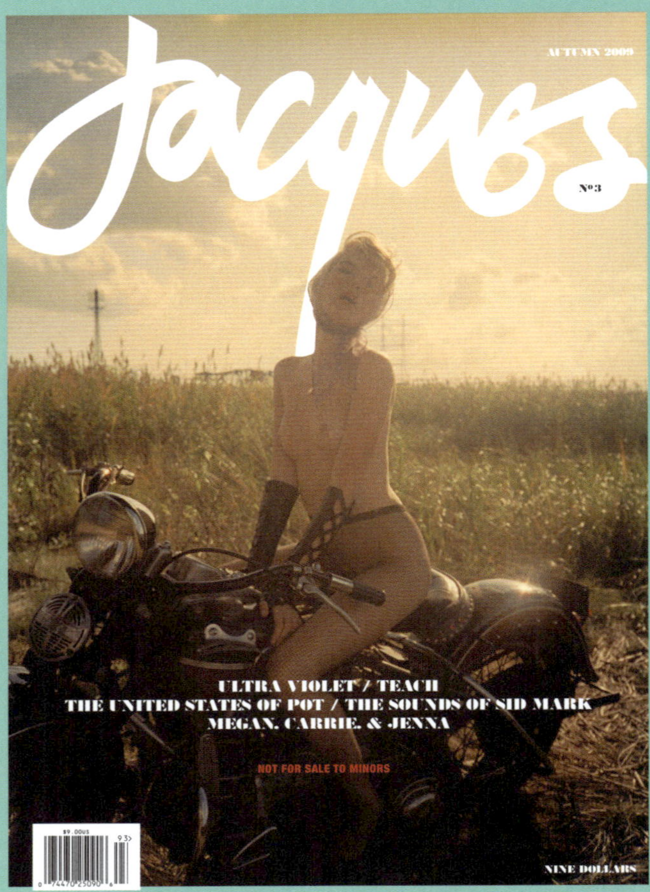

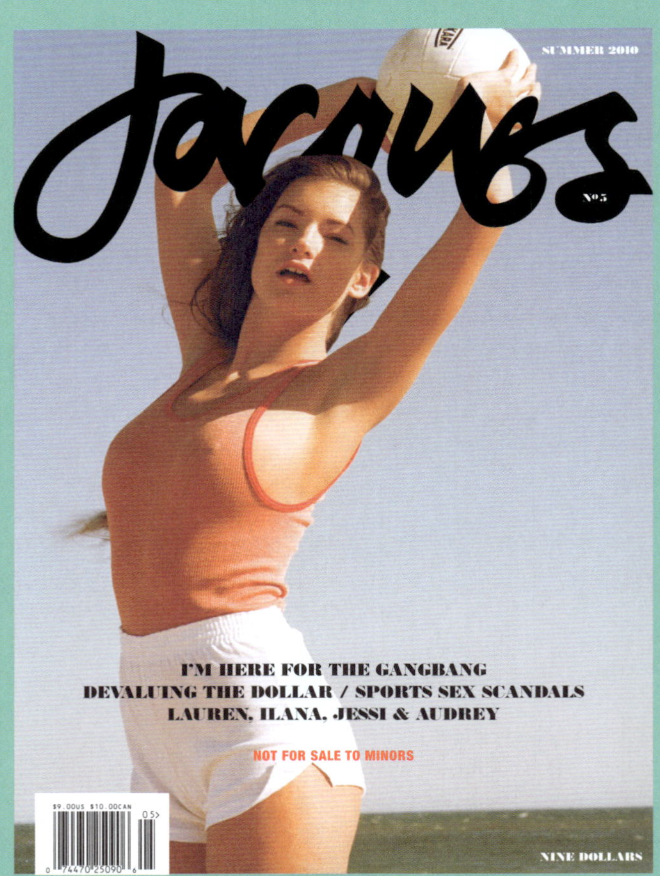

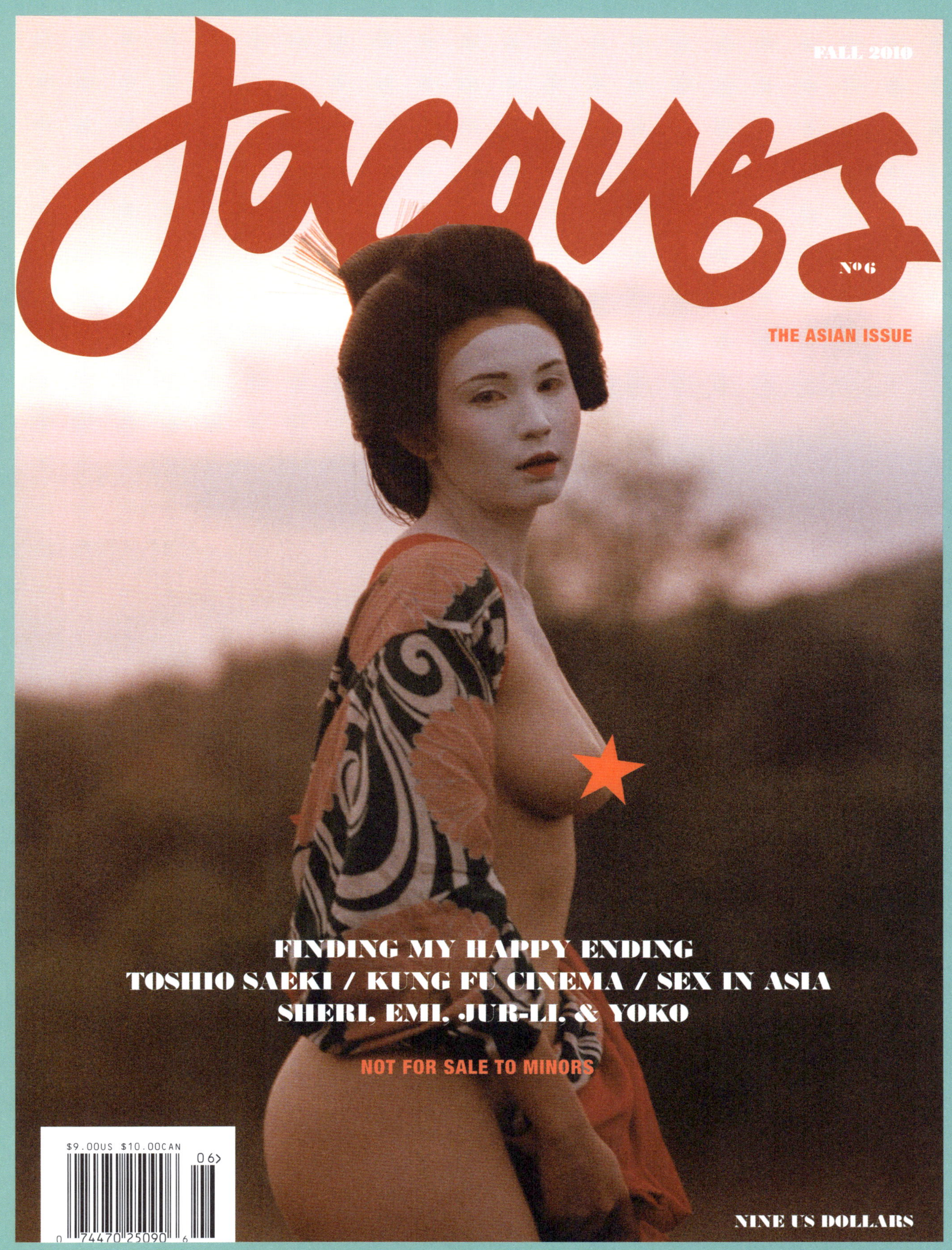

FALL 2010
Jacques
Nº 6
THE ASIAN ISSUE
FINDING MY HAPPY ENDING
TOSHIO SAEKI / KUNG FU CINEMA / SEX IN ASIA
SHERI, EMI, JUR-LI, & YOKO
NOT FOR SALE TO MINORS
$9.00US $10.00CAN
NINE US DOLLARS

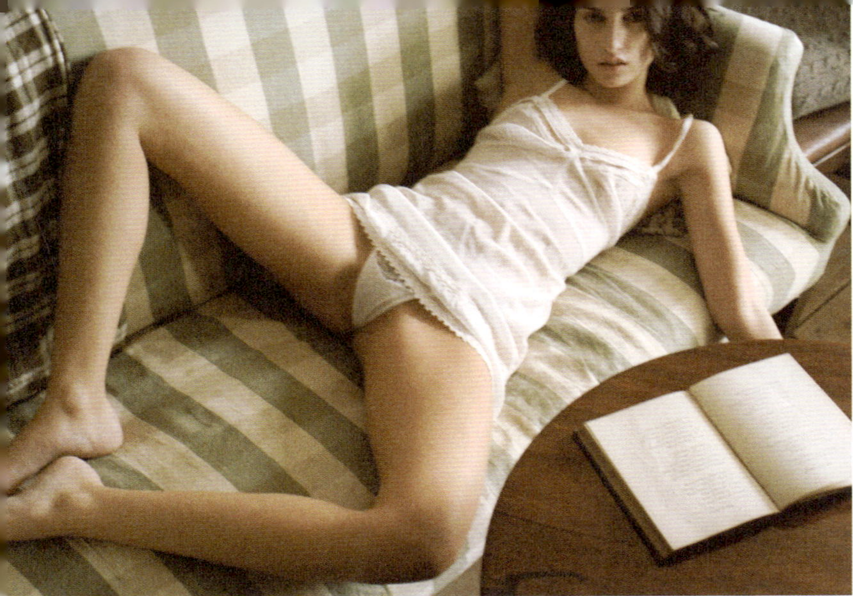

I don't feel special or anything. It's just funny. I'm an ex stripper. Who did he think he was playing with? I know how to get what I want. I told him *'you've had your taste, you want to see me again you have to book me for a shoot'*. The very next day my booker called to let me know Terry booked me.

The shoot was not that great though. I was having a miscarriage (I didn't let him know, I put a smile on my face and pretended nothing was wrong). But I still got what I wanted.

I would die for two things in life. My art and my children.

What is that role? Is the point of the magazine to sexually arouse readers, or are you working in a vacuum of nostalgia?

I like to turn people on. It's what I do best. I just do it in a different way.

The design of the magazines feels retro. Is that a deliberate direction?

Well my soon to be ex husband is 14 years older than me. What can I say? I like old.

Personally I could do older. The young bloods get too excited. But my therapist says I need to stop. So I'm trying new things. My third child's father (the one I'm pregnant with now) is only 5 and a half years older than me. It's actually inspired me to make a few new changes to the magazine.

Jacques has more in common with sex in advertising; it's a tease rather than hardcore digital porn. Is there a point at which an image becomes too explicit for Jacques to publish? Pubic hair? Genitalia?

I'm planning to challenge this in my new beginnings with *Jacques*. My husband made me feel really bad about spread legs. He talks about empowering women. But now that my eyes are really open, I see that with him it's actually about control. It's not because of our pussy, it's what makes us woman. I still prefer hair, but why be ashamed. Is it dirty? Is it vulgar? I don't really know... but I intend to find out.

Do you have a favourite shoot that best represents the mood and tone of Jacques?

I love them all. They're all my babies.

Who buys/reads Jacques? Men and women?

It may be the men who buy it but as soon as they get home, the girlfriends/wives snatch them.

How do you picture readers enjoying and making use of the magazine?

Hopefully how I do. On my boyfriends chest when I'm...

The traditional frame of reference for sex magazines is that it's a male business exploiting women. How does Jacques differ from this model?

I don't believe that crap for one minute. Trust me. Some women, including myself, love being sexual and powerful. I think *Jacques* portrays women as real, as what they are.

What fantasy THEY want to be for the day. *Jacques* differs because I am giving them a chance to be in control of what they want. Not what the men want.

But at the same time it is nice to bow down and please. Maybe the magazine has a nice compromise to it that I am unaware of?

Would you ever add men to the shoots?

I plan on it now that Jonathan is gone. But, I have weird taste. I like a good hairy chest and real muscles. You know, the kind men get from building stuff, lifting furniture, etc. Not fake gym muscles.

The magazine was launched by you and Jonathan Leder as a male-female team. Do you anticipate significant changes now that you are the lead editor?

I was always in charge. My husband just put restrictions on me and I would back down because we had children and he would get physical with me. Now that I have broken free I expect it to be better.

What are your future plans for the magazine?

Not sure. I never really had plans for the magazine to begin with. I just do what I want, cross my fingers, hope it works.

Any other comments/points you'd like to add?

In five years and two kids later and pregnant with my third I haven't been in front of the camera. I am now returning. And I'm taking it off for *Jacques*.

"WHEN I STARTED MODELLING EVERY AGENCY TOLD ME MY HIPS WERE TOO BIG, MY BOOBS WERE TOO BIG. BUT I WAS COMFORTABLE WITH MY BODY – I'D BEEN A STRIPPER FOR THREE YEARS IN TAMPA, FLORIDA AND STARTED DOING BURLESQUE WHEN I MOVED TO NEW YORK – AND THE PHOTOGRAPHERS LOVED ME. BRUCE WEBBER LOVED THE WAY I STRIPPED."

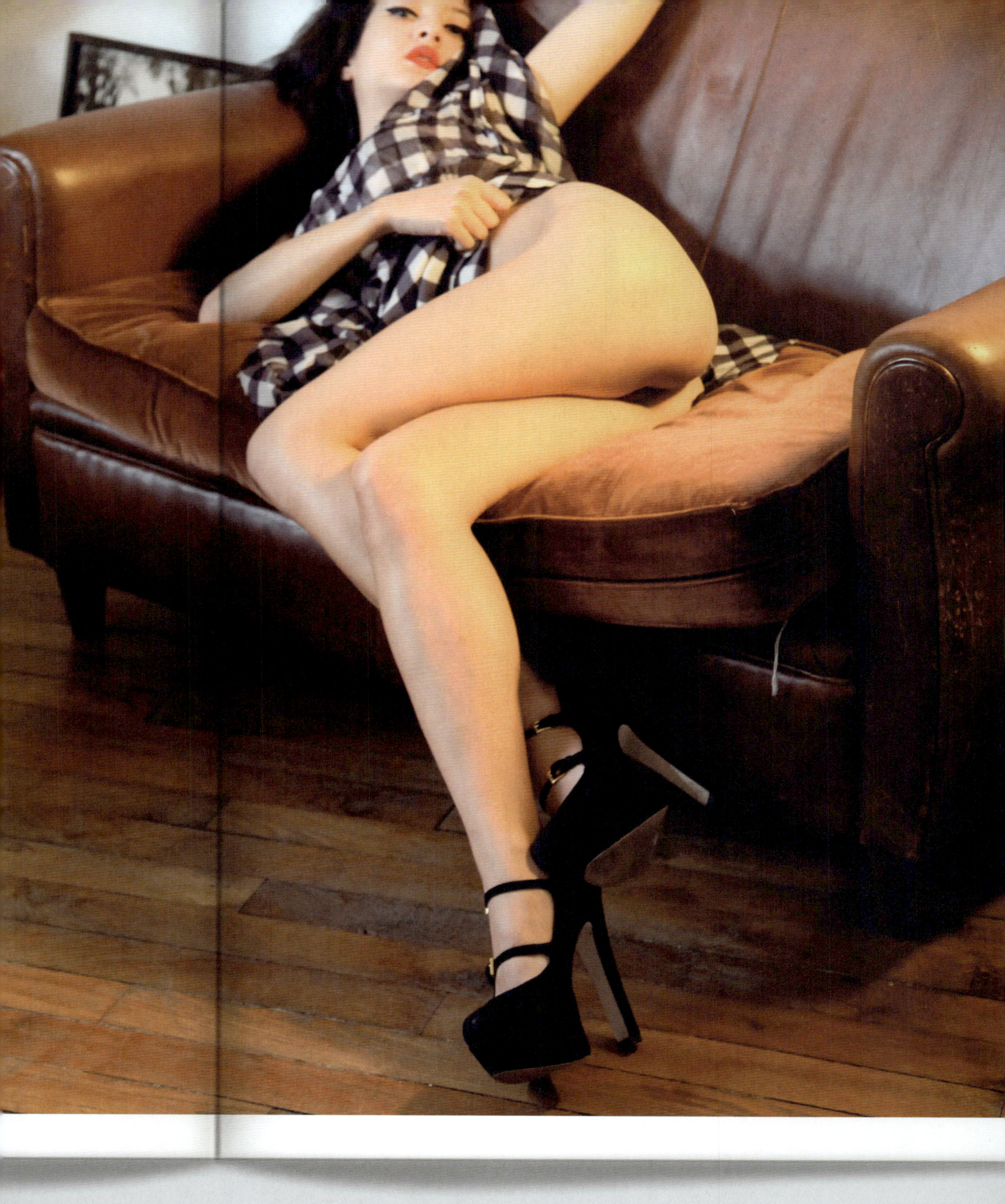

EROTICISM IN
FRAGMENTS

Edwarda emerged from the singular desire of a
25-year-old girl, Sam Guelimi, longing to express
a hushed sensitivity. A missing button, a lost glove,
a silk ribbon all came to embody silent eroticism.
Inspired by George Bataille's novel *Madame Edwarda*,
where the author explores the contradictory,
sometimes-destructive nature of sexuality, Guelimi
too seeks its constant ambivalence and porousness.
Today the founder, who is also the creative director,
is allowing her personal tastes and lustful memories
to guide her — moments of her past, a line of a book,
or an inch of a painting find themselves amplified
and sublimated throughout the issues.
Far from a news-based editorial structure, *Edwarda* offers
texts by authors (dead or alive) and discussions between
philosophers; the photo shoots resemble personal diaries
following various women into intimacy, some snapshot
style, some more theatrical.

INTERVIEW BY ALICE PFEIFFER.
PORTRAIT BY SÉBASTIEN AGNETTI.

WWW.EDWARDA.FR

Currently celebrating its second anniversary, *Edwarda* has also published books of photos and has held exhibitions in Paris.

If Bataille described Madame Edwarda as the *"lustful key to internal life"*, this modern-day interpretation is certainly true of Sam's concealed existence.

"THE IMAGES ARE, TO ME, FRAGMENTS OF STORIES. YOU CHOSE TO ENTER AT A SPECIFIC MOMENT, NOT BEFORE, NOT AFTER."

Hello Sam, how did you end up where you are today?

I was simply allergic to university, to the obligatory lectures, and the alarm clock early in the morning. So I preferred staying at home, watching films, listening to music and reading books. One author led me to another. What are the consequences of this solitary education? To this day, there are still names I can't pronounce properly, having never shared my new knowledge in fancy parties (where you never learn much more than the correct pronunciation of the artist you admire). And by the way, another one of my weaknesses is that I can't measure anything: I don't know what level zero is of intimacy. I owe the woman I am today to my friends. I have played and I have dreamed, and I have refined who I am through them.

Are there any specific moments in history, art, any places, that are key to who you are, and what you've put into *Edwarda* ?

I've come to realise that the people that surround and have accompanied me to this day can't be separated from the different pre-furnished flats I've had to live in and move from every three months (no warrantee or anything needed to move into those!) — these were often highly unlikely cohabitations.

First, rue de Savoie (by Saint-Michel): I lived with Dirty de Bataille, Loulou, PJ Harvey, Felicidad de Berthet, Marcello Mastroianni (in *La Dolce Vita* by Federico Fellini).

All I wore was a dress that you button in the front, which looked like the one Isabelle Adjani wore in *L'Eté Meurtrier*. There she is, sweating, and dancing at the firemen's ball. Or Marlon Brando, in *The Fugitive Kind...*

Secondly, rue de Charonne (by Bastille): *Sugar Kane* (Marilyn Monroe in Some Like It Hot), Stendhal and his fiascos, *Betty Blue* (played by Béatrice Dalle), saying, with this artificial voice: *"you were going to have a chilli all to yourself with the heat!"* I spent all my money on Belle Époque champagne because I loved the bottle. Dominique Ristori (the director of the Common Research Centre, an institute of the European Commission), then my neighbour, used to leave an article from *La Recherche* (the leading scientific research magazine). It started with *"and in the morning, right when she was about to leave, by foot..."*

Thirdly, rue Saint Honoré (by Place Vendôme): Ingrid Caven, *Albertine* by Proust, *the Prince of New York* (Abel Ferrara). This is when I met Jefferson (John Jefferson Selve, today editor-in-chief of *Edwarda*). We were drunk and danced to Maria Callas, a smell of pomegranate hanging in the air, which came from Santa Maria Novella, in Florence.

} p.49

Sam Guelimi shot by
Sébastien Agnetti

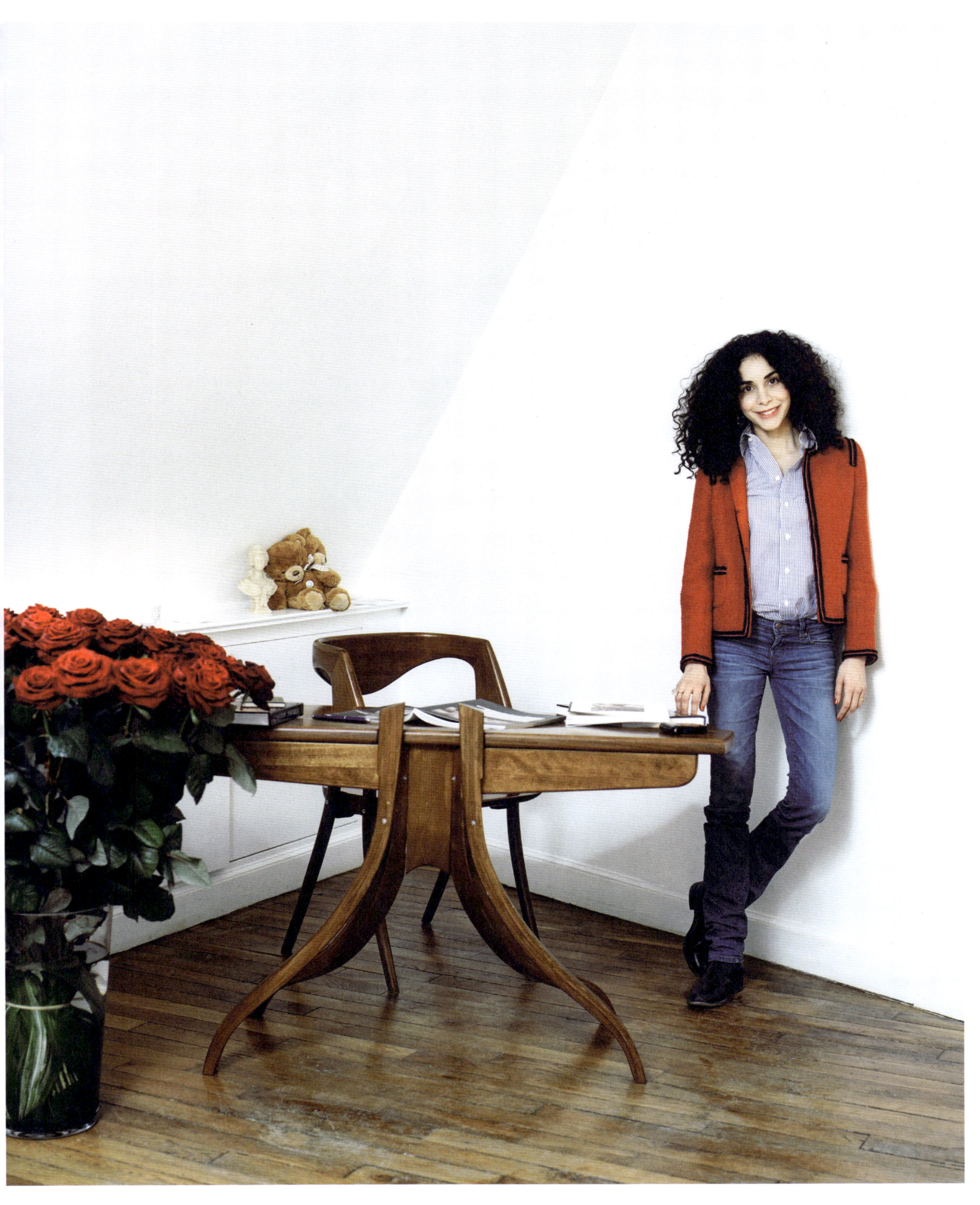

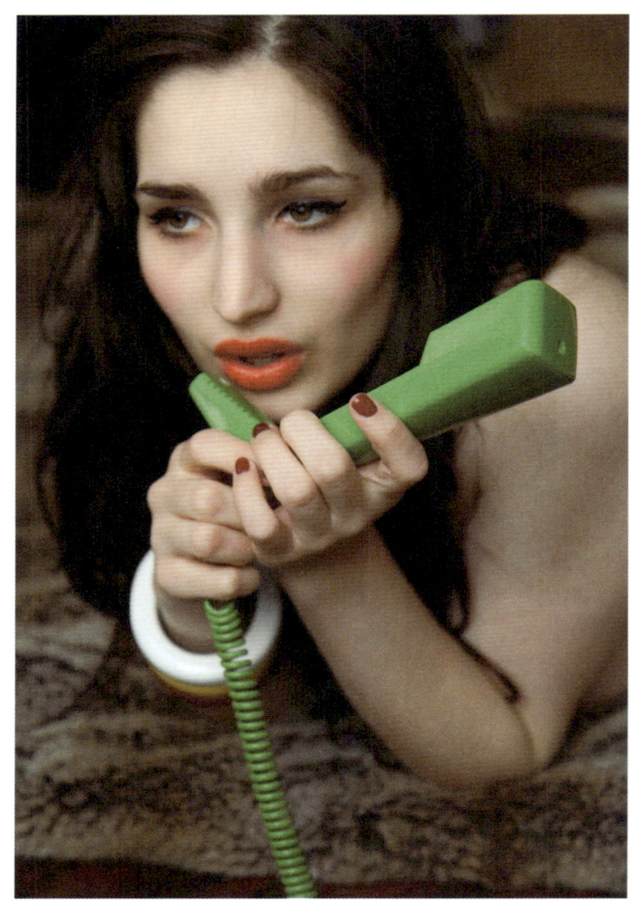

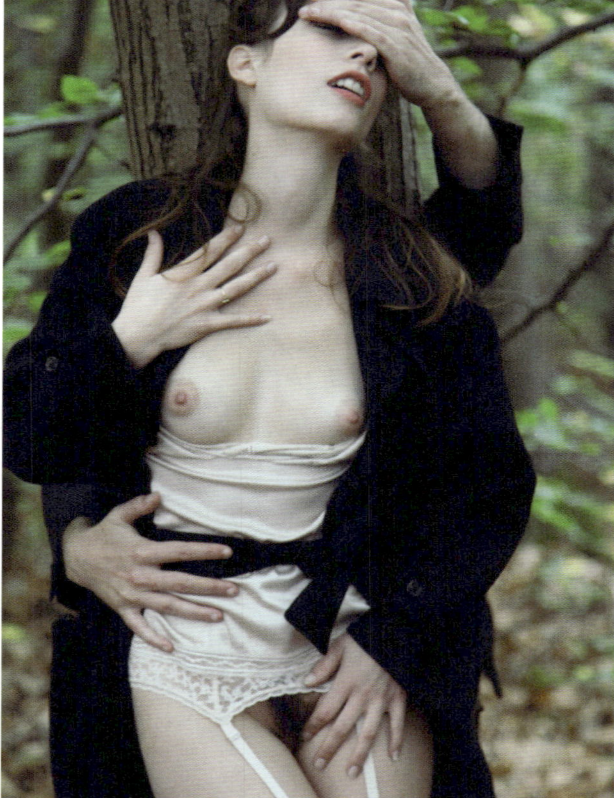

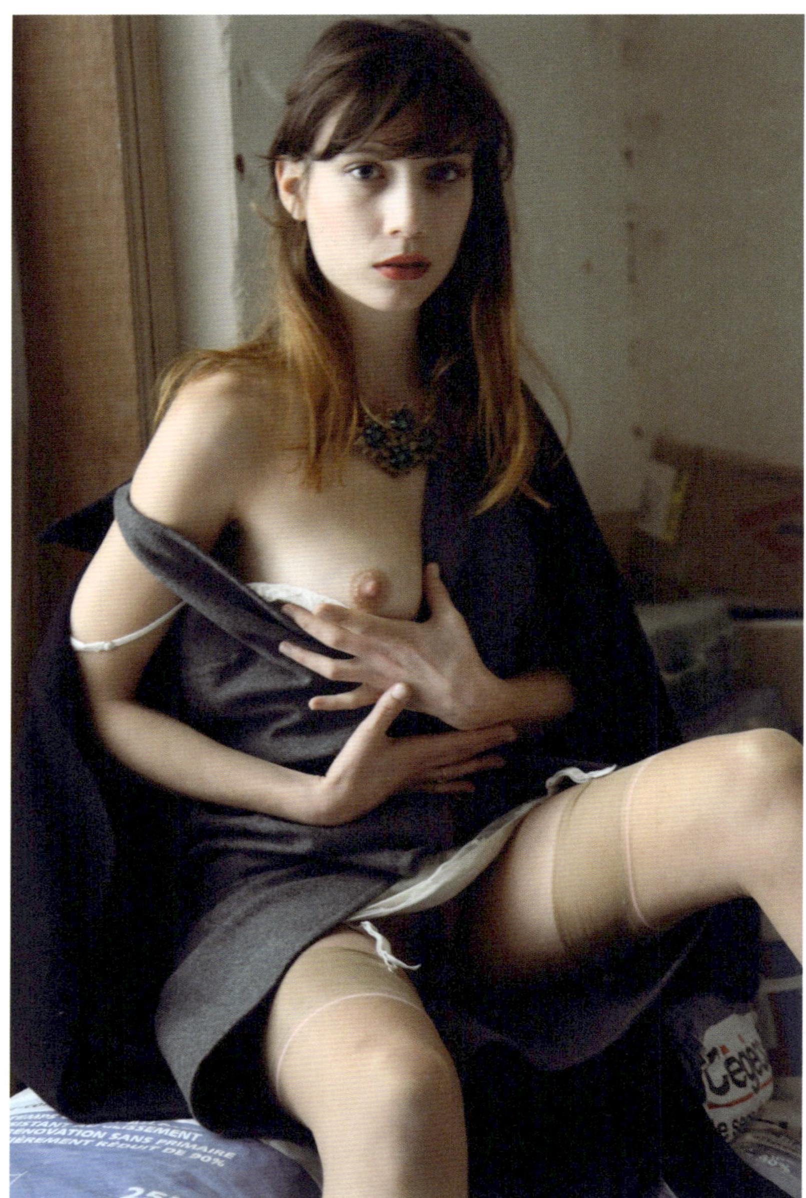

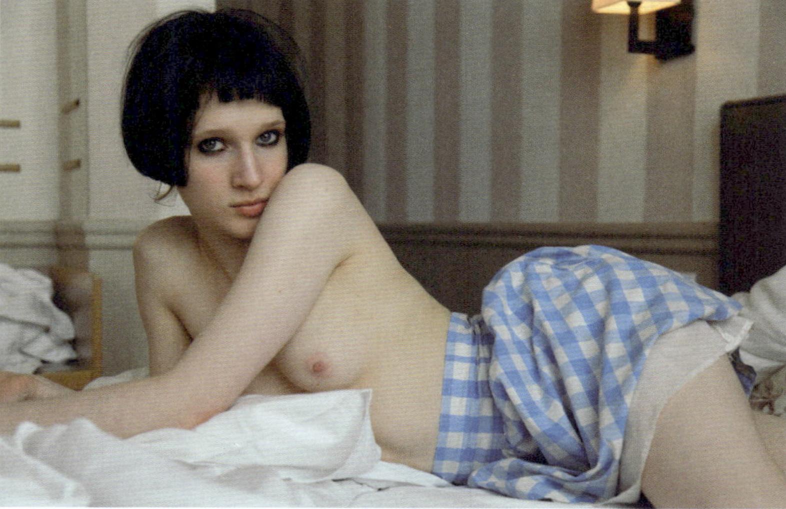

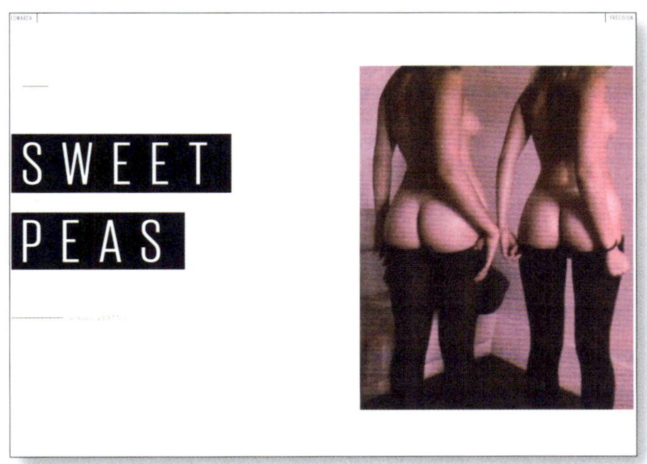

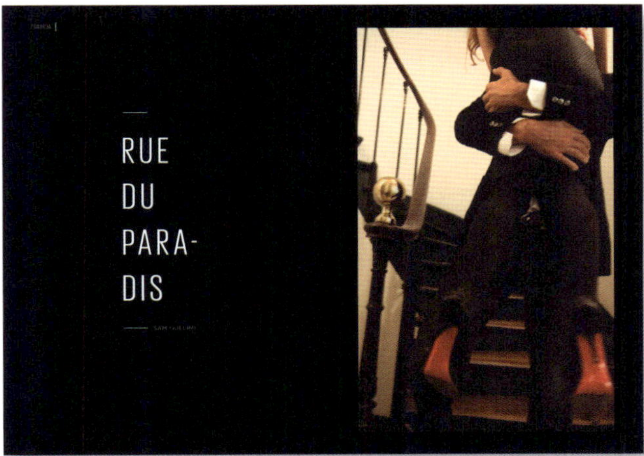

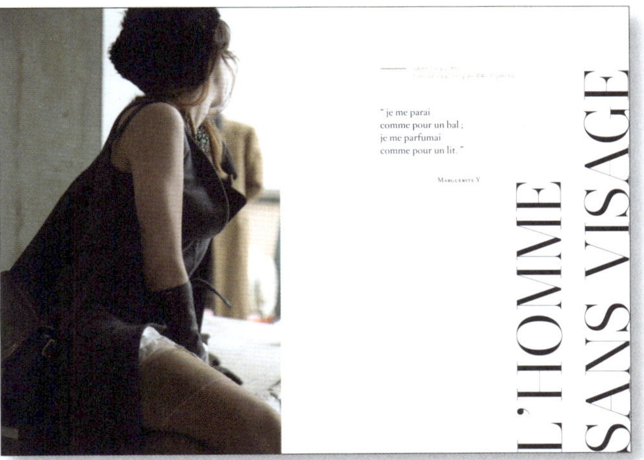

The funny part is that each of these apartments, for their peculiar connections, could have led to an issue of *Edwarda*.

How did *Edwarda* come about? What was the concept, and the desire behind it?

I had the strong desire for this internal erotic life to be inscribed, to find an incarnation. My friends John Jefferson, Dominique Ristori, and then Ferdinand Gouzon *(writer and journalist)*, became part of this. Other people, more discreet ones, helped me finance this dream publication.

Did you feel a certain cultural void? Something missing in the field of magazines?

No, what was lacking came from within myself. *Edwarda* was both madness and a necessity: I dreamed of a place where people could meet, where hypersensitivity would be the leading strength.

Why are you so attracted to eroticism?

Eroticism to me is delight. I want to indulge myself in this delighful experience.

What kind of eroticism are you talking about, and how do you maintain this across the issues?

The eroticism I wanted to talk about is called The Game. We play with sentences, colours, the creases in clothes, a haggard face when the body is open, gazes that grab you... these are rules you invent. All we want is for our images to be accessible, for it to be easy to penetrate them... and not so easy to leave them!

What has the evolution been since the early days of *Edwarda*?

From one issue to the next, it became obvious to us that we were chasing something unattainable: disorder. We, who feared the end of *Edwarda*, had it wrong. We never ended up being satisfied with the issue that came before, ultimately that meant that we still had a few more stories to invent: the starting point could be a ribbon around a tree for example (in the last issue: precision).

What are you trying to prove or break down about contemporary society and its relation to sexuality?

Our preoccupations are a lot more personal. For example, I discovered that, to me, Eroticism and joy form an indivisible whole. *Edwarda* is a lot closer to precepts than concepts.

Let's talk about photography. What 'use', what vision and place do the photo shoots have? A series of photos where sexuality naturally seeps in, or a sexualized fashion shoot?

As I told you, in *Edwarda*, eroticism is something that inscribes itself and finds an incarnation. Therefore, the images

} p.52

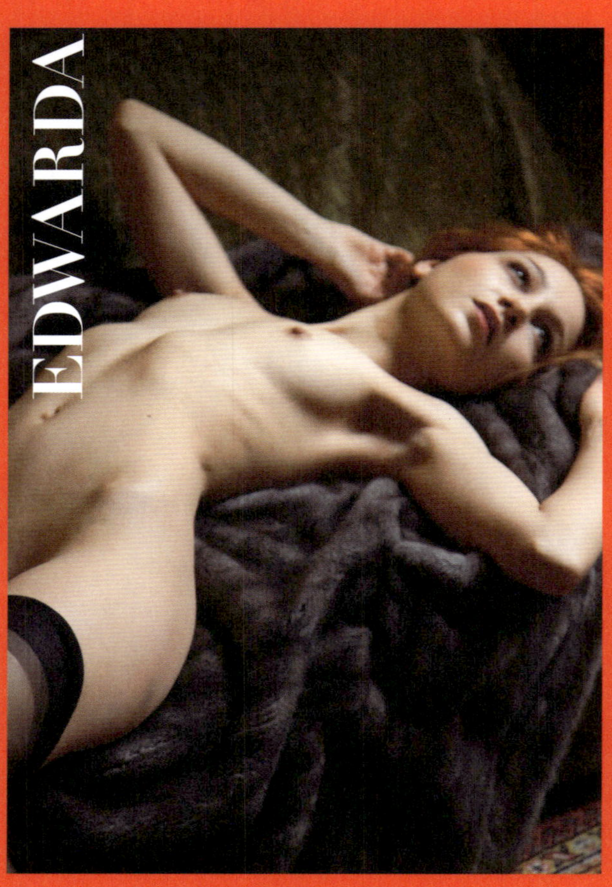

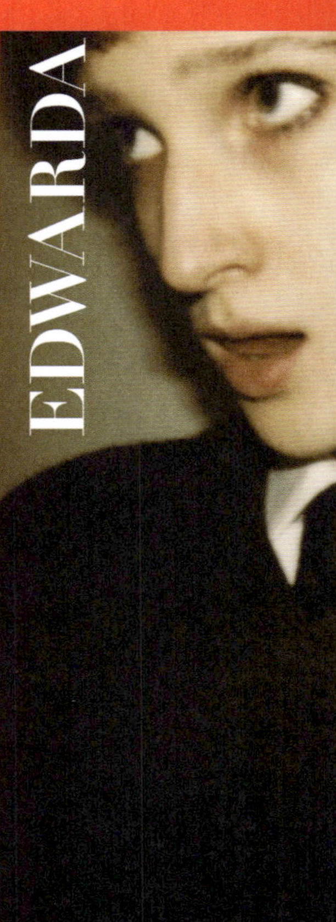

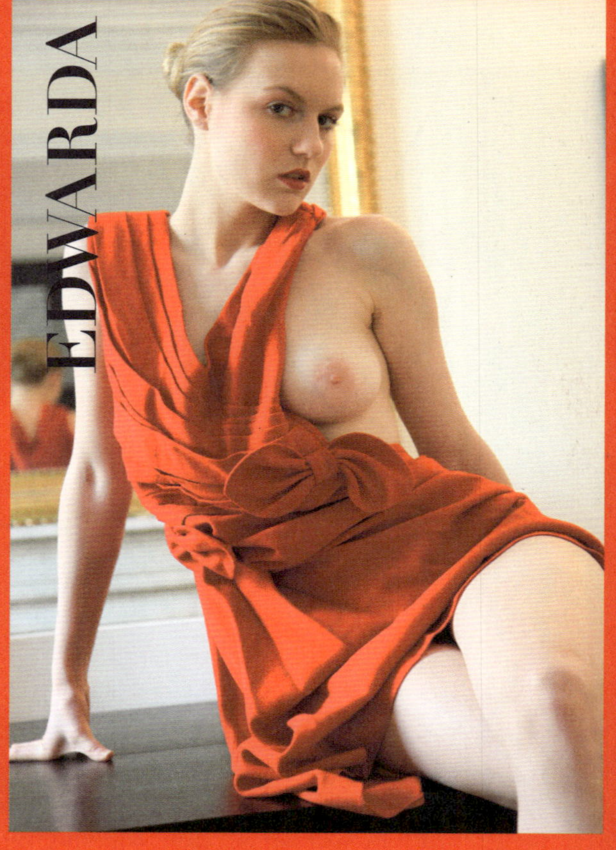

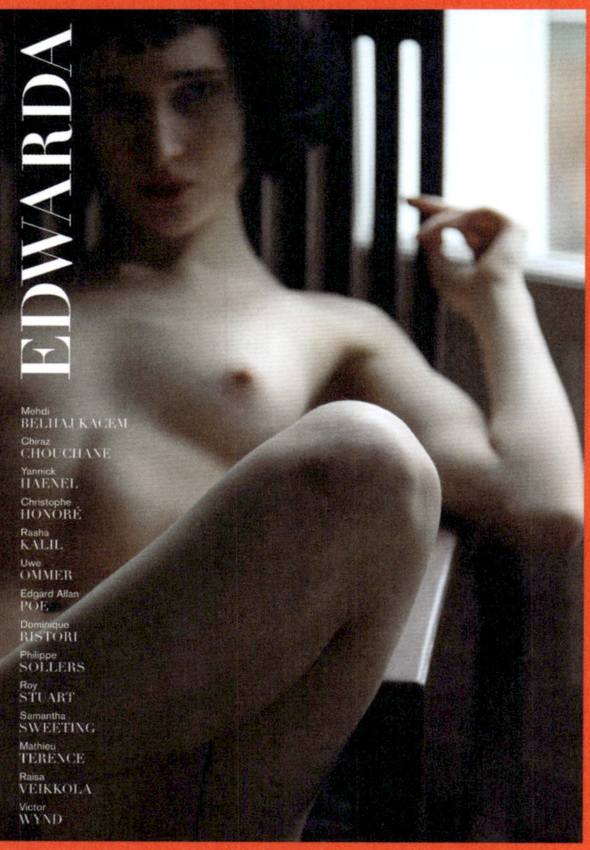

Mehdi
BELHAJ KACEM

Chiraz
CHOUCHANE

Yannick
HAENEL

Christophe
HONORÉ

Rasha
KALIL

Uwe
OMMER

Edgard Allan
POE

Dominique
RISTORI

Philippe
SOLLERS

Roy
STUART

Samantha
SWEETING

Mathieu
TERENCE

Raisa
VEIKKOLA

Victor
WYND

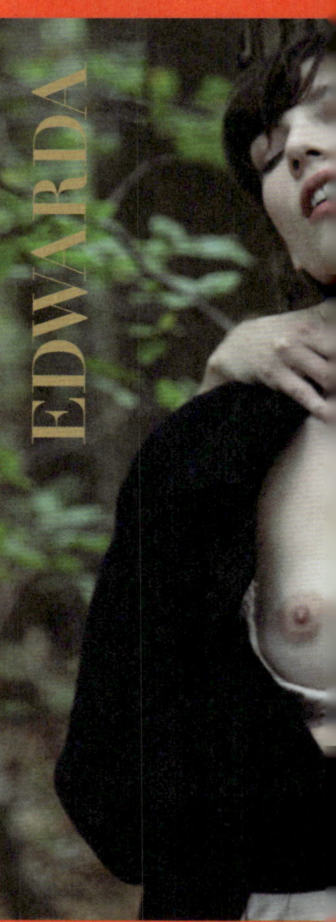

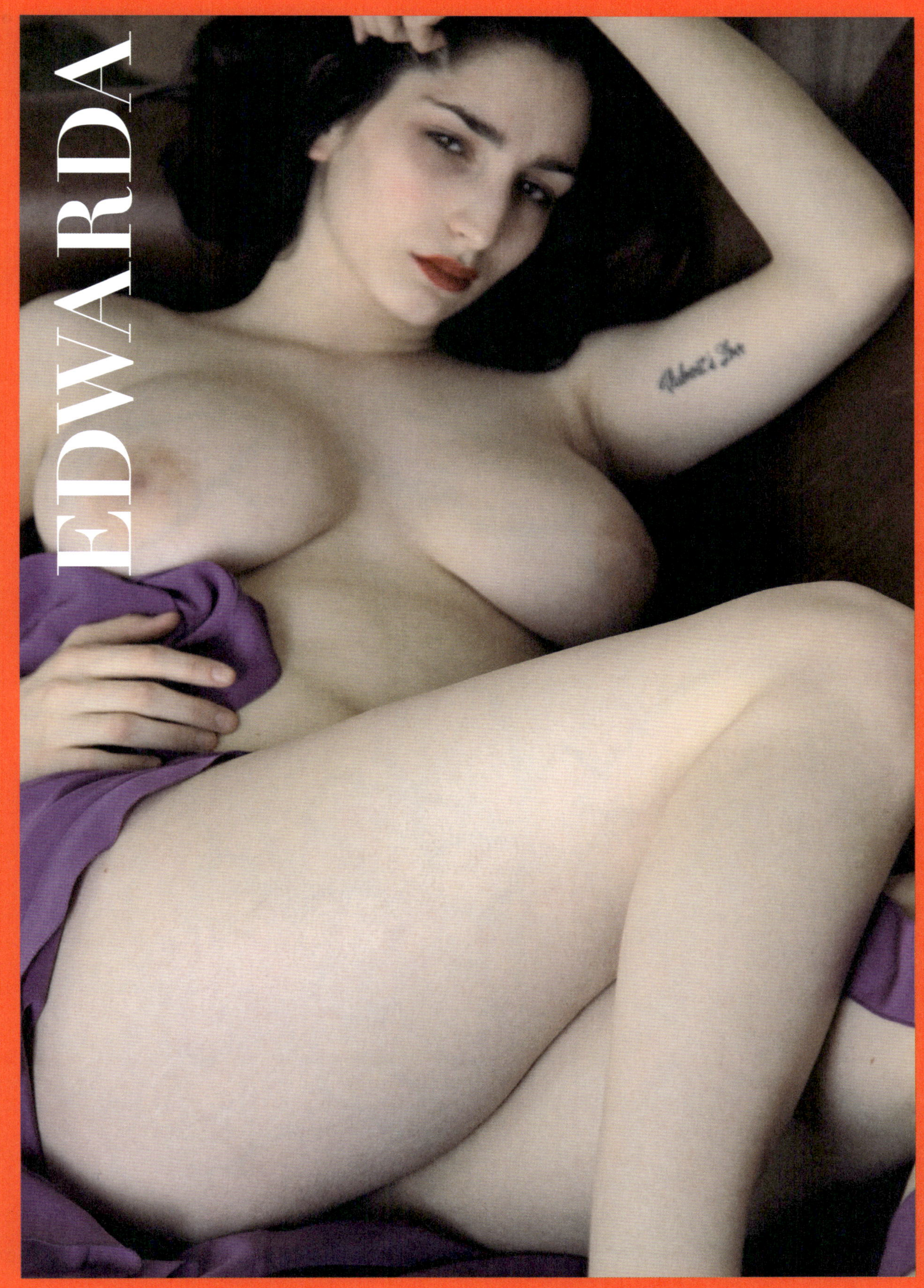

EDWARDA

are, to me, fragments of stories. You chose to enter at a specific moment, not before, not after. When she is still wearing her clothes or when she unties her hair... and then you daydream about what happens next... guessing is desiring...

You have also been involved in various projects surrounding the magazine, correct?

Yes, after a first exhibition of my photographs at Ofr *[Paris-based bookshop and art space]*, also celebrating the launch of issue 6, another show is currently in the pipelines. It will take place in April, at the Galerie Libertine in Brussels.

This will also coincide with *Fatales*, the planned title for spring. I am also working on group shows based around the images produced for *Edwarda*. Selecting and guiding photographers, depending on the theme and their sensitivity, is an important part of my work; it also includes finding the perfect model for the shoot, that I then dress with my clothes (or rather, undress).

The moment I most love is the editing. What is exciting to me, is that I have to pick one story from thousands of options. It is subjectivity that gives the magazine its singularity.

So it's a multi-media and multi-layered sensitivity you are promoting?

Yes, every issue is the outcome of meetings and collaborations with writers and filmmakers. Those lead to a text or an image that wouldn't have been born otherwise. I love the idea that there are sentences that have yet to be written, floating between the writer and me, which one day inscribe themselves onto the pages of *Edwarda*.

Essentially *Edwarda* is privileged enough not to have to bend to the need for news but rather to allow encounters to bloom naturally and out of our love for something specific. From one issue to the next, collaborators grow increasingly closer to *Edwarda*. I remember my first meeting with writer Yannick Haenel, in a Parisian café. Because we got on so well, a beautiful text was born, *The solitude of Anna Thomson* - that evening, we felt that it was going to overwhelm both of us. I could also tell you about Mathieu Terence. We met at Café de Flore, we were shy, and thus nothing happened. As he was about to leave, he gave me *Les Jeunes Filles de l'Ombre*. And that's when I really got to know him-after I read the short stories. It was magical, because I realised that we dreamed of the same women, women who were equally desirable as they were intelligent. I mean a sensitive intelligence. Since then, he has written six short stories for *Edwarda*, which, I hope, we can gather and publish. I can also tell you that Dominique Ristory and myself are thinking hard about a book that would tell a story, with a mixture of words and images.

How do you keep the magazine alive, business-wise?

I admit we are very lucky. *Edwarda* is an independent publication. The generosity of various art patrons that supported us when we launched the magazine has ultimately enabled its freedom. The readers, some of whom are loyal subscribers, allow us to finance the printing. But today, we need to think of advertising to help *Edwarda* grow. This would allow us for example, to have access to exceptional places for photo shoots, which our current production doesn't allow. Or to cover *Edwarda* models in beautiful dresses and sumptuous jewellery: my wardrobe is limited! We are in contact with several advertisers who seem to understand us, and the upcoming collaborations won't only be commercial but creative. Others, less bold, will probably not even grant us a meeting. But we aren't as touchy as in the beginning. We cope with those refusals.

Do you have any idea of your circulation and readership?

Around 3000 readers show interest and loyalty. We always try to improve our work, to make them shiver and show them secret passages.

Who are they?

We don't know that, but they are part of our quest for beauty and sensuality. Because of these non-utilitarian concerns, *Edwarda* is a luxury publication.

Where do you draw the line between eroticism and vulgarity?

Being vulgar isn't the point. *Edwarda* has a transient aesthetic proposition. We are experimenting. It can be successful, but we are never safe from landing beside the point. We will be vulgar...when we fail. And we get close, because we don't want to be cautious and stop earlier. Erotic excitement is at the border. It implies taking risks.

Vulgarity isn't excess like it is portrayed today: too much lipstick, too many curves – these overly feminine signs don't scare us. We play with them, we invite a dissonance, because it's from discordance that the blur emerges. Not in the linear, the smooth. What if vulgarity was equal to conformity? Desire is never vulgar.

Unconsciously we all have limits, and that's for the best. We're lucky to be able to play with those. We are going to take good care of these limits, otherwise the game is over: there is no more transgression today... the fun is about stopping right on time.

You've been compared to *l'Imparfaite* before, as they also are an erotic magazine, which emerged round the same time. What is the main difference between *Edwarda* and *l'Imparfaite*?

There is one major difference: they graduated from Sciences Po, I didn't!

"EDWARDA WAS BOTH MADNESS AND A NECESSITY: I DREAMED OF A PLACE WHERE PEOPLE COULD MEET, WHERE HYPERSENSITIVITY WOULD BE THE LEADING STRENGTH."

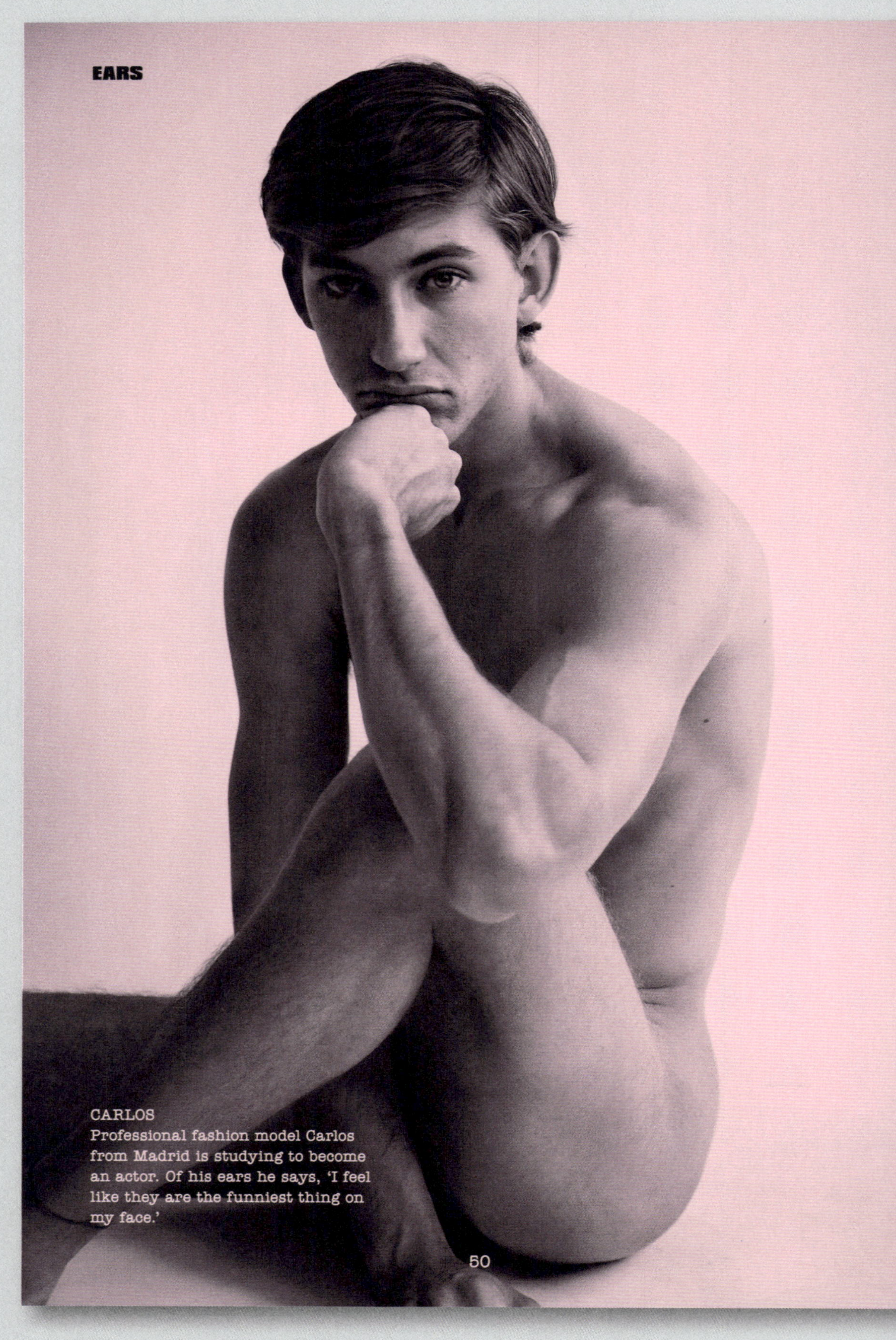

CARLOS
Professional fashion model Carlos
from Madrid is studying to become
an actor. Of his ears he says, 'I feel
like they are the funniest thing on
my face.'

THE SILENT REVOLUTION

Journalist Gert Jonkers met editorial designer Jop van Bennekom back in 1998 while editing Dutch monthly magazine *Blvd*. They worked together at that magazine for less than a year, but it was long enough to establish the foundation of a friendship and creative partnership that would invigorate modern independent publishing.

Two years later they launched their first magazine together. Called *Butt*, it was a proud "fag mag" for "interesting homosexuals and the men who love them." Uncensored and sexually explicit, the plan for the magazine was simple; it would publish candid conversations between gay men. Ten years later, it's stayed true to that manifesto and, with it, helped re-define gay culture. The magazine became a positive, life-affirming influence on its readers.

Interview by Steven Gregor.
Photography by Andrea Larsson.

In the same period, the duo also launched biannual style magazines *Fantastic Man* and *The Gentlewoman* (the latter is edited by Penny Martin, Professor of Fashion Imagery at the London College of Fashion). These magazines have adopted the same genre-challenging editorial philosophy as *Butt* and confirmed Gert and Jop's publishing credentials.

A surprise to many of its readers, late last year the duo published the final issue of *Butt*.

"GAY CULTURE IS VERY DIFFERENT TODAY THAN IT WAS 10 YEARS AGO, IT'S MUCH MORE DEMOCRATIC."

Why did you start *Butt*?

Gert: There was something seriously lacking in gay media. Magazines had no relationship with us and with being gay. We enjoyed American magazines like *Index* and *Straight to Hell*... and some fanzines from the west coast in the US we'd somehow stumbled upon. But there wasn't anything that felt close to us in a geographical sense.

What didn't you like about gay magazines around that time?

Jop: We hated gay magazines and we didn't like gay culture. Around that time it was so incredibly uncool to be gay. It was a total cliché, so mainstream. We responded to that by making something that was subculture... where being gay and thinking in a different way could be inspiring. We wanted to create a magazine for men who thought about things in a new way. It was also about being brutally honest. The whole magazine was Q and A: just men chatting.

What was different about *Butt*?

Jop: Butt was about gay men identifying more with men than with women. That was something seriously lacking in gay media... even in the porn that was around at the time. And that's completely changed. I'm pleased that things have changed in gay culture. The focus has shifted to masculinity.

Generally speaking, do you think gay magazines are better today than they were back then?

Jop: Gay culture is very different today than it was 10 years ago, it's much more democratic.

Gert: The gay scene has changed a lot... it's constantly changing. So the need for a gay publication changes.

Jop: Yeah, gay magazines have improved... many have re-invented themselves as fashion magazines. And that was a big shift with *Butt*. A lot of people who started out reading *Butt* switched to *Fantastic Man*.

So, did *Butt* have a younger readership?

Jop: Yeah, *Butt* magazine had a lot of younger readers. Especially when we started being distributed in all American Apparel stores. American Apparel bought loads of copies of the magazine. And all of a sudden *Butt* started to reach people in places like Columbus, Ohio and Mexico City and all over the world. It was really great.

***Butt* was a celebration of being queer, of sex and the body... without resorting to the body fascism so common in gay culture. Did you expect *Butt* to become such a positive role model?**

} p.59

Gert Jonkers and
Jop van Bennekom shot by
Andreas Larsson

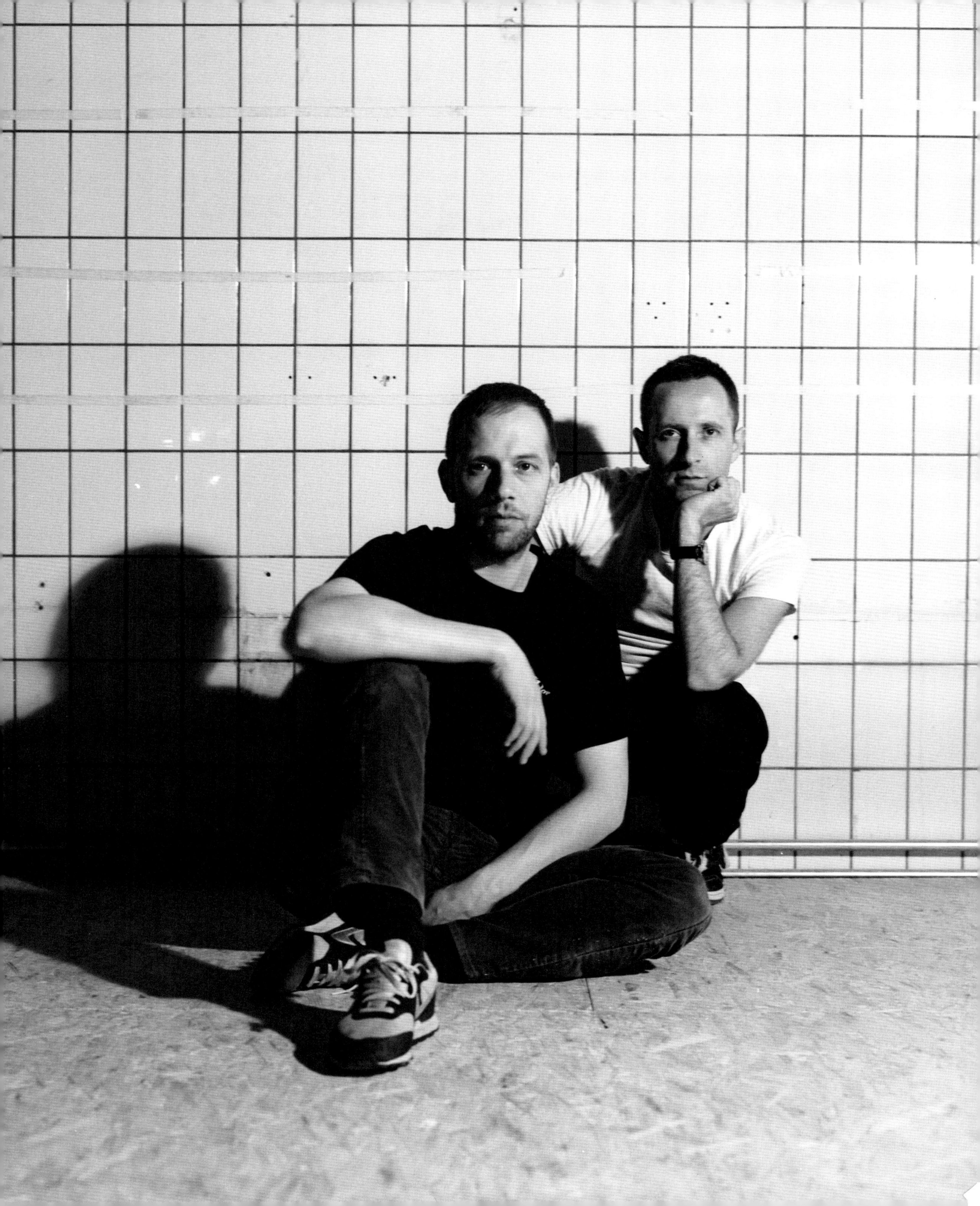

Magazines that inspired Gert & Jop

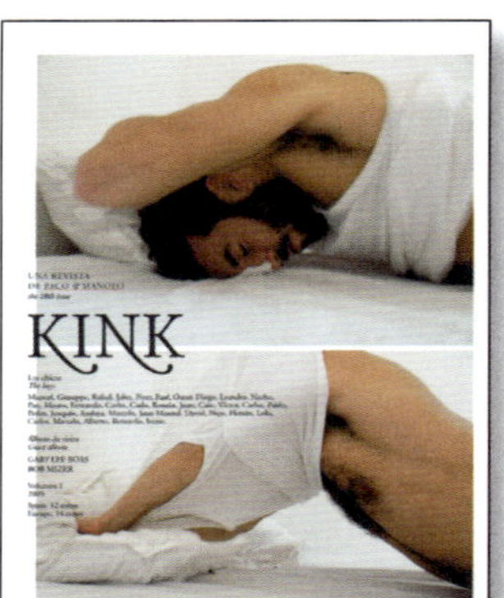

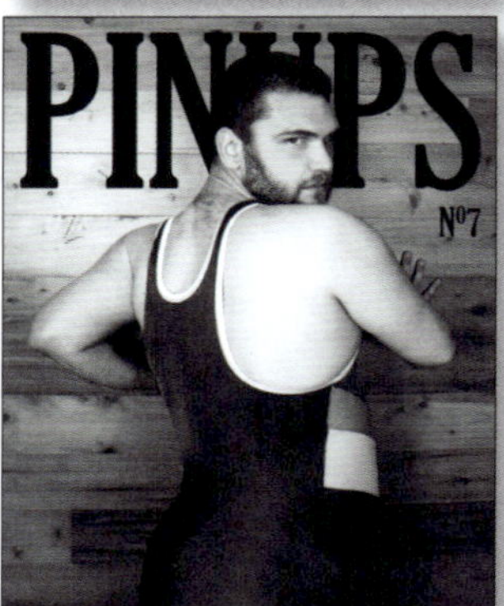

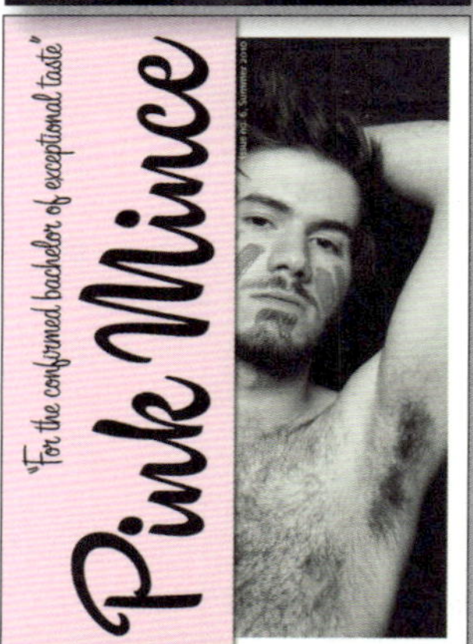

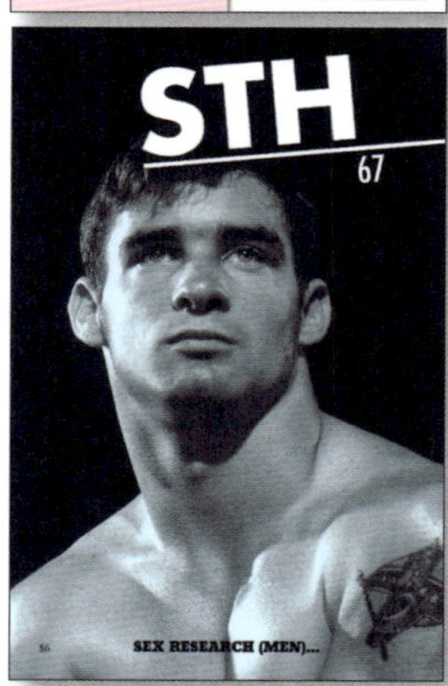

Fantastic Man & the gentlewoman
Gert & Jop's current projects

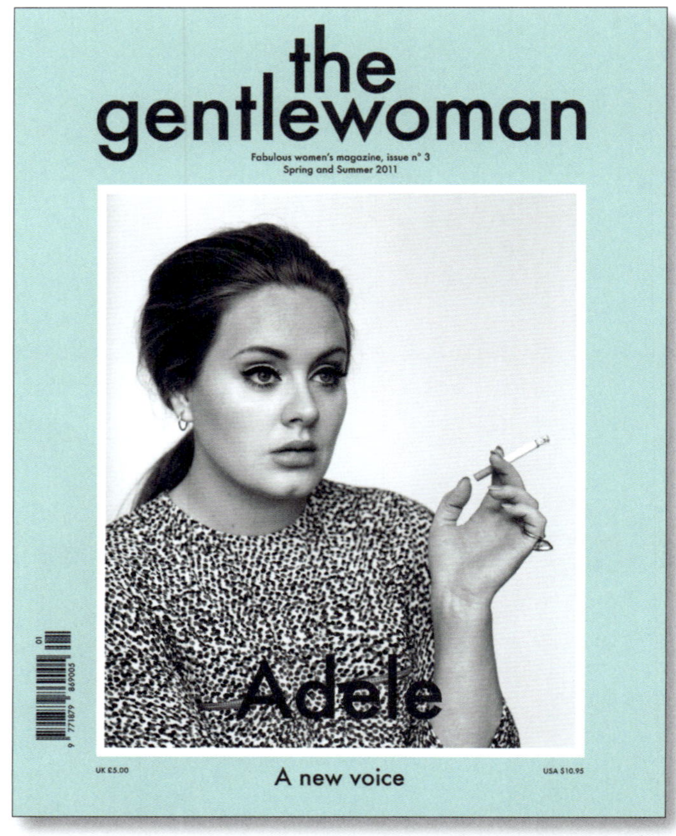

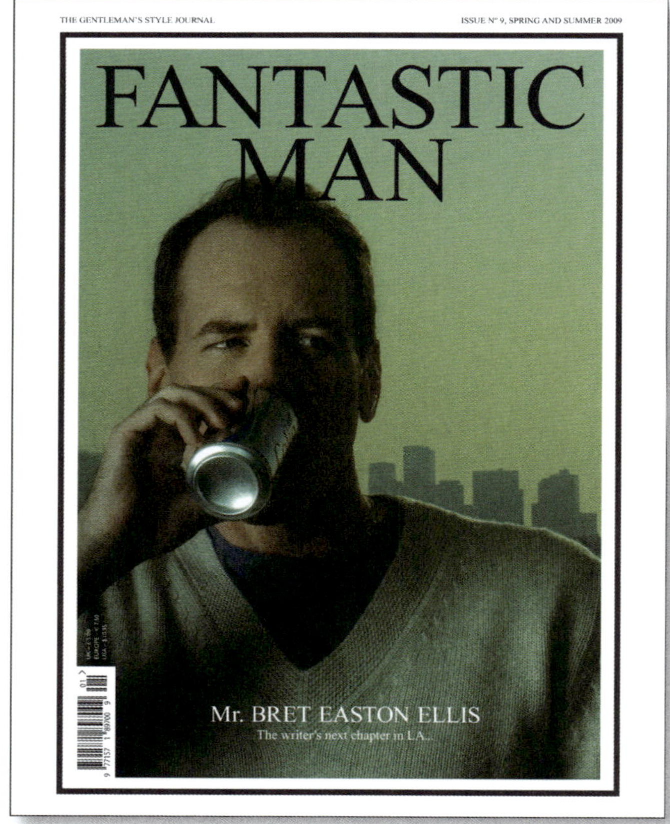

Butt inside spreads

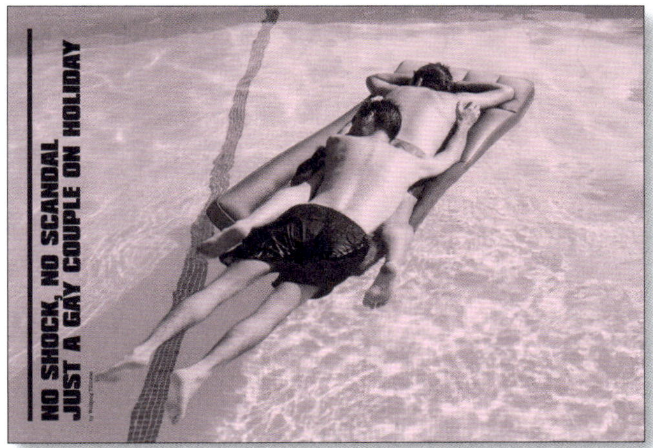

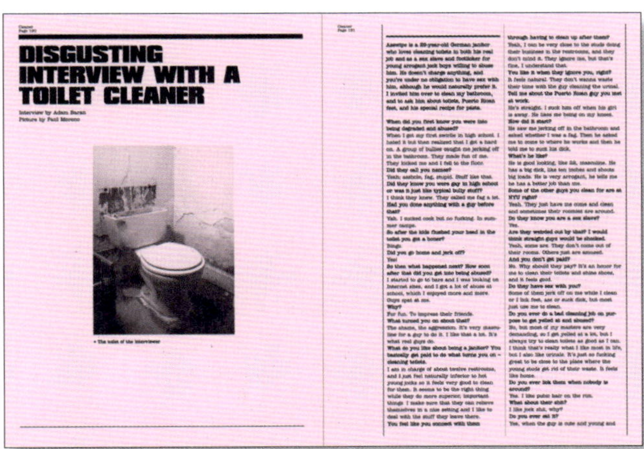

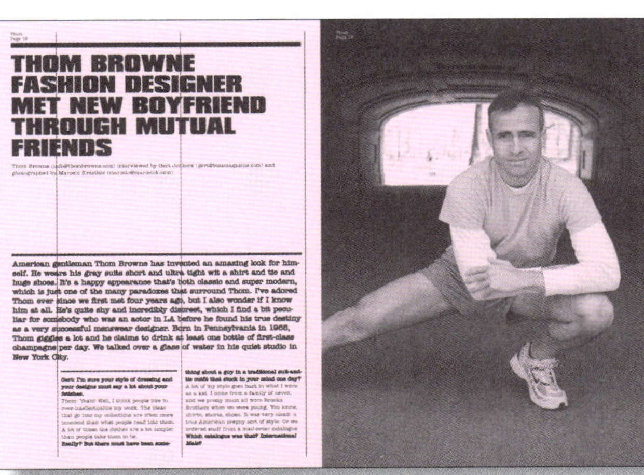

<u>Jop:</u> I think the 20s is such an informative period. Often, gay men especially have a lot of things to sort out. And *Butt* magazine really spoke to those people.

So, editorially and stylistically, do you think there are similarities between *Butt* and *Fantastic Man*? And, indeed, *The Gentlewoman* too?

<u>Gert:</u> [Surprised] You think there are similarities between *The Gentlewoman* and *Butt*?

Well, in that both *Butt* and *The Gentlewoman* are respectful of the people they profile. Many gay magazines and women's titles push an unhealthy notion of body image… and they like to mock their peers. Your titles are the antidote to this.

<u>Jop:</u> They're all magazines about people. I think they're quite similar in that respect. It's hard for us to say because we're so close to them. We tried to do something a little different with *The Gentlewoman*, but maybe we didn't succeed.

<u>Gert:</u> Each is about honesty and grounded in reality. Being based in reality has always been very important to us. And they all have our tone of voice, that's unavoidable.

***Butt*'s design was quite unique, delineated text – set in the traditional (old fashioned, even) American Typewriter typeface – and reportage-style photography. How do you describe it?**

<u>Jop:</u> *Butt*'s design aesthetic is grounded in the idea of absolute necessity. Black and white, printed on pink paper. It looks sexy. Super simple and straightforward.

<u>Gert:</u> The utility of newspapers was another inspiration. The idea for *Butt* was simple. We published conversations between homosexuals. We'd always been more interested in newspapers than traditional glossy magazines. Rule number one for *Butt* has been to keep it real and to keep it simple.

Were you inspired by any other magazines?

<u>Jop:</u> Andy Warhol's *Interview*, of course. And we looked at *Straight to Hell* magazine.

Visually, the magazine didn't change… it didn't evolve.

<u>Jop:</u> I didn't know how to improve it. We felt it was perfect. We worked on the first issue for more than a year.

And, what about the magazine's photographic style? Images were not re-touched… you even published covers with red eye. How do you describe the photographic style?

<u>Jop:</u> It's also super straightforward. Honest. No one's acting or pretending to be someone else. It's relaxed.

In the proceeding 10 years, did you feel pressure to become more outrageous or explicit?

}p.62

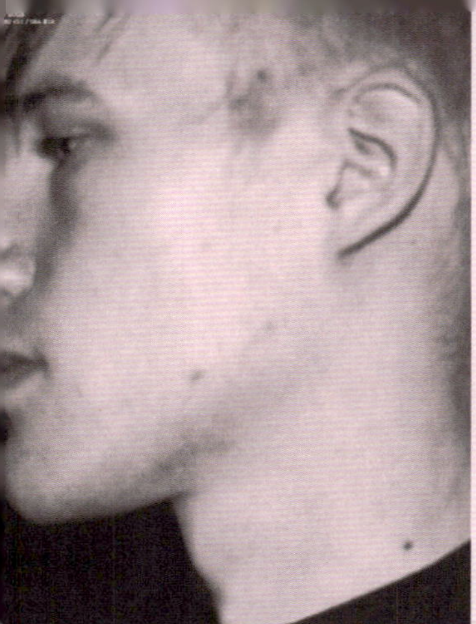
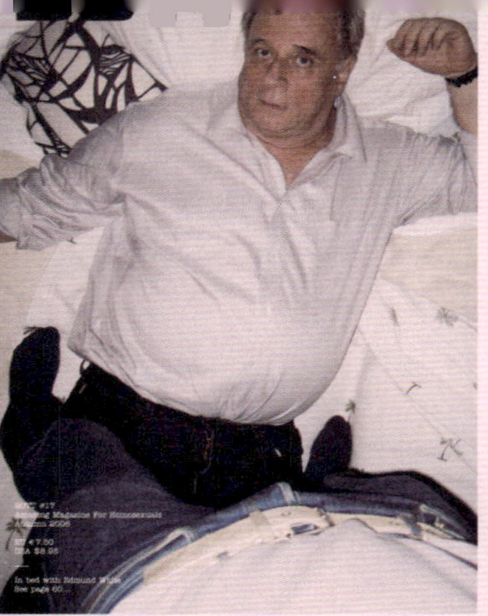
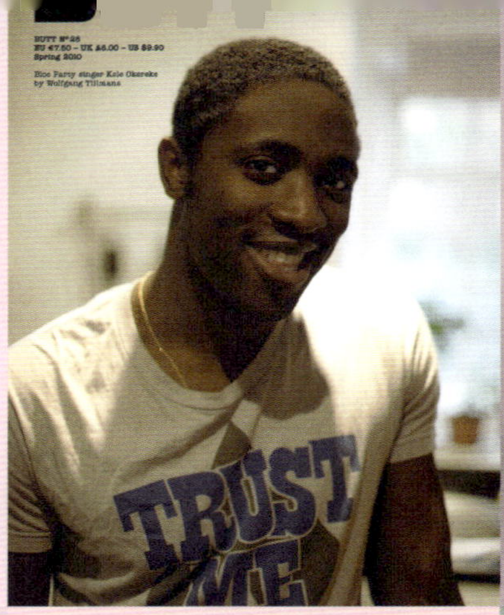
TRUST
ME
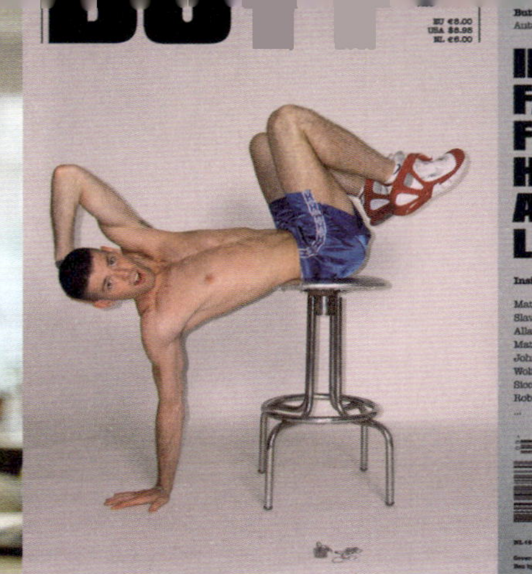
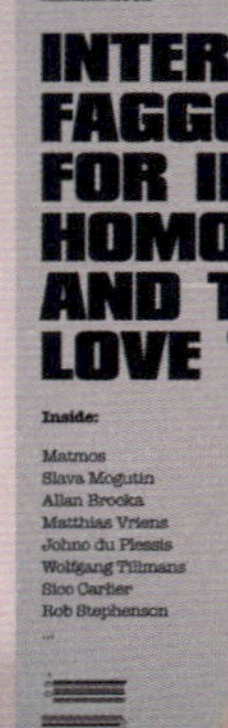
Butt Magazine #5
Autumn 2002
INTERN
FAGGO
FOR IN
HOMOS
AND TH
LOVE T
Inside:
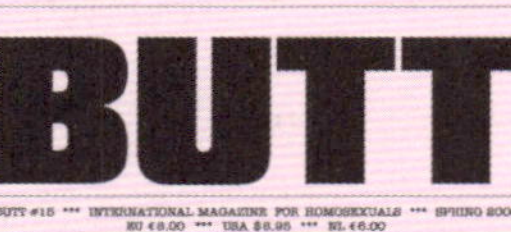
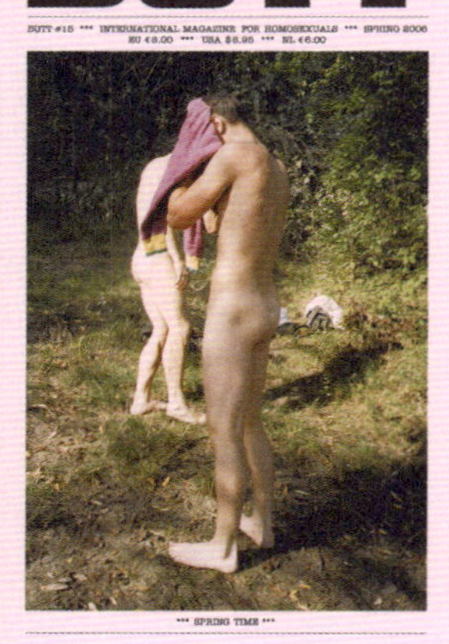
BUTT
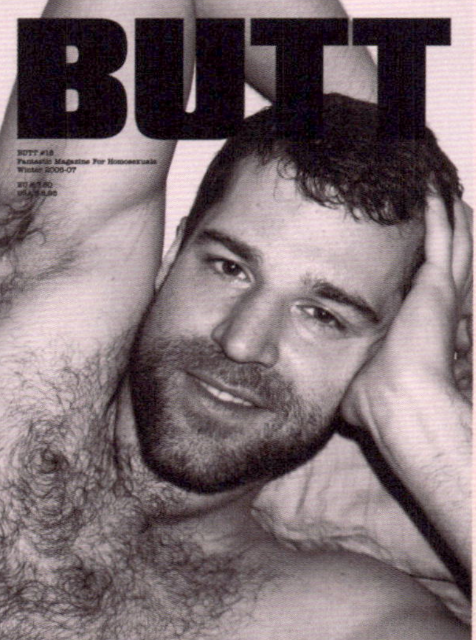
BUTT
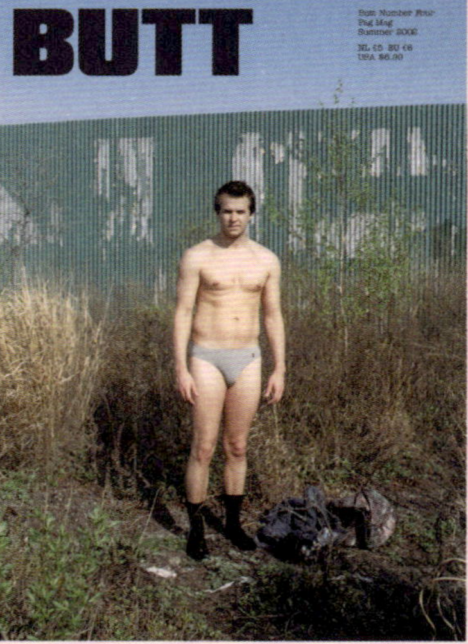
BUTT
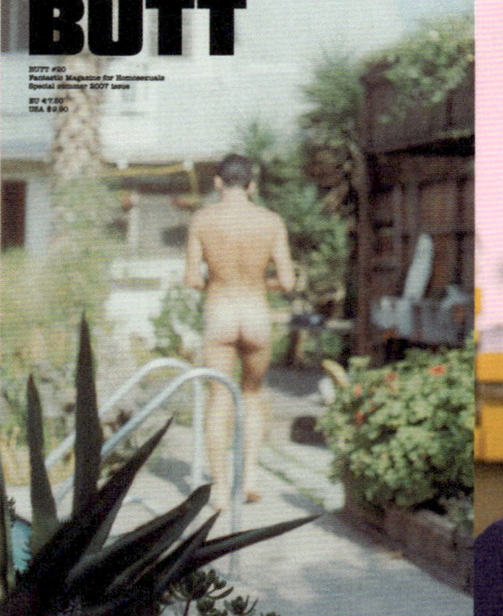
BUTT
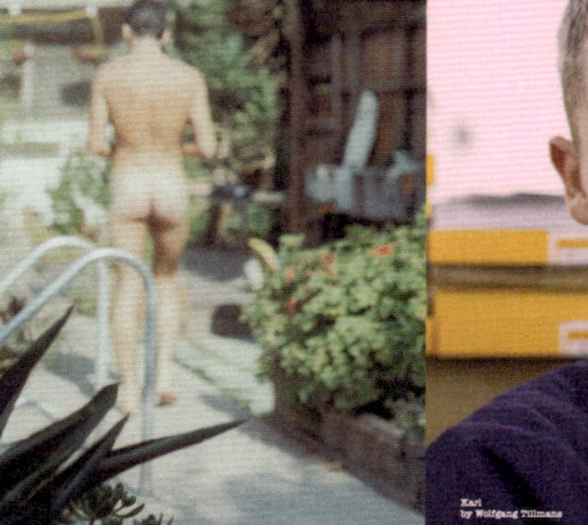
BU
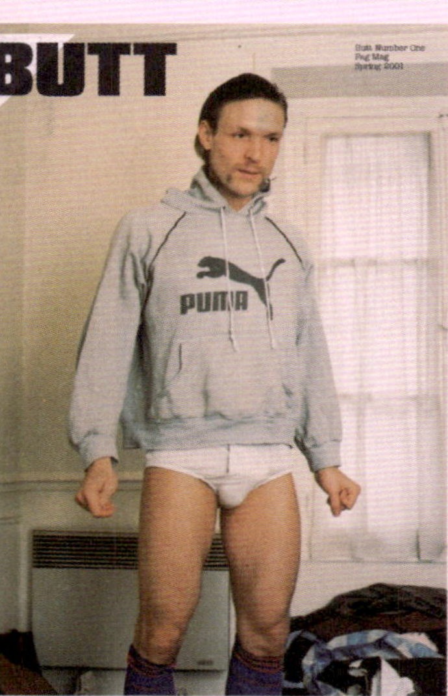
BUTT
PUMA
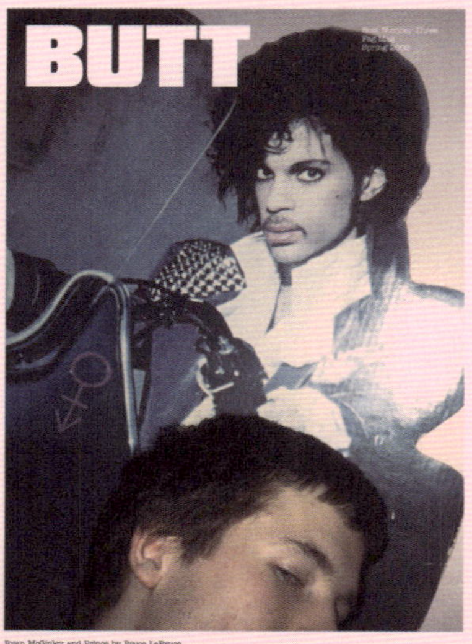
BUTT
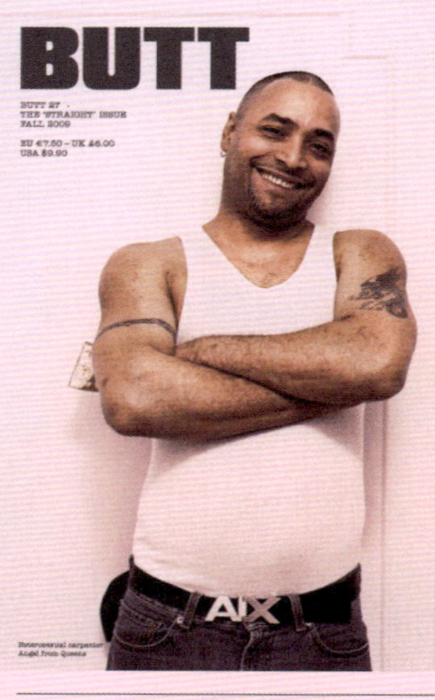
BUTT
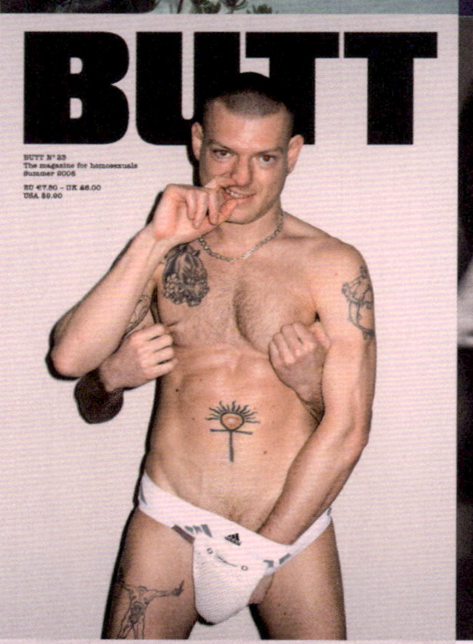
BUTT
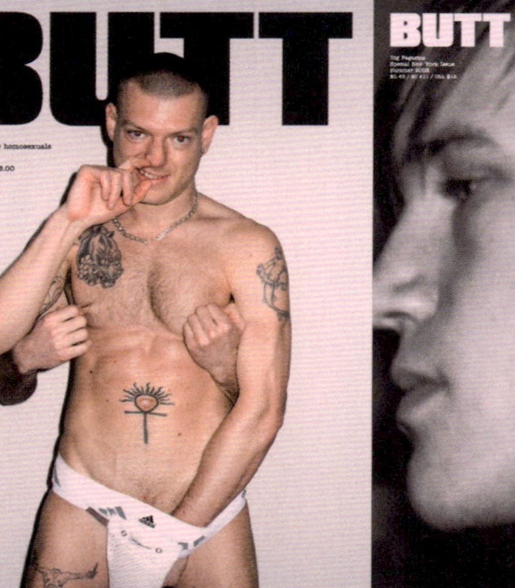
BU
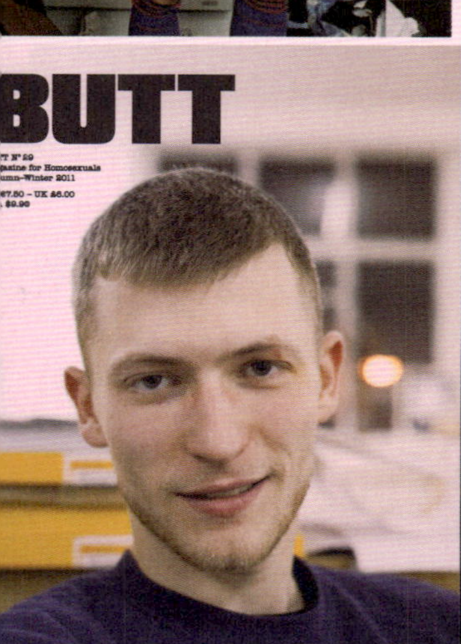
BUTT
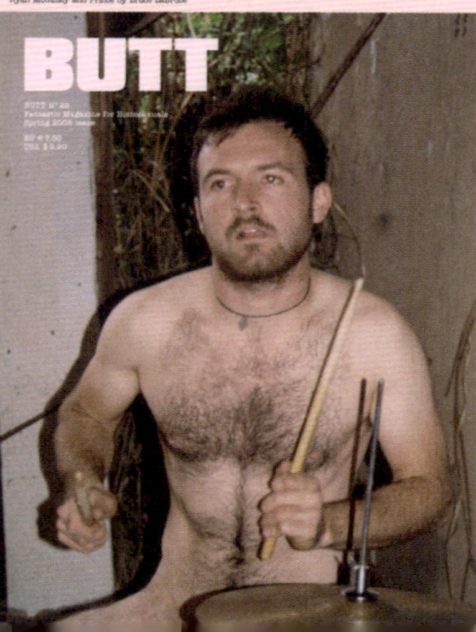
BUTT
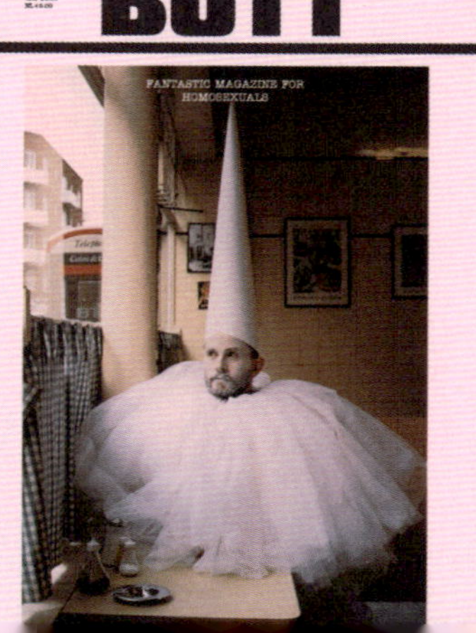
BUTT
FANTASTIC MAGAZINE FOR
HOMOSEXUALS
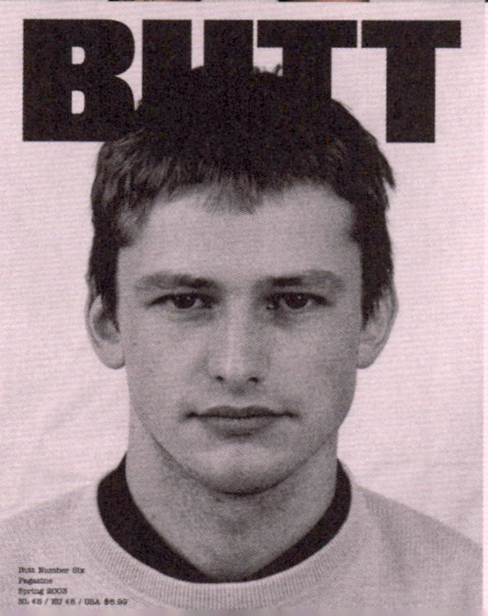
BUTT
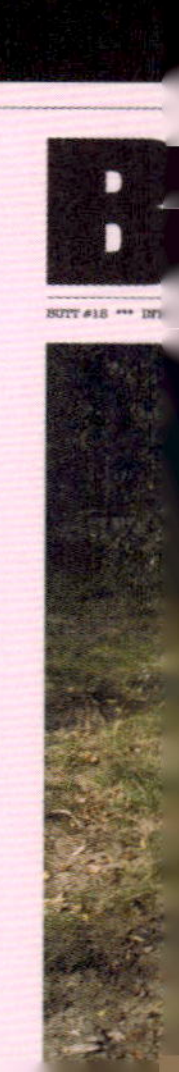

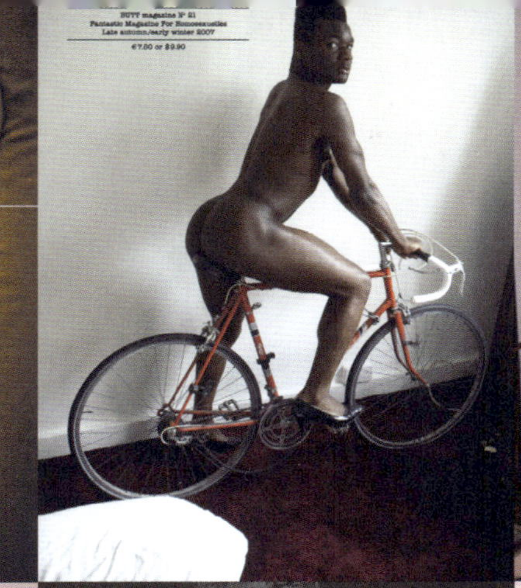
BUTT magazine Nº 21
Fantastic Magazine for Homosexuals
Late autumn/early winter 2007
€7.00 or $9.00

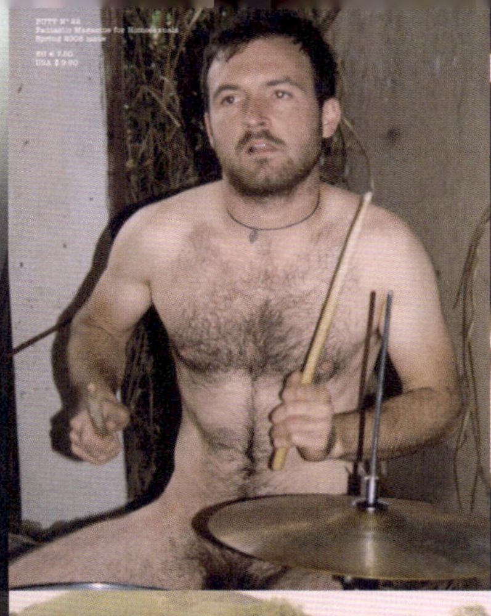
Fantastic Magazine for Homosexuals
€7.00 or $9.00

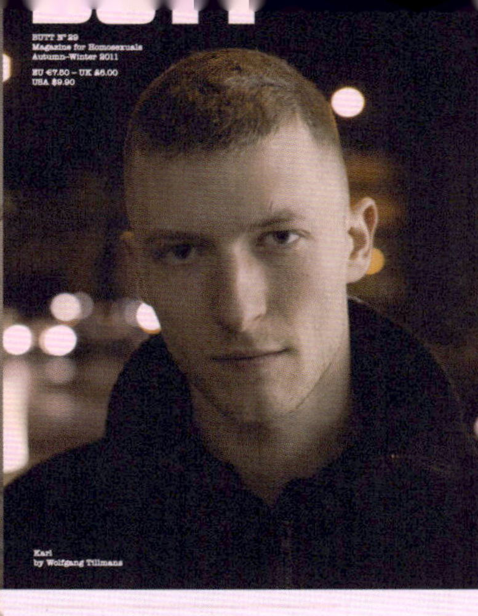
BUTT Nº 39
Magazine for Homosexuals
Autumn-Winter 2011
EU €7.50 · UK €6.00
USA $9.00

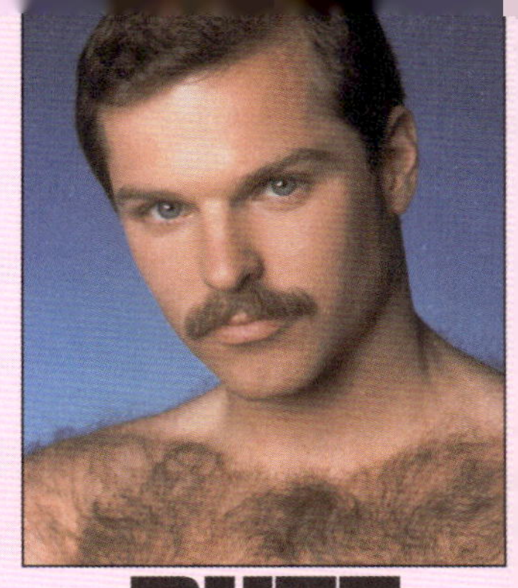
BUTT
BUTT #11 – AUTUMN 2004
FANTASTIC MAGAZINE FOR HOMOSEXUALS

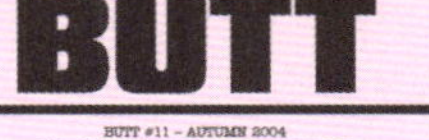
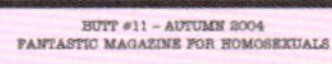

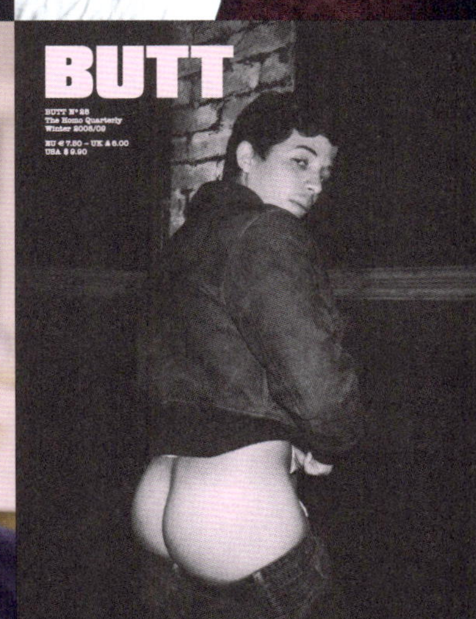
BUTT
BUTT Nº 23
The Homo Quarterly
Winter 2007/08
USA $9.90

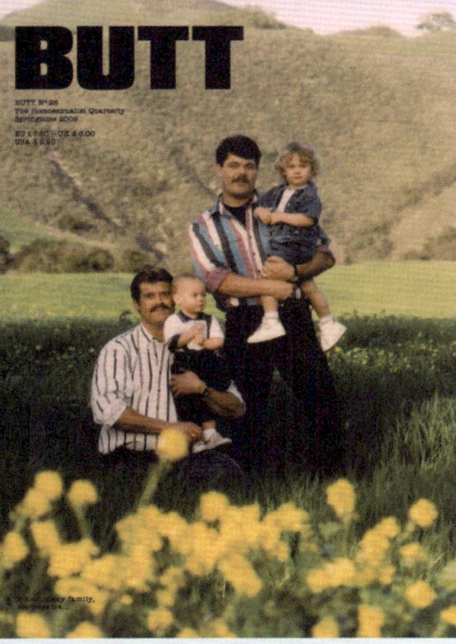
BUTT
BUTT Nº 24
The Homosexual Quarterly
Spring 2008
EU €7.50 · UK €6.00
USA $9.90

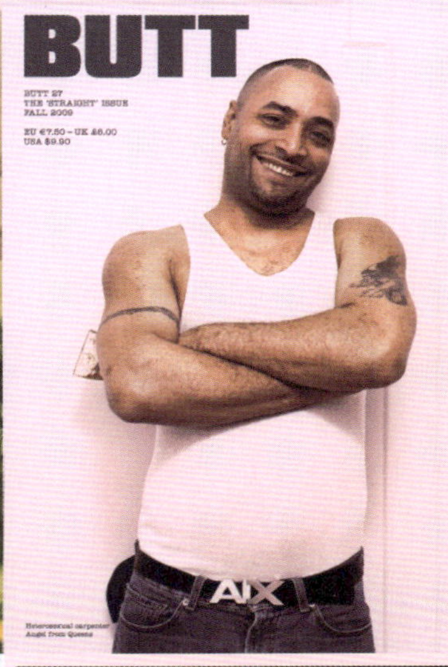
BUTT
BUTT 27
THE STRAIGHT ISSUE
FALL 2009
EU €7.50 · UK €6.00
USA $9.90

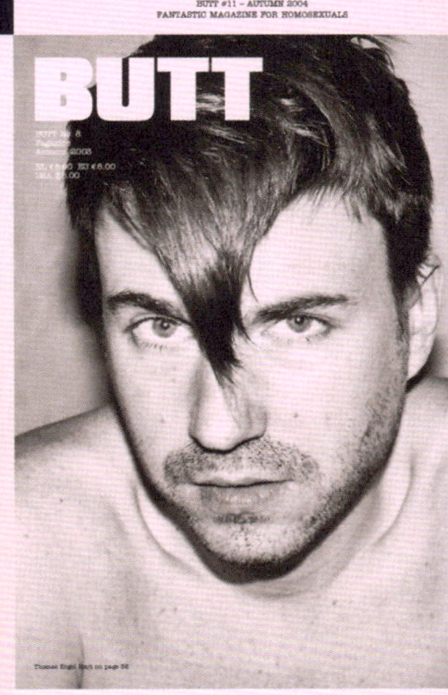
BUTT
BUTT Nº 6
Summer 2005
EU €7.50 · UK €6.00
USA $9.00

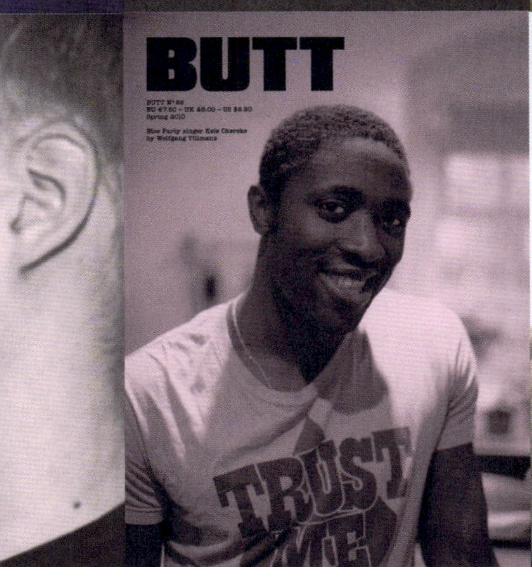
BUTT
BUTT Nº 22
The Homo Quarterly
Spring 2007

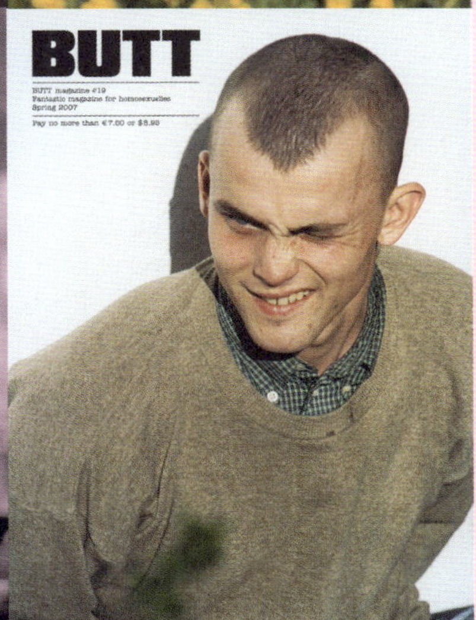
BUTT
BUTT magazine #19
Fantastic magazine for homosexuals
Spring 2007
Pay no more than €7.00 or $5.90

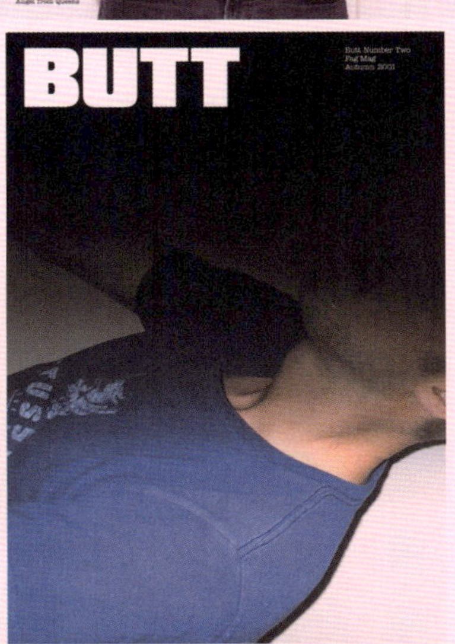
BUTT
Butt Number Two
Fag Mag
Autumn 2001

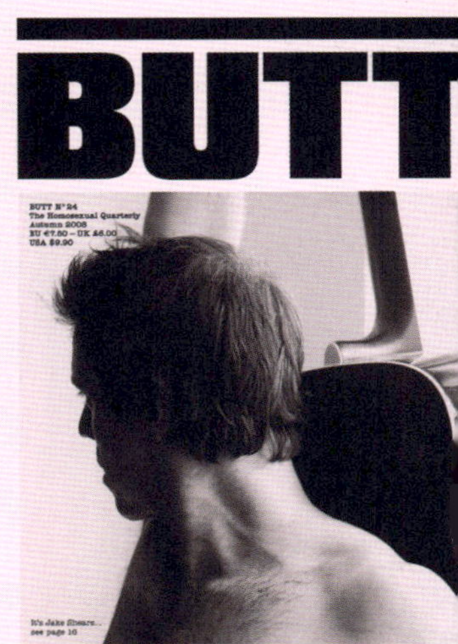
BUTT
BUTT Nº 24
The Homosexual Quarterly
Autumn 2008
USA $9.90

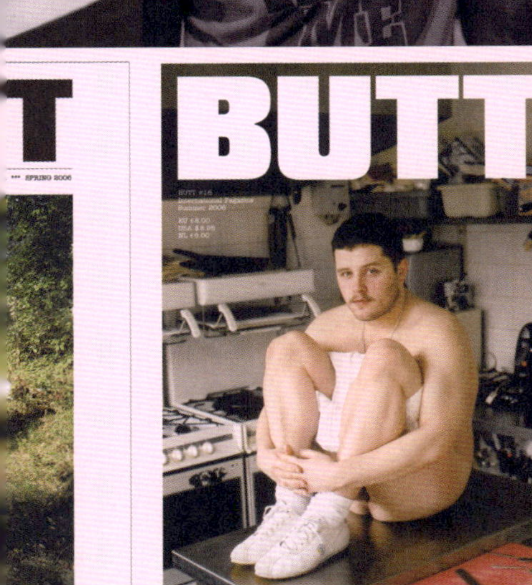
BUTT
SPRING 2006
BUTT #16
International Fagazine
Summer 2006

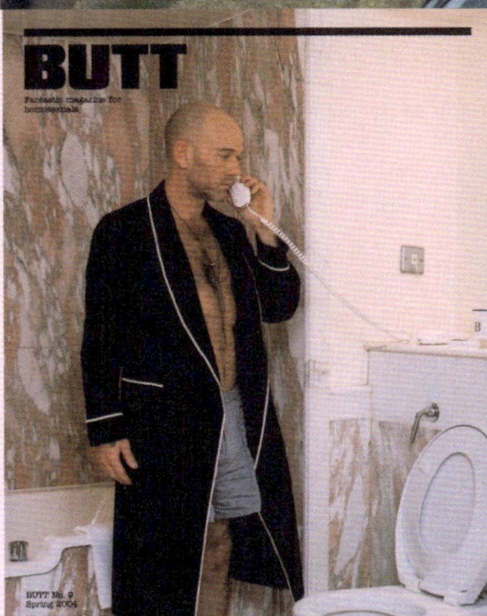
BUTT
Fantastic magazine for
homosexuals
BUTT No. 9
Spring 2004

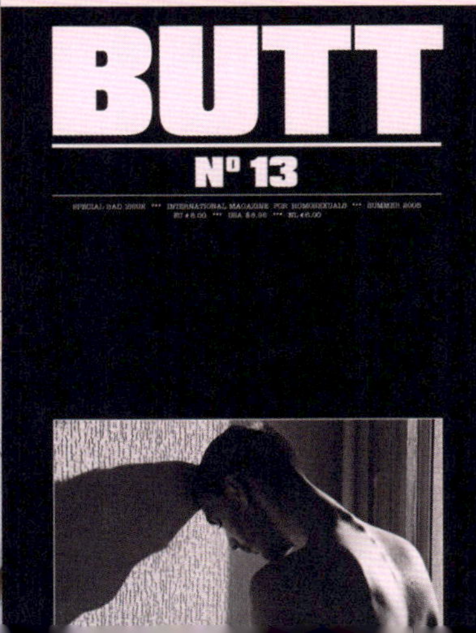
BUTT
Nº 13
SPECIAL SAD ISSUE · INTERNATIONAL MAGAZINE FOR HOMOSEXUALS · SUMMER 2005
EU €6.00 · USA $6.00 · NL €6.00

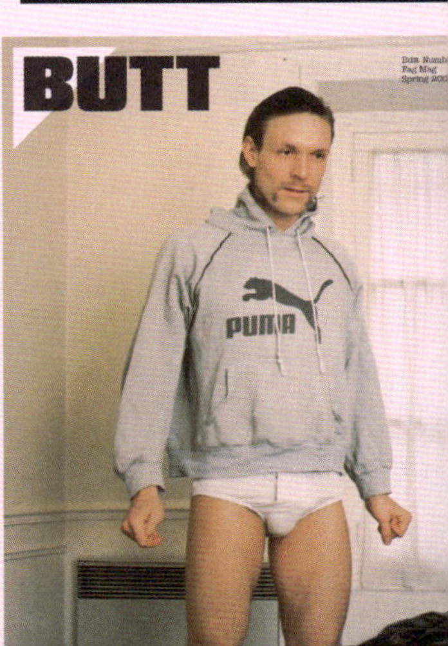
BUTT
Butt Number
Fag Mag
Spring 2002

Jop: Yeah. We tried a few things in one or two issues. But I don't think it worked. For instance, if you show a guy with a hard-on, other things get lost – the person disappears, they become objectified. It's a fine line between sex and sexy that we tried to balance.

What about the business of publishing a magazine like *Butt*? Was it difficult?

Jop: We printed the first issue with savings. And we sold ads for 150 guilders, about £50. The motivation to publish *Butt* was never financial. We never made a penny from the magazine.

Gert: We didn't get into publishing for commercial reasons. I think we should have done something else if we wanted to make a lot of money.

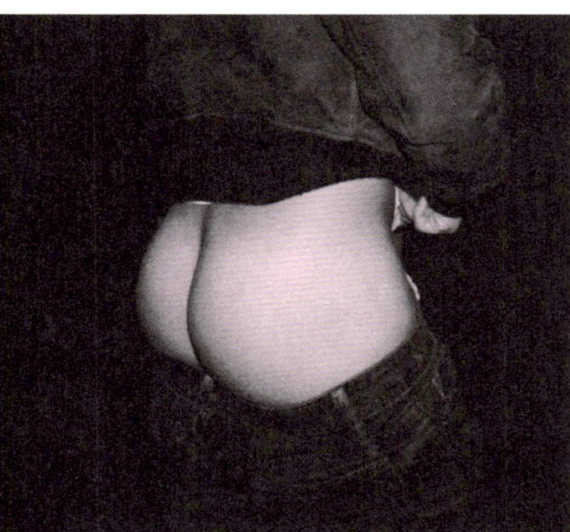

Early on, was distribution tricky?

Gert: Interestingly, one of the complaints we received over the years was how hard it was to find *Butt*. When we first started we found it difficult clicking into an existing distribution system. We weren't pornographic enough for porn distribution but we were too pornographic for regular magazine distribution. So we had to organise distribution ourselves.

Looking back, what are the highlights?

Jop: A real highlight for us is that it grew. There were so many people reading the magazine... and there were so many influential gay men reading the magazine. It established a very dedicated readership in just two-or-three years, even when it was still quite difficult to find [in stores]. Then we had a few celebrities in the magazine... and we could just get away with what we were doing, on our own terms.

And we were being asked to host *Butt* parties all over the world. All of a sudden we had fans. The magazine didn't just have readers, it had fans. That was very special.

And, of course, there's the *Butt* website. It hosts a forum of members, affectionately known as Buttheads.

Gert: There are over 10,000 fans on there! We wanted to build a community with *Butt*, a platform where people could share ideas, interests and dislikes. The internet is very good for that.

Jop: A lot of people have met others and been dating through that network. It's amazing. The most exciting thing about it is that it just works.

Were you contacted by a lot of readers wanting to contribute to the magazine?

Jop: Yeah. Around 2006 and 2007 there were a number of readers who became contributors... and then went on to become professional photographers or writers. That was a very inspiring shift.

Gert: We were always very excited by the willingness of people to get involved. Sometimes we said yes, sometimes we said no.

After 29 issues, why the decision to stop publishing *Butt*?

Gert: We made *Butt* for ourselves. We were making a magazine we wanted to read. That's why we created it. And the moment we started to feel less excited about it was the right time to move on.

Jop: We tried a few things... we tried to find a new editor. We worked with other people. We moved to New York for two years. We tried different things to make it work but we were never one hundred per cent satisfied with it.

Gert: It has always been super well received, and that's been exciting for us. Even after the first issue, there was an immediate response. People were excited about the magazine... and that level of enthusiasm continued. I hope that feeling remains. I hope people have a great...

I don't want to say I hope people remember it. That makes it seem like a thing of the past. And it's not. *Butt*'s content has never been all that timely. You can read an issue from seven years ago as if it's the current issue. It's almost like a book in that way.

Taschen published an anthology of *Butt*'s first five years back in 2006. Will there be another book?

Gert: Maybe we need to publish another book. It's not so much a matter of wanting or not wanting to do it, but actually finding the time to do it.

Jop: It would be nice to bring together an overview of everything we've done, maybe a book or some kind of archive.

What would you like *Butt*'s legacy to be?

Jop: Time will tell. It's not for me to say. We may have had an influence on gay culture, but it's certainly not the magazine's legacy that every gay man wears a beard.

What will younger fans read now, post *Butt*?

Jop: [Laughs] They should start their own magazine.

WE MADE BUTT FOR OURSELVES. WE WERE MAKING A MAGAZINE WE WANTED TO READ. THAT'S WHY WE CREATED IT.

L'IMPARFAITE OR THE ANTHROPOLOGY OF SEXUALITY

'L'Imparfaite', a twist on a French conjugation tense, is the lovechild of Science-Po *(Paris' leading school for Political and Social Science)* graduates. Although the magazine was born while its founders were still studying, it has since bloomed into a mature, established publication for self-claimed *"obedient perverts."*
Closer to Judith Butler than to the Marquis de Sade, *l'Imparfaite* proposes an in-depth, critical content borrowing from research, and political or gender studies tools; it studies rather than romanticizes the plurality of sexual discourses.

Interview by Alice Pfeiffer.
Portrait by Sébastien Agnetti.

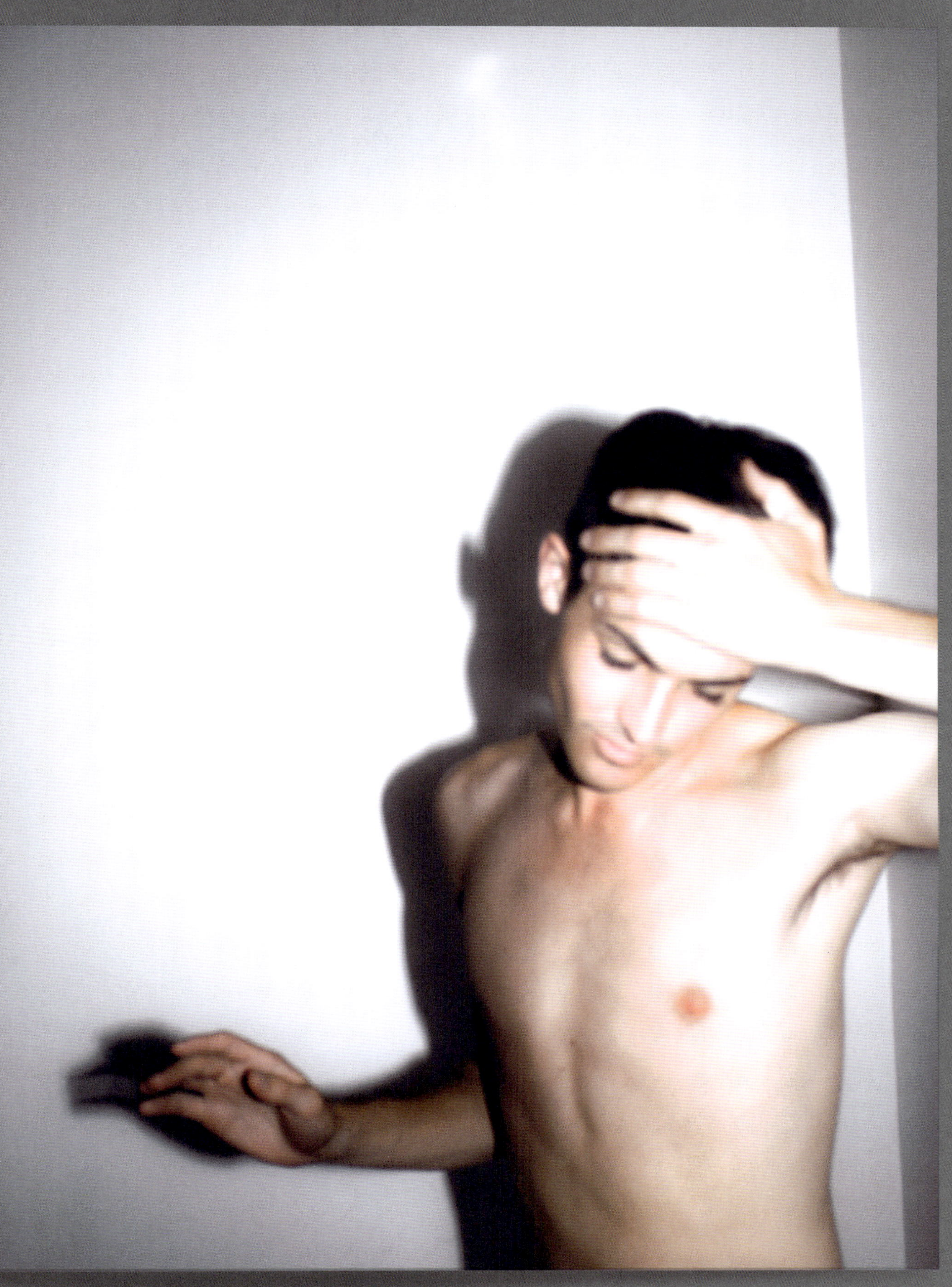

The magazine reinforces its contemporary dimension by conducting investigative reporting on various issues and oddities in society.
The photographic dimension is also key: raw at times, subdued at others, it opts for an aesthetic that is both sensitive and cerebral.
The team also uses *l'Imparfaite* as a platform for young photographers they scout worldwide – an approach that landed them in last year's Hyères Photography Festival.
Damien Bright, co-founder of the magazine talks about losing the Science-Po label, finding eroticism on the Internet and at the Louvre, and tying sexuality to post-human theory.

"BEHIND EVERY EROTIC STORY, THERE IS A HUMAN STORY – ONE THAT ENCOMPASSES A SOCIAL, POLITICAL, AND AESTHETIC DISCOURSE. IT IS PRECISELY THIS STORY WE ATTEMPT TO TELL."

Can you tell me about yourselves? Who are you, and why are you here today?

The founders of *l'Imparfaite* met in the classrooms of Science-Po *(Paris)*. Today no longer studying, they are pursuing this adventure full heartedly, and have since been joined by other young students and professionals.

The team consists of journalists, researchers, artists, French people, and foreigners. It is this diversity of specialty and origin that gives us our strength. As for myself, I am Australian, and have a background in political sociology.

Have any specific moments, memories, or influences in your teenage years contributed to the birth of *l'Imparfaite*?

I am still glued to the photos of Bill Henson and Philip Lorca Dicorcia. I totally assume my fandom of the anthropologist Donna Haraway, and to the discovery, last year, of the Australian novelist Christos Tsiolkas, an absolute must. My most memorable erotic memories were a matter of difficulty and deliquescence, of the connection between love, sex, and foreignness.

How did *l'Imparfaite* come about, was erotic press something you were especially interested in?

We discovered a number of erotic student publications abroad. It is a genre we wanted to question by bringing together several disciplines, approaches and visions, in one unique issue. We wanted to address the various issues linked to sexuality and desire, with multiple gazes – which felt like a natural engagement, and an extremely stimulating one too. We enjoyed the experience, we received positive feedback, and we decided to keep going, and to become more professional. Today, we are preparing the fifth issue of the publication.

What did you want to bring to the world of publishing, or to the culture surrounding you?

A quick look at the offer in kiosks will tell you that the tendency is either going in the way of pornography, or of women's magazines, with expressions which are interesting but more indirect, expressed through art or contemporary

} p.68

Damien Bright shot by
Sébastien Agnetti

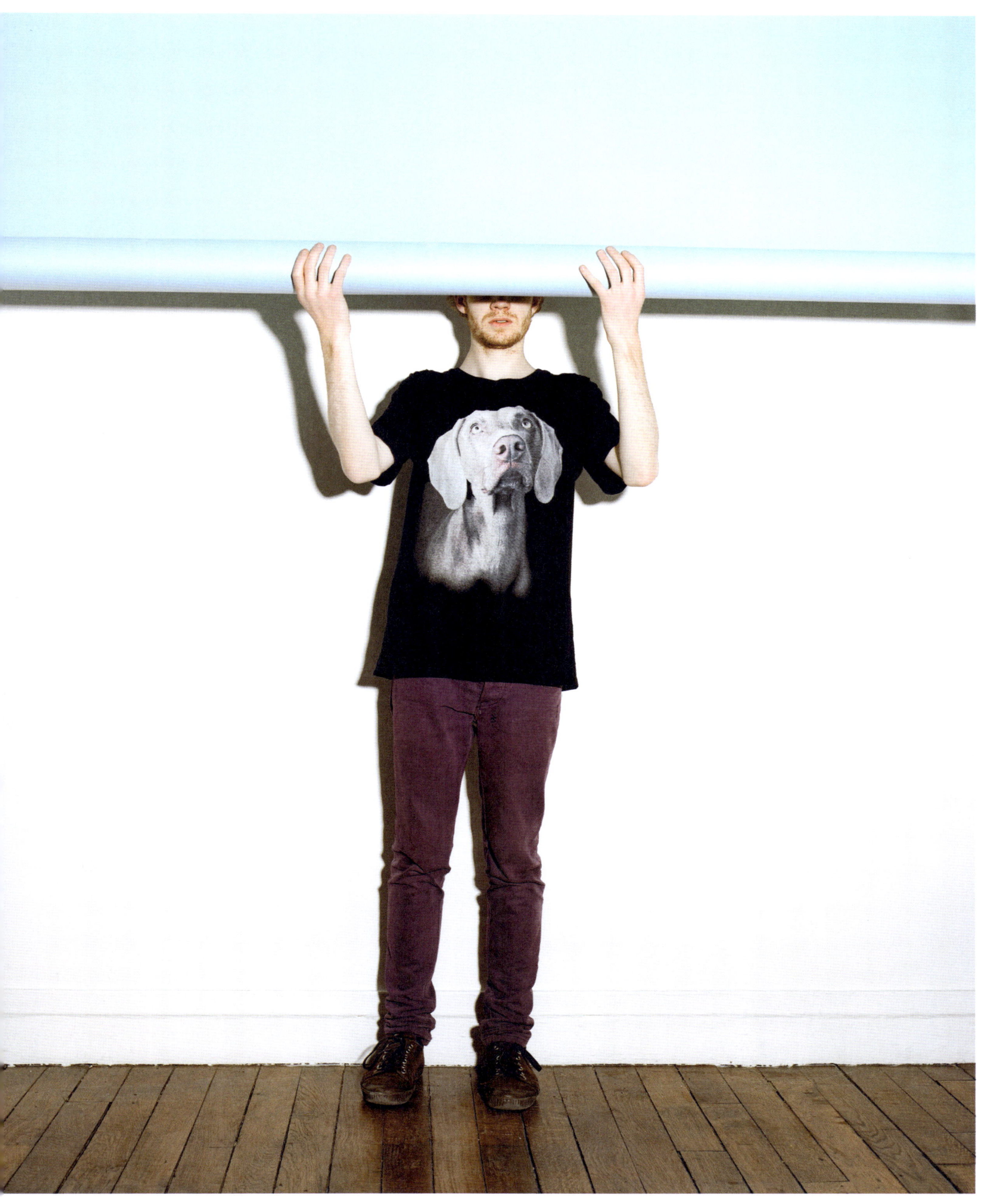

art. We wanted to offer different angles of analysis, and to confront different disciplines, to propose a view that is more open, a topic that concerns us all.

Why were you drawn to eroticism to the point of creating a magazine about it?

There are several reasons for that: its long history; its cultural and political multiplicity; its mutations when faced with technology; its practices; historical changes. In short, it is safe to say it is a fluid topic, at the crossroads of numerous issues in society, all of which interest us.

Indeed, Eroticism is endless – which aspects of it did you want to address as a first priority?

We talk about an eroticism open and without determinism that one can find as much within Internet memes, as in paintings at the Louvre, in the apartment of your neighbour as well as in San Francisco in 1970. We are very interested in erotic practices in all their diversities, and the meaning you can find in them.

Do you fear not being able to maintain this quest?

No, given eroticism's multiplicity, it is a topic one can keep digging further into, issue after issue.

Do you feel *l'Imparfaite* has changed much since its launch?

The team has grown, we have strengthened and diversified our graphic identity, we are developing our online presence, our international outlook, and our pertinence vis-à-vis the journalistic and artistic worlds. We have transcended a certain 'Science-Po' labelling that marked us a lot during our first two issues.

Yet, as graduates from a *grande école*, do you think an underlying intellectual questioning drives *l'Imparfaite*?

We don't claim a specific school of thought, nor a scholarly ambition, but aim for a constant examination. Indeed, we like, for example, to confront very contrasted, opposed points of views in two different articles, or in two-pronged interviews. Say, the surprising meeting to discuss bisexuality between the writer Mazarine Pingeot *[daughter of ex-French president François Mitterand]* and the deputy director for culture of Paris Christophe Girard. This plural speech implies nevertheless an openness to various approaches such as gender studies, sociology of change, news reporting etc…without heralding in one particular school of thought. In a similar approach, we visited, in 2010, La Fistinière *[The house of Fisting, France]*. It is a guesthouse dedicated to the homosexual subculture of fisting. We wanted to meet its participants, collect their impressions—an experience that was later repeated by more famous media. We encourage all our contributors to offer readings, words, thoughts, both clearly

} p.72

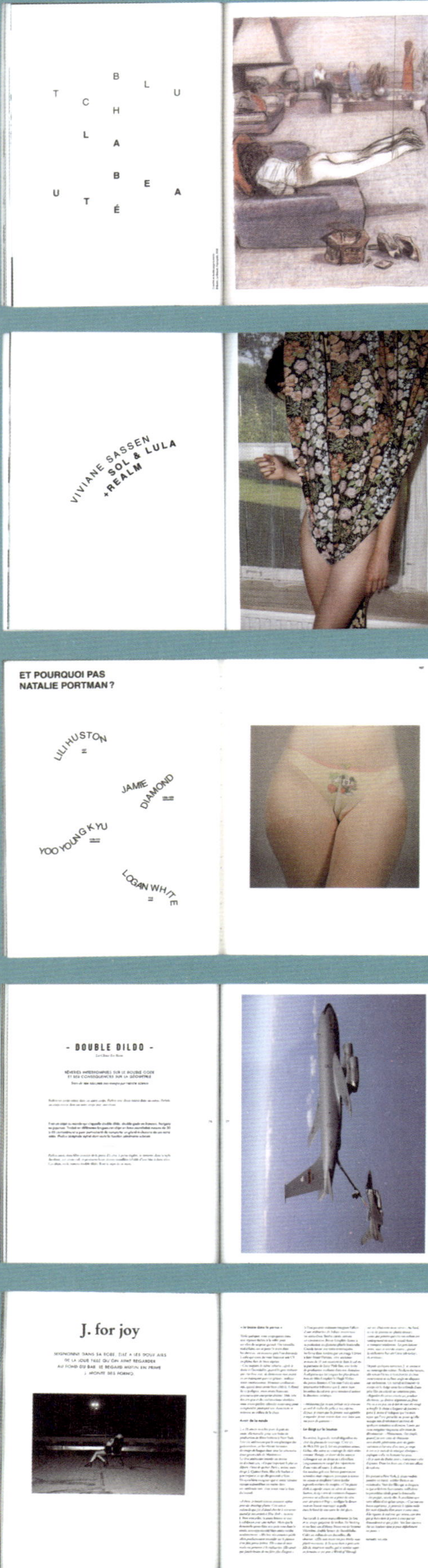

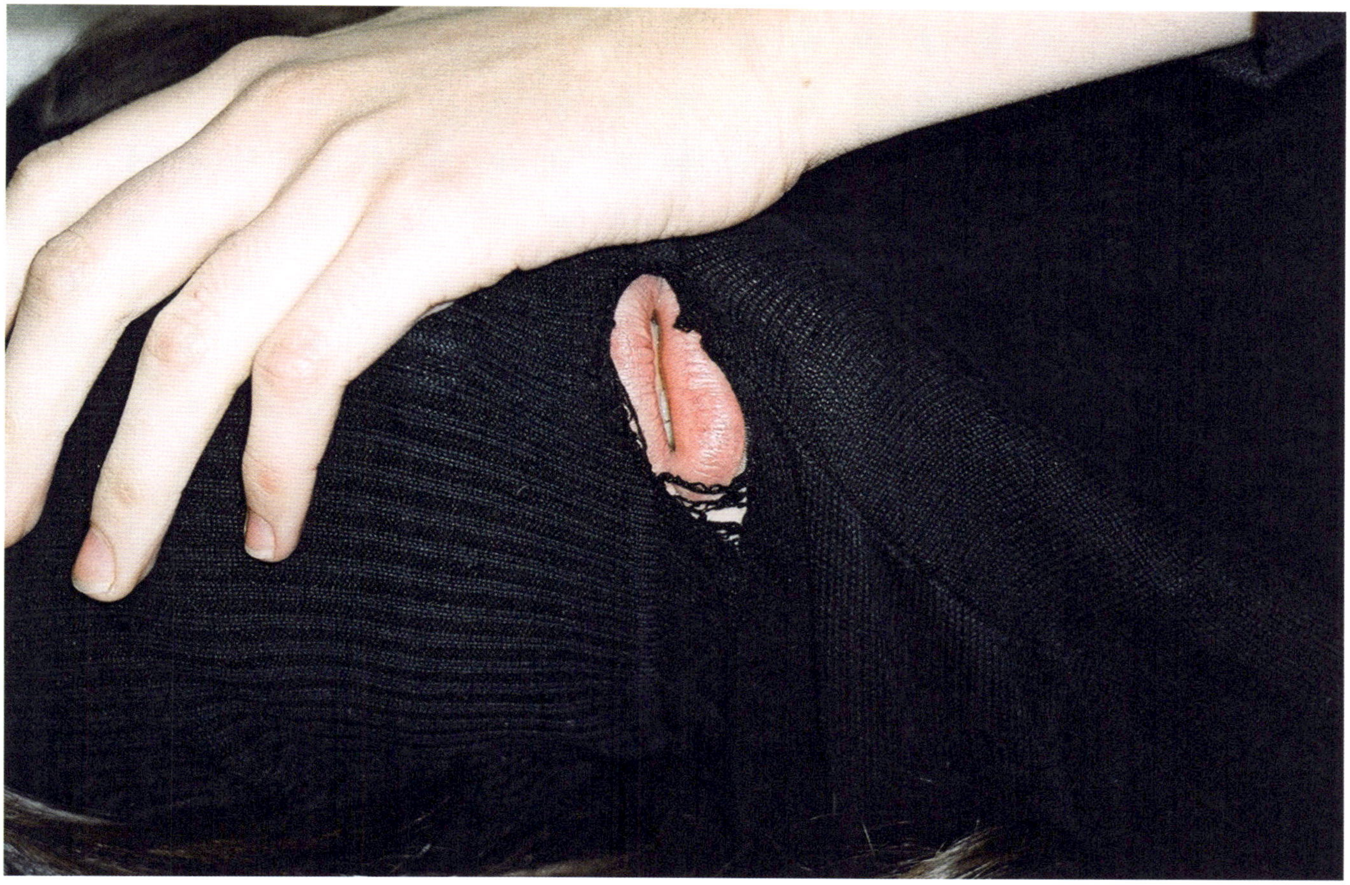

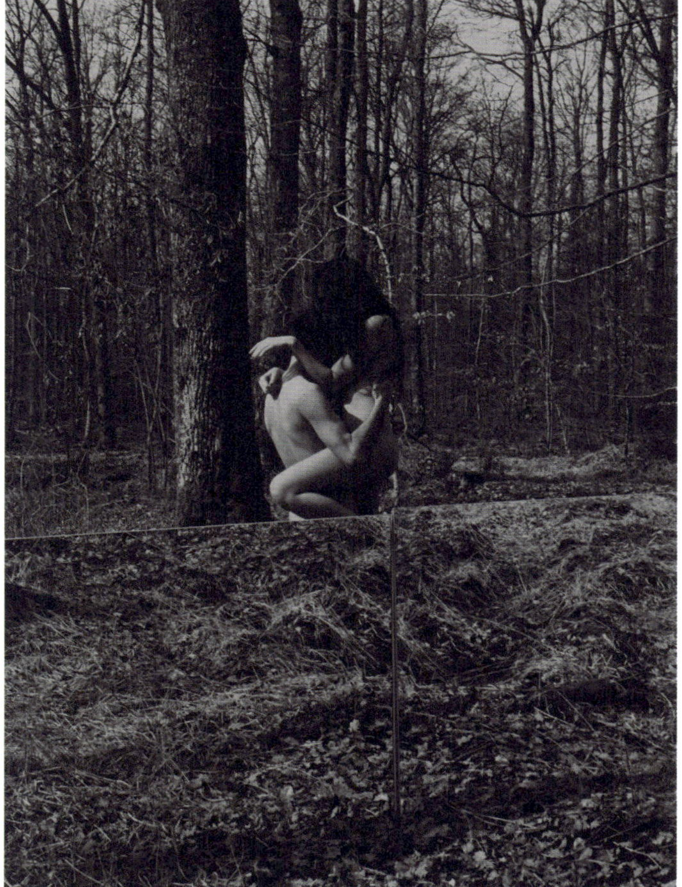

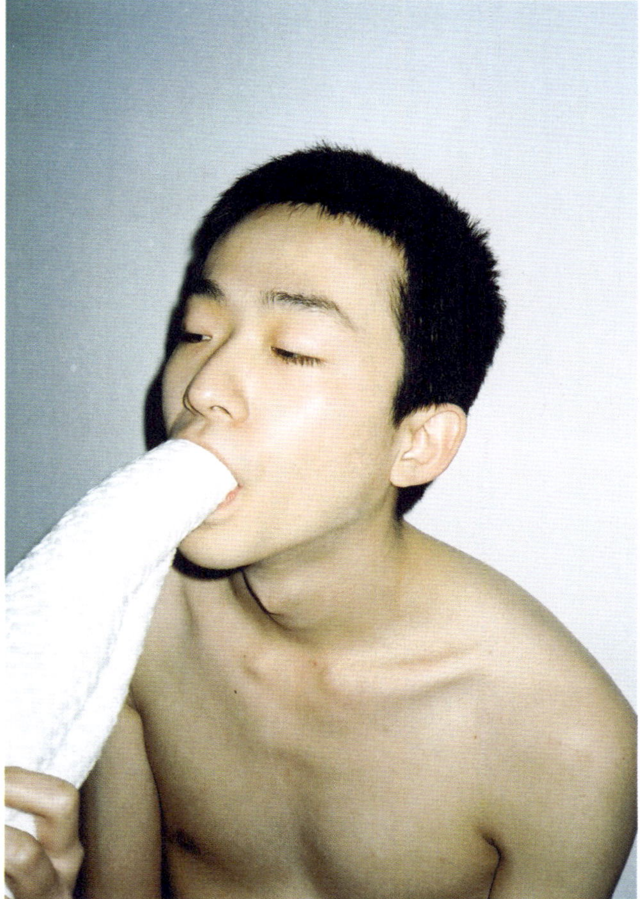

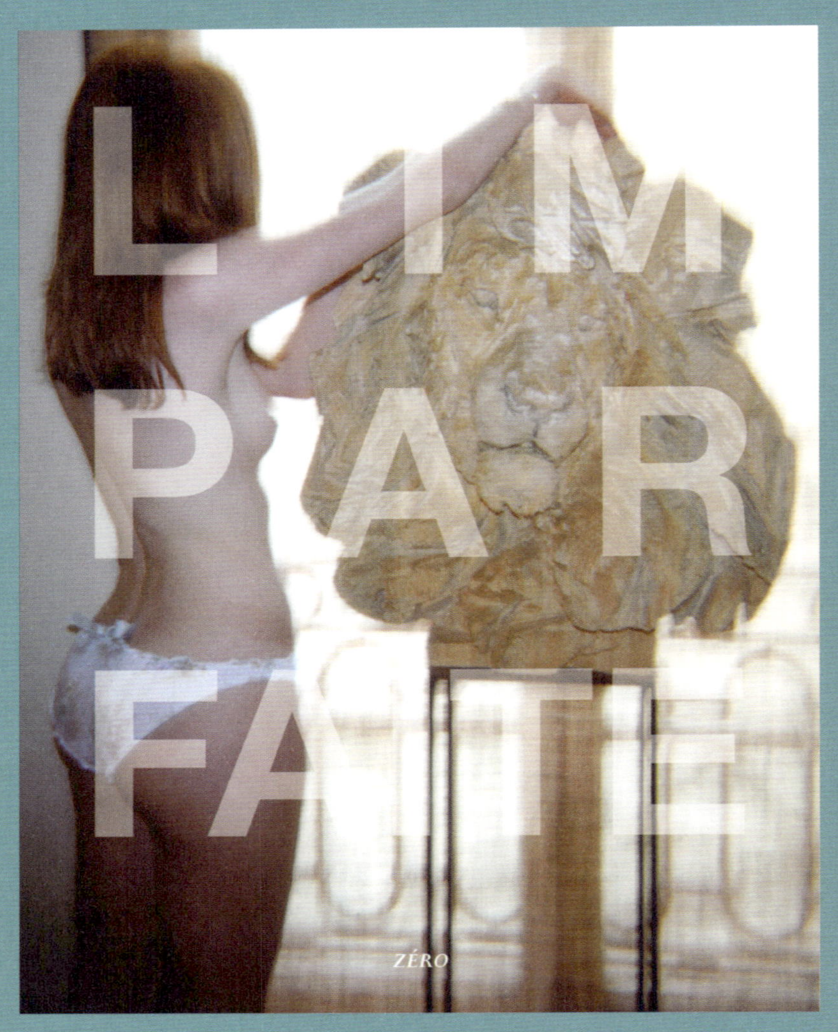
L IM
PAR
FAITE
ZÉRO

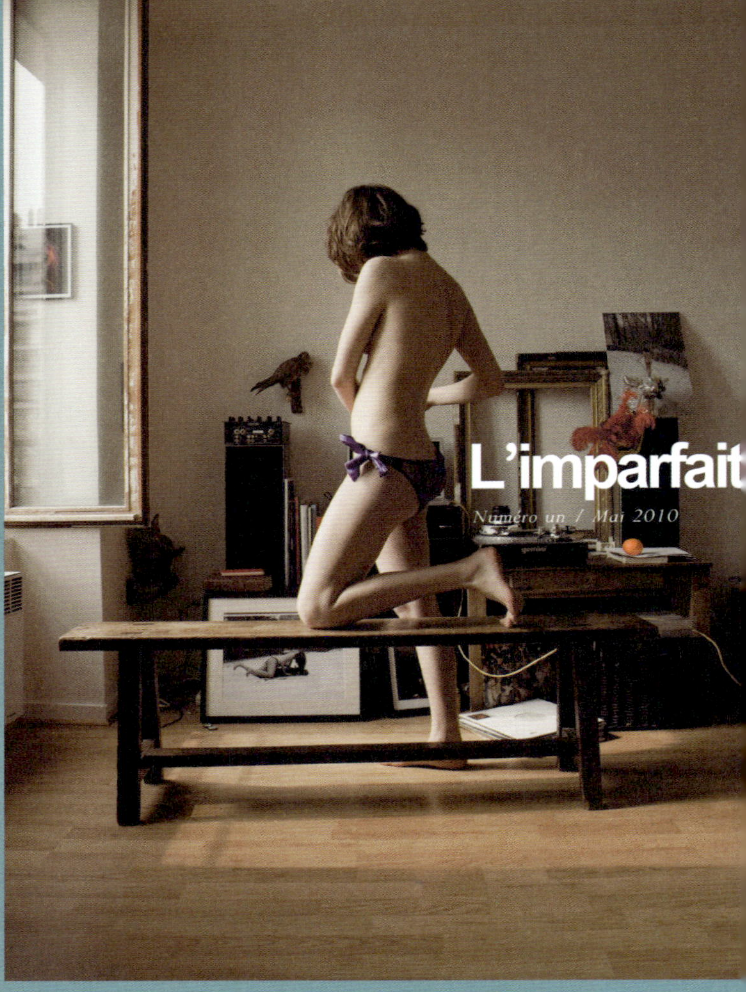
L'imparfait
Numéro un / Mai 2010

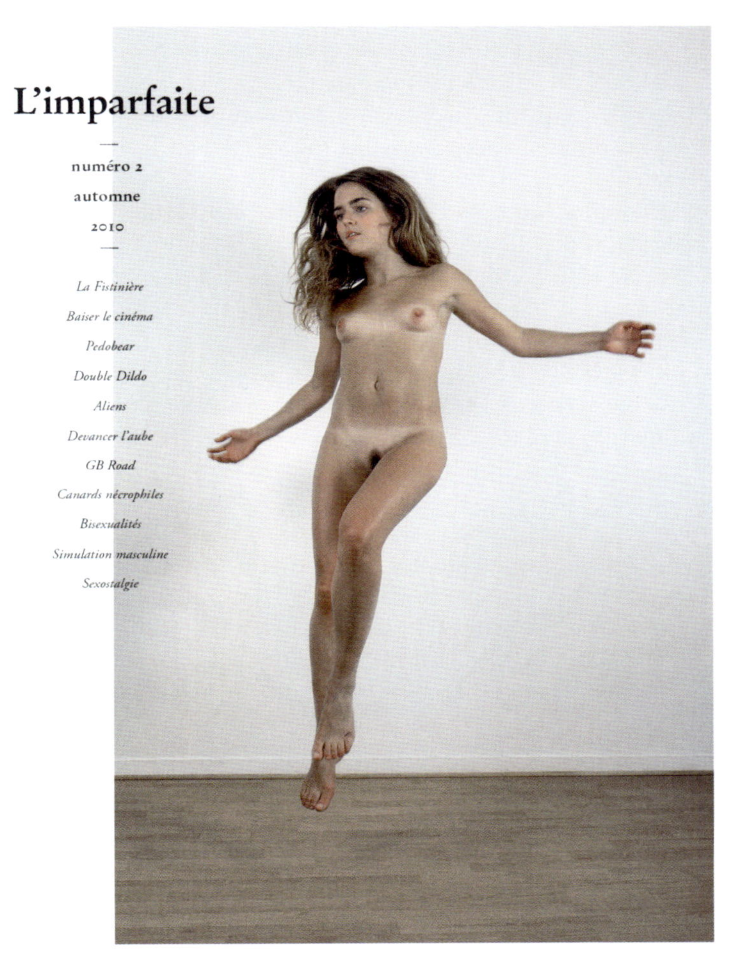
L'imparfaite
numéro 2
automne
2010
La Fistinière
Baiser le cinéma
Pedobear
Double Dildo
Aliens
Devancer l'aube
GB Road
Canards nécrophiles
Bisexualités
Simulation masculine
Sexostalgie

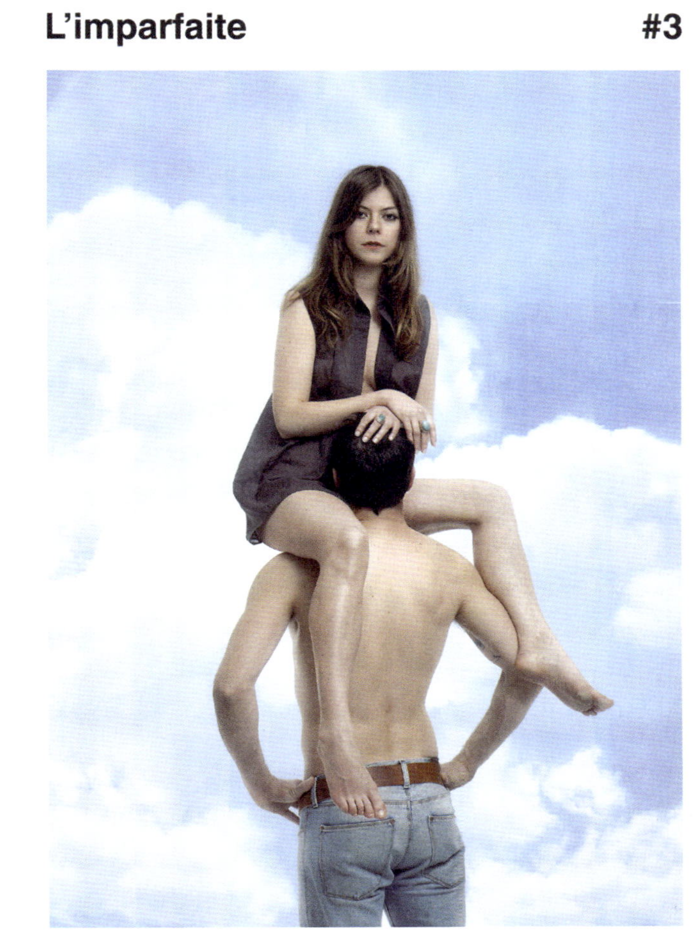
L'imparfaite
#3

argued and strong. Today, this is what gives the publication its diversity and its eroticism.

What is the connection between intellectualism, photography and eroticism? Is this something you toy with in *l'Imparfaite*?

Fashion and fashion photography have played an important role in the history of sexuality and eroticism, and we admit we play with this aspect in our photography. But, more importantly, we are after original, innovative pieces on eroticism. Our art direction does a thorough job in looking for young photographers with a real point of view, a vision, a real statement; it is a real satisfaction that those we spot end up being shown in galleries and other publications. In the third issue, the young Chinese photographer Ren Hang has since found a soaring fame; our interaction with him was particularly intense, as we, relied on Google Translate for the communication, and he, on his passings through Hong-Kong to send us images, away from the censorship.

You were involved in the Hyères Festival amongst other projects. Is there anything else in the pipeline?

We are currently working on the preparation of the next issue, to be released in Spring 2012. There will be new collaborations and original series. We are also preparing a totally new website, and a special launch event as we do for every issue.

What about the less fun aspect of things – the business side? It's a tough time for printed press, how do you manage to stay alive?

Our readership feels especially committed to the publication. They also follow us online through our blog and Facebook page. This allows us to maintain a constant communication between the launch of each issue. As far as partnerships and advertisers are concerned, we are always open to a fruitful cooperation. This can go from buying a simple page of advertising to a joint artistic direction. We have had numerous positive experiences in this area, from event planning to conducting market research. Above all, *l'Imparfaite* is a collective that promotes open-mindedness. Some like the idea, others less.

Do you know what the circulation and readership of *l'Imparfaite* is?

We are widely distributed in France, in Europe and internationally. Our readership is extremely varied; it includes all age groups, social backgrounds, nationalities and genders. This broadness in reach, which happened early on, confirmed the pertinence of our approach. As for the circulation, it varies from issue to issue. The two first issues have been sold out for quite a while now.

What is the limit between vulgarity and eroticism? Do you have conscious boundaries you will never cross?

Eroticism is a human sentiment, a lived experience. In that sense, what is vulgar to one can be all too banal to another. These oppositions don't interest us as much as the meaning that can be attached to the actual experiences. In the past, we have addressed so-called 'vulgar' topics, such as the bukkake *[a sexual practice that consists of several men simultaneously ejaculating on the same woman or man]*. We have also discussed fisting – but have always made sure we gave a voice to the protagonists. Behind every erotic story, there is a human story – one that encompasses a social, political, and aesthetic discourse. It is precisely this story we attempt to tell.

You have been compared to *Edwarda* in the past, another erotic publication which emerged in the same period. What is the main difference between you two?

To us, *Edwarda* represents another outlook on eroticism – one more centered around a salon representation, from literature, of a femininity especially aestheticized.

Edwarda focuses on heterocentric photography and on fiction texts by famous writers, living or dead. We on the other hand prefer original productions of young talents, and want to focus on the transversal approach between sociology and journalism.

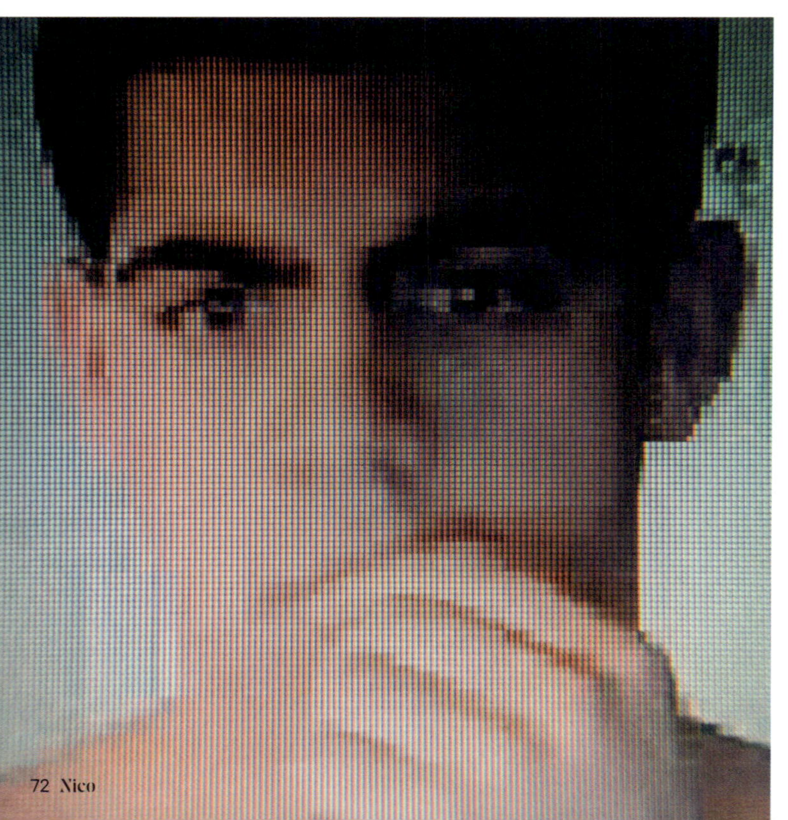

"WE ARE VERY
INTERESTED
IN EROTIC
PRACTICES IN
ALL THEIR
DIVERSITIES,
AND THE
MEANING YOU
CAN FIND IN
THEM."

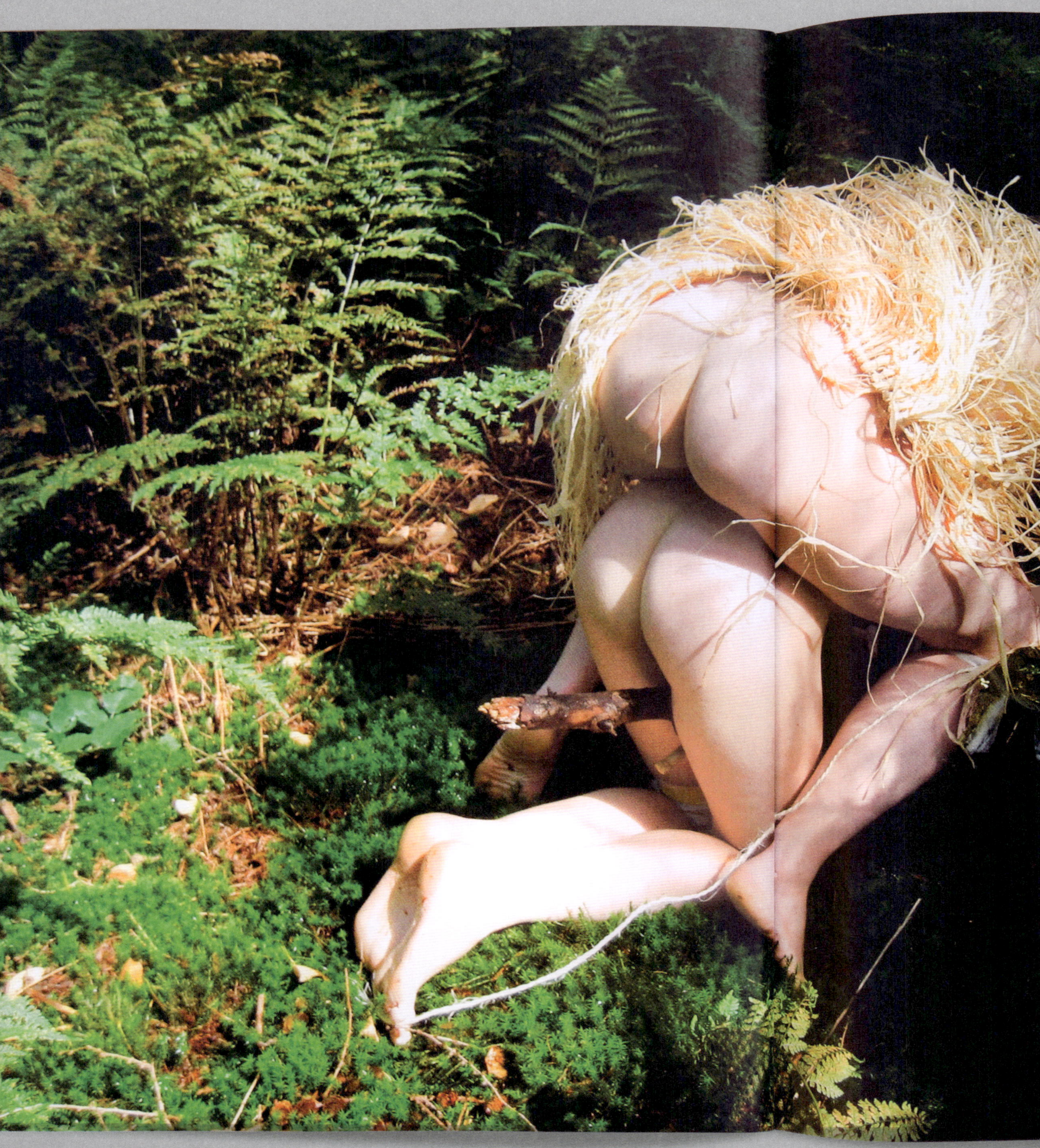

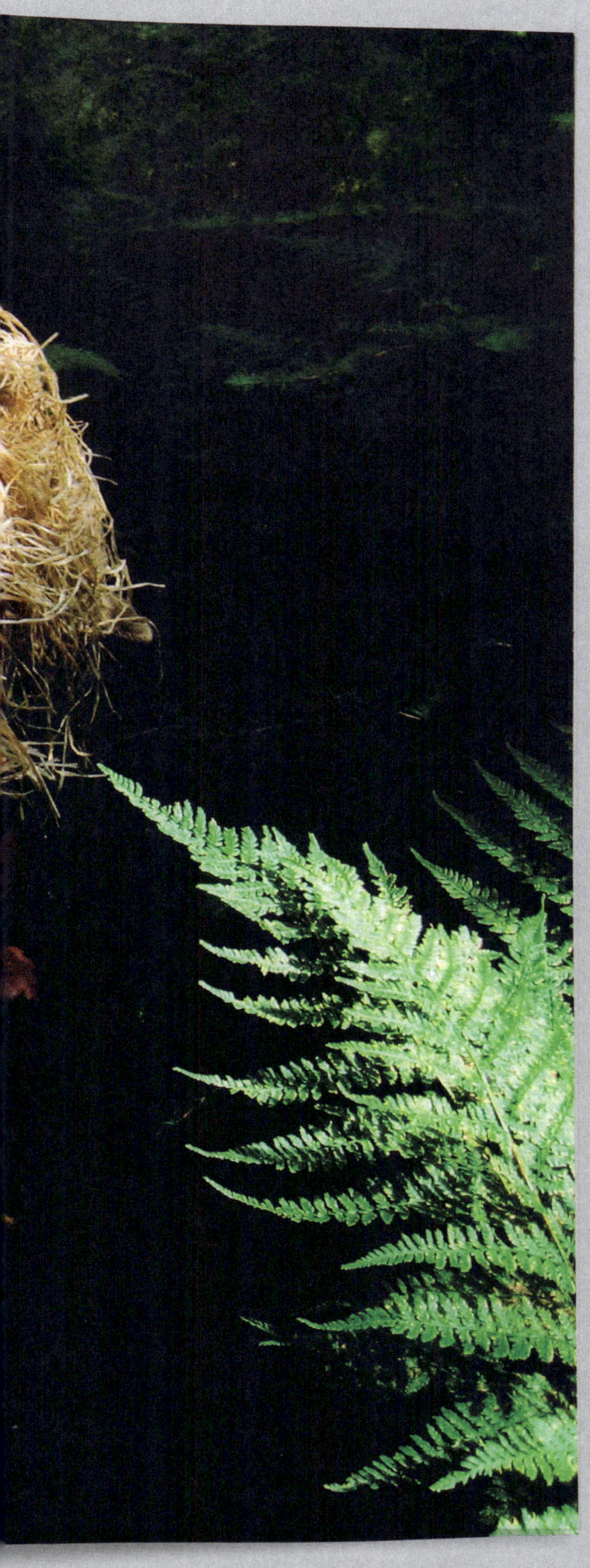

NOT ONLY GIRLS LIKE US

It's almost been a decade since scene-marketing specialist Jessica Gysel launched *GLU* magazine, about and for lesbians. After a restyling, the content and readership have been expanded. And so has the title. Find out everything you always wanted to know about the independent magazine *Girls Like Us*.

INTERVIEW BY MEREL KORKHUIS.
PORTRAIT BY TANIA THEODOROU.

WWW.GLUMAGAZINE.COM

"WE STILL FEATURE SEXY IMAGES, BUT IT'S MORE ART THAN EROTICISM NOW."

First of all where does the great, ambiguous, name come from?

For years a friend of mine from Paris was dreaming of starting her own record label especially for (lesbian) women. By the time I launched *GLU* I needed a strong name and she still didn't use hers. So I simply asked if I could have it. I love it because it refers to girls who have the same sexual preference we have.

So what is it, *Girls Like Us* or *GLU*?

When the first issue came out in 2002, I only used *GLU*. It made sense because the magazine was compact. Since the restyling, that also resulted in a bigger magazine size, I prefer *Girls Like Us*, although *GLU* is still used a lot. *Girls Like Us* feels a bit more dignified and mature somehow, less *fanziney*.

What exactly did you change during the restyling?

Besides the size, the main difference is the target group and, related to that, the content. *GLU* was a niche magazine especially made for lesbian women. Not just the target group consisted of lesbian women; we also only featured lesbian women. Since the restyling we shifted the focus from lesbians to feminism. Sure we lost part of our readers, but we also had a lot of new arising.

How is that mutation visible in the magazine?

The content is broader in every aspect. We still feature sexy images, but it's more art than eroticism now. And we changed the layout drastically. *Girls Like Us* art director Vela Arbutina, who is hetero by the way, decided to use a different font. She chose Gill Sans, because the creator, Eric Gill, was sexually confused. Vela thought it would be a nice inside joke. She also decided to add a fifth Pantone colour to every issue. So the magazine is printed in cyan, magenta, yellow and black, and then we always use a fifth one. The first time we did it, we went for purple. Another link to the gay scene and to Lavender, a gay action group from the seventies. We've also decided to make *Girls Like Us* less tough and a bit more elegant and soft. More appealing in a way. The paper had to be more tactile and the text has more space than before. To ease the eyes. Other than that we try to avoid rules. The only returning element is the picture of the Greek island Lesbos on the inside cover. Maybe the new layout can best be described as sexiness and aesthetics with a twist.

} *p.78*

Jessica Gysel shot by
Tania Theodorou

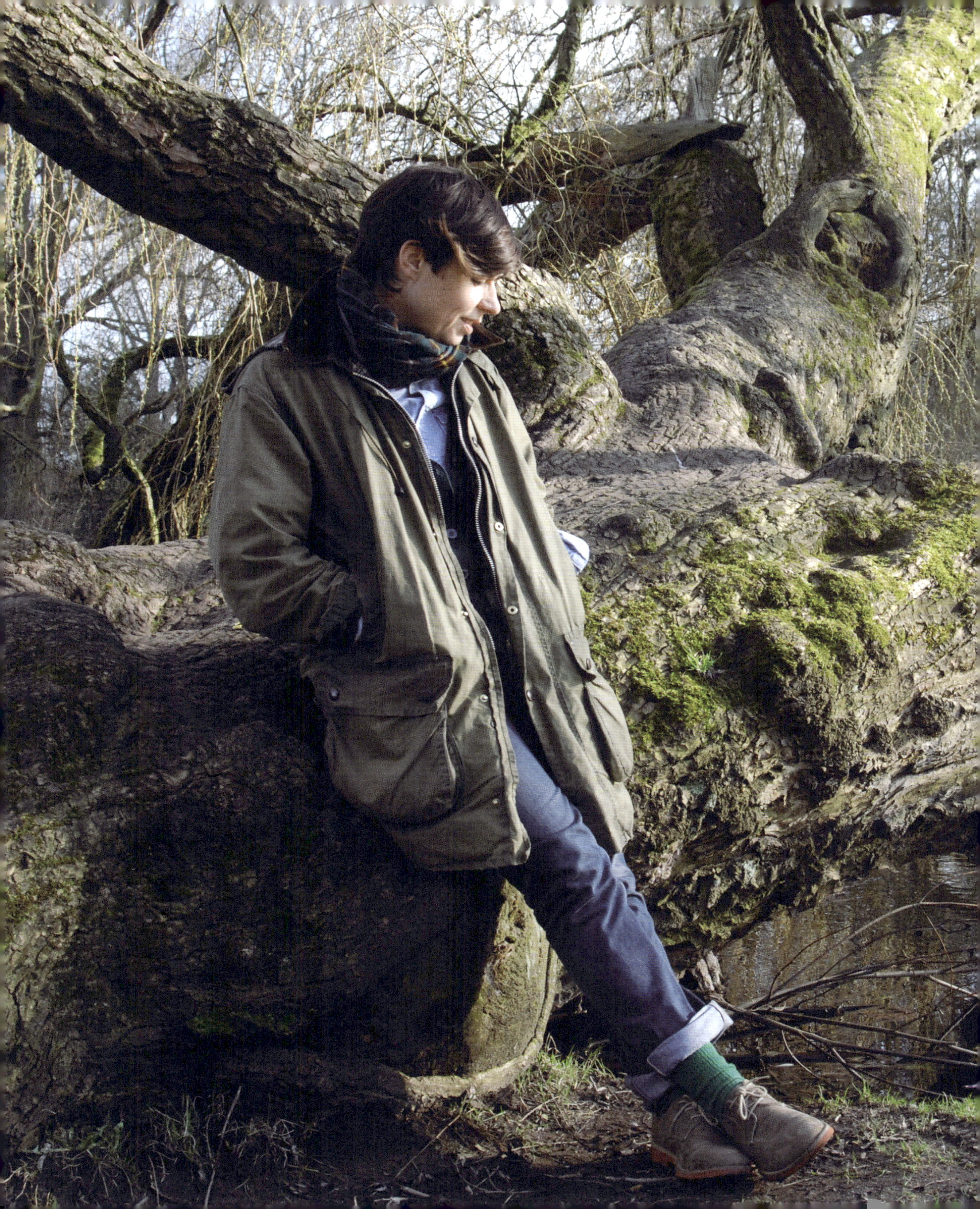

And content-wise?

In the old version we only had three types of features. Conversations, photo specials and the Archive. In the last case we featured images and information from Lesbian archives all over the world. Almost every big city has one. We went to Los Angeles, New York, Berlin, etc. After eight issues I felt like we needed something new. We'd featured nearly all the important people in the lesbian scene. We were done. We needed more art. A lot of interesting things happen in that scene. Of course we still focus on strong women. But since the restyling we also publish essays, screenplays, short stories, collages and 3D interviews. We ask three people to interview one and the same person and publish the three interviews in one article. All in all, the magazine is less caught in a format. And that's something I'm extremely happy about. I collect the content in a random way. The network that surrounds me comes with suggestions, I see interesting stuff, and it all goes very organically. Eclectic is the magic word. This automatically means we don't publish *Girls Like Us* on a set frequency. It's published when it's finished. That's more or less twice a year. And that's enough. It's not a time-phased magazine, we don't feature season-based collections for example, so it's not a problem if it's in stores for quite a long time. I even like it that way. We also noticed an issue of *Girls Like Us* sits around a subscribers' or buyers' house longer than you would expect. Maybe even for six months or so. It's not necessary to raise the frequency. And last but not least; the less issues you make, the more of a collector's item they become.

How did the restyling change your readership?

It shifted from mainly lesbians to a broader audience such as both gay and hetero artists, gallerists, curators, stylists, designers, musicians, performers and those working in creative industries and media. And at book and magazine fairs I notice many graphic design students are interested.

Let's go back to the beginning. Why did you launch *GLU*?

There were many mainstream lifestyle magazines for lesbians on the market, like *Diva* from England and *Curve* from the US. All very good, but containing a lot of fashion and practical information on adoption for example. Don't get me wrong, it's interesting to know what your options are if you are a lesbian couple and you want to adopt a child, but I wanted to make a more edgy magazine.

What was your big example?

I'm friends with Gert Jonkers and Job van Bennekom, founders of *Butt* magazine (2001-2011). *Butt* was a pink pocketsize magazine by and for male homosexuals. Gert and Job motivated me to create a similar version for lesbians.

} p.82

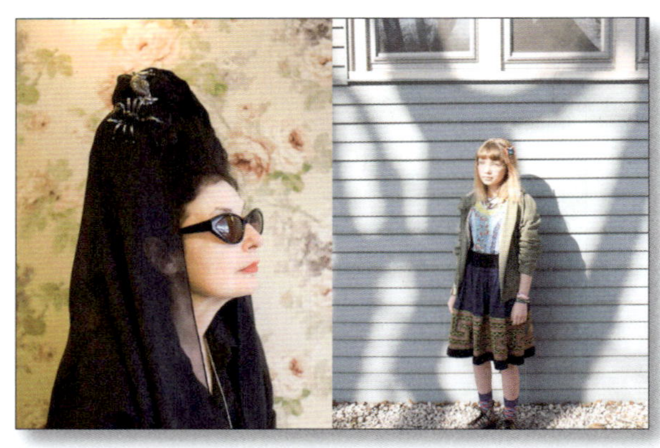

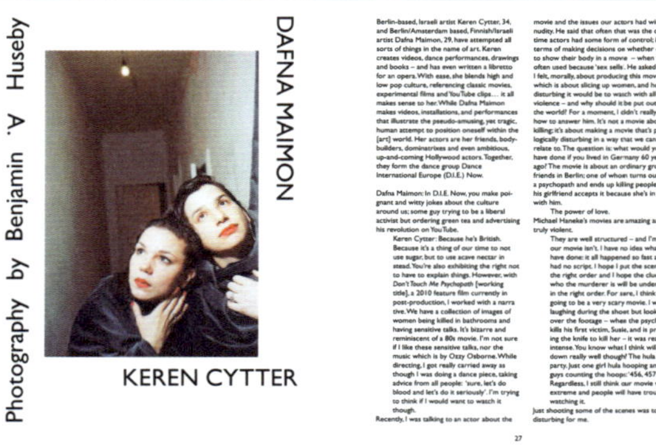

Berlin-based, Israeli artist Keren Cytter, 34, and Berlin/Amsterdam based, Finnish/Israeli artist Dafna Maimon, 29, have attempted all sorts of things in the name of art. Keren creates videos, dance performances, drawings and books — and has even written a libretto for an opera. With ease, she blends high and low pop culture, referencing classic movies, experimental films and YouTube clips… it all makes sense to her. While Dafna Maimon makes videos, installations, and performances that illustrate the pseudo-amusing, yet tragic, human attempt to position oneself within the [art] world. Her actors are her friends, bodybuilders, dominatrixes and even ambitious, up-and-coming Hollywood actors. Together, they form the dance group Dance International Europe (D.I.E.) Now.

Dafna Maimon: In D.I.E. Now, you make poignant and witty jokes about the culture around us; some guy trying to be a liberal activist but ordering green tea and advertising his revolution on YouTube.

Keren Cytter: Because he's British. Because it's a thing of our time to not use sugar, but to use acave nectar instead. You're also exhibiting the right not to have to explain things. However, with *Don't Touch Me Psychopath* [working title], a 2010 feature film currently in post-production, I worked with a narrative. We have a collection of images of women being killed in bathrooms and having sensitive talks. It's bizarre and reminiscent of a 80s movie. I'm not sure if I like these sensitive talks, nor the music which is by Ozzy Osborne. While directing, I got really carried away as though I was doing a dance piece, taking advice from all people: 'sure, let's do blood and let's do it seriously'. I'm trying to think if I would want to watch it though.

Recently, I was talking to an actor about the movie and the issues our actors had with nudity. He said that often that was the only time actors had some form of control; in terms of making decisions oe whether or not to show their body in a movie — when it's so often used because 'sex sells'. He asked how I felt, morally, about producing this movie which is about slicing up women, and how disturbing it would be to watch with all its violence — and why should it be put out into the world? For a moment, I didn't really know how to answer him. It's not a movie about killing; it's about making a movie that's psychologically disturbing in a way that we can also relate to. The question is: what would you have done if you lived in Germany 60 years ago? The movie is about an ordinary group of friends in Berlin; one of whom turns out to be a psychopath and ends up killing people. And his girlfriend accepts it because she's in love with him.

The power of love.

Michael Haneke's movies are amazing and truly violent.

They are well structured — and I'm afraid our movie isn't. I have no idea what we have done: it all happened so fast and we had no script. I hope I put the scenes in the right order and I hope the clues to who the murderer is will be understood in the right order. For sure, I think it's going to be a very scary movie. I was laughing during the shoot but looking over the footage — when the psychopath kills his first victim, Susie, and is preparing the knife to kill her — it was really intense. You know what I think will go down really well though? The hula hoop party. Just one girl hula hooping and two guys counting the hoops: '456, 457, 458…' Regardless, I still think our movie will be extreme and people will have trouble watching it.

Just shooting some of the scenes was too disturbing for me.

27

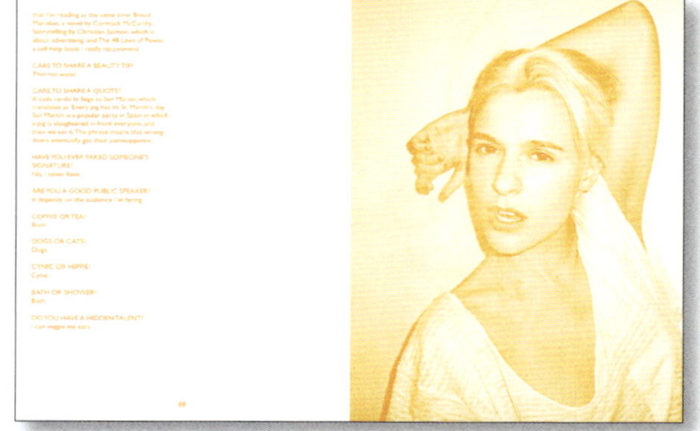

Selection of inspirational covers.

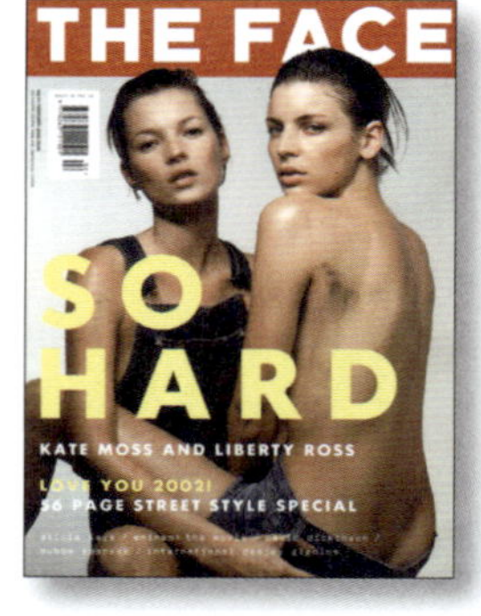

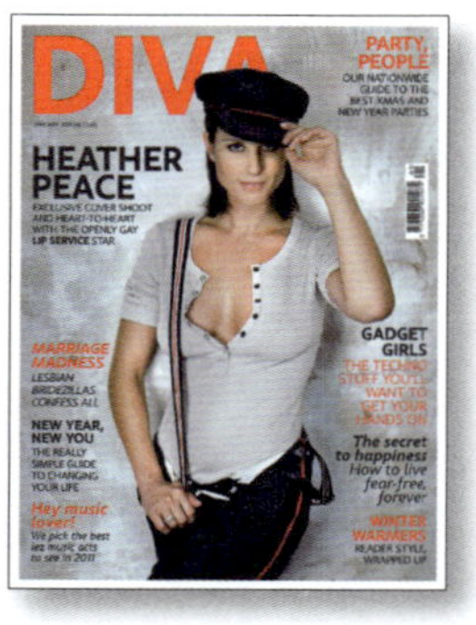

Fumble in the Jungle

CONCEPT BY MELANIE BONAJO AND EMMELINE DE MOOIJ
PHOTOGRAPHY BY MELANIE BONAJO

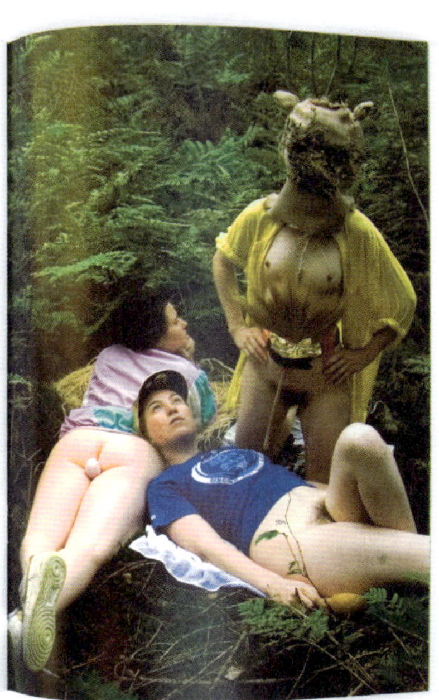

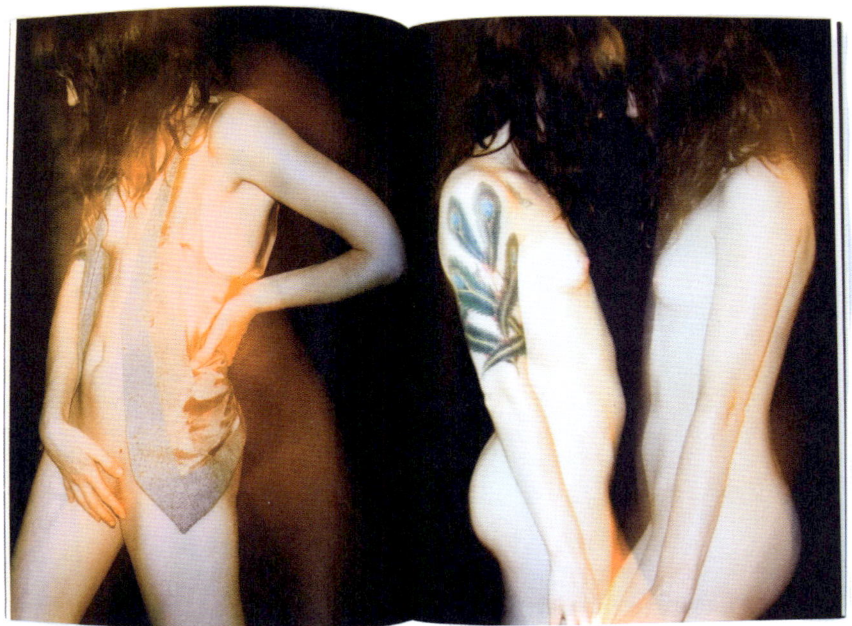

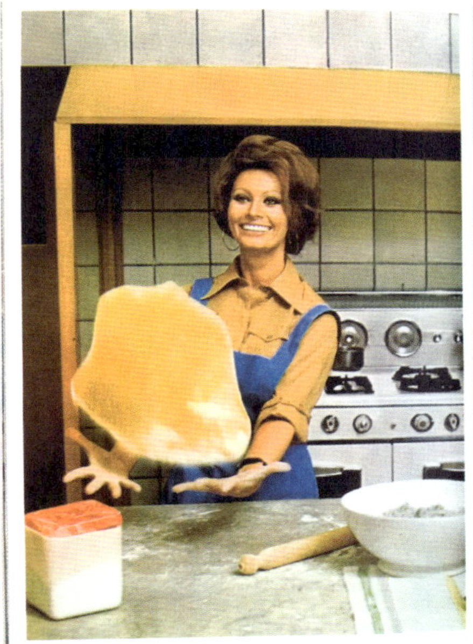

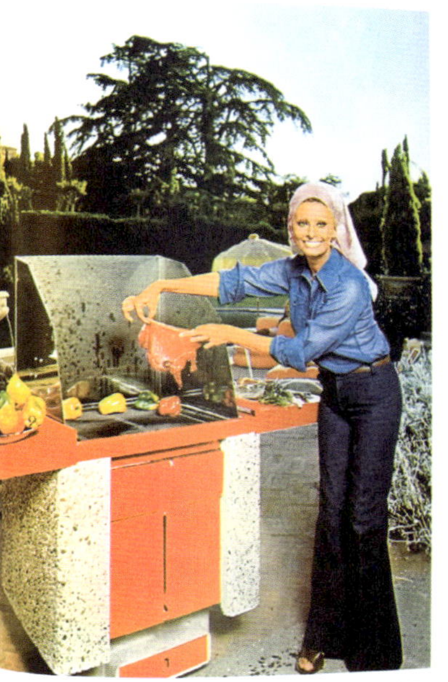

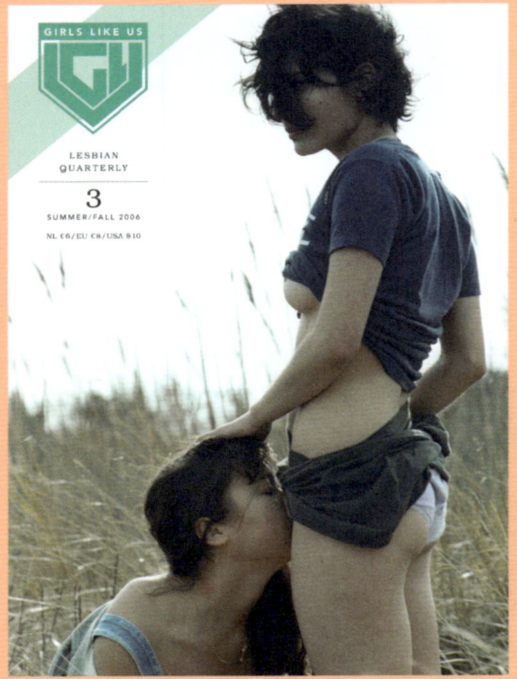

GIRLS LIKE US
GLU
LESBIAN
QUARTERLY
3
SUMMER/FALL 2006
NL €6/EU €8/USA $10

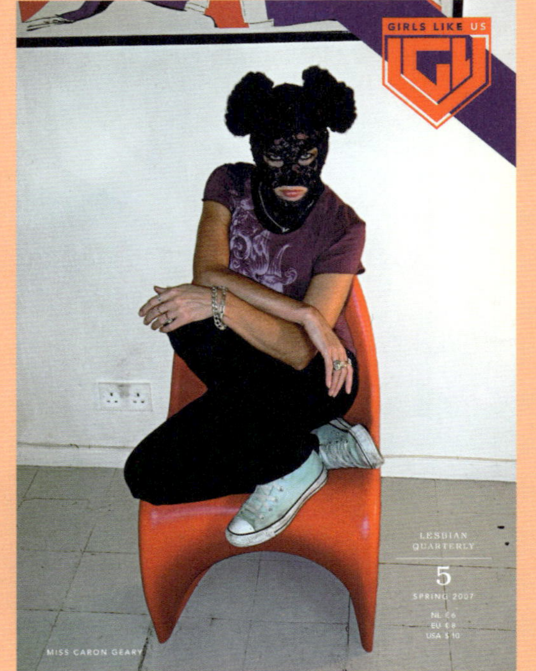

GIRLS LIKE US
GLU
LESBIAN
QUARTERLY
5
SPRING 2007
NL €6
EU €8
USA $10
MISS CARON GEARY

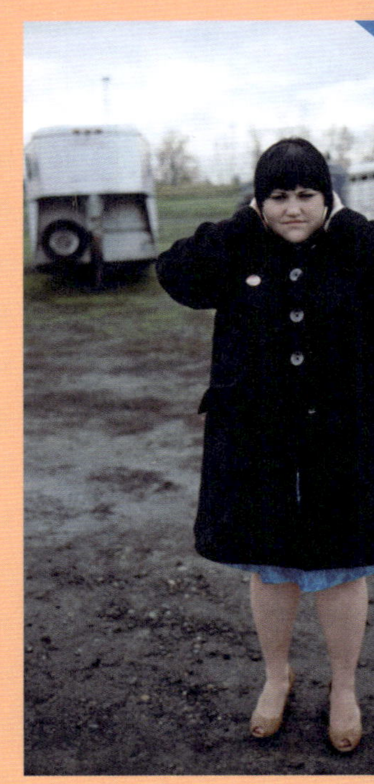

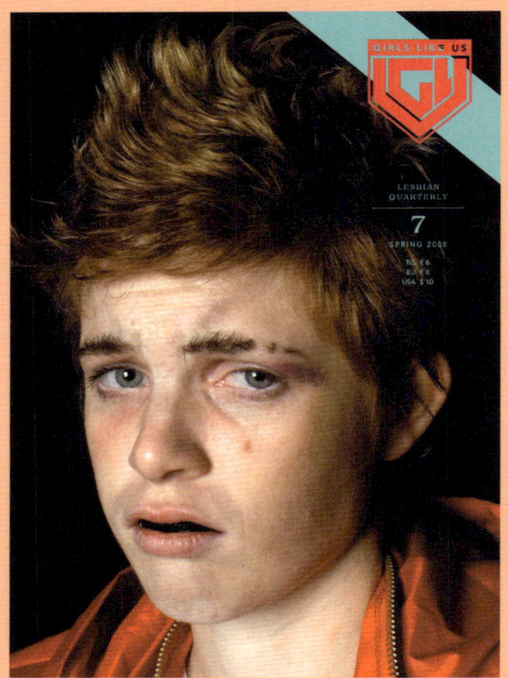

GIRLS LIKE US
GLU
LESBIAN
QUARTERLY
7
SPRING 2008
NL €6
EU €8
USA $10

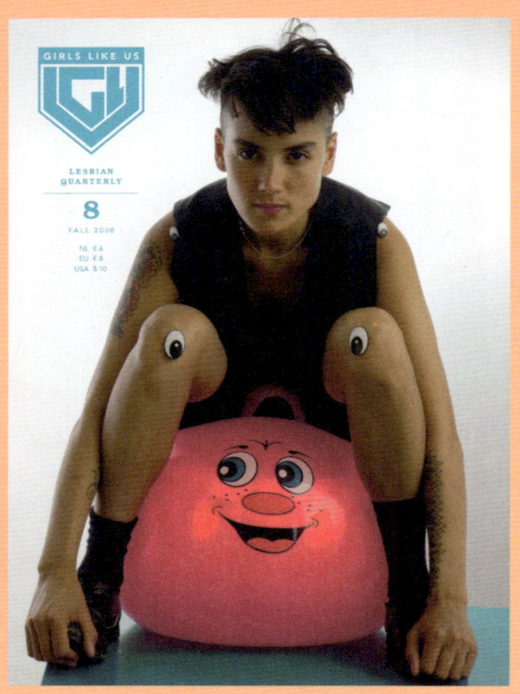

GIRLS LIKE US
GLU
LESBIAN
QUARTERLY
8
FALL 2008
NL €6
EU €8
USA $10

Girl
Volume 2 - Issue I
Us

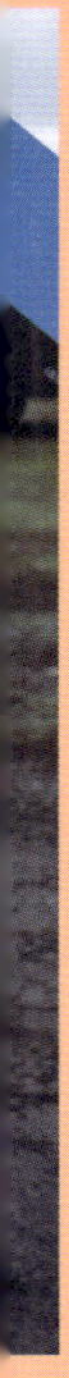

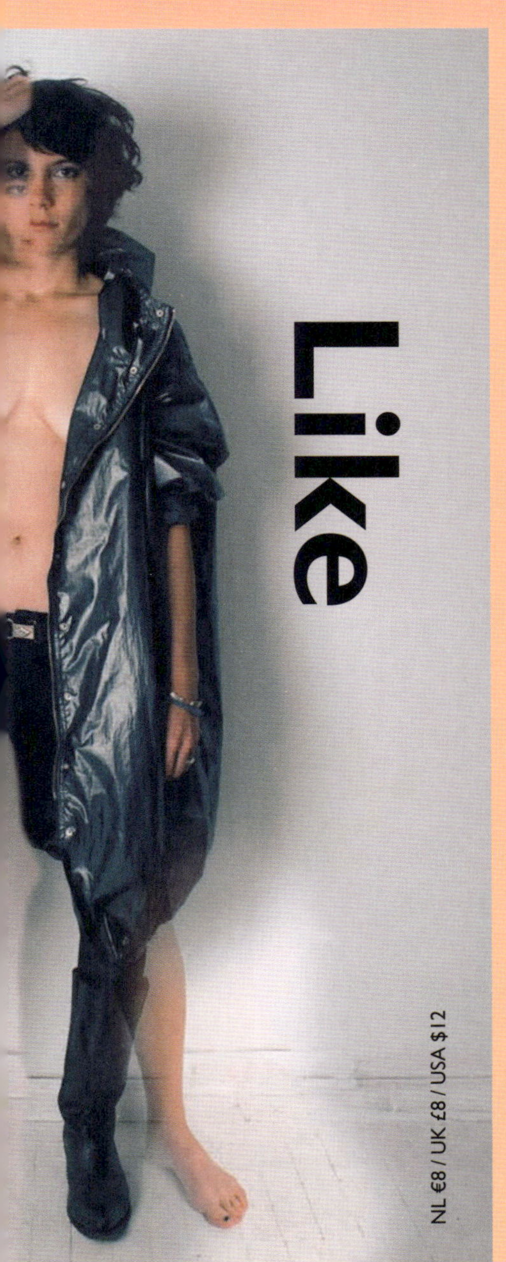
Like
NL €8 / UK £8 / USA $12

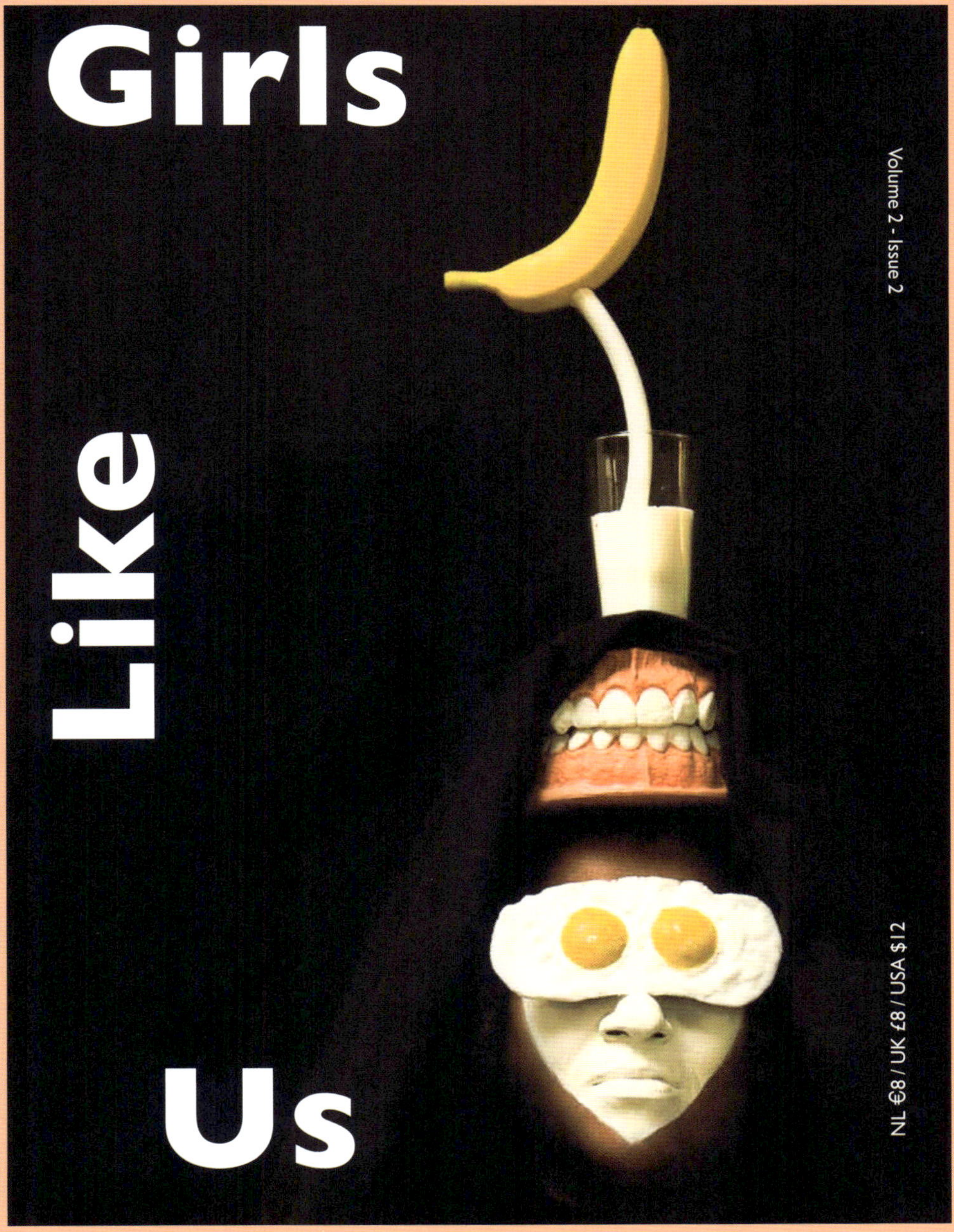

Girls
Like
Us
Volume 2 - Issue 2
NL €8 / UK £8 / USA $12

My first three issues were even called *Kutt* (Kut is the not so civil Dutch word for vagina). But I soon realized I wanted to be completely independent so I started *GLU*. At the moment I don't read a lot of magazines. I like *Index* because of the interviews that are more like conversations than Q&A and *The Face*. And I'm subscribed to *The New York Times*, but that's about it. Most magazine makers are too focused on retro right now, and I've had it with retro. That's also why we stopped publishing those lesbian archives in *Girls Like Us*.

You started a magazine, just like that. What is your background?

I studied communication mainly in Gent and partly in Amsterdam. My graduation project was an analysis of scene marketing. I researched how brands can reach certain sub cultures and specific target groups. And I still work in that field. Brands like Nike and Lee jeans asked me to develop concepts for specific target groups and a Dutch fashion brand for women just asked me to create an identity book, based on interviews with different types of creative women. And also for *Girls Like Us* I use my education to reach the right advertising clients. For example the back page of *Girls Like Us* is always covered with a custom-made advertisement of American Apparel. And this fashion brand also sells my magazine in their stores worldwide. Comme des Garçons is a brand I would really like to work with in the future.

Talking about distribution, what's your strategy?

Girls Like Us is for sale worldwide at arty bookstores, gay bookstores, some concept stores and American Apparel. I'm happy about all those points of sale, but I'm still hoping for more art and fashion oriented selling points In terms of subscriptions, you could say 700 subscribers. Not a lot, but I certainly don't complain. Most of our magazines go to Europe and the US. Some to Japan and some to Brazil. And I can imagine and hope some will go to Cape Town, South Africa in the future.

We're doing this interview in your living room in Amsterdam. Did you always make *Girls Like Us* from home?

Not always. In the past I had a studio and also my graphic designers have their studio space. We also had interns at certain points, but we don't have a headquarters or anything like that. Vela and I travel a lot, but we're both based in Amsterdam. I think the city has had a big influence on our work. If we would have been based in New York, I would have never met the founders of *Butt* and maybe never launched a magazine like *Girls Like Us*. And Vela studied at both Central Saint Martin's in London and the Rietveld Academy in Amsterdam. No doubt these influences are visible in her work somehow.

Are you satisfied the way *Girls Like Us* is at the moment?

Yes, but things can always be even better. So I'm planning to make future issues even more accessible, for example by adding an editorial. It would be nice to be able to pay all my bills with *Girls Like Us*, but I don't expect it to come that far. I have to be realistic I'm always thinking of new ways to extent the Girls Like Us brand. For example with parties with the same name and same look and feel. I'm not afraid blogs will beat magazines. As long as you add something valuable to the paper version, printed magazines will never die. I'm not per se dreaming of a bigger brand awareness, but if a huge newspaper wants to write about us; great! Strange for a marketing person to say, I know, but I'm just more focused on the content than on the marketing. After almost ten years I still love making this magazine. It's a great outlet for my personal opinion, a great way to stay updated and a great way to meet interesting people. It's nice to have a voice in a debate. There's still a lot to tell. But I'm not in a hurry. I want to continue making *Girls Like Us* for the rest of my life. There's more to come!

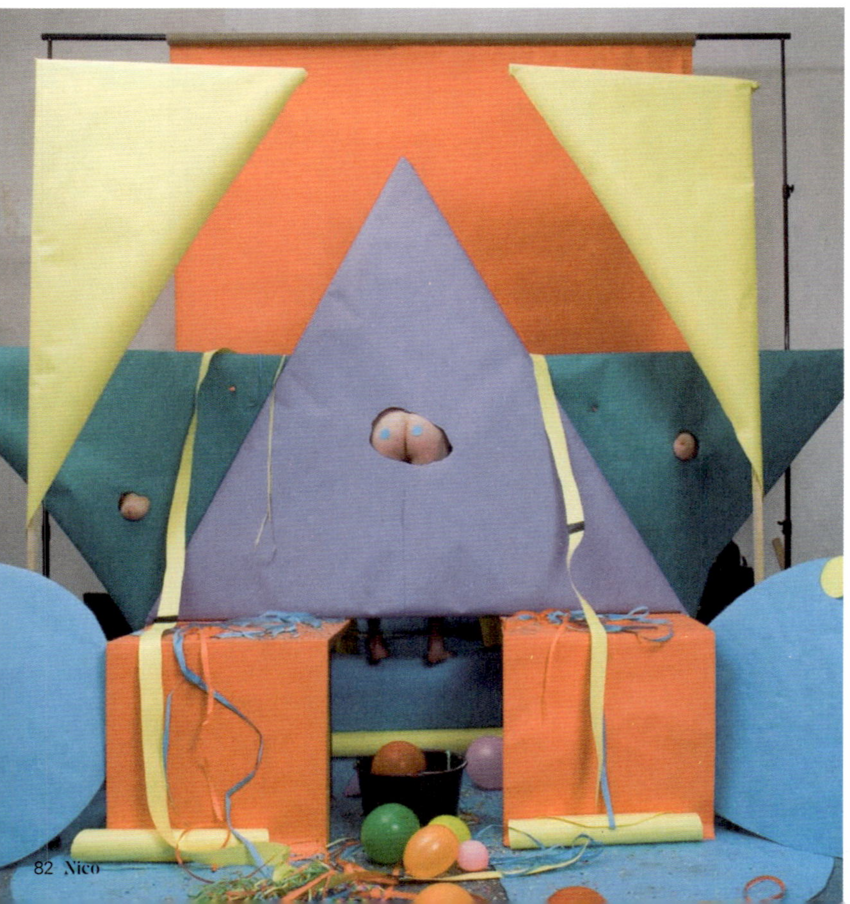

“I'M NOT AFRAID
BLOGS WILL BEAT
MAGAZINES.
AS LONG AS YOU
ADD SOMETHING
VALUABLE
TO THE PAPER
VERSION, PRINTED
MAGAZINES
WILL NEVER DIE.”

THE SINUOUS LINES OF PANTYHOSE

He talks about his work as escapism and a common
ground for those in need of experimenting with
desire. It´s not whether it´s sexy, erotic or fetish but rather
a sensible approach to one´s secret perception of beauty.
Howard Chu, on his own since 2002 after graduating from
Brooks Institute of Photography and later on assisting
some of New York's professional photographers, is now
making an impact on New York and the world.
Pantyhose, his fanzine is getting our attention.

INTERVIEW BY VICTOR ZABROCKIS
PORTRAIT BY HOWARD CHU

WWW.HOWARDCHUSTUDIO.COM

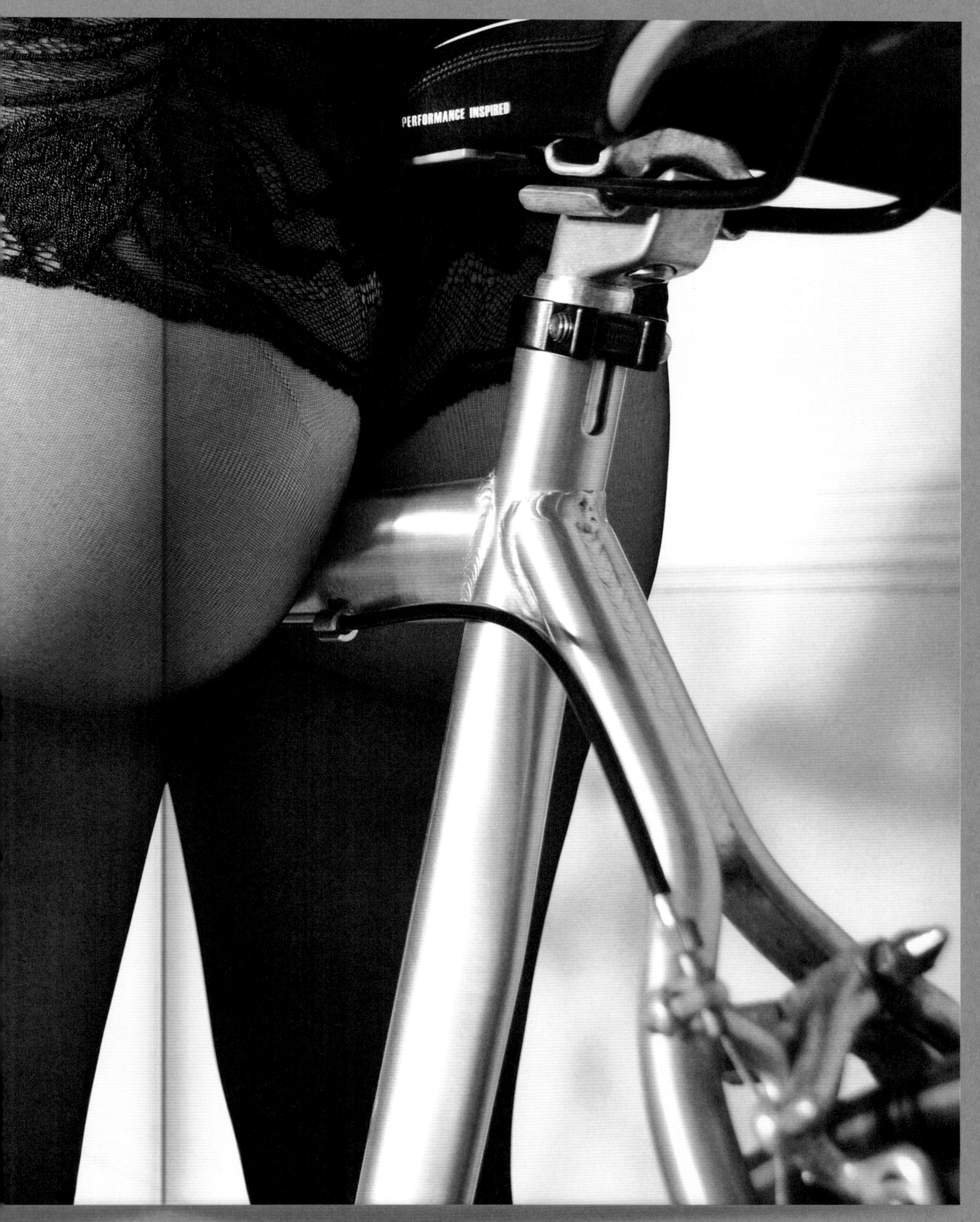
PERFORMANCE INSPIRED

Can you tell us a bit about your background?

I was born and raised in South Korea. We moved to Los Angeles when I was 5 because my father got a job in the US. A year later he got an opportunity to open his own company in Korea so we moved back. I was only little and we didn't stay in America too long but I remember a lot of things, like going to pre-school and watching American TV shows like the *Donny and Marie Show*.

I think living in America for that short time made a big impact on me. We got green cards when I was 14 and we came to Los Angeles (where I have an uncle and aunt) for 2 weeks every year. I remember getting really excited to come to the US because it was just so different from Korea. We watched MTV all day and bought the latest trends in clothes and shoes. Then we would go back to Korea, you couldn't really wear the American clothes there because they were too colourful or would standout. I was different from my friends; I never looked or dressed like them. Looking back, I never felt I fit in, as I was growing up in Korea.

My grandfather was a famous author in Korea. He passed away one month before I was born. He had two brothers, one was a poet and the other a filmmaker. I've met the poet a few times but not the filmmaker. Even though I had a lot of creative uncles, I can't say creativity or creative people always surrounded me.

What kind of environment did you grow up in?

When I was 13-14 I was having a hard time figuring out what I wanted to be when I grew up. I knew I couldn't sit at the same desk and work 9 to 5 everyday. I told my parents I couldn't do that but I didn't know what else I could do. When my mom saw that I was enjoying taking photos, she enlisted me into a lot of photo contests and I won quite a bit. I think it clicked with her that maybe I could make a living taking photos. We didn't know anyone who was a photographer and didn't know if you could make a living with it. She did some research and asked around, and found out that it was a real profession and you could make a career out of it.

My parents were very different from other parents. They were very open to a lot of things. I went to an all-boys Junior High and High School in Korea and there was maybe one school I knew of that was co-ed and the rest were all boys or all girls. In Korea we believe that dating is the biggest distraction for young students from getting into University. So they do all they can to prevent students from dating. It's very unnatural if you think about it. Of course at that age you want to have a girlfriend, maybe it's not too serious but you want to know what girls are all about. If you're told you're not supposed to meet

} p.89

"MY PARENTS WERE VERY DIFFERENT FROM OTHER PARENTS. THEY WERE VERY OPEN TO A LOT OF THINGS."

PANTYHOSE VIDEO

Howard Chu
autoportrait
}

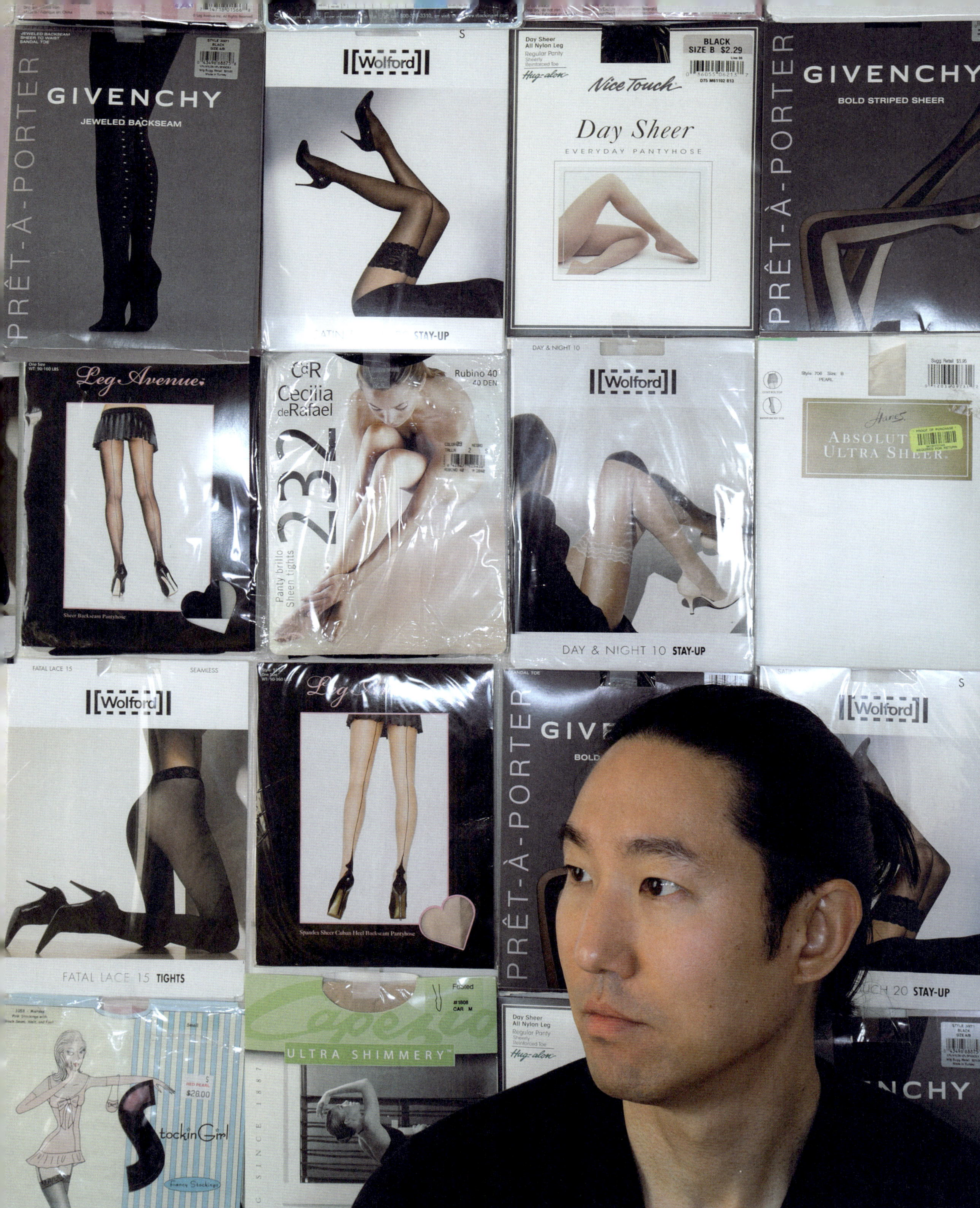
GIVENCHY
PRÊT-À-PORTER
JEWELED BACKSEAM
[Wolford]
Nice Touch
Day Sheer
EVERYDAY PANTYHOSE
GIVENCHY
PRÊT-À-PORTER
BOLD STRIPED SHEER
STAY-UP
Leg Avenue
Sheer Backseam Pantyhose
CdR
Ceciia
deRafael
Rubino 40
40 DEN
232
Panty brillo
Sheer tights
[Wolford]
ABSOLUT
ULTRA SHEER.
Hanes
DAY & NIGHT 10 STAY-UP
FATAL LACE 15
SEAMLESS
[Wolford]
Leg
Spandex Sheer Cuban Heel Backseam Pantyhose
GIVE
PRÊT-À-PORTER
BOLD
[Wolford]
FATAL LACE 15 TIGHTS
ULTRA SHIMMERY
SINCE 1887
StockinGirl
Day Sheer
All Nylon Leg
Regular Panty
Hug-alon
TOUCH 20 STAY-UP
NCHY

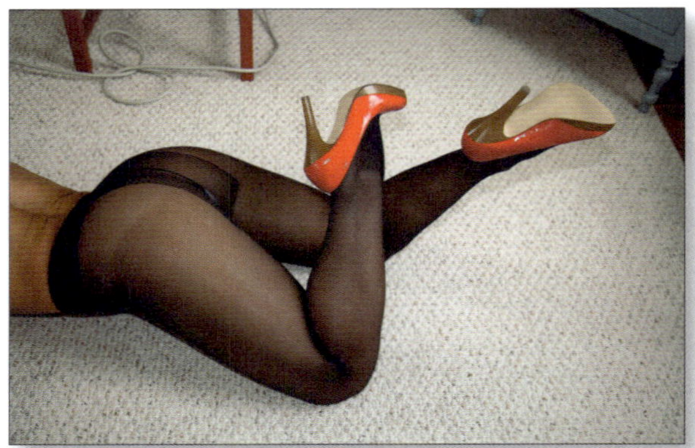

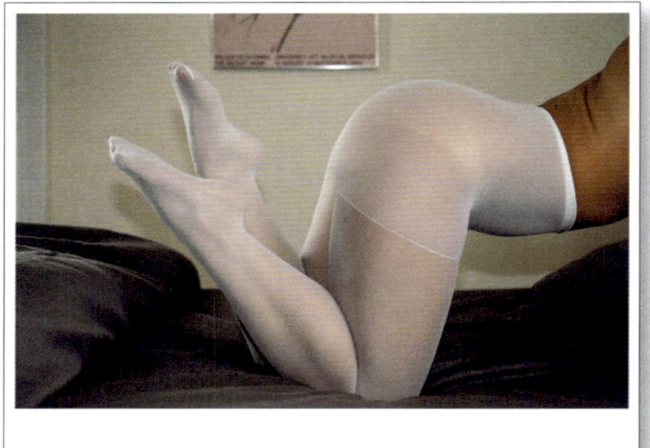

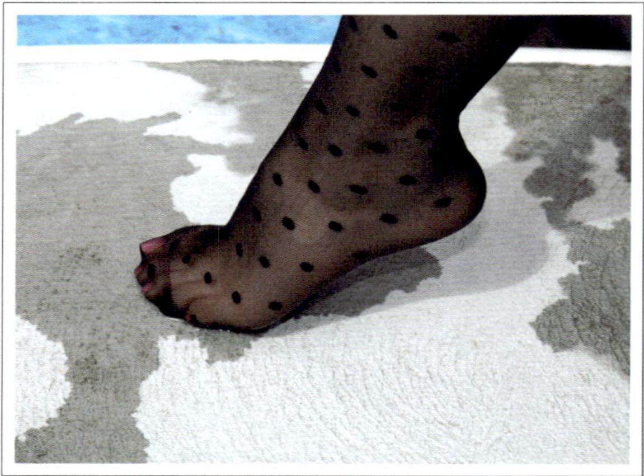

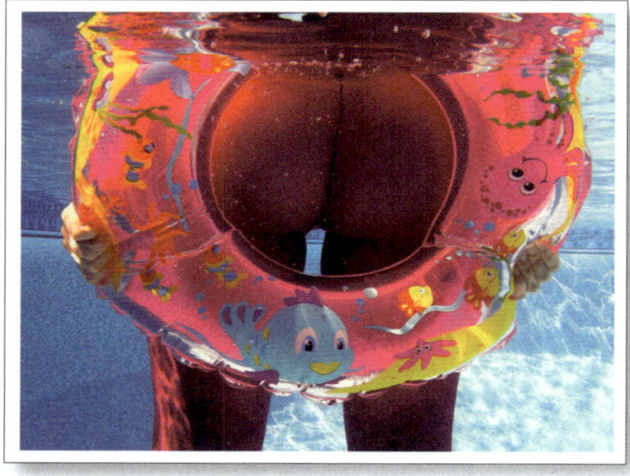

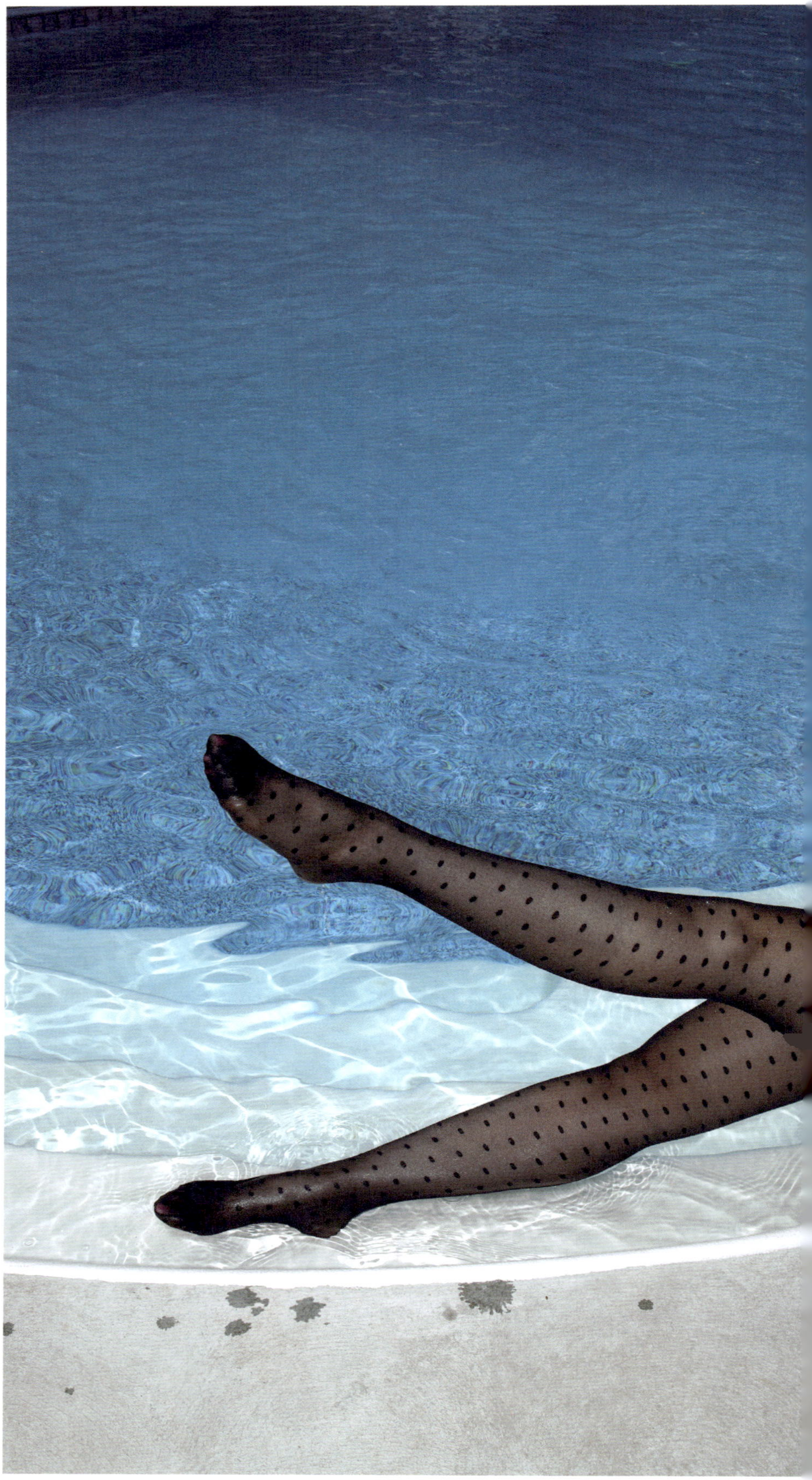

them it makes you want to meet them even more. But this was not allowed at that time and if you got caught seeing a girl a teacher would punish you. My teacher slapped my face when I got caught meeting a girl secretly. He wanted to have a parent-teacher meeting and have a talk. To my surprise my mom defended me saying that there is nothing wrong with boys at my age wanting to meet a girl. She said she doesn't really understand why teachers make a big deal out of it and make students secretly meet girls. After that the teacher didn't really bother me much, he just left me alone. That was really great. I felt like I was untouchable!

Where did you grow up?

After graduating High School in Korea I moved to the US permanently, mainly to attend photography school in Santa Barbara, California. My parents came with me and helped me settle in and then they went back to Korea. I was all alone and free to do as I pleased. I really had a great time living in the US and going to photography school. I practically lived in the school photo lab day and night, taking pictures and making prints, loving every minute of it. I really didn't do much else.

When did you start calling yourself a photographer?

I guess I knew I was a photographer when I was 16. My mother had a friend who knew a man who taught photography, she hired him to be my private photography teacher. We met once a week, every Saturday for a year. He was the president of the Korean Photography Association. He took me under his wing and taught me everything he knew about photography. He taught me how to frame, crop and see things you might miss in everyday life. He taught me to see objects as lines and shapes, lights and shadows. To look at small details in everyday objects on the streets or make something ugly into something beautiful. He definitely had a different eye. I owe everything I know about photography to him.

Do you remember your first erotic picture?

The first time I saw a naked photo of a girl was when I was about 10. An older kid who lived next door showed my friends and me a torn out page from *Playboy* magazine of a naked girl. She was showing her pubic hair and everything. We didn't know what we were looking at but I felt we were doing something bad and it made my heart beat so fast.

The first erotic photo I took was a topless photo of a model. I was testing to get more photos for my portfolio in NY. I think I did that because I couldn't borrow any clothes to photograph. I was very new and didn't have any connections. I was so nervous to see this model topless standing in front of me. The pictures came out ok. I didn't really know what I was doing.

Was it then that you started playing with sensuality as a theme or fetish?

I don't really remember when I had my first encounter with pantyhose. I always liked the soft feeling of pantyhose as long as I can remember.

My first masturbation was with pantyhose and I think that's when I associated sex or pleasure with pantyhose. I didn't know I had a fetish back then or that my interest in pantyhose was a fetish.

Did you explore your pantyhose theme while at Brooks Institute of Photography?

No. I was still learning about photography when I was in school. All the technical stuff.

When did you make it to New York?

I got an internship for a month with a well-known fashion photographer in NY while I was in school. He offered me an assisting position if I finished school and moved to NY. So I did. It all happened really fast.

When I was in school, I thought once I graduated I would open my own studio and start shooting and making money right away. When I finished my internship I realized that wasn't the case. I had no connections and I didn't even have a real portfolio. I needed to learn how the fashion photography world worked, build my portfolio and learn how business was conducted.

Did it start as a theme and later become a fetish or the other way around?

I was photographing everything but pantyhose. I couldn't photograph a girl in pantyhose before *Pantyhose*. I was very insecure about my fetish and I kept it a secret. Once I made *Pantyhose* issue N° 1 I knew that's what I wanted to do.

Do you think your work will evolve into more intimate realms of pantyhose and sex?

What I'm doing right now is just a foundation. I want people to associate the word pantyhose with my work. Every time you hear or see pantyhose you have *Pantyhose* images in your head. I have a much bigger vision for *Pantyhose*, that everyone has to wait and see. I can't share it right now.

How much do you know about the history of pantyhose?

I know a little about the history of pantyhose, but I'm not a pantyhose historian. The history of it didn't really influence me.

How did you get to know Elmer Batters' work and why do you like it?

I came across his book *From the Tip of the Toes to the Top of the Hose*, at a bookstore where they sold erotic books. It was packaged in an actual nylon and of course that caught my

} p.90

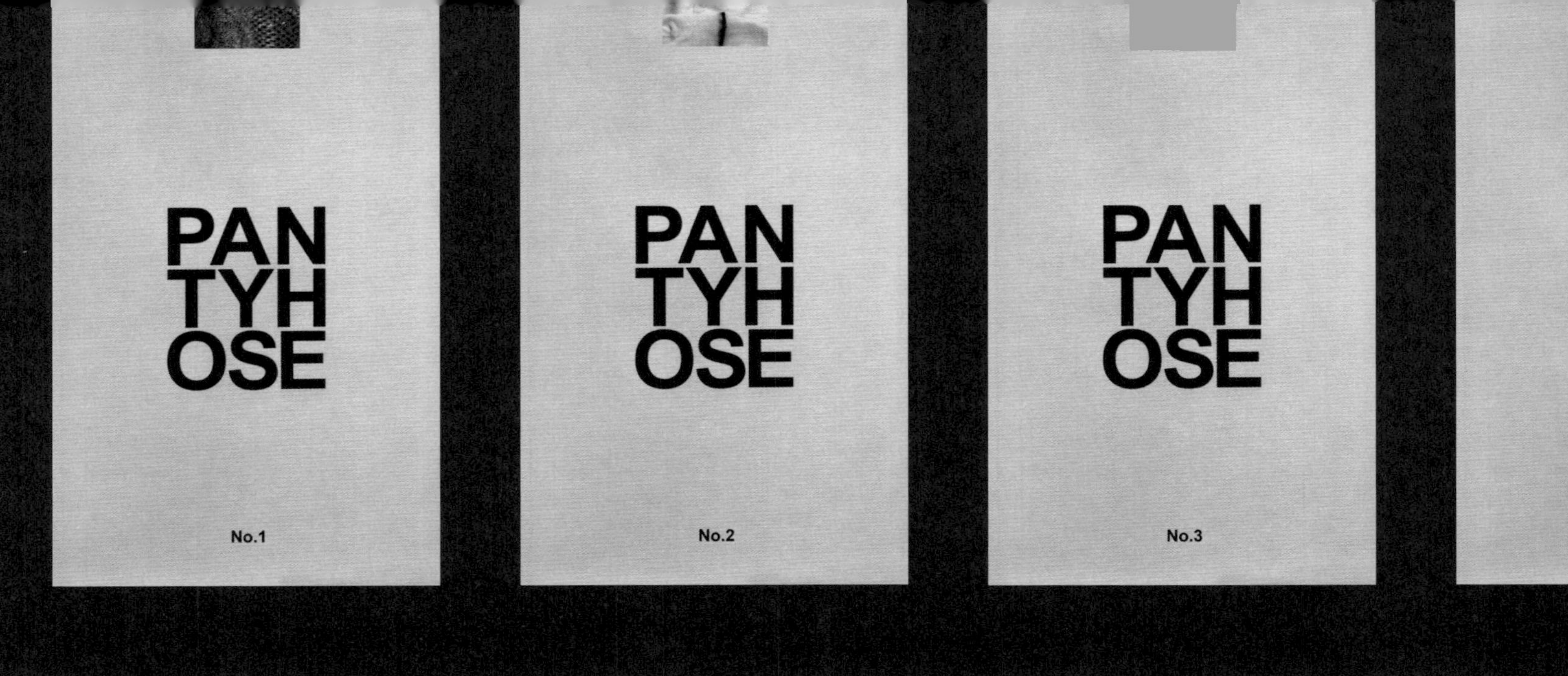

attention. But I couldn't buy it. I was too embarrassed to bring it to the cashier and let them know what I was buying.

He is the only photographer I know of from that time period that photographed his own fetish, rather than photographing for other people and their fetishes. I thought it was so bold of him to do that. Something I couldn't even imagine at that time.

Do you know other photographers that share your fetish for pantyhose?

I don't really know any other photographer with a pantyhose fetish. There are thousands of pantyhose fetish sites and someone had to take all those photos but I don't know of them.

Will you ever invite others to show their work at *Pantyhose*?

Not really. My intention was not to make a magazine with other people's photos. I think that becomes a whole other thing. Now you are a publisher, editor, etc.

Does your sexual partner share this fetish with you too?

She doesn't have a pantyhose fetish, but she accepts mine and understands it. She wishes she had a fetish but she doesn't. My wife is the one who encouraged me to shoot women wearing pantyhose. It all began when I took a photo of her wearing pantyhose. She made me feel like it's ok to take a photo of it and I felt such a satisfaction afterwards. Like I finally found what my thing was. Until then I always struggled to find what my path or style was. I tried everything, every style of photography you can imagine but in the end I was never satisfied with my work. There was something missing and I didn't know what. My wife is at every shoot for *Pantyhose*. I think having her there makes the models feel more comfortable. She also knows my style and will tell me if something is working or not or if I should move on to the next shot. She helps put together the looks (which pantyhose and shoes work together) and a lot of times will have to straighten the seams of the pantyhose on the models!

You see, until I met her, I did my best to hide my fetish from everyone. As I was growing up I thought I was the only one who had this fetish and I was terrified if someone found out about it. Before there was Internet porn, I discovered a porn magazine called *Leg Show* and was very excited to know I wasn't the only one. Still I wouldn't dare to tell anyone about it.

Once I was taking photos for a fashion magazine, it was a lingerie story, the stylist had stockings and pantyhose and I told him not to use them. I was just so nervous that anyone on the set would find out I had a pantyhose fetish.

Do you know what it feels like to wear pantyhose?

I kind of do. When I was about 9 years old I wore them under my pants and went to school. It was wintertime and I thought *"why don't I wear them instead of long johns?"* I was so young and I didn't even know what sex or a fetish was. I just thought why not? I forgot that I was wearing pantyhose that day and in the evening my mom accidentally found out and asked why I was wearing them and I couldn't answer because I didn't know why I did it. I think I said I was cold or something. Looking back I was

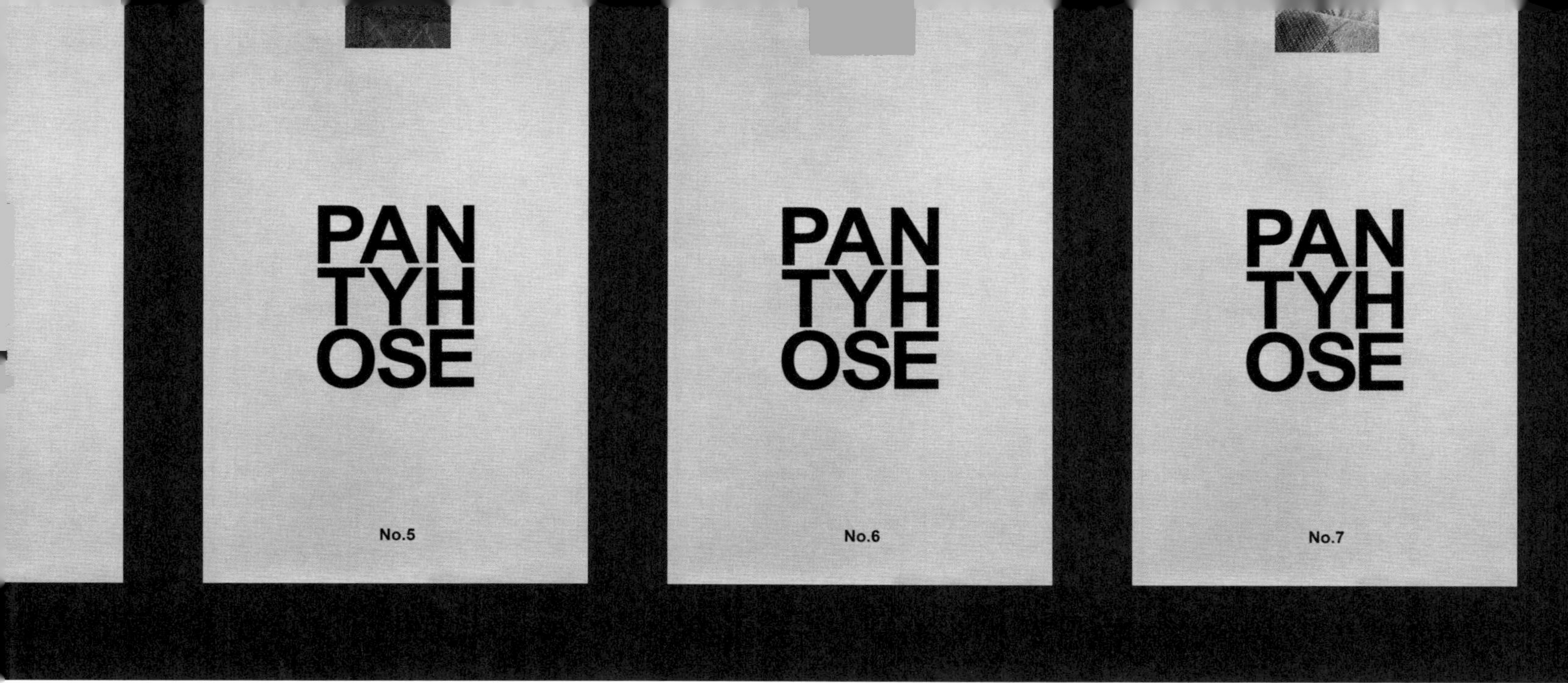

so innocent. I know a lot of men who like to wear them and it's another fetish. Not for me. I feel like it's cross-dressing and I don't a have desire to do that.

What is the relationship of your work with architecture?

This goes back to my first photography teacher again. The way he taught me to see lines and shapes in objects is in every photo I take. Then it evolved after I discovered the Japanese architect Tadao Ando. His work touched me deeply and it reconnected me to why I became a photographer in the first place.

How come you rarely show faces?

In the beginning I wanted to focus on my fetish. Like let's get to the point. If I take a photo of a girl's legs wearing pantyhose you know what I'm trying to say. Now it's more like a play. You can put any face you want on the model when you look at those photos. I wanted viewers to imagine and dream and put any girl they wished in the photos. I include the photos of the backgrounds or surroundings to show viewers where I'm shooting so they will have a sense of the space and location. Once I read somewhere that what's going on outside of the camera frame is as important as what is in the frame. I took it literally.

Why *Pantyhose*?

Pantyhose is a perfect word to describe how I feel about my fetish. Lingerie sounds expensive and foreign to me. Nylon or hosiery is too broad. Stocking is a whole other fetish. Pantyhose sounds very ordinary and familiar to me. In Korea they call pantyhose "panty stockings." I guess they mean stockings with a panty built in-that kind of makes sense...

What have you learned from it so far?

Technically I learned to be very simple. I used to love to set up complicated lighting with many strobes in the studios and use a Hasselblad medium format camera with a digital back attached and tethered to a computer. People always told me how beautiful my lighting was when they saw my work. That really pissed me off. Making beautiful light is a gaffer's (lighting technician) job and I considered myself a photographer. So when I started taking photos for *Pantyhose* I wanted to keep it simple, my camera, my subject and me. The more I shot this way, the more I really loved it. It was like going back to when I was starting to take photos. I was wandering around the streets all day with my 35mm camera. So I sold all of my strobes, my Hasselblad and bought a digital SLR camera and haven't looked back ever since.

Would you ever tell *Nico* readers a secret no one knows about you?

Me trying on pantyhose is a secret I never told anyone.

Do you get aroused when taking pictures?

It used to turn me on physically in the very beginning, but then it went away as I really got into it. I have a lot of other things to think about when I'm taking pictures, exposure, composition, what's in the background and so on. The pantyhose give me a focal point and the story of every issue revolves around it.

} p.92

Do you think your work will evolve into more erotic stuff?

I believe in imagination. I think of my pictures as a starting point of imagination for every individual. It can go whichever direction they like. If I show the models' face and vagina in every photo, for example, there is no room for fantasy. I think you get bored with the picture faster when you see everything.

What is success to you?

Success to me is balancing all the areas of your life. Money, family, yourself, health and your work all coming together. You can be a millionaire but miserable and alone or enlightened but sick and broke.

So success is about balancing all the different areas of your life and making them work. It is also about doing what you love everyday, learning from your every experience and growing.

Do you consider your work art?

Ahh, the art or not the art question! I have thought about this in the past but I don't anymore. I don't ask those questions anymore with my work. I just create it and let others categorize it for me.

I've seen my photos on many blogs. When I see them on a fetish blog they don't look like art, yet when I see them on an art blog, they look like art. It's really funny to see how the context in which you see my images changes the way they can be perceived as art or fetish photography. You can ask me this question again after my gallery show but for now I prefer being a photographer better than an artist.

Will you separate Pantyhose magazine from your studio?

I have thought about that lately. It seems *Pantyhose* has its own life and I'm seriously considering giving it its own space. I think I'll know what to do when the time is right.

How do you make a living?

I accept commissioned work mostly from fashion and advertising. Sometimes I work on commissioned work for days and sometimes I do nothing but work on *Pantyhose*. I kind of like the break from each one. It helps me think and grow. They both help each other. I might get an idea to use in an advertising shoot from *Pantyhose* and for *Pantyhose* from an advertising shoot.

Who would you like to photograph if you could?

I came across a lot of women on pantyhose photo sites or blogs that I wanted to photograph but I don't know their names. I'm not even sure if they are real fetish models or not. I like unknown, real-looking women. Not so perfect looking. I think perfection is boring.

If I have to choose well-known people, I would say Daisy Lowe or Katy Perry. They just look good in pantyhose and they seem fun to work with.

Tell us about your dreams.

I've been having this dream where I need to go to the bathroom. I'm in a public bathroom and every stall is dirty and wet and I can't even step into it. I look for a different one and it's dirty again. I keep looking for one and end up waking up. I googled about this dream and some sites say that dreams which contain a toilet mean that we want to rid ourselves of burdens, releasing and letting go of toxic feelings and thoughts. I guess it's a good dream to have then.

Are you happy?

Yes I am. I have a lot of good things going on in my life to be happy about. I focus mostly on what I have rather than what I don't have and I'm grateful for all of those things. I'm very happy to do this interview with *nico* for example. Thank you and I really appreciate it.

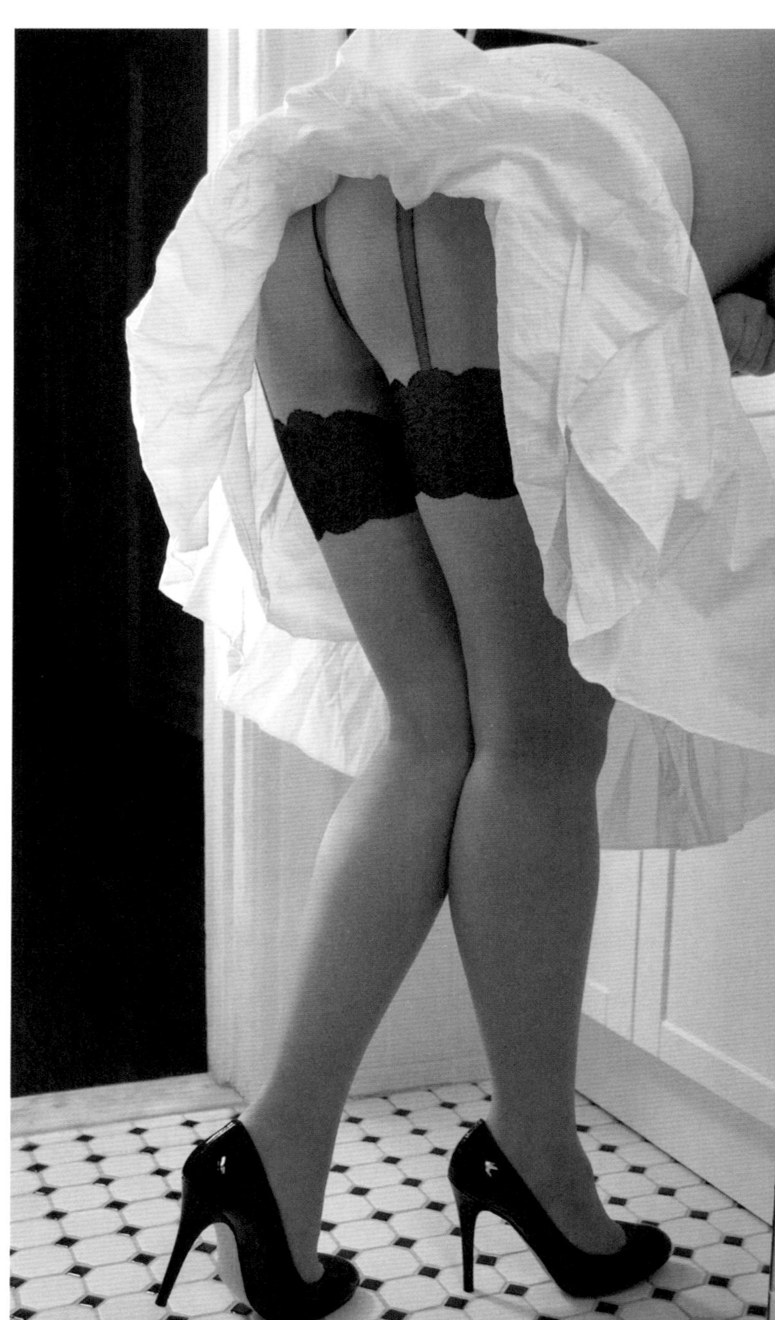

"I WAS VERY INSECURE ABOUT MY FETISH AND I KEPT IT A SECRET. ONCE I MADE PANTYHOSE ISSUE NO.1 I KNEW THAT'S WHAT I WANTED TO DO."

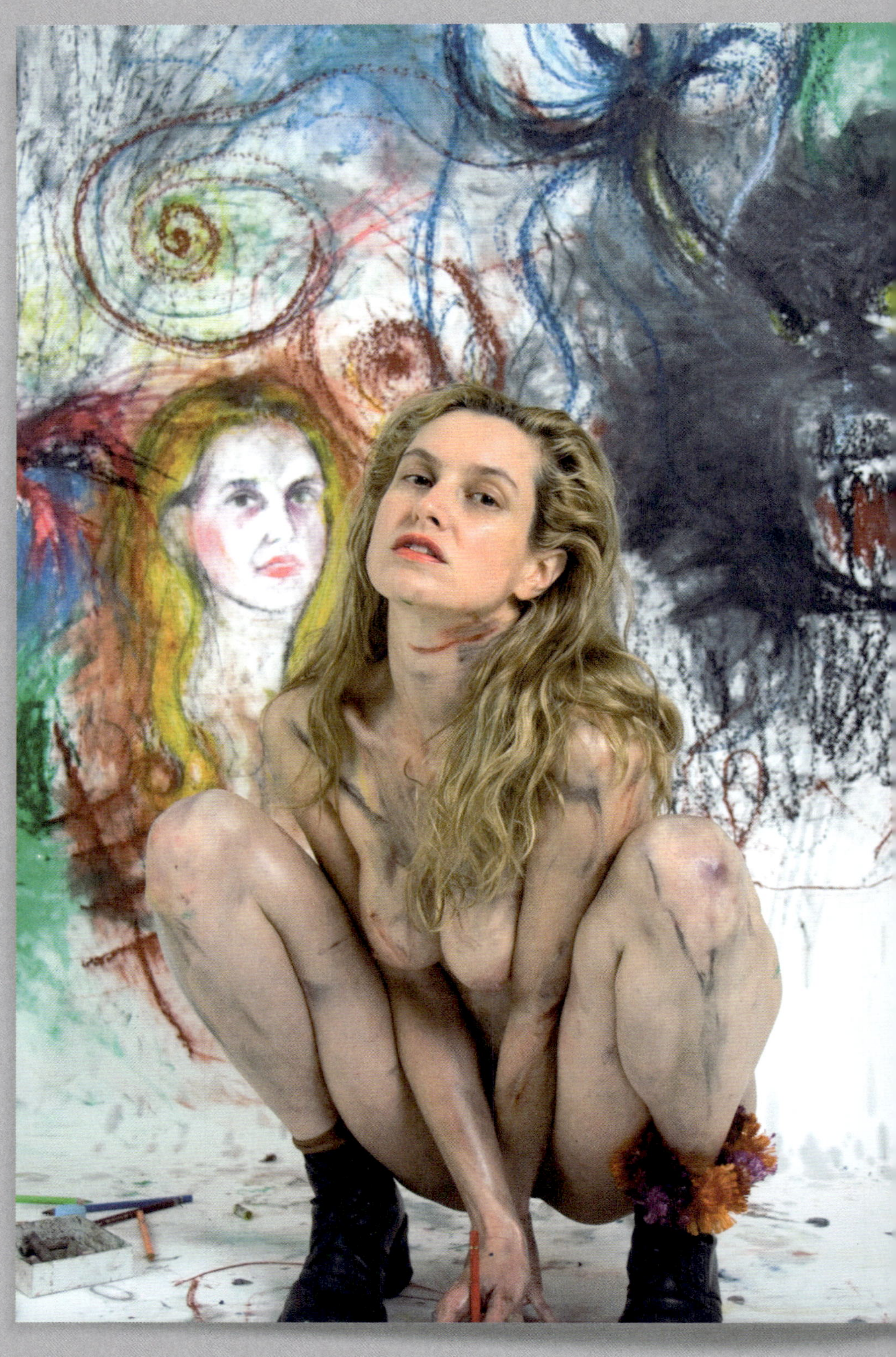

STICK PHOTOSHOP UP YOUR ARSE!

Published and self-funded by two friends in Cologne, the bi-annual sibling magazines *Jungsheft* and *Giddyheft* put ordinary aroused people on pornographic display. Aimed at women and men respectively, the almost pocket-sized pamphlets seek to establish themselves as an alternative to traditionally polished, yawningly predictable and over-stylized printed porn.

Interview by Gintare Parulyte.
Portrait by Sandra Stein.

By uniting pictures and texts and peeling off the superfluous and the fake, the magazines expose volunteering participants in their intimate, attention-seeking horny state.

"IMAGINE TWO STRANGERS ARRIVE AT YOUR FLAT AND ASK YOU TO UNDRESS IN FRONT OF THEIR CAMERA JUST BECAUSE YOU MENTIONED SOMETHING ON A RANDOM DRUNK NIGHT."

Elke, when and how did the magazine originate?

Jungsheft was a silly idea that Nicole and I came up with during our holiday in Greece in 2003. It stems from a desire to see and show *"normal"* naked men in print, something we had not come across back then. We were quite motivated and started asking around for men willing to take off their clothes. Our plan was to make black and white photocopies of these pictures and sell them, but once we found some guys, after what turned out to be a difficult search, we thought that it would be a shame to only do photocopies. So, we decided to use our savings, print a thousand copies, in colour this time, and force everybody to buy it. This is where it all began. And, indeed, things continued from there on. The first *Jungsheft* came out in 2005. Two years later, after receiving many emails from men who loved the idea and wanted a mag of their own, we decided to create the *Giddyheft*. Their requests brought the female version to life.

Which magazine is more popular?

Weirdly enough, both magazines are sold equally, simply because most people order both issues at the same time. Of course there are people who only buy one magazine, but I'd say that roughly 70% buy both simultaneously.

Did you have any magazine-related experience prior to that?

The magazine idea was supposed to be a joke and we were absolutely inexperienced, which means that legal, commercial or financial implications hadn't even crossed our minds. This obviously led to many mistakes along the way. Simple stuff. For instance, our magazine was called differently at the beginning. We simply didn't know that one had to check the name before bringing a product out to the public. We never made the boys sign a contract in order to transfer the rights to us, since we were the ones distributing the pictures later on and so on. There are so many things to respect when dealing with pornography and we didn't know any of them. I can frankly admit that had we known all of this beforehand, we would have never done it in the first place.

When did the problems disappear?

You are literally thrown into the whole chaos. When you are sued, your reaction is obviously *"Shit!"*, but then you learn from it. We haven't had any problems for a while now, but you do learn from these experiences step by step: How to find the boys, which arguments to use in order to make them take their clothes off and so on. We are still learning.

} *p.99*

Elke Kuhlen shot by
Sandra Stein

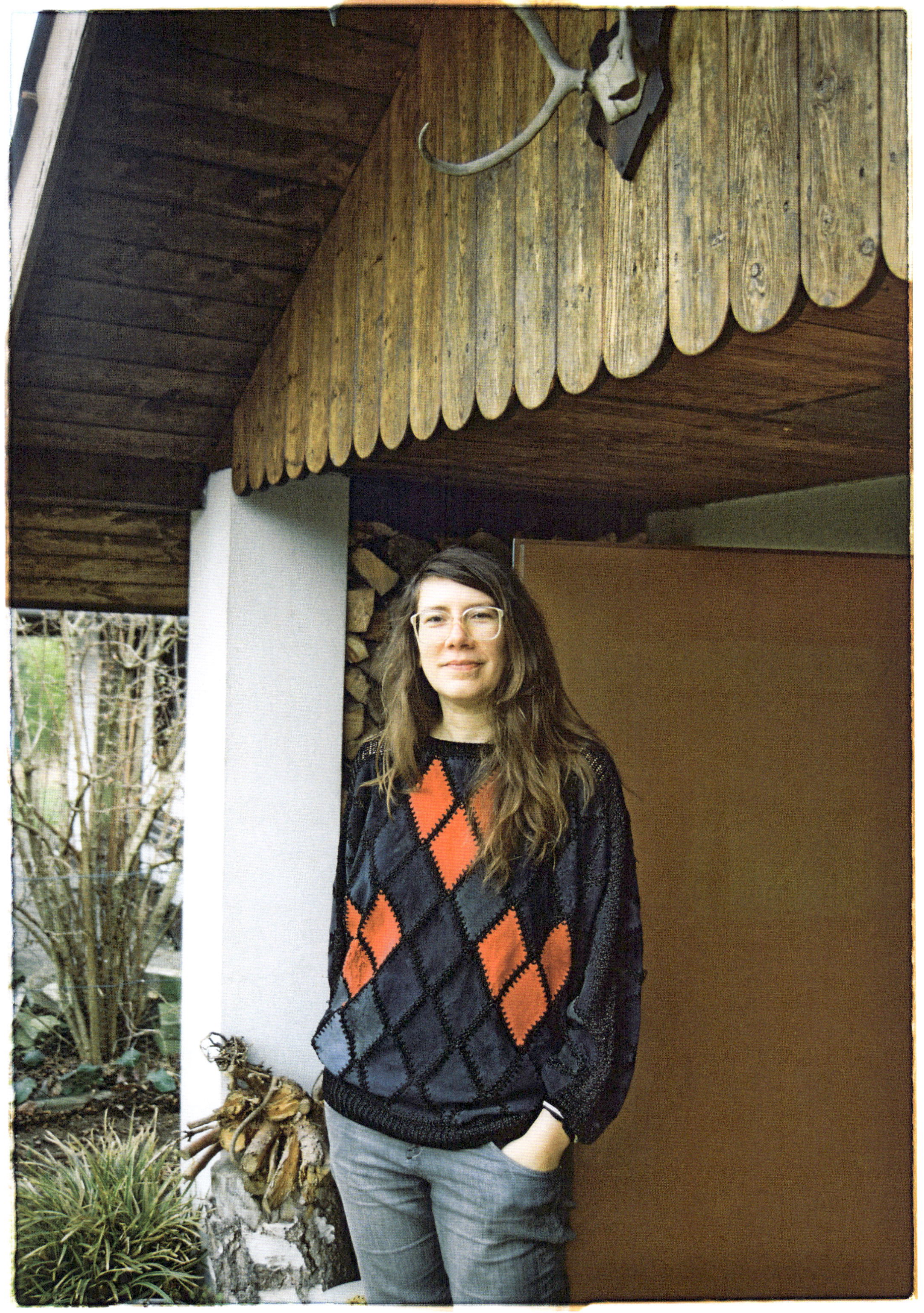

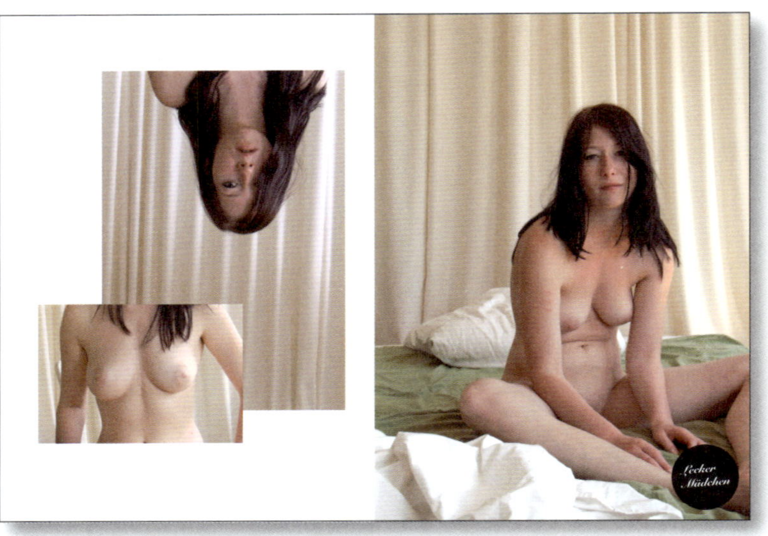

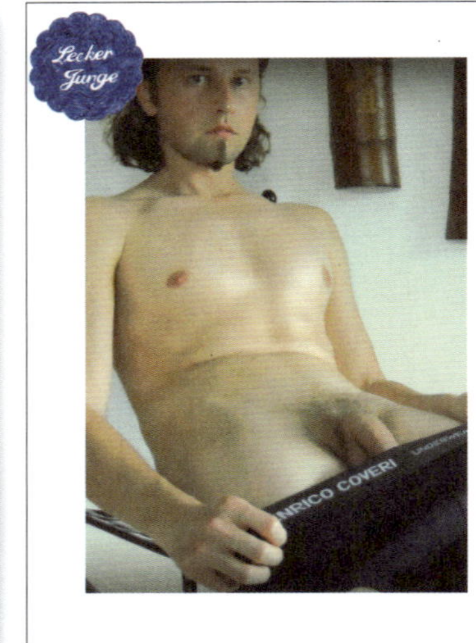

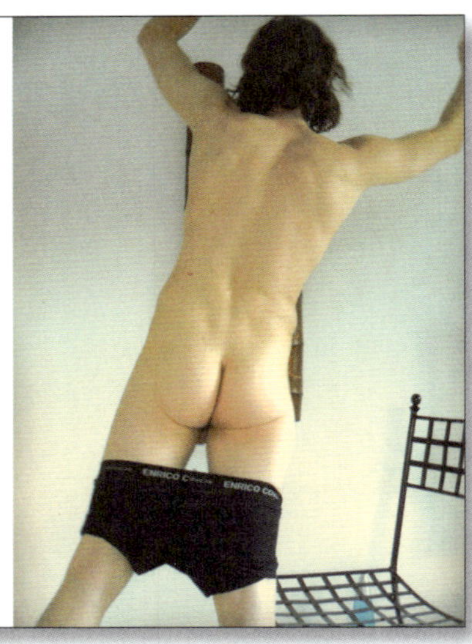

VORZEITIGE EJAKULATION

TEXT UWE KRETSCHMER ILLU VANESSA WEBER

SCHOENE BESCHERUNG

Das zu frühe Kommen von Männern ist ein allen vertrautes und doch sehr schambehaftetes Thema. Um die verfrühte Ejakulation zu verstehen, muss mensch zunächst die männliche Ejakulation selbst verstehen. Sich sexuell zu befreien heißt immer auch sich von falschen Vorstellungen zu lösen, die uns sexuell einengen. Und das Abspritzen ist ein Kapitel der menschlichen Sexualität, über das zwar viel geredet, von dem aber tatsächlich wenig gewusst wird.

DER MYTHOS DES MAENNLICHEN ERGUSSES

Wie kaum ein anderer Aspekt menschlicher Biologie ist die Ejakulation von Mythen verklärt. Da ist zuerst mal der von der Fortpflanzung, wo das Ejakulat zum Saft des Lebens erkoren wird. Daran knüpfte die fixe Idee an, Sex wäre ein Mittel zum Zweck, ein notwendiges Übel zur Kinderzeugung. Hier entspringt dann wohl die Vorstellung, Ziel und Zweck von Sex sei die Absonderung des männlichen Sekrets. Die leicht wahnsinnig wirkende Annahme, es ginge beim Sex ausschließlich um männliche Sekretabsonderung oder männliche Befriedigung ist leider immer noch weit verbreitet. Das zeigt sich nicht zuletzt darin, dass die Mainstream-Pornographie durch den Cumshot noch immer das Abspritzen als Höhe-, Ziel und Endpunkt menschlicher Sexualität darstellt. Der Mann selbst hat dann auch oft ein ambivalentes Verhältnis zu dieser Ausscheidung. Er wünscht sich im Mund und auf seine Sexualpartner_in kommen zu dürfen, ob er das auch selber gerne hätte ist aber fraglich. Eine Freundin erzählte mir gar mal, dass ihr Freund gekränkt sei, wenn sie seinen „Schmodder" wieder ausspucke. Auch wenn es sicher gut für jeden Menschen wäre sich vor nix Körpereigenem zu ekeln, besonders im Sexuellen ist das von großem Vorteil, wird jeder Mann, der sein Sperma mal in den Mund nimmt, es dort eine halbe Minute behält und dann schluckt, seine Sexualpartner_in fortan sicher weniger aktiv seine Gurgel- und Schluckphantasien zutragen.

ORGASMUS UNGLEICH EJAKULATION

Wer abspritzt hatte nicht automatisch einen Orgasmus und umgekehrt! Tatsächlich ist es sogar möglich, Männer die aus religiösen oder anderen Gründen ihren Schwanz nicht anfassen dürfen, zu entsaften, indem man bei ihnen per Druck auf die Prostata eine quasi mechanische Ejakulation auslöst. Bei diesem Ejakulieren kann natürlich von Orgasmus keine Rede sein, und es wird klar, dass Ejakulation und Orgasmus nicht dasselbe. Auch Pornodarsteller die stehend und zielend, innerhalb von 30 Sekunden per Handbetrieb kommen müssen, dürften wohl weniger orgastisch empfinden, und wer schon mal eine Spermaprobe abgeben durfte, weiß auch dass das mit Orgasmus nicht viel zu tun hat.

Ursächlich ist hier, dass der männliche Orgasmus im Gehirn ausgelöst wird und nicht im Schwanz oder sonst wo. Eine Skala der Intensität

39

DICK TRIX

TEXT & FOTOS LORD LÖRES

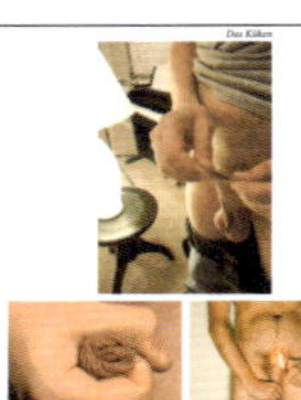
Das Küken

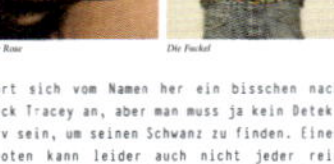
Die Rose   Die Fackel

Hört sich vom Namen her ein bisschen nach Dick Tracey an, aber man muss ja kein Detektiv sein, um seinen Schwanz zu finden. Einen Knoten kann leider auch nicht jeder rein machen, also muss Mann sich mit anderen Spiele-eien begnügen.

Bei "wetten, dass..." war ich damit noch nicht, aber ich möchte behaupten, das jahrelange Übung mich zu einem wahrlichen Meister der Schwanz-Akkrobatik gemacht hat. Ob Segelsch.ff, Hamburger oder Didgeridoo, so einiges wurde mittlerweile in mein festes Repertoire aufgenommen und ich appeliere an die Damenwelt gerne einmal diesem Schauspiel der Körperteile beizuwohnen.

Euer Lord Löres

39

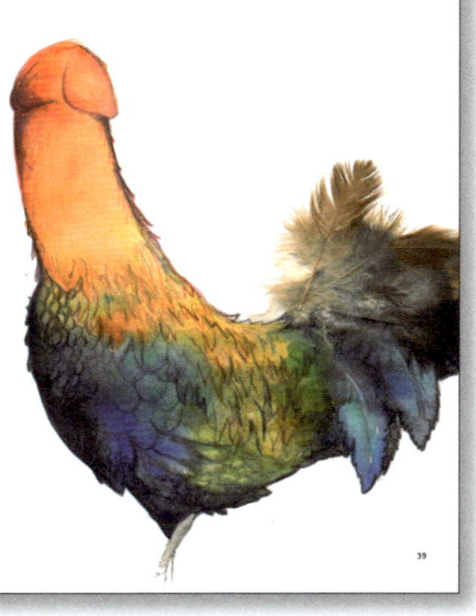

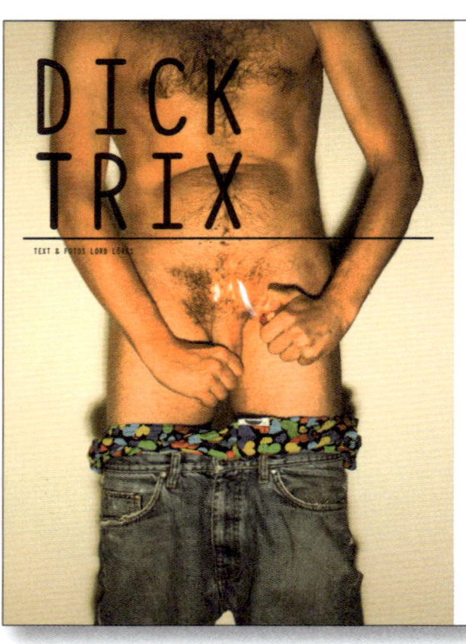

55

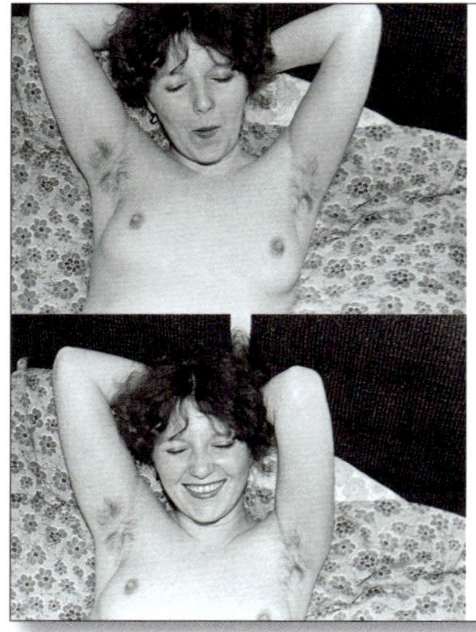

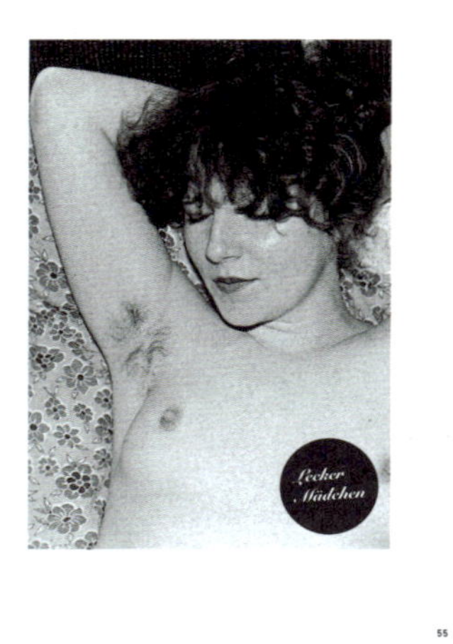

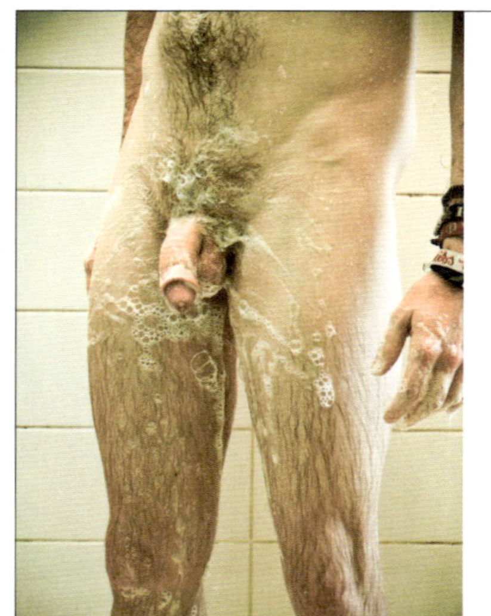

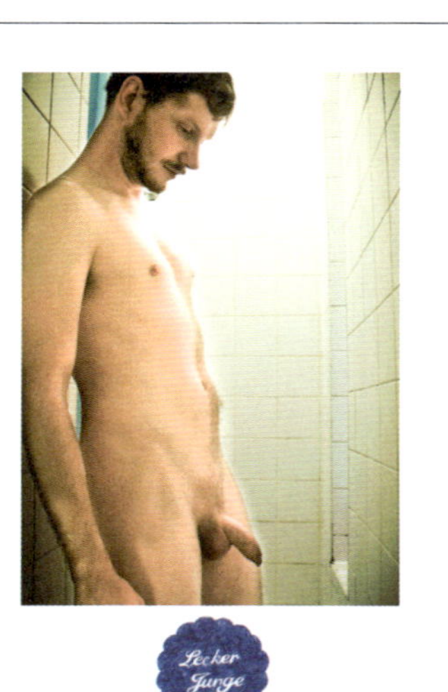

51

Has this project become your full-time job?

That would be nice, but no, there's no money to be made with these magazines. It's our hobby that we both spend time on after work. My day job consists of booking bands for festivals, whereas Nicole works for a company that manufactures drinks.

How did you choose the visual identity? What about content and format?

I would say that the style, or the visual appearance, is a direct combination of a lack of financial means and absolute and naïve subjectivity. We decided to print on an A5 format simply because it turned out to be much cheaper than the A4 option. We were very lucky that a friend of mine suggested designing the magazine. She created the basic layout for the very first issue. We're currently collaborating with a third graphic designer, a natural consequence of our inability to remunerate our contributors, yet the graphic backbone is still the same as in the first issue. We are very reliant on other people and their time schedules because of the extremely DIY character of the magazine. We wanted everything to be as "normal" and "ordinary" as possible. We don't use any retouching software or special lighting and styling in the creation of our pictures because we want it to be all about reality. But at the same time it is because we don't even have the money for it.

How did you proceed before your first issue, where and how did you find the people?

First, we asked our friends. Obviously nobody was willing to do it. Then the search went as follows: *"I am telling this to you and you tell it to your sister and her roommate might agree to do it"*. Once I received a tentative response, I called the person and said, *"Hello, apparently you said that you wouldn't mind taking your clothes off"*.

Like "Yeah, you said so after two bottles of champagne, remember?"

It really went along these lines. Whilst working on our first issue, we sometimes arrived at a person's place and they would say: *"Who the fuck are you?"* Imagine two strangers arrive at your flat and ask you to undress in front of their camera just because you mentioned something on a random drunk night.

How are the pictures taken?

Sometimes people take pictures themselves, sometimes we ask photographer friends for help. What happens more often, and what is aesthetically more appealing, is that pictures get taken by the respective partners of the volunteers. This doesn't necessarily make the pictures look better, but people are definitely more at ease, which in the end is of utmost importance. I'd also say that half of the people are friends of friends of friends. By the way, if there is anybody you can think of, please let me know what their favourite drink is, ok?

Of course! Have there ever been any cases of people regretting having posed?

Absolutely. This happens regularly, men being happy that an issue was sold out and would never be available again. I can understand that, since so many people took their decisions spontaneously.

Any anecdotes about people on the pictures being recognized?

That does happen from time to time. Once we didn't have enough girls for the *Giddyheft* so I begged a friend, who finally agreed to save me from publishing blank pages. One day she went to a café for a professional meeting that was related to her very serious and important position in a famous daily newspaper. A guy approached her and told her: *"Hey, weren't you in a magazine recently?"* Thinking that he was referring to her job, she proudly answered, *"Yeah, sure, I was"*. It turned out the guy meant the *Giddyheft* and congratulated her on dealing with it in such a relaxed way. I am not trying to fool anybody, the amount of magazines published is clearly fairly small and copies are not sold everywhere, but situations like that are bound to occur.

How many copies were printed in the beginning and how many do you issue now?

We went from 1000 to 5000.

What is the most common praise you get?

We get many emails from our readers, which is really sweet. They are relieved about the existence of a "real" and simple magazine. The problem is that there really isn't a middle way in the world of printed porn. You either have super polished models or the cliché girl from Eastern Europe with her legs spread on a leather couch. It is truly difficult to find people like you and I in those magazines, which is absolutely absurd when you think about it. If there had already been something like that on the market, I wouldn't have wanted to make it. I would have gone to the shop and bought it, instead of going through so much stress.

What is the main criticism you come across?

If we do get any, which is rare, it is mostly related to texts, which I can understand. We don't always have well-written articles or well-researched topics because, again, we don't have the means. We are happy when people are motivated to write for us, but there are times when stuff arrives that we are not very fond of, but still include in the mag to avoid having empty pages.

} p.102

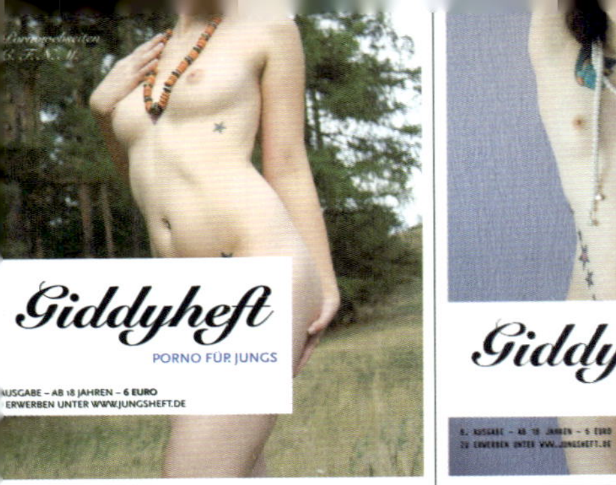
Giddyheft
PORNO FÜR JUNGS
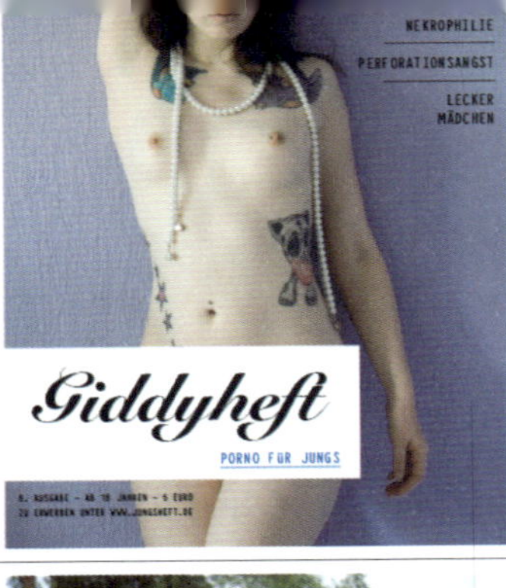
Giddyheft
PORNO FÜR JUNGS
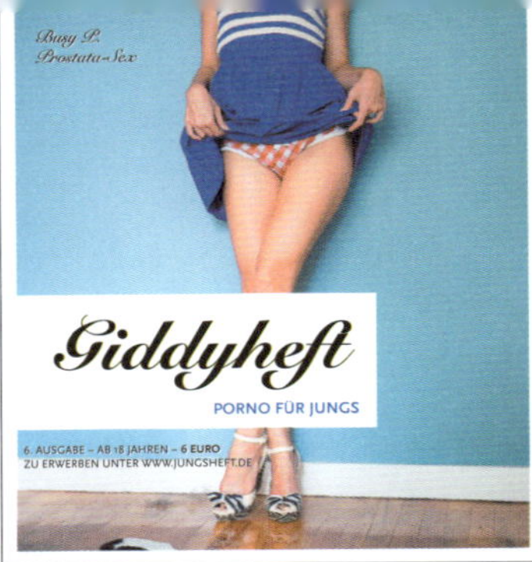
Giddyheft
PORNO FÜR JUNGS
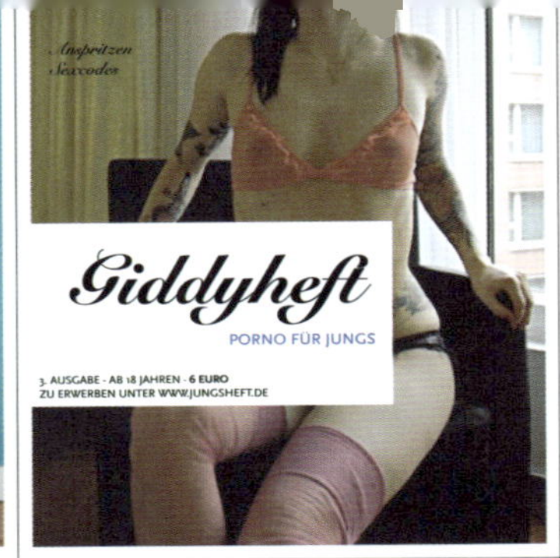
Giddyheft
PORNO FÜR JUNGS
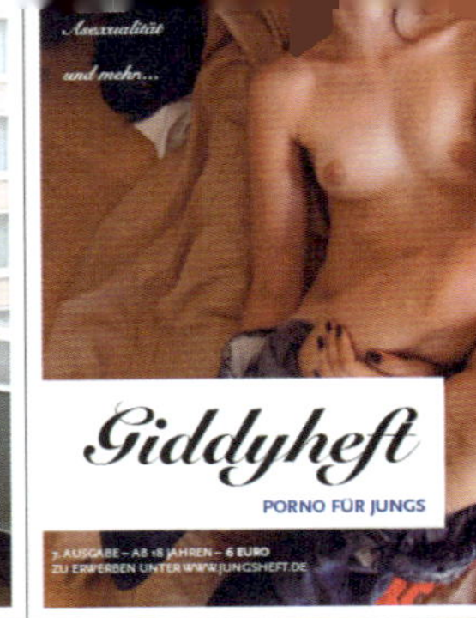
Giddyheft
PORNO FÜR JUNGS
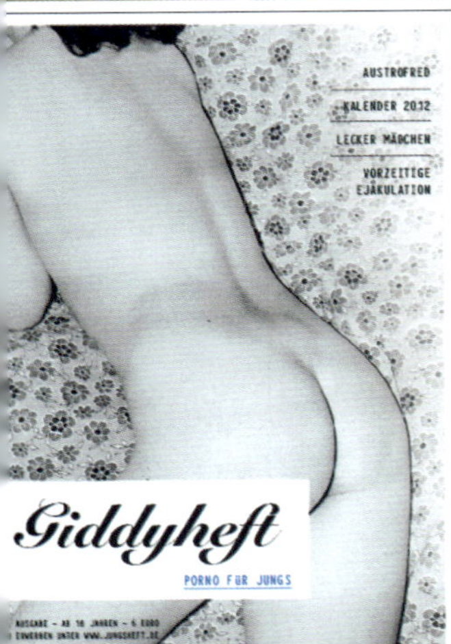
Giddyheft
PORNO FÜR JUNGS
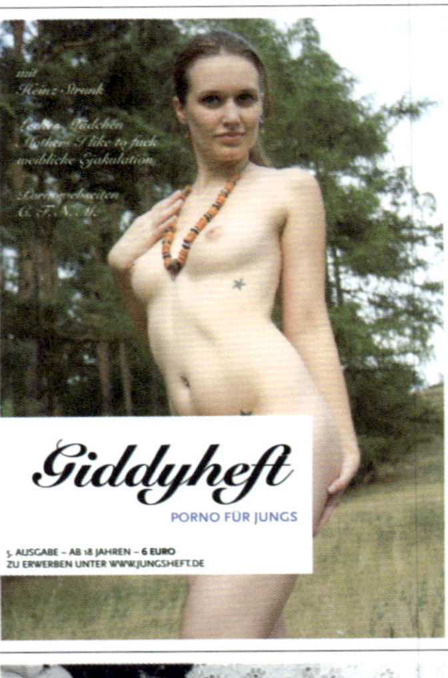
Giddyheft
PORNO FÜR JUNGS
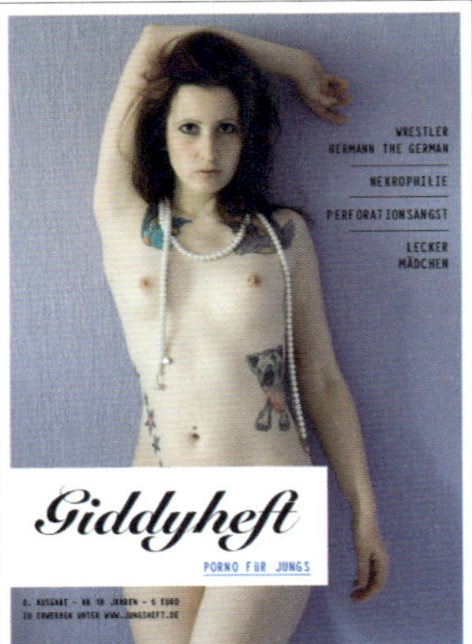
Giddyheft
PORNO FÜR JUNGS
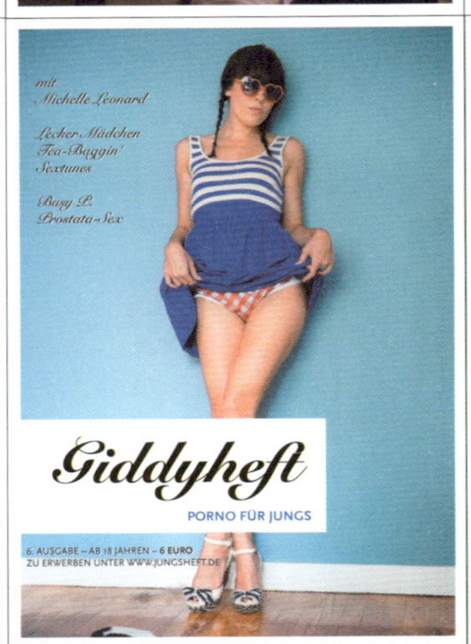
Giddyheft
PORNO FÜR JUNGS
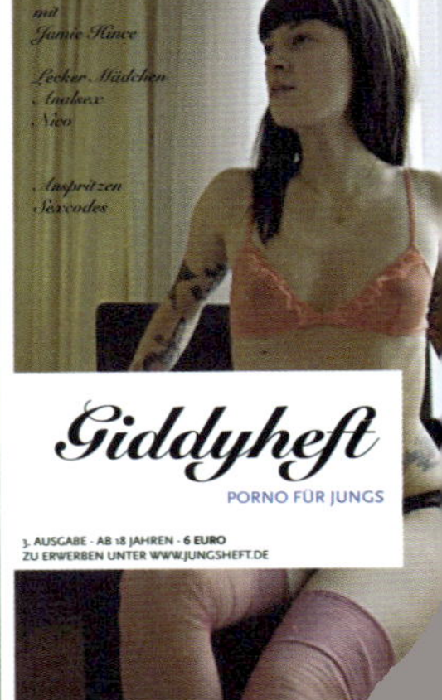
Giddyheft
PORNO FÜR JUNGS
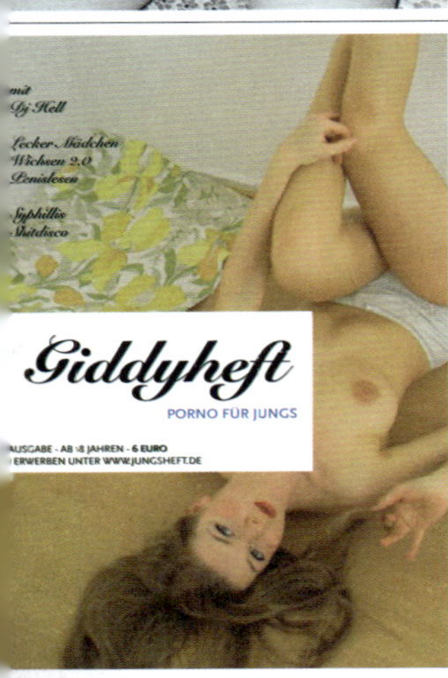
Giddyheft
PORNO FÜR JUNGS
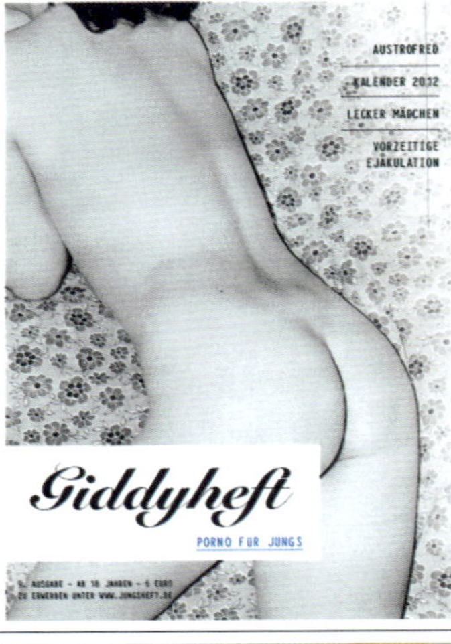
Giddyheft
PORNO FÜR JUNGS
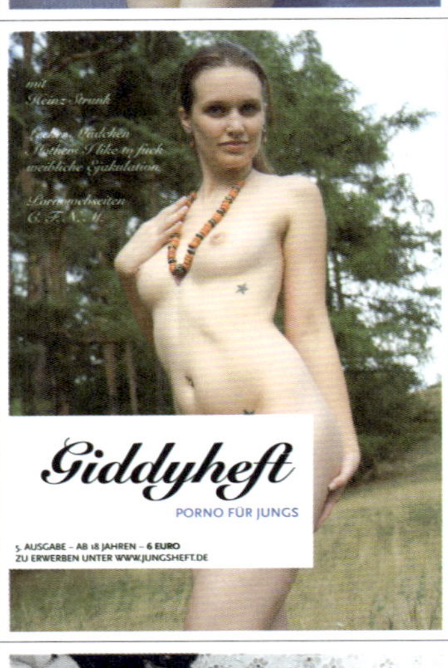
Giddyheft
PORNO FÜR JUNGS
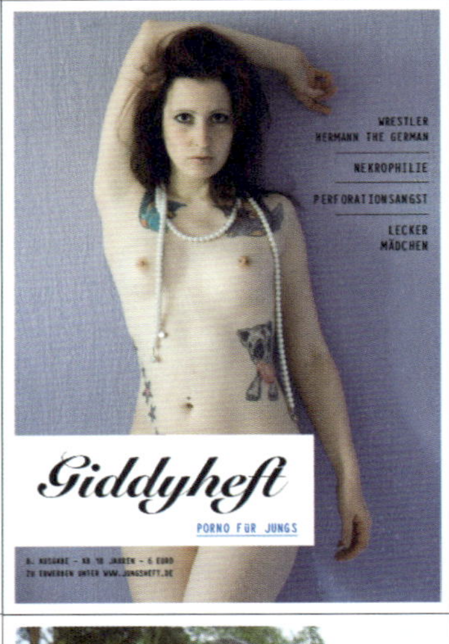
Giddyheft
PORNO FÜR JUNGS
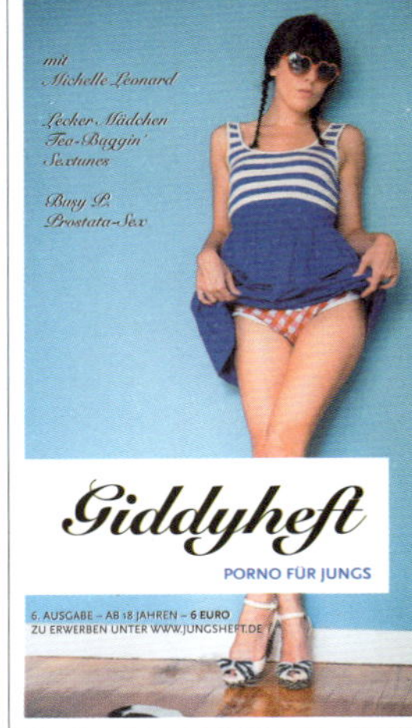
Giddyheft
PORNO FÜR JUNGS
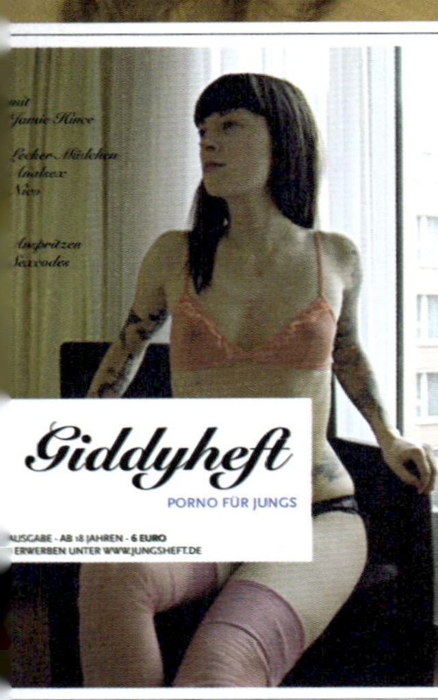
Giddyheft
PORNO FÜR JUNGS
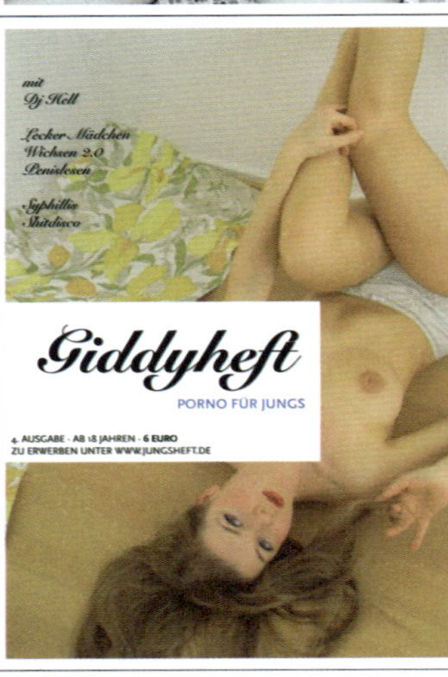
Giddyheft
PORNO FÜR JUNGS
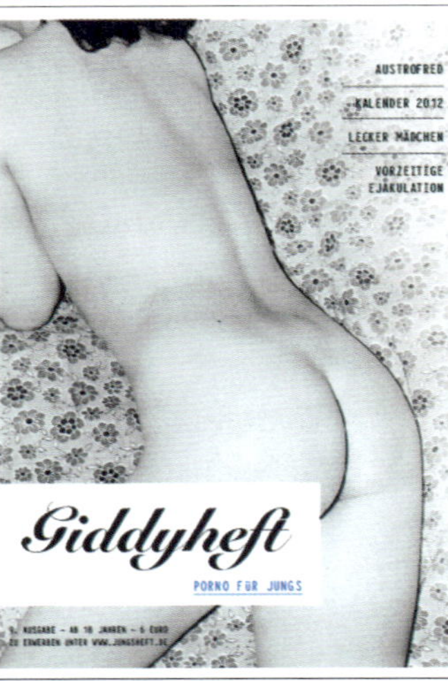
Giddyheft
PORNO FÜR JUNGS
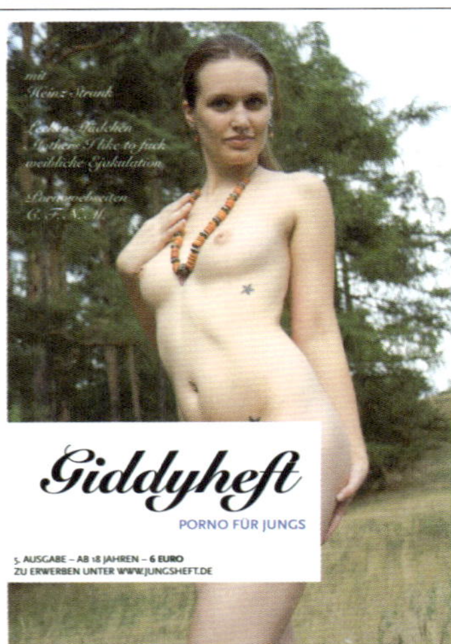
Giddyheft
PORNO FÜR JUNGS
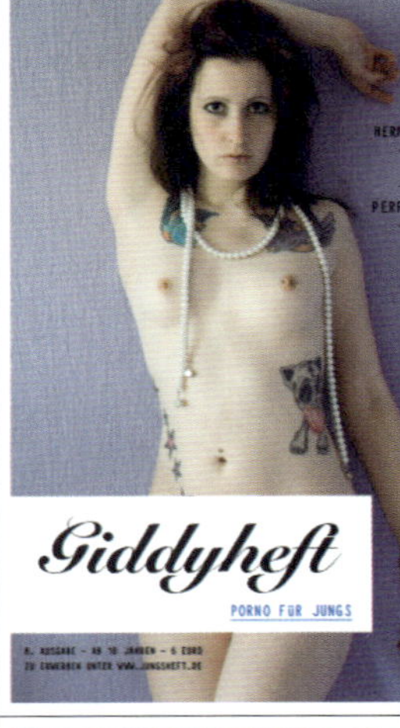
Giddyheft
PORNO FÜR JUNGS
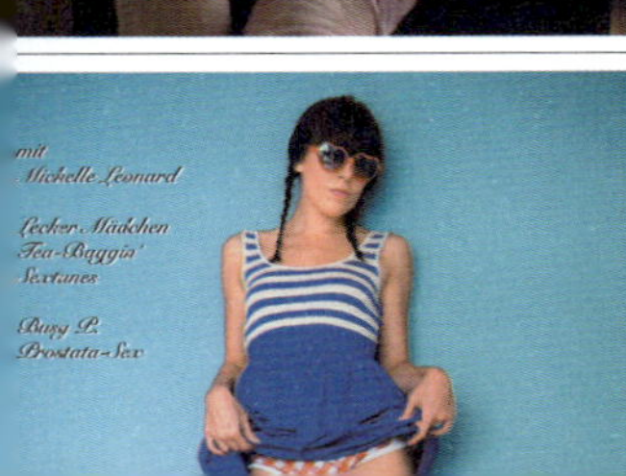
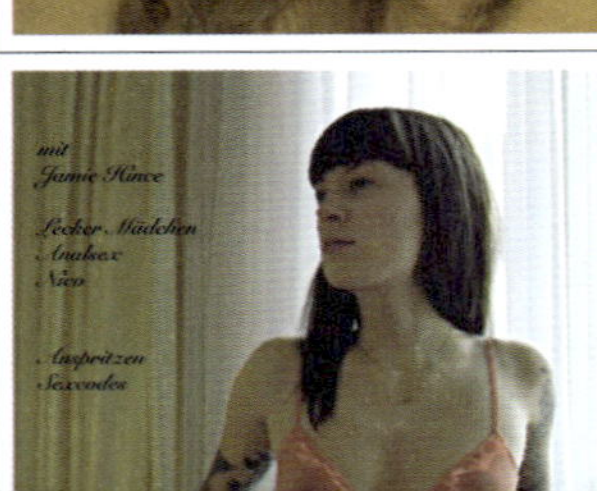
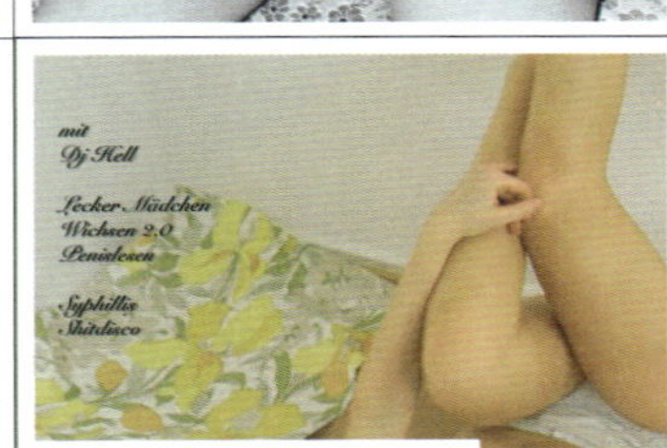
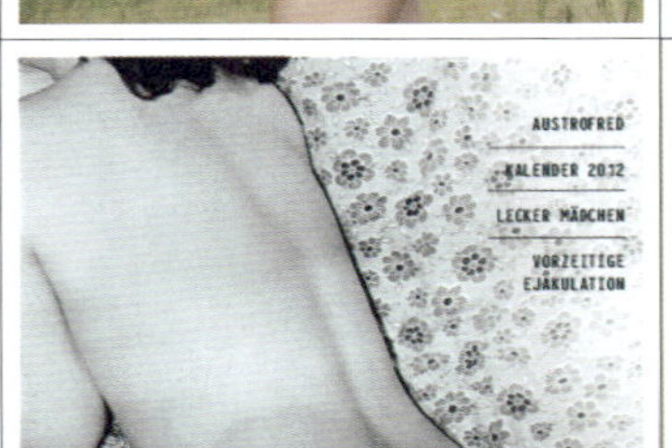
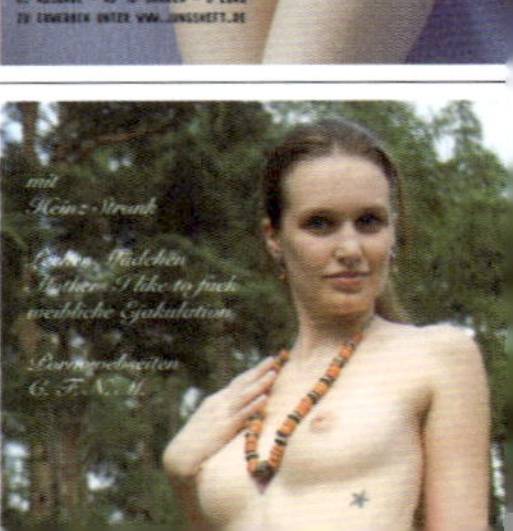

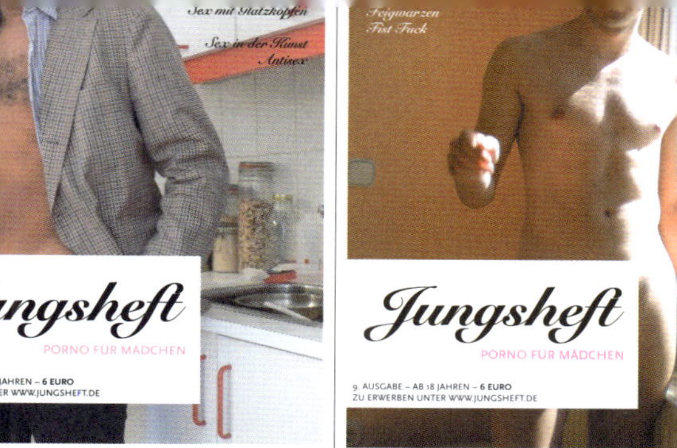
ngsheft
JAHREN – 6 EURO
ER WWW.JUNGSHEFT.DE
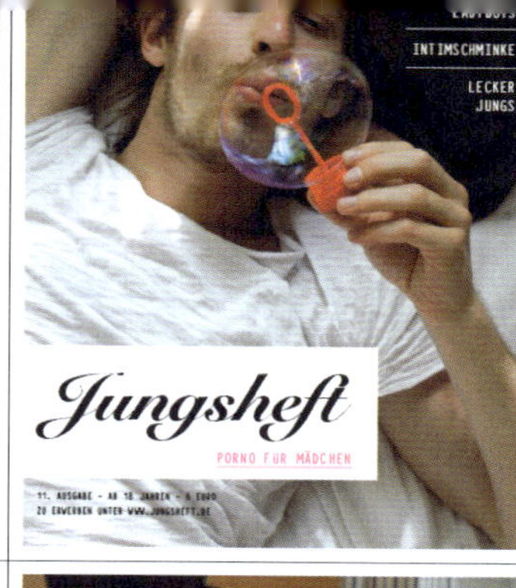
Jungsheft
PORNO FÜR MÄDCHEN
9. AUSGABE – AB 18 JAHREN – 6 EURO
ZU ERWERBEN UNTER WWW.JUNGSHEFT.DE
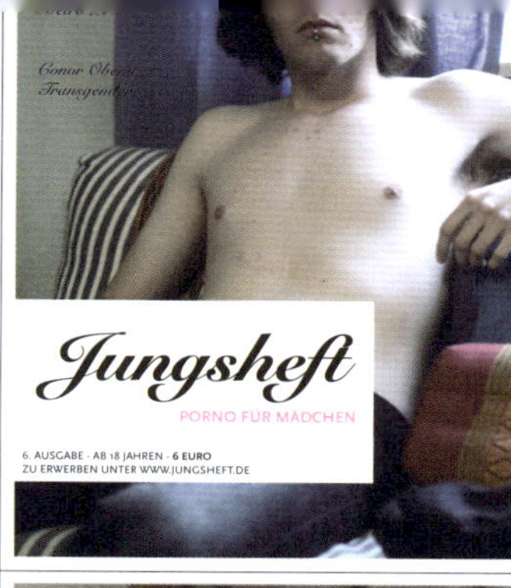
Jungsheft
PORNO FÜR MÄDCHEN
11. AUSGABE – AB 18 JAHREN – 6 EURO
ZU ERWERBEN UNTER WWW.JUNGSHEFT.DE
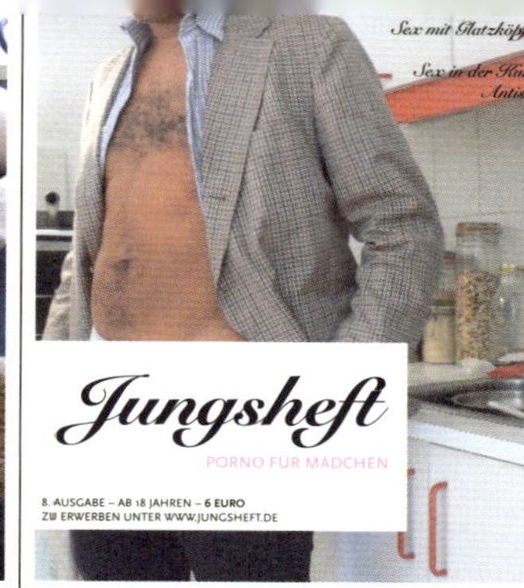
Jungsheft
PORNO FÜR MÄDCHEN
6. AUSGABE – AB 18 JAHREN – 6 EURO
ZU ERWERBEN UNTER WWW.JUNGSHEFT.DE
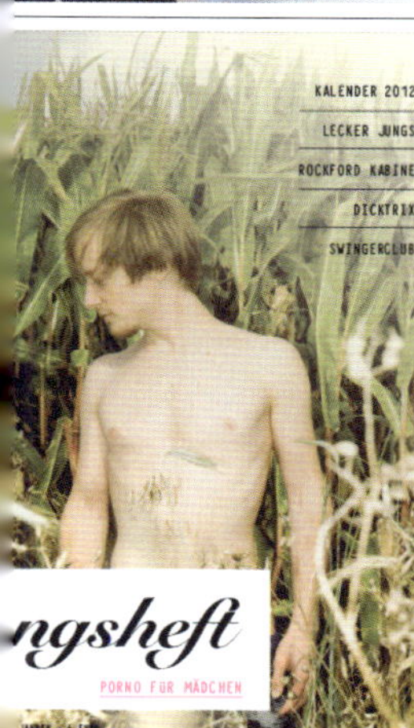
Jungsheft
PORNO FÜR MÄDCHEN
8. AUSGABE – AB 18 JAHREN – 6 EURO
ZU ERWERBEN UNTER WWW.JUNGSHEFT.DE

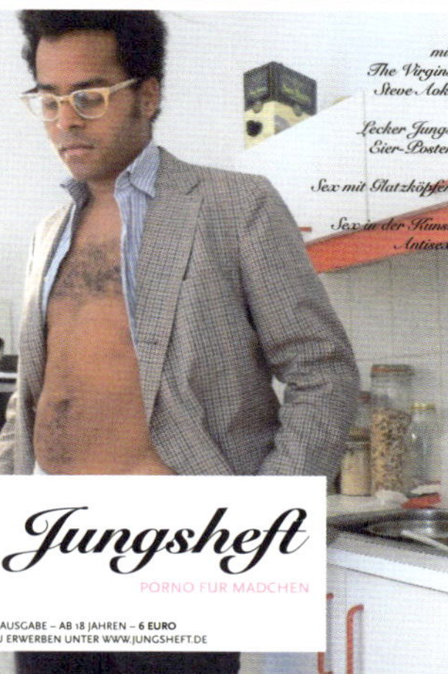
KALENDER 2012
LECKER JUNGS
ROCKFORD KABINE
DICKTRIX
SWINGERCLUB

ngsheft
PORNO FÜR MÄDCHEN
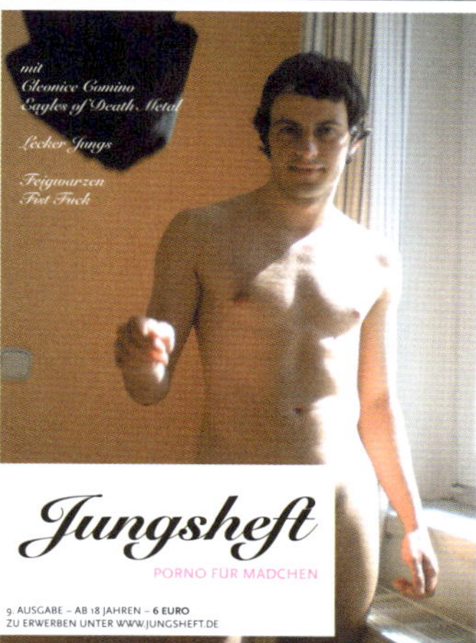
Jungsheft
PORNO FÜR MÄDCHEN
8. AUSGABE – AB 18 JAHREN – 6 EURO
ZU ERWERBEN UNTER WWW.JUNGSHEFT.DE
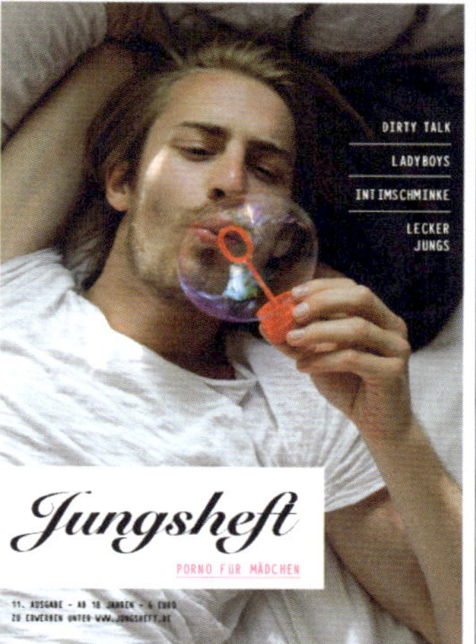
mit
Cleonice Comino
Eagles of Death Metal
Lecker Jungs
Feigwarzen
Fist Fuck

Jungsheft
PORNO FÜR MÄDCHEN
9. AUSGABE – AB 18 JAHREN – 6 EURO
ZU ERWERBEN UNTER WWW.JUNGSHEFT.DE
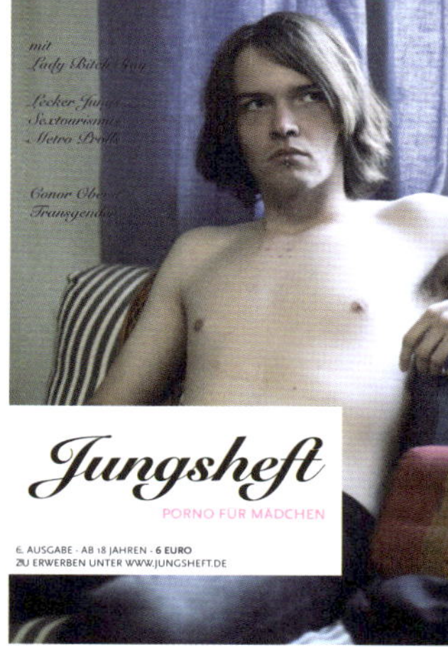
Jungsheft
PORNO FÜR MÄDCHEN
11. AUSGABE – AB 18 JAHREN – 6 EURO
ZU ERWERBEN UNTER WWW.JUNGSHEFT.DE
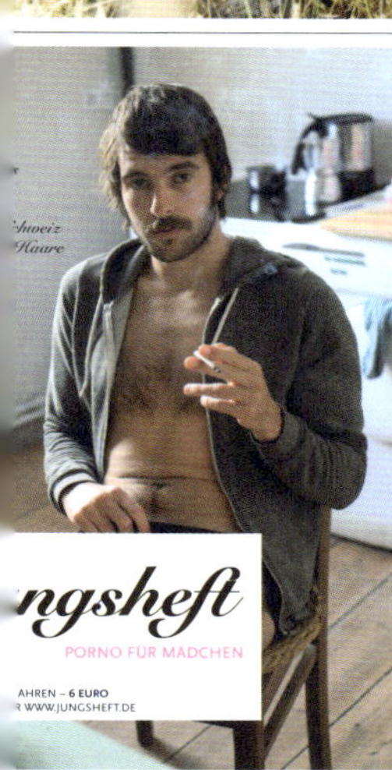
DIRTY TALK
LADYBOYS
INTIMSCHMINKE
LECKER JUNGS

Jungsheft
PORNO FÜR MÄDCHEN
6. AUSGABE – AB 18 JAHREN – 6 EURO
ZU ERWERBEN UNTER WWW.JUNGSHEFT.DE

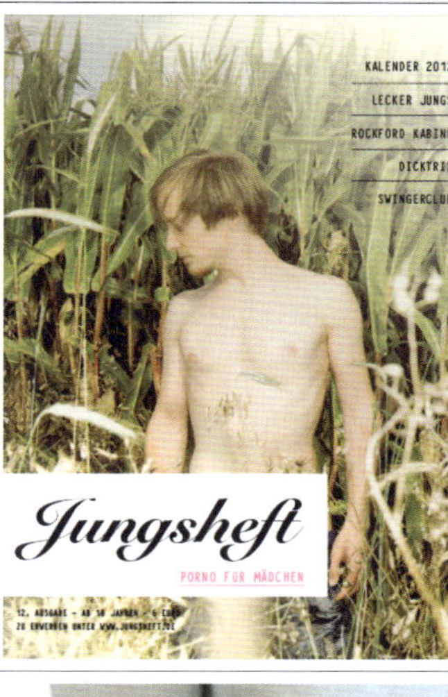
ngsheft
PORNO FÜR MÄDCHEN
JAHREN – 6 EURO
WWW.JUNGSHEFT.DE
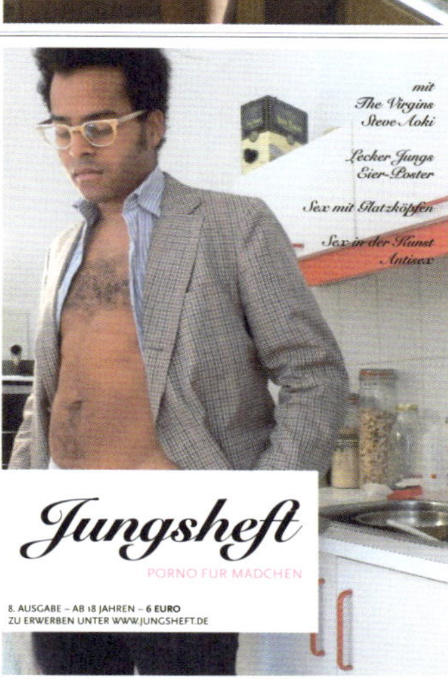
KALENDER 2012
LECKER JUNGS
ROCKFORD KABINE
DICKTRIX
SWINGERCLUB

Jungsheft
PORNO FÜR MÄDCHEN
12. AUSGABE – AB 18 JAHREN – 6 EURO
ZU ERWERBEN UNTER WWW.JUNGSHEFT.DE
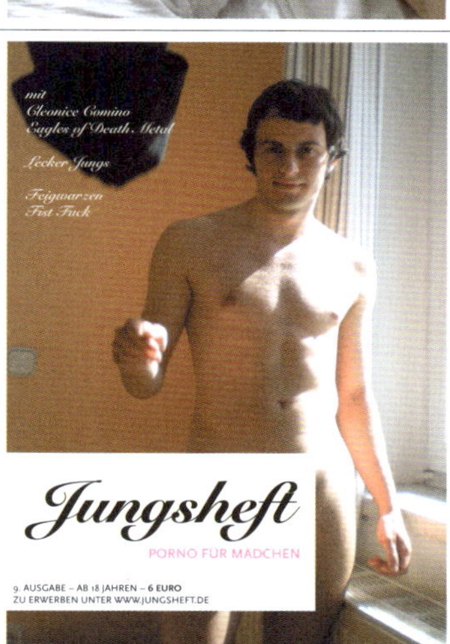
Jungsheft
PORNO FÜR MÄDCHEN
8. AUSGABE – AB 18 JAHREN – 6 EURO
ZU ERWERBEN UNTER WWW.JUNGSHEFT.DE
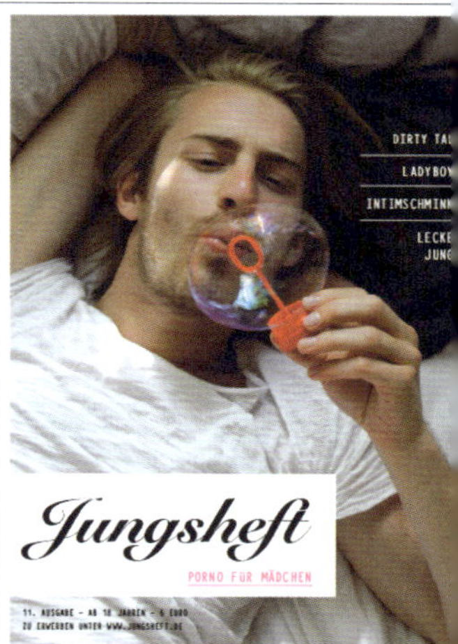
mit
The Virgins
Steve Aoki
Lecker Jungs
Eier-Poster
Sex mit Glatzköpfen
Sex in der Kunst
Antisex

Jungsheft
PORNO FÜR MÄDCHEN
9. AUSGABE – AB 18 JAHREN – 6 EURO
ZU ERWERBEN UNTER WWW.JUNGSHEFT.DE
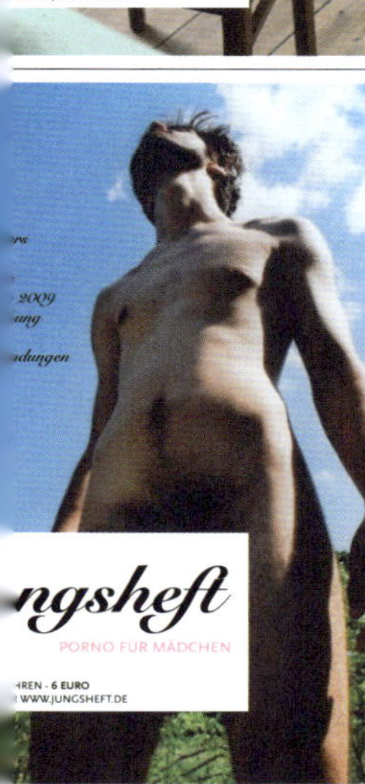
DIRTY TALK
LADYBOYS
INTIMSCHMINKE
LECKER JUNGS

Jungsheft
PORNO FÜR MÄDCHEN

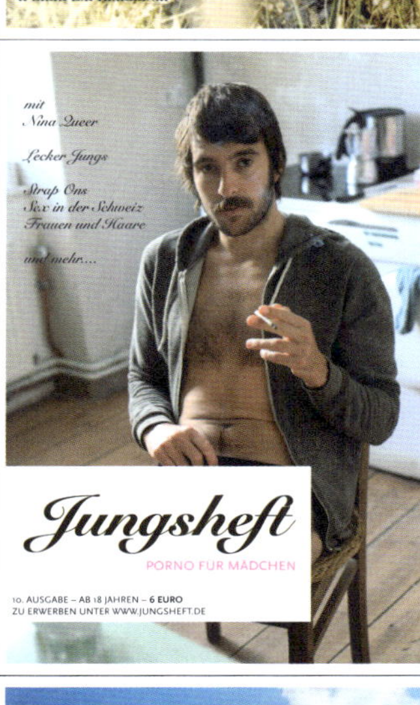
mit
Nina Queer
Lecker Jungs
Strap Ons
Sex in der Schweiz
Frauen und Haare
und mehr…

Jungsheft
PORNO FÜR MÄDCHEN
10. AUSGABE – AB 18 JAHREN – 6 EURO
ZU ERWERBEN UNTER WWW.JUNGSHEFT.DE
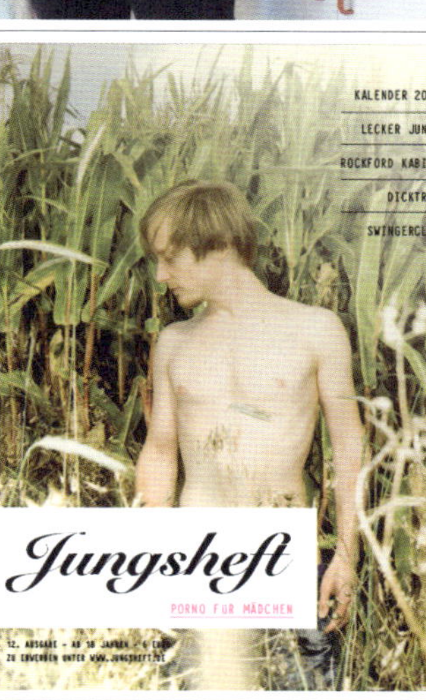
KALENDER 2012
LECKER JUNGS
ROCKFORD KABINE
DICKTRIX
SWINGERCLUB

Jungsheft
PORNO FÜR MÄDCHEN
12. AUSGABE – AB 18 JAHREN – 6 EURO
ZU ERWERBEN UNTER WWW.JUNGSHEFT.DE
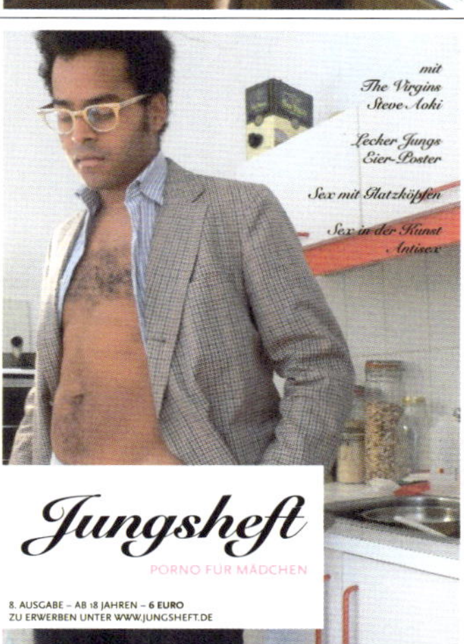
mit
The Virgins
Steve Aoki
Lecker Jungs
Eier-Poster
Sex mit Glatzköpfen
Sex in der Kunst
Antisex

Jungsheft
PORNO FÜR MÄDCHEN
8. AUSGABE – AB 18 JAHREN – 6 EURO
ZU ERWERBEN UNTER WWW.JUNGSHEFT.DE
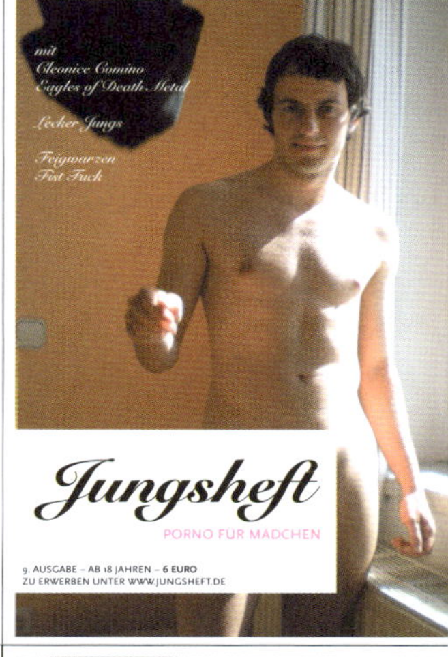
mit
Cleonice Comino
Eagles of Death Metal
Lecker Jungs
Feigwarzen
Fist Fuck

Jungsheft
PORNO FÜR MÄDCHEN
9. AUSGABE – AB 18 JAHREN – 6 EURO
ZU ERWERBEN UNTER WWW.JUNGSHEFT.DE

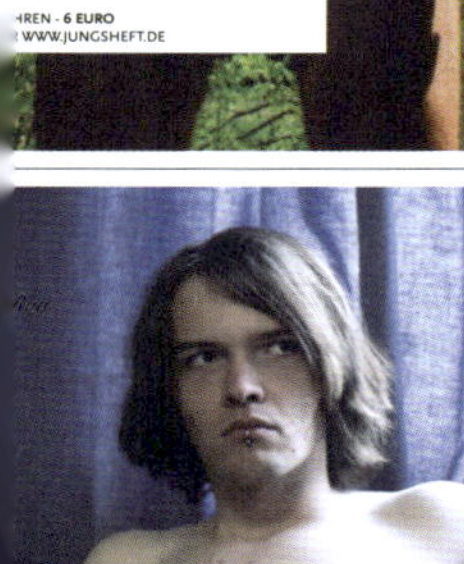
ngsheft
PORNO FÜR MÄDCHEN
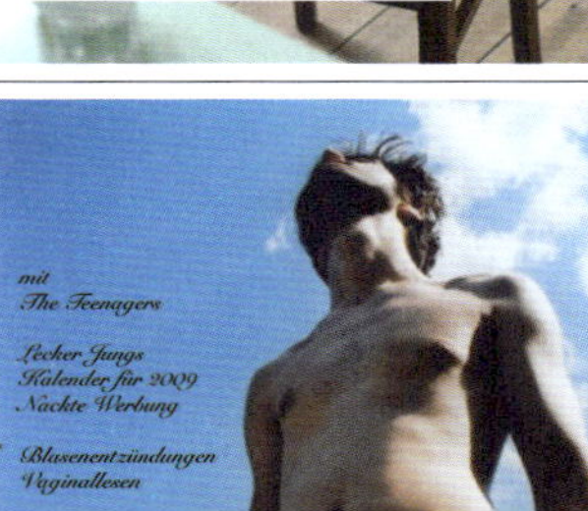
mit
The Teenagers
Lecker Jungs
Kalender für 2009
Nackte Werbung
Blasenentzündungen
Vaginalfloßen
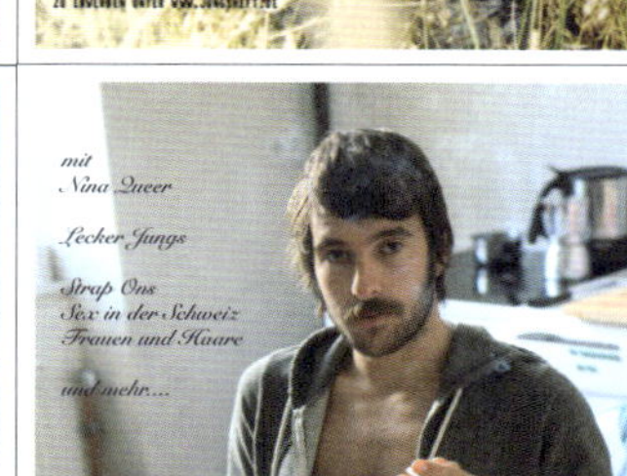
mit
Nina Queer
Lecker Jungs
Strap Ons
Sex in der Schweiz
Frauen und Haare
und mehr…
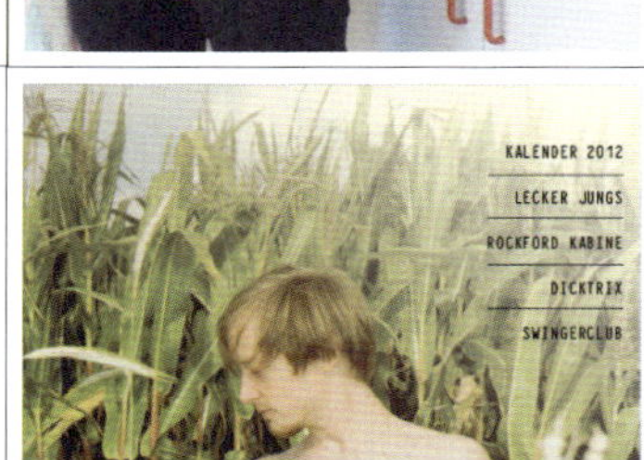
KALENDER 2012
LECKER JUNGS
ROCKFORD KABINE
DICKTRIX
SWINGERCLUB
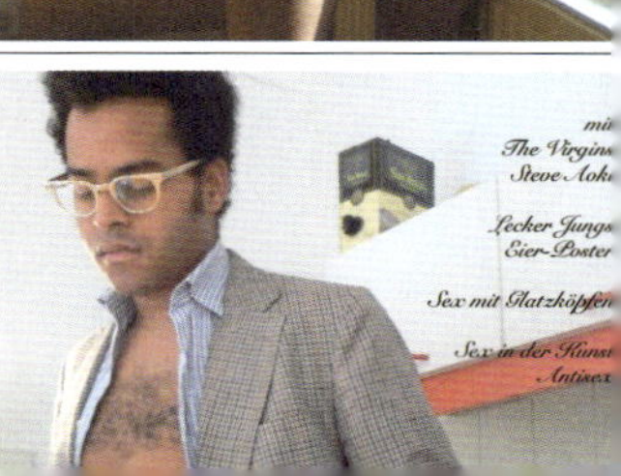
mit
The Virgins
Steve Aoki
Lecker Jungs
Eier-Poster
Sex mit Glatzköpfen
Sex in der Kunst

In regards to pictures, sometimes somebody would send us a complaint and say something along the lines of *"I love beautiful and muscular guys with beautiful tattoos, why are there none in your mag?"* All I can write back is: *"Yeah, great idea, we'd love to, but unfortunately we don't happen to have any available at the moment, thank you."*

Which audience did you target when creating the magazine?

Initially, we didn't really think about it. If there ever was a target, then it would have been us. Again, a lot was related to our lack of cash and professional experience in the field. Today I would say that readers are women between 18 and 40 living in big cities. We know this since we ship the ordered magazine ourselves, a task that requires the biggest amount of time in this adventure.

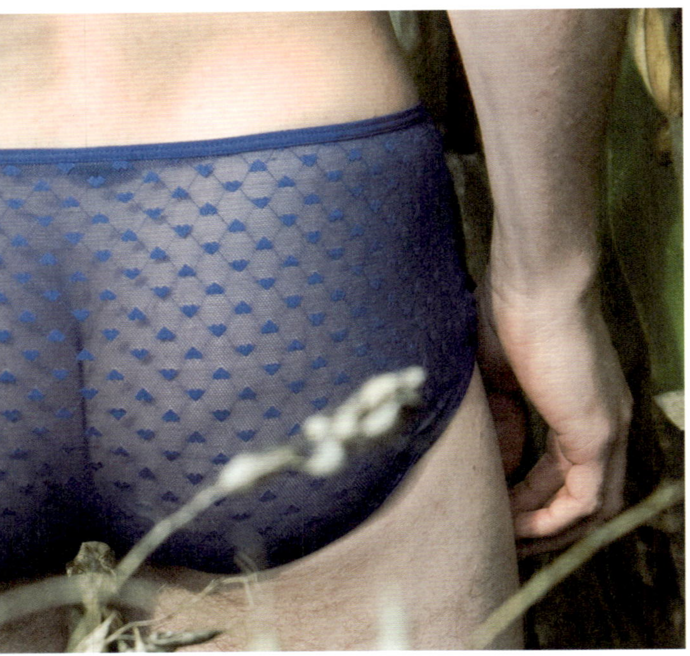

Where can your magazines be found?

Most sales are done over the Internet, not in shops. However, some places specialize in magazines and we try to sell ours there too, such as the House of Photography in Hamburg or Do you read me? in Berlin. They sell many copies and are just really cute shops. Most copies are sold in Germany, Switzerland and Austria, because the magazine is in German. Our next goal is to create a pdf or an app version of it in English in order to become more up-to-date and reach out to a larger readership.

After reading and seeing so much porn over the past few years, is there still anything that shocks or surprises you?

Absolutely, especially ideas for articles that people come up with, such as texts on polygamist political parties or fisting introduction courses, all things I've obviously never heard of.

How about you and Nicole, were you into porn before launching the magazine?

Not at all, I would say that we were, and still are, normal mid-thirties users, you know what I mean? It's not like I've ever spent my free time attending some kind of sex meetings or browsing porn websites. Yes, I have watched porn already, but I was never an addict.

What have been some of the highlights since the launch?

In the issue 8 of the *Jungsheft,* we featured Twin Shadow, whose music I am a big fan of and who undressed for the mag. He contacted us himself which was really nice. Also, one of our first issues featured an article on Wimster, hipster men that are wimps, which I found very appropriate. These guys often indulge themselves in sadness and melancholia, yet are overly eager to look good. Personal experience reports are great too, like the one of a guy who claims that men come better and quicker if you touch their prostate properly.

Have the magazines influenced your sex life? Do you feel like you've become a bigger expert?

I wouldn't say so, no, since - without going to extremes - I have always had a personal, yet open relationship to sex. Just because someone claims that men come better when their prostate is rubbed, that doesn't mean that you go home and squeeze your arm into your boyfriend's arse. Or like fisting: it has never been my thing, and it probably never will be, no matter how many articles people write about it.

I loved the pictures of the guy who transforms his penis into vaginas or hamburgers by merely squeezing and reshaping his dick!

Isn't he great? The guy who sent this is just absolutely fantastic and great fun. I really hope that he comes up with more shapes in the near future. His ideas are really inspiring and so easy to follow at home!

How long do you think the magic of *"girl or boy next door"* porn can be sustained?

Good question. I hope that it will last for a while. No matter how weird it sounds, I really do have the impression that porn for women is an attractive proposition. It's been like that for a while now and I think there is no end in sight. However, our magazines are clearly a niche product since the majority of women out there are still craving pictures of sexy muscular men instead of real ones. Only a very particular kind of woman desires to see a picture of an aroused hungry indie boy with a few tattoos.

"THE PROBLEM IS THAT THERE REALLY ISN'T A MIDDLE WAY IN THE WORLD OF PRINTED PORN. YOU EITHER HAVE SUPER POLISHED MODELS OR THE CLICHÉ GIRL FROM EASTERN EUROPE WITH HER LEGS SPREAD ON A LEATHER COUCH."

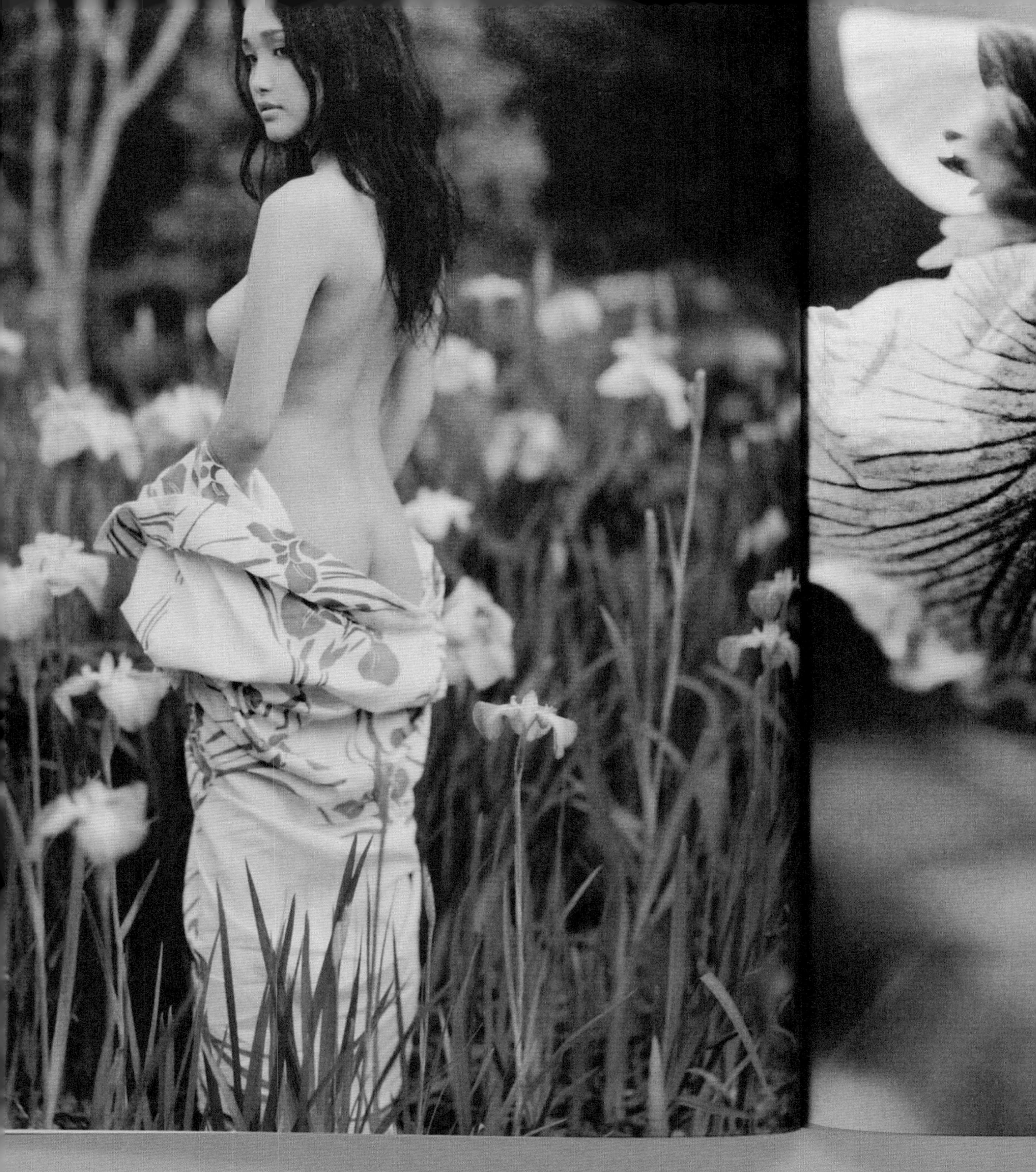

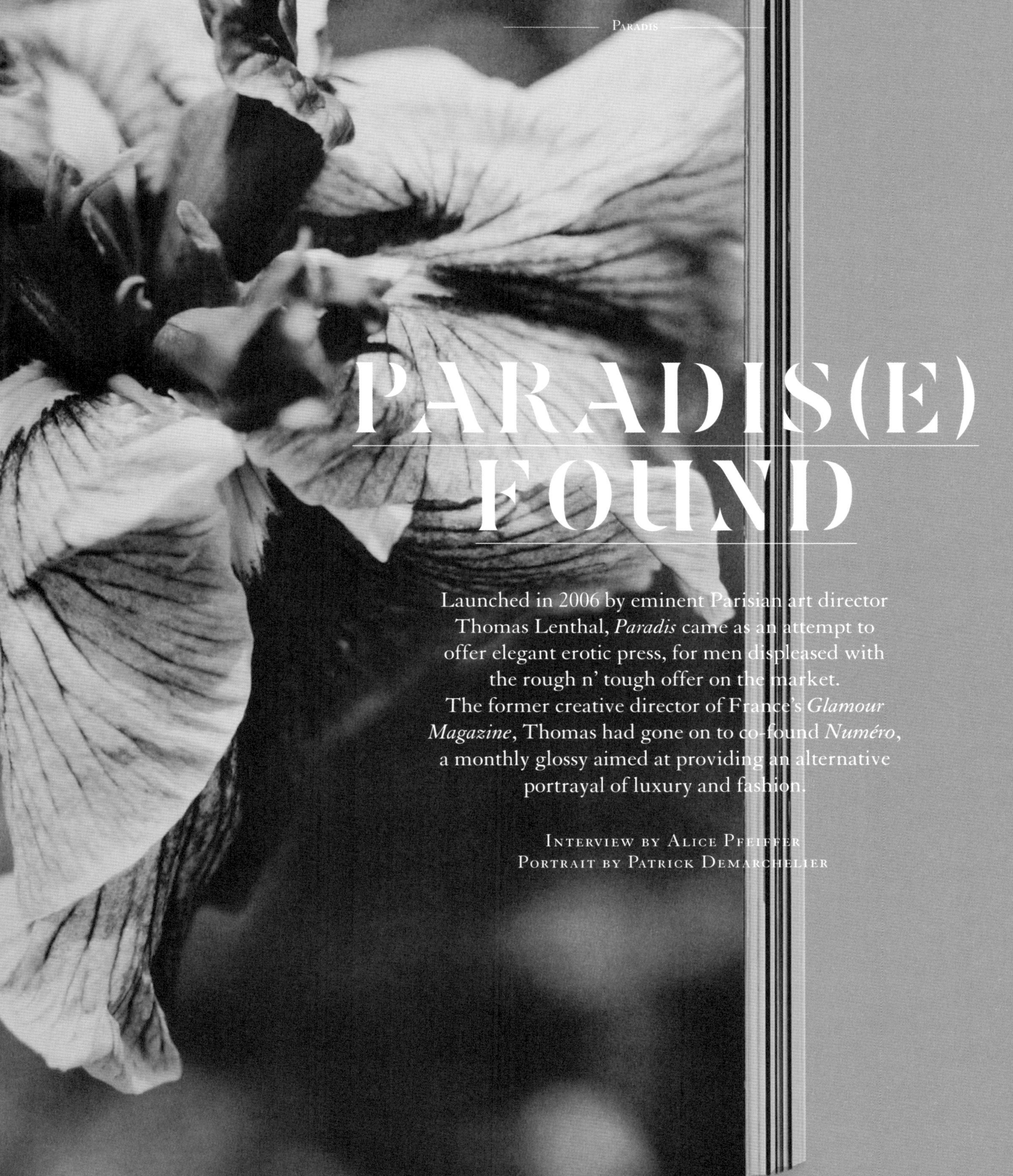

PARADIS(E) FOUND

Launched in 2006 by eminent Parisian art director
Thomas Lenthal, *Paradis* came as an attempt to
offer elegant erotic press, for men displeased with
the rough n' tough offer on the market.
The former creative director of France's *Glamour
Magazine*, Thomas had gone on to co-found *Numéro*,
a monthly glossy aimed at providing an alternative
portrayal of luxury and fashion.

Interview by Alice Pfeiffer
Portrait by Patrick Demarchelier

Today, *Paradis* has introduced a sensual, stripped down (both literally and figuratively) pathway for sartorial photographers to experiment in. An annual, book-like publication, it allows for extensive features and photo shoots, all without a hint of product placement. Maria Carla Boscono shot by Juergen Teller taking a naked nap on the kitchen table, Anouck Lepère by Jock Sturgis tanning in the nude — a departure from fashion without losing its high-end finishing. A self-proclaimed *"magazine for the modern man,"* Lenthal's heaven on paper hopes to intrigue a few women too.

About to release its 6th issue, *Paradis* was awarded the best magazine prize by the influential Club des Directeurs Artistiques in 2008 and now exists in an English language edition too. In the meantime, its founder and publisher still finds the time to direct campaigns for the likes of Christian Dior, Yves Saint Laurent or Missoni.

Nico speaks to Thomas Lenthal about the difference between eroticism and pornography, Carine Roitfeld, and *l'amour toujours.*

What was the initial pitch?

When I first started *Paradis* six years ago, the aim was to encapsulate several things that, at the time, were totally missing in the French male press. At the start, its ambitions were a lot more mainstream than what they have become: *Paradis* was a form of pastiche — in the literal sense of the term — of *Lui [iconic French men's lifestyle magazine, 1963-1987]*, which had struck me and an entire generation of men. *Lui* could have been considered as a French *Playboy* Magazine, a way of looking at eroticism in a far less American manner. The girls in it weren't canons of beauty, they didn't follow one single morpho-type. They weren't just chicks with big boobs. Rather, the magazine offered a plethora of archetypes, and found beauty in a myriad of girls. *Paradis* kicked off with the ambition of being a neo-*Lui*, a publication that would invoke the same hedonistic frame of mind; later, it turned into something more niche.

What kind of man were you addressing?

A man who didn't recognize himself in the existing magazines, who found them too brute-like. The only press of quality was gay press. I thought, why doesn't a single descent photographer shoot for any of the straight magazines available?

You mentioned *Paradis* was more mainstream when it started – what did you leave behind and why?

The first issue was a lot more generalist, it even had a car in it! Today, I don't recognize myself in it at all. We soon dropped this mainstream ambition because doing a mainstream lifestyle magazine for men is practically an industrial project. I wanted to keep the home-made aspect. What felt more important was to infuse some eroticism in the French media landscape.

When *Paradis* was launched, it was also Carine Roitfeld's heyday at French *Vogue*, where boobs were on display to accompany a nail varnish feature. Is that something you agree with?

Sure, you might think it's unnecessary to show sex to sell nails. But I think Carine Roitfeld had an intuition — an unconscious one, knowing her —, that the language of fashion is inevitably linked to the language of eroticism. And even if you think breasts and nail polish are totally disconnected, nail polish is sold because there is an erotic benefit to it.

} *p.109*

Thomas Lenthal shot by
Patrick Demarchelier

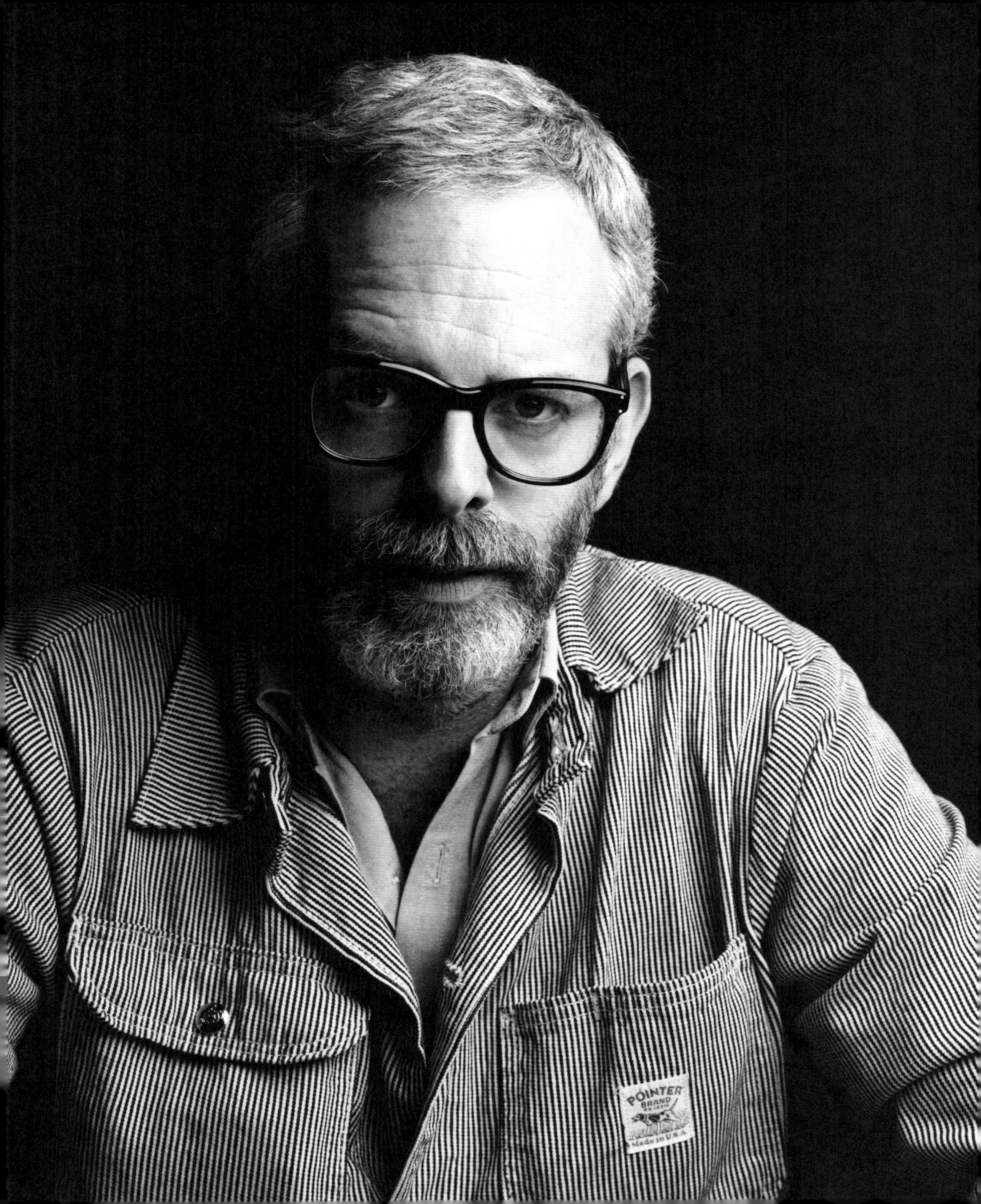

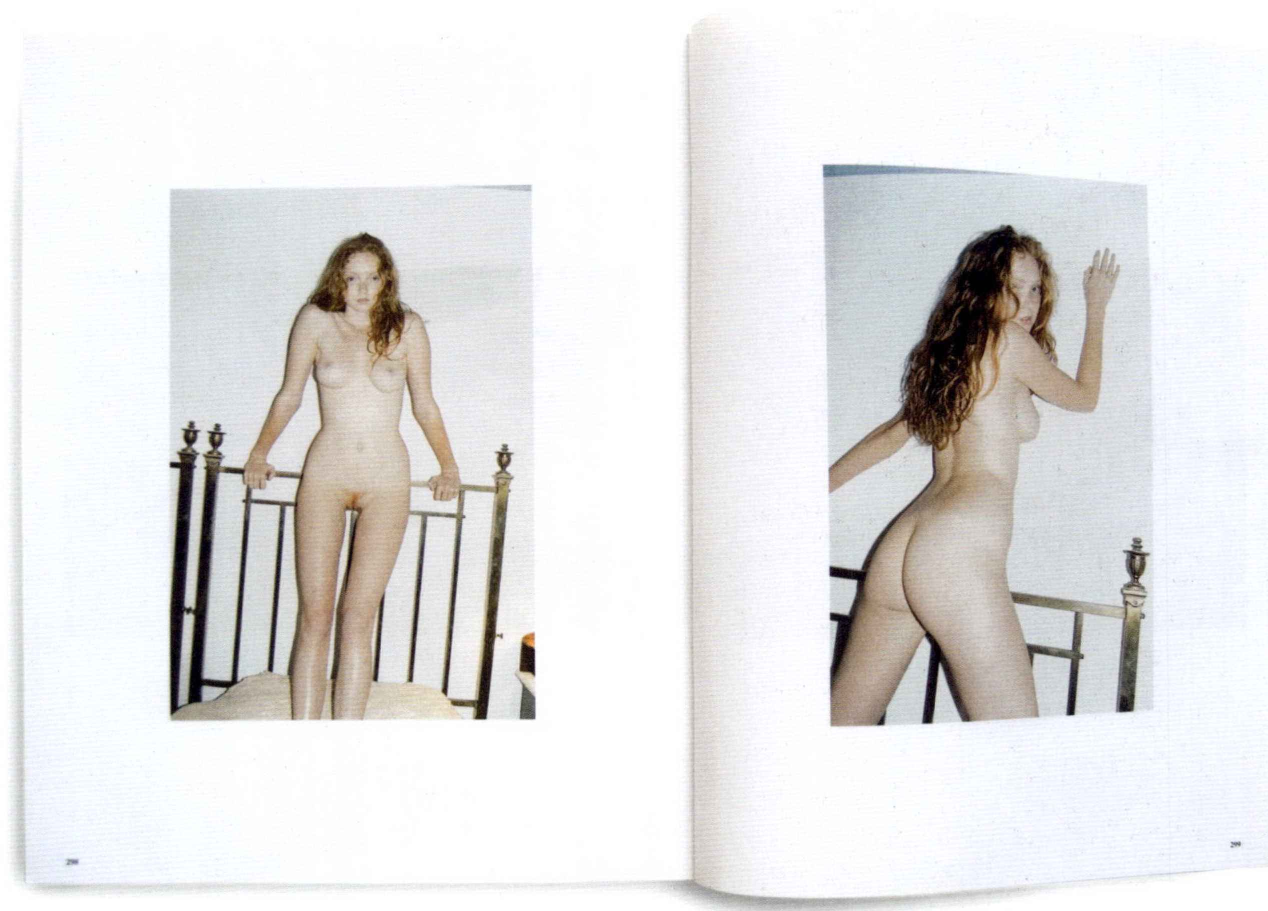

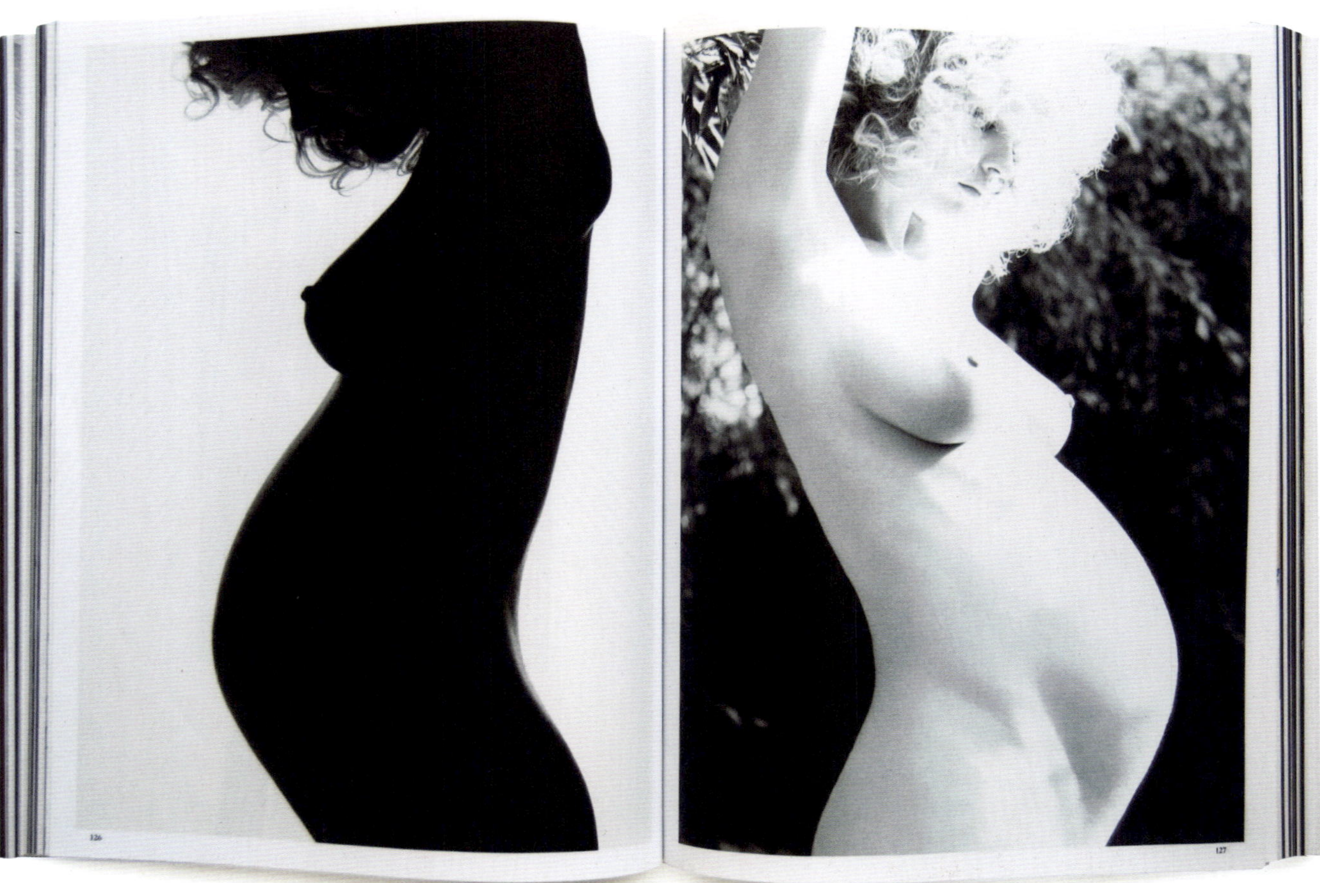

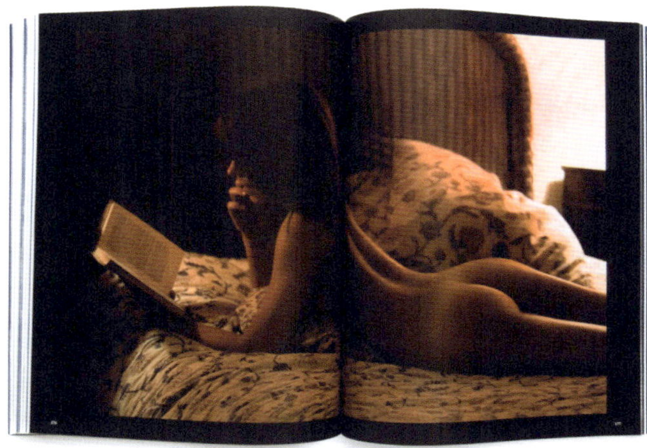

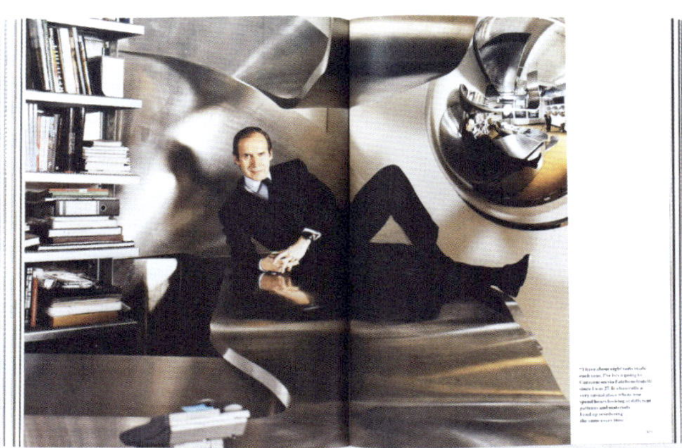

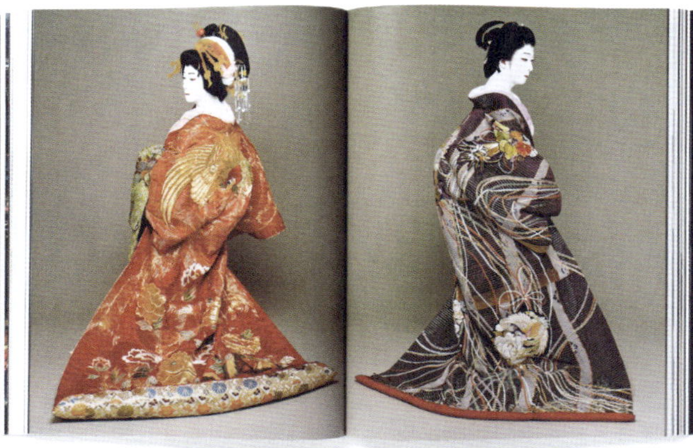

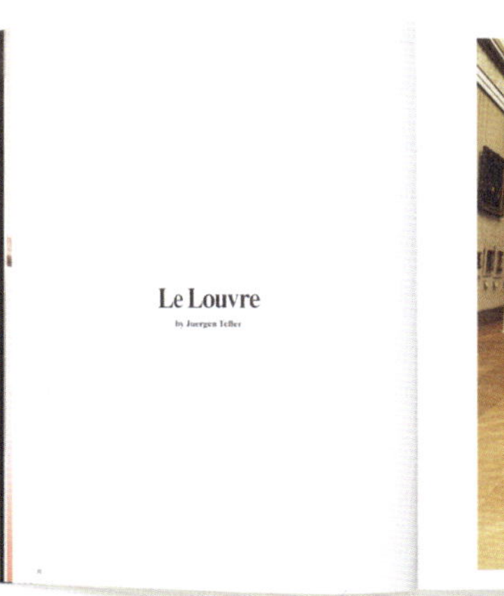
Le Louvre
by Juergen Teller

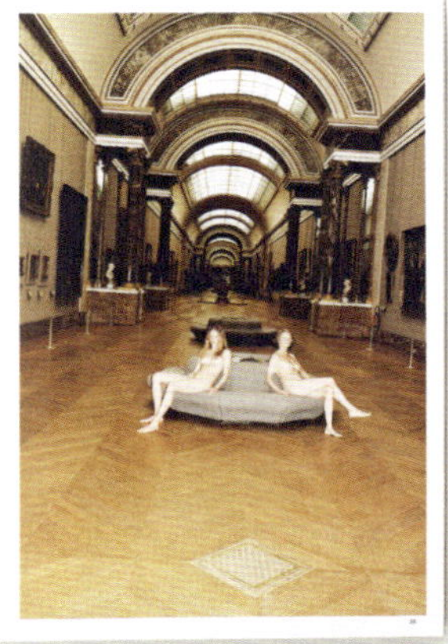

What is your personal definition of eroticism?

To be erotic, a woman must be a subject. There must be a promise that the other exists. This means there is a possible dialogue, not necessarily a verbal one, but at least the possibility of an encounter, a little bit of love. Not marriage and children material, but some form of fleeting feelings. In *Lui*, the girls looked at you, didn't look like idiots. They were alive.

France is famous for its outspoken relationship to sex – is your magazine's approach 'French' in that sense?

It's funny you'd ask – that's in fact a question almost all foreign media asked when we first launched *Paradis*. I suppose that over here, it is so unproblematic to portray sex that we didn't even think about it. It didn't feel like a topic. Rather, the challenge was to depict sex for certain straight men, and hopefully appeal to a couple of girls too. And it does, which is an immense compliment. In France, sensual things of life are infused with culture: food, sex. It's also a way of detaching yourself from those.

In the 5th issue, we feature Charlotte Rampling and Raquel Zimmerman nude at the Musée du Louvre, and I think we've departed from an erotic problematic. I don't think it's a turn on, I don't even know if it can still be considered erotic.

Apart from *Lui,* what other teenage memories have contributed to *Paradis*?

Italian 60s and 70s pseudo-sexy cinema showed a touching eroticism, with extraordinary actresses. I long for the country to start producing that sort of feature again. There are several films with images that still haunt me. *Til God do us part* by Luigi Comencini is one of them. I also saw *Belle de Jour* by Luis Buñuel when I was thirteen and it blew my mind.

What are the traces of *Numéro* in *Paradis*?

There are quite visible traces, since 90 percent of the photographers featured come from fashion. Yet *Paradis* is freed from any commercial constraints, since there are very few things to sell. When you do a fashion magazine, you do propaganda for brands, which is less the case for *Paradis*. We featured some fashion at the beginning, which we've stopped doing.

Yet you appeal to a fashion audience – would you say fashion is perhaps more of an aesthetic discourse than a subject, and can therefore seep into non-fashion publications?

Although I don't feel I have something original enough to say about fashion to create a magazine about it today, it's true that people in the field have a certain ambition. A desire of extreme quality. Fashion is couture, and couture is ultimate exigency. In that sense the world and culture of

} *p.112*

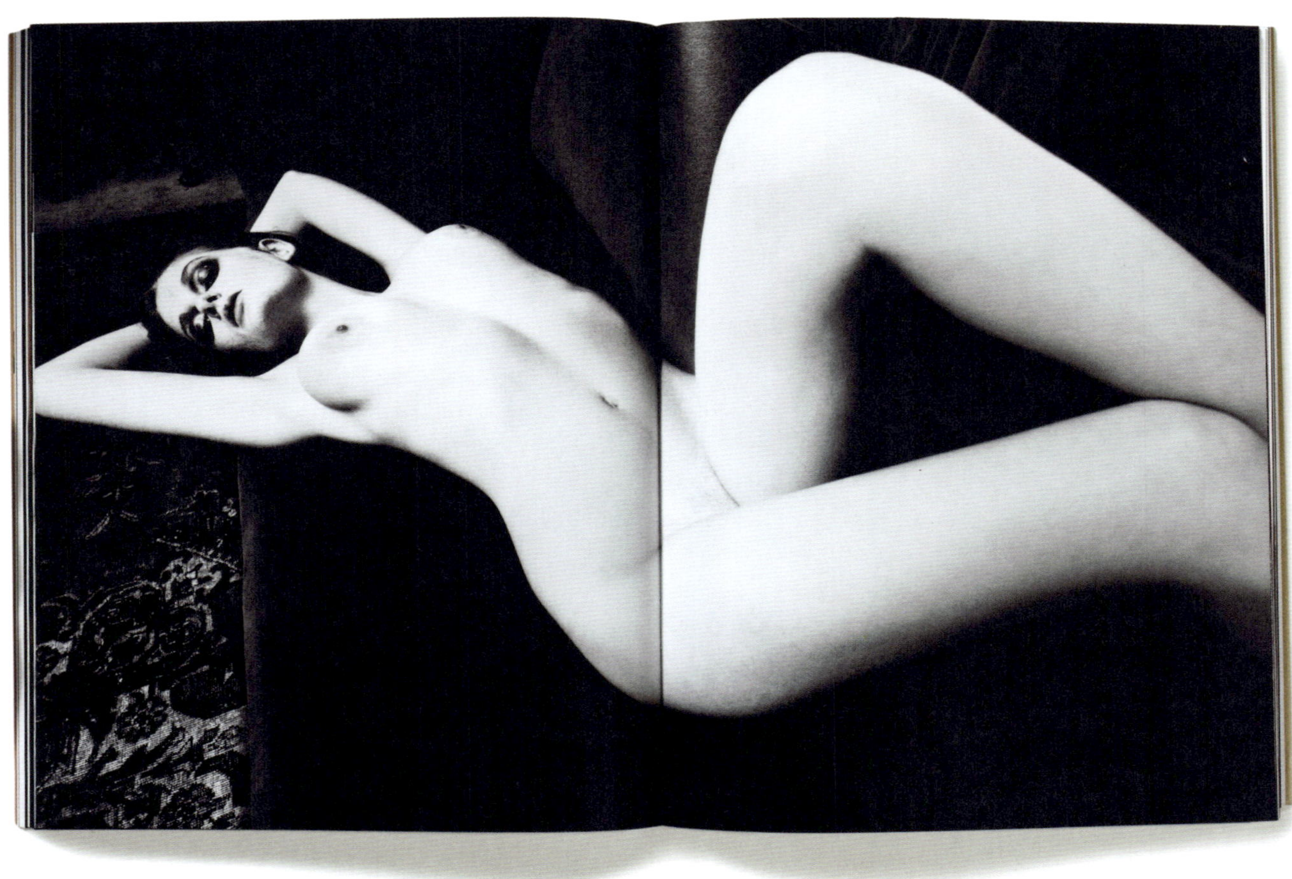

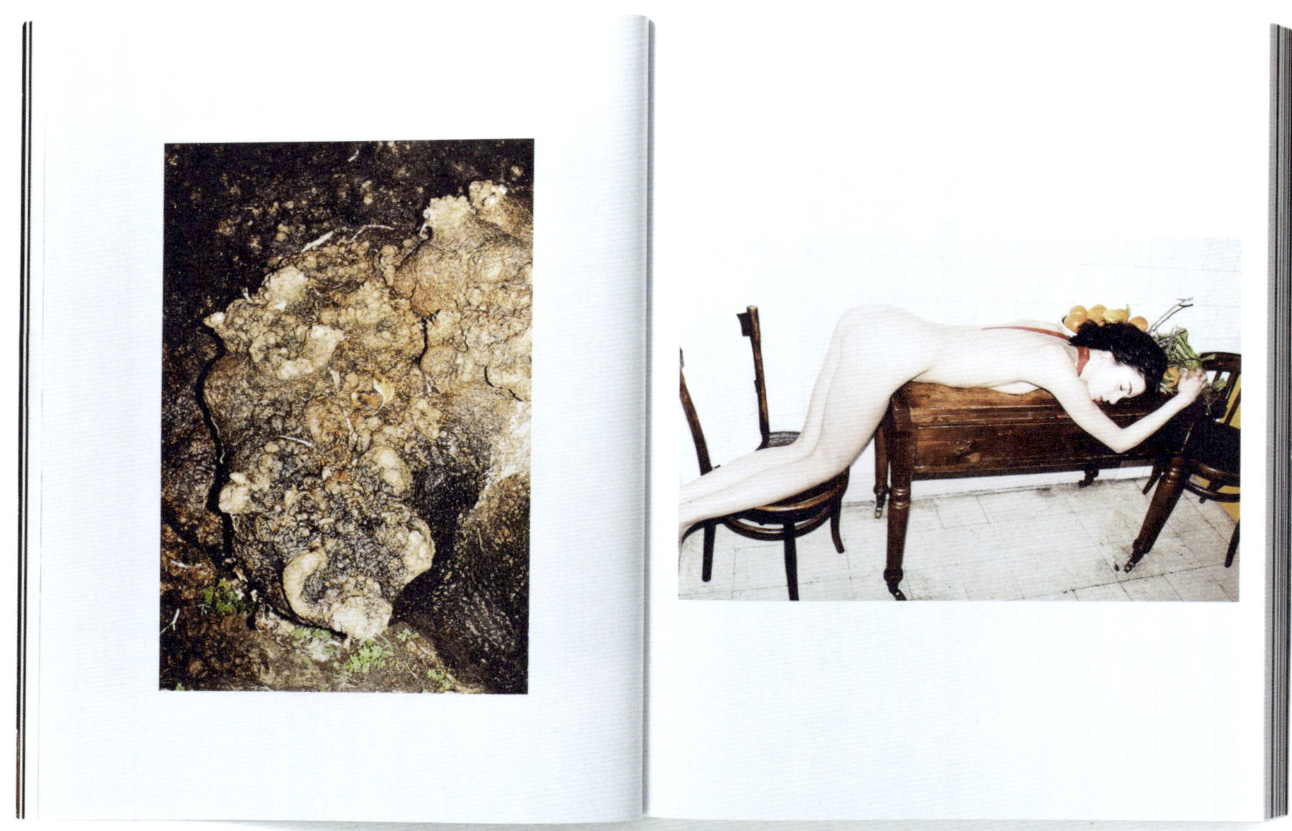

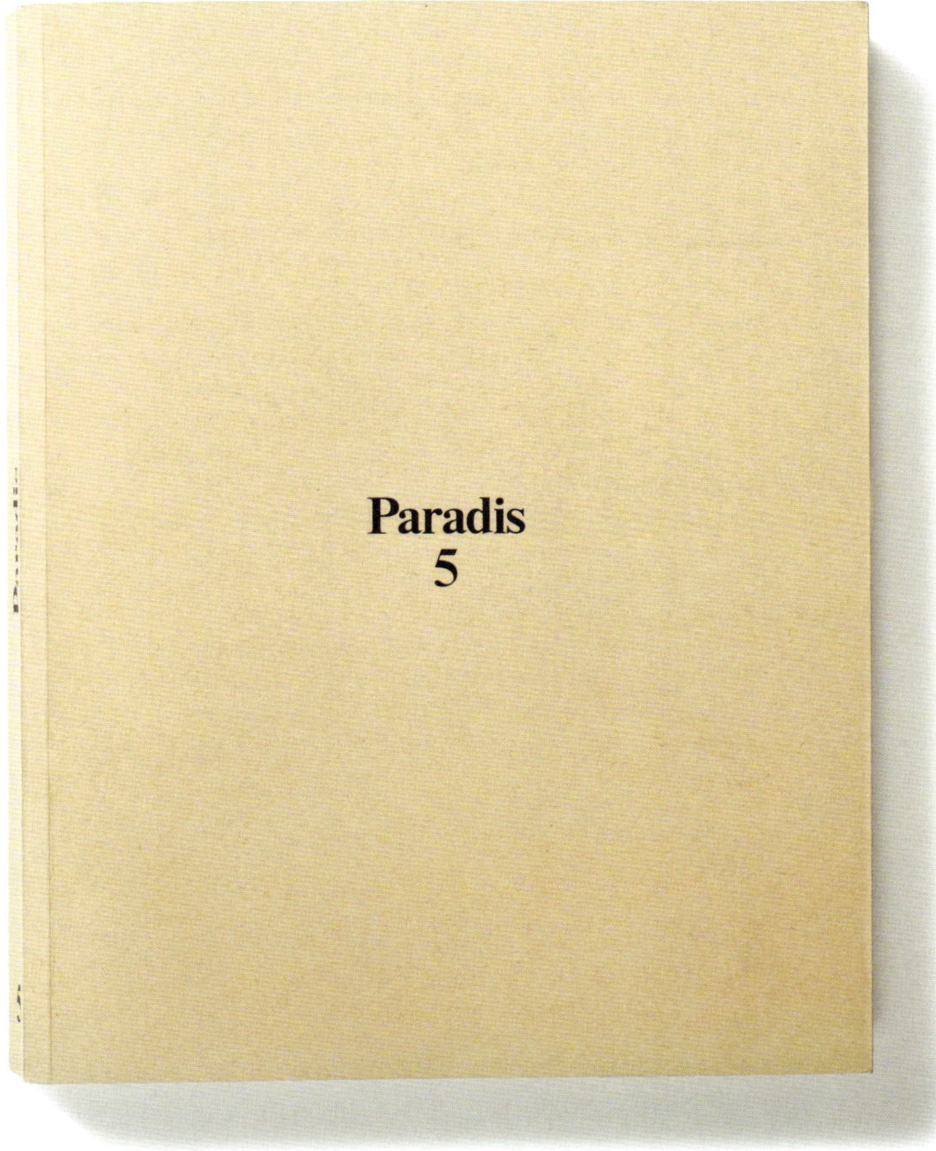
Paradis
5

fashion tend to create a quality chain. My aim today is to take fashion photographers toward non-fashion projects: for example, I asked Juergen Teller to try nude photography for the first time.

What can you do that you couldn't have dreamed off in a fashion publication?

To try out projects simply for the fun of them, without any restrictions. For example, to go back to Juergen Teller, in the next issue of *Paradis*, he has a series coming out which is 100 pages long. That's something you could never do in the fashion press, not even in *Vogue*. It's odd to operate in a media field that has its own economic rules, and to totally bypass them. *Paradis* is an object of pleasure, perhaps that's the eroticism we're actually going on about!

But how do you keep it alive financially?

I have a parallel activity; *Paradis* is a practically self-financed project. It's not terribly expensive to make because we have enough advertising pages. We cover our costs but certainly don't make any money from it. But it's a real joy to make it.

What editorial challenges did you give yourself?

We tried out things that have since been done by other magazines – for example, we had, very very long interviews of people who were very old, and totally without news, nothing to sell. Don't get me wrong, this isn't an act of media bravery, but it's just that when you come out once a year, you have the time to get interviews you really want, you think in a more long-term manner, and have a more outspread search for remarkable things.

Even though you give a new freedom to contributors, do you feel the magazine has basic rules it needs to stick to?

This is hard to say, because it is a project that grows with us. Its contours shift incessantly. Yes, the magazine fits within the frame I give it, but it's an extremely fluid frame.

What is the difference between pornography and eroticism?

Eroticism is a promise of life, porn a promise of death. It's a cult of death. In pornography, there is also an outrageous desire to punish women. But eroticism is filled with unpredictability.

Also, porn can be a little like looking at a dessert on a fast food menu. Nothing unexpected will happen, the entire experience is foreseeable, and in that sense, it's already dead.

And when does eroticism become mere vulgarity?

It becomes vulgar when it's contemptuous. It becomes vulgar when it's malicious, when it makes you feel ill-at-ease. All of a sudden you can feel the power relation and it simply makes you uncomfortable. This, I would say, is vulgar.

Talking of surprises – would it be relevant to work with someone who solely works on nude photography?

The photographers who spend a lifetime shooting naked girls aren't that interested in photography, if you ask me. They're interested in seeing the girls naked. Although it's perfectly understandable that a man might dream of sleeping with a different girl every day, shooting a different nude every day is slightly disturbing. That said, I've commissioned a series to Japanese photographer Kishin Shinoyama, who's done nude in the past and in his case I don't find it problematic, his work goes beyond that.

Since this is a magazine for and by straight men, could you ever consider using gay imagery?

If I don't, it is because gay sensitivity has put an elaborate imagery into place, and I don't think I could do it better myself, nor have anything more interesting to offer.

How about lesbian imagery?

I suppose I have yet to find what lesbian aesthetics are exactly, by and for lesbians. I don't mean lesbian films and works don't exist of course, but I still don't cease, or am able to spot a 'typical' lesbian style. But I'd be very open to find out more about it. I'm open to... not everything, but quite a few things.

"EROTICISM IS A PROMISE OF LIFE, PORN A PROMISE OF DEATH. IT'S A CULT OF DEATH. IN PORNOGRAPHY, THERE IS ALSO AN OUTRAGEOUS DESIRE TO PUNISH WOMEN. BUT EROTICISM IS FILLED WITH UNPREDICTABILITY."

FROM EROTICA TO PORNOGRAPHY TO EROTICA AGAIN… THE 360° HISTORY OF MEN'S MAGAZINES

By Samir "Mr. Magazine™" Husni, Ph.D.

Two important births were recorded in the year 1953, as to which one would be considered the most erotic is anyone's guess: the wailing arrival of Mr. Magazine™ (complete with tie and mustache), and the humble entry of *Playboy* (the first issue was produced in Hugh Hefner's Hyde Park kitchen), and since this article is about the history of men's magazines, let's talk about *Playboy*.

Playboy was, and still is, for that matter, an icon in men's magazines. It reigned supreme until 1980 and its writers have produced some of the best interviews in the business to date. From Miles Davis and Jackie Gleason way back in 1962, to one of its most famous with Jimmy Carter (he was not yet president at the time) who admitted to *Playboy*'s Robert Scheer that he had lusted in his heart. *Playboy* set a precedent for the magazine interview. It's hard to believe that a publication of *Playboy*'s magnitude and stamina started so humbly in 1953.

With a little over $8000, partially borrowed from his brother and mother, Hugh Hefner created a brand that became an empire. From using a picture of Marilyn Monroe (which was originally a calendar pin-up) as the first centrefold, to photographs of people like Drew Barrymore (January, 1995), Daryl Hannah (November, 2003), and Deborah Gibson (March, 2005), *Playboy* brought a different style and class to men's magazines, legitimising erotica as no other magazine had before it.

It was exciting times for adult-entertainment; especially men's magazines.

But to discuss the history of men's magazines, one has to go back to the beginning; the very beginning. Erotic images and personifications have been a part of our human development since the dawn of time; from the Greeks to the Romans, the depiction of the human body (*au naturel*) has both fascinated and captivated. In countries like Nepal, Japan, and China, illustrations of sex and erotic art have specific spiritual meanings within their native religions. For some cultures from the ancient world, erotica was considered prestigious and displayed prominently throughout their everyday lives. For example, the Romans had the habit of etching their depictions upon pottery or lamps. One such piece was discovered and dated at somewhere around the 1st century AD; it had been ornately etched to show off a woman having sexual intercourse with two men simultaneously. Quite progressive, even by today's rather relaxed standards.

Such openness and blatant affinity for the naked form, sex, and erotica was acceptable behavior, it was thought to be the highest form of flattery to celebrate the nude body. From great works of art such as the sculptures of the Greek gods in ancient times, to Rodin's "The Thinker", naked hasn't always meant disgraceful; in fact, quite the opposite. Beauty and the delight of the senses personified these pieces and bringing joy to the beholder was their creators' intent. Not to offend or repulse.

It wasn't until the Victorian era that the line between erotic beauty and distasteful imagery (pornography, as it is called today) was drawn. And then in 1864 the first modern definition of the word "pornography" appeared in Webster's Dictionary. This was the moment that defined the term "explicit pictures." But, unlike other word definitions, pornography's definition reached as high as the United States Supreme Court, the highest judicial entity in the country where the justices opted

> page 117

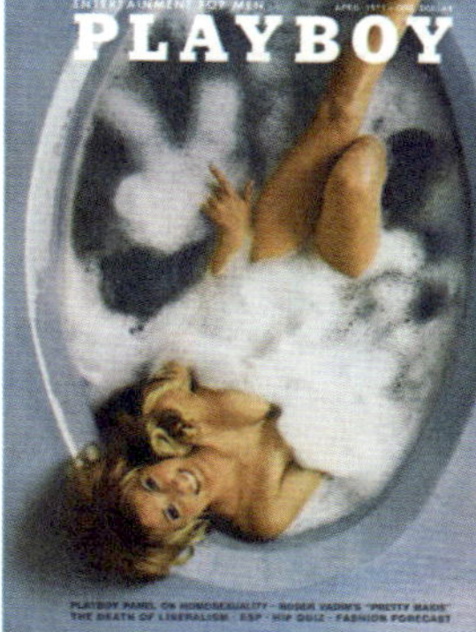

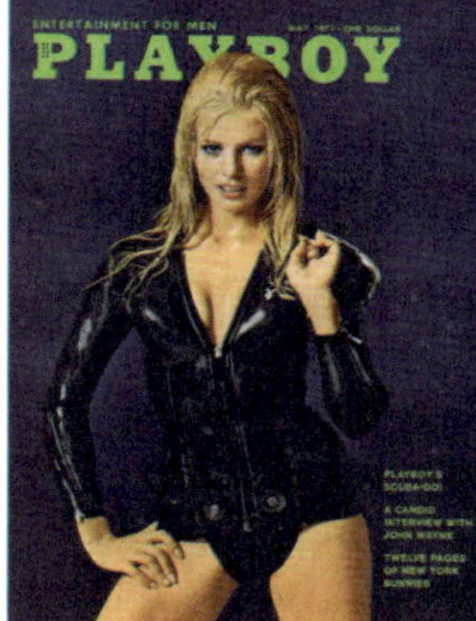

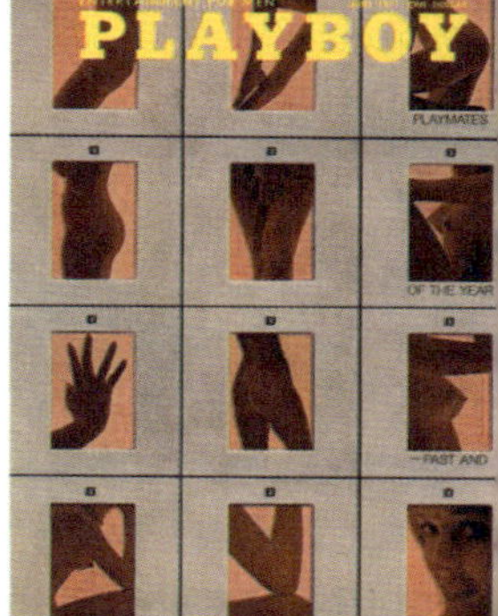

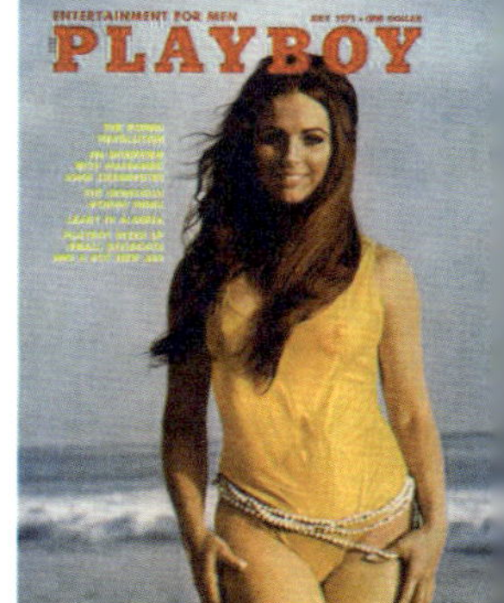

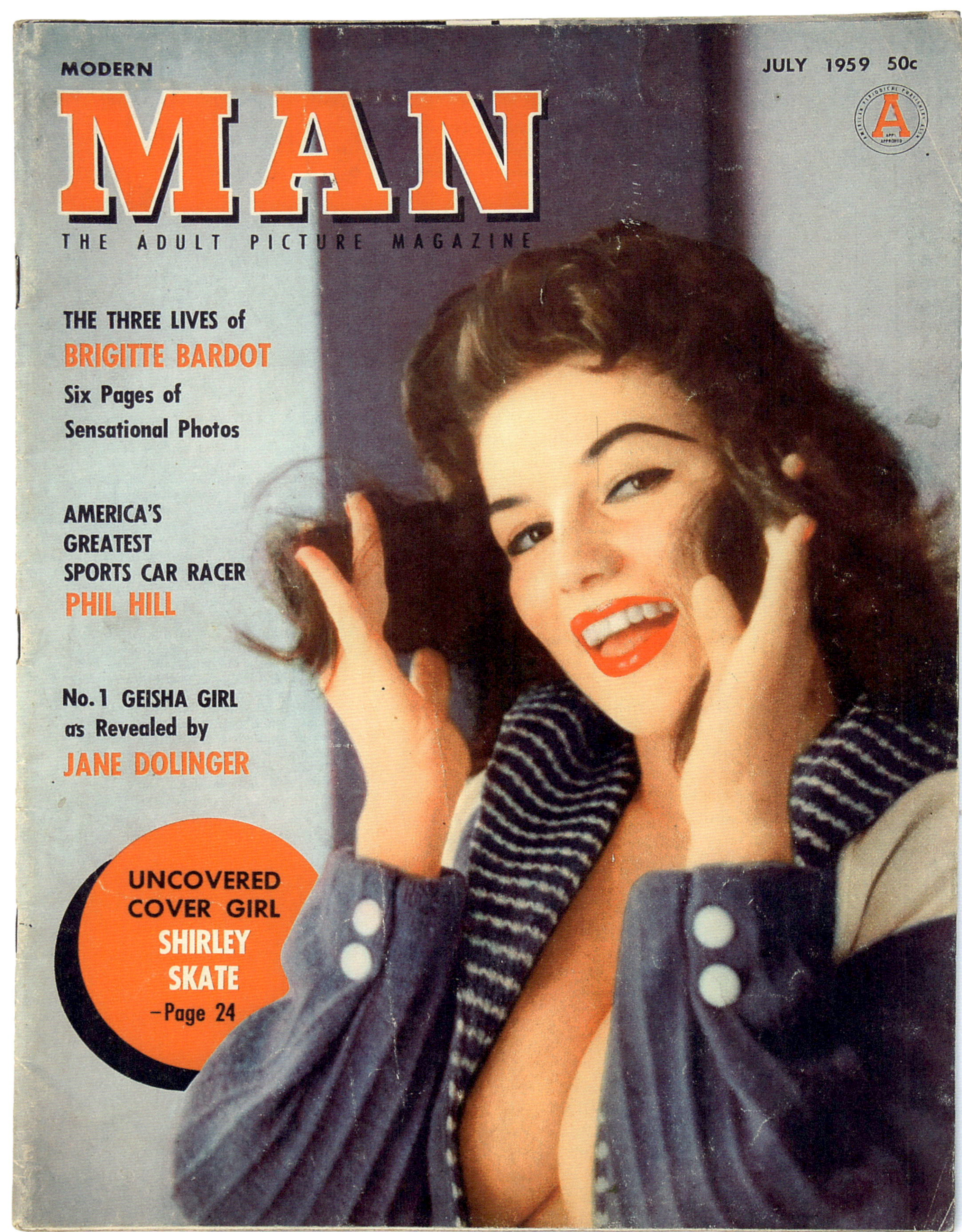

Modern Man cover , July 1959

The Birth of the Erotic Magazine

for a very lucrative definition, *"we know it when we see it."* So is the centrefold porn or erotica, that is and will continue to be the question for some time to come.

Before Hef and the multiplication of his bunnies, a genre of men's magazines called Men's Adventure existed, consisting of titles like Argosy (December, 1882) the longest-running and considered by some the best of the genre, *Stag* (first published in June, 1937), *Swank* (1940s), and *For Men Only* (December, 1957). These magazines alluded to sex and the unclad female body, without the in-your-face style that was just around the corner. The boundaries of explicit were about to be stretched beyond the extreme and parts of the country just weren't ready for it especially in the very conservative South.

In 1965, in the United Kingdom, a magazine was born that would eventually, four years later, be sold in the United States. And it was sure to rock the realms of decency where men's magazines were concerned with tremendous waves. That magazine was called *Penthouse* and it was delivered into the world by a man named Bob Guccione. It began with a softcore style that combined pictorials with lifestyle articles that appealed to men. It was a huge success.

Penthouse and *Playboy* soon became rivals for the public's affection, each publication trying to outdo the other by going a little farther with every photo they included between their pages. And so began the "Pubic Wars" a phrase coined by Hefner, with a tongue-in-cheek twist on the Roman/Carthage battles dubbed the Punic Wars. It pushed both empires to obvious extremes.

Having started *Penthouse* in England, Guccione had been showing pubic hair for a while in his UK editions. The Europeans had a far more liberal attitude toward the forbidden areas on the male/female form. Not to be outdone, Hefner decided that he had to compete with the new kid on the block, which on occasion was surpassing him in sales and circulation numbers. So risking obscenity charges here in the States, since it was extremely forbidden to photograph pubic hair or genitals in any capacity, *Playboy* began to show glimpses of pubic hair about nine months after *Penthouse* (June 1970). Needless to say, the ensuing battle was both entertaining and sublimely ridiculous.

Eventually the two magazines would move in entirely different directions, with *Playboy* assuming a more passively softcore lean, focusing more on hiring extremely well-known and talented authors to pen their features, and *Penthouse* gravitating toward even raunchier photos, ultimately delving into hardcore porn and spreads showing women urinating; something deemed unacceptable and disgusting in the erotic magazine world. Since 2004, *Penthouse* has been under new management

> page 122

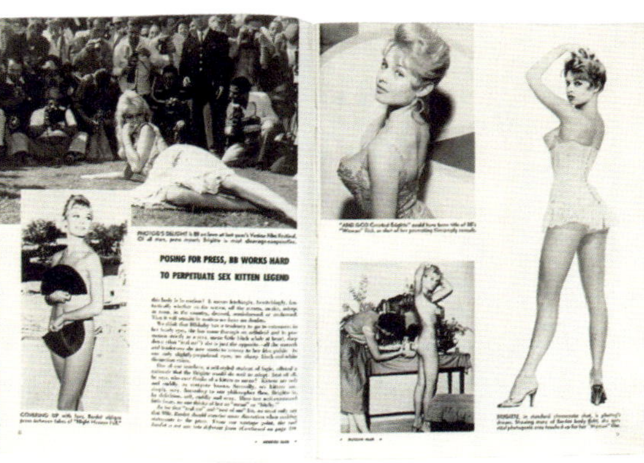

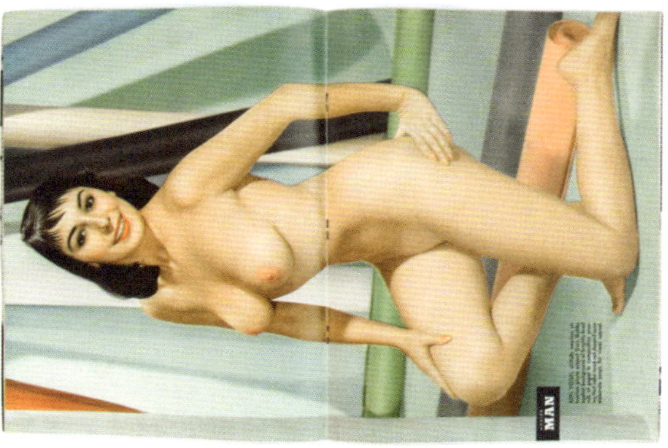

Modern Man Inside spreads ,
July 1959

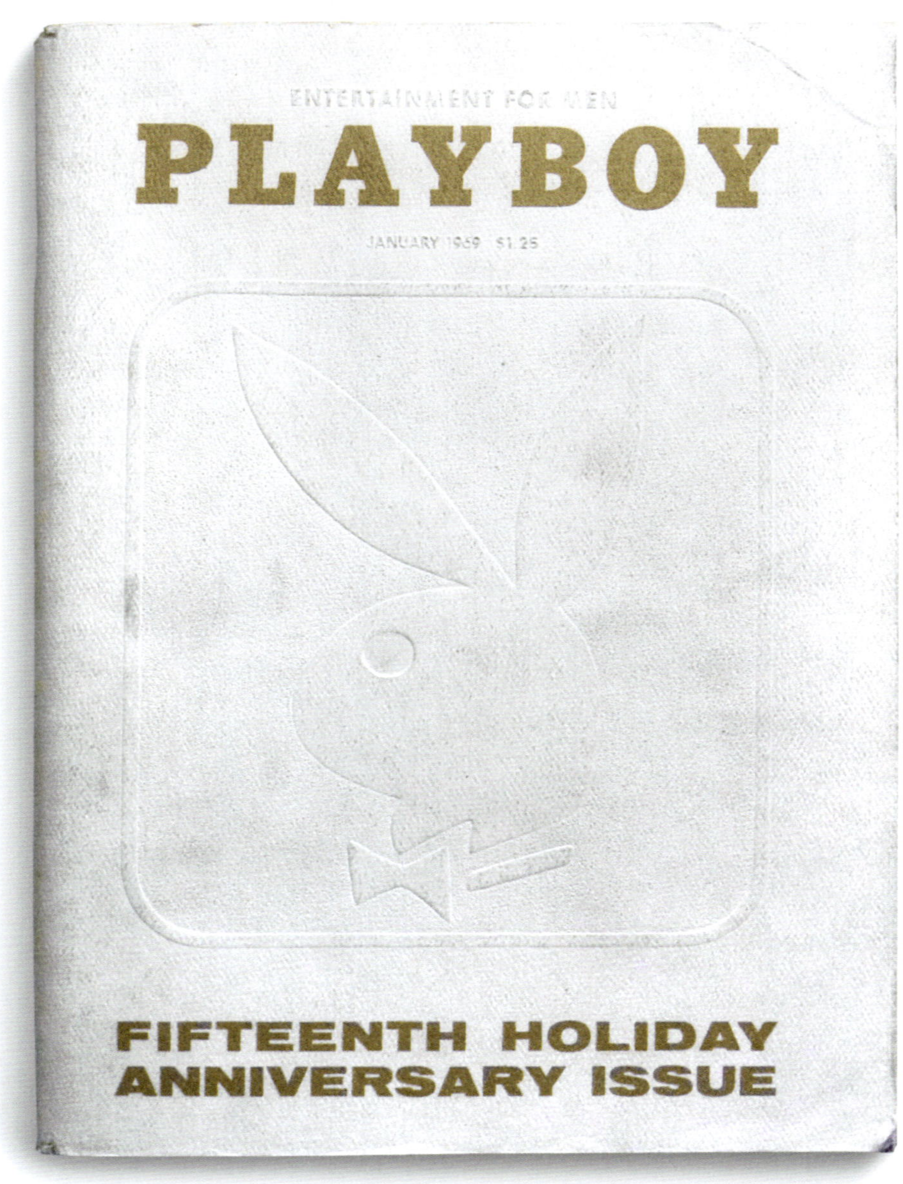

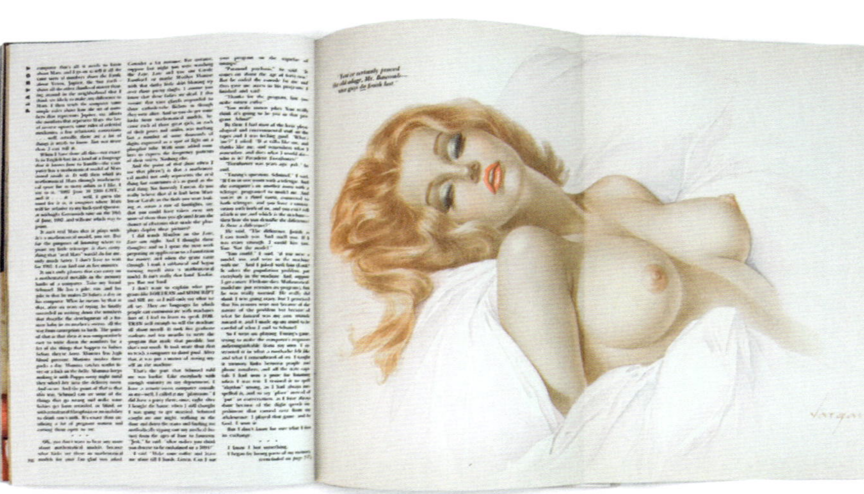

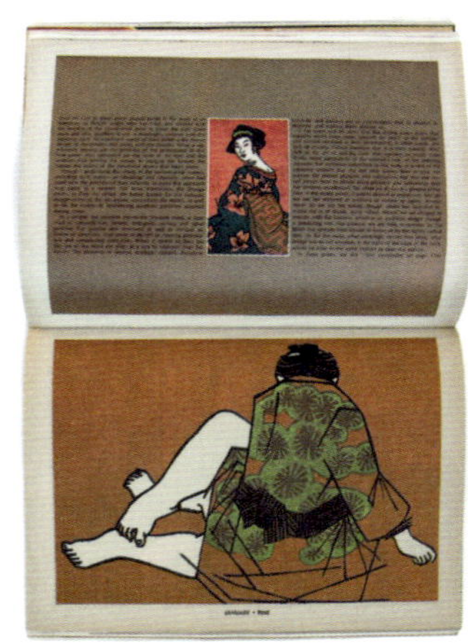

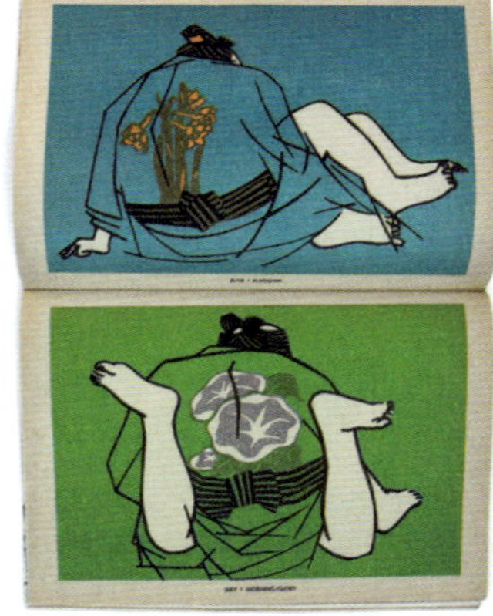

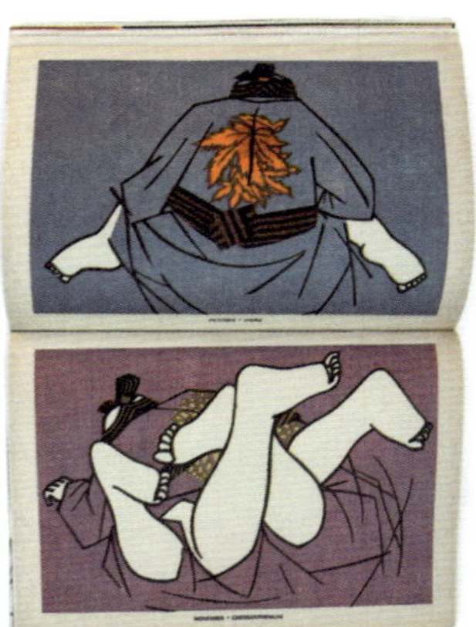

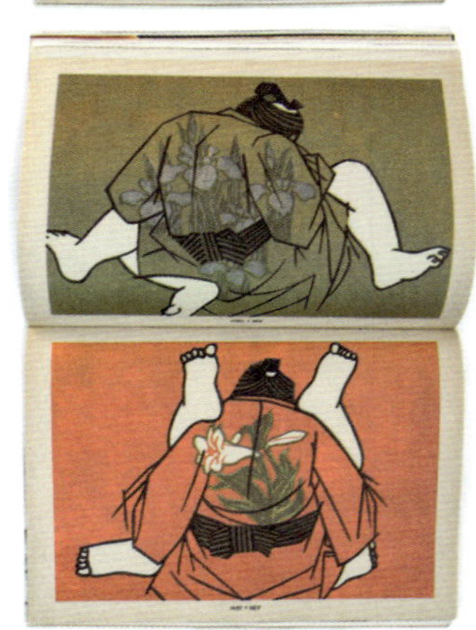

Playboy cover & inside spreads, January 1969, 15th birthday issue

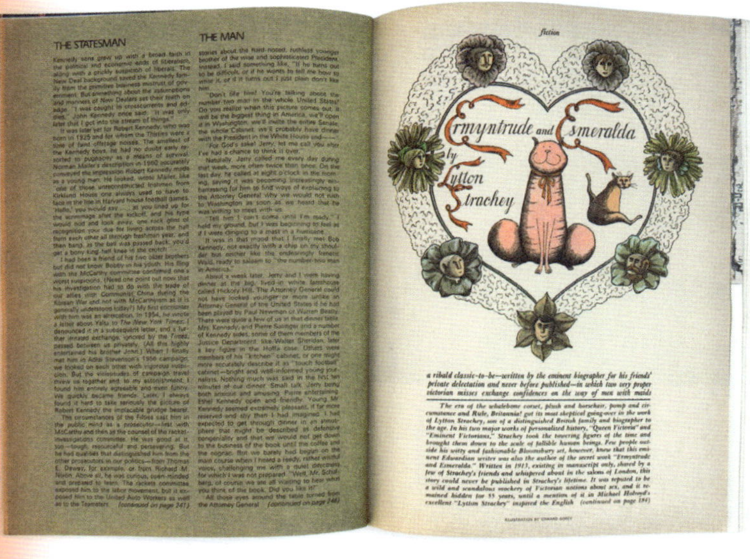

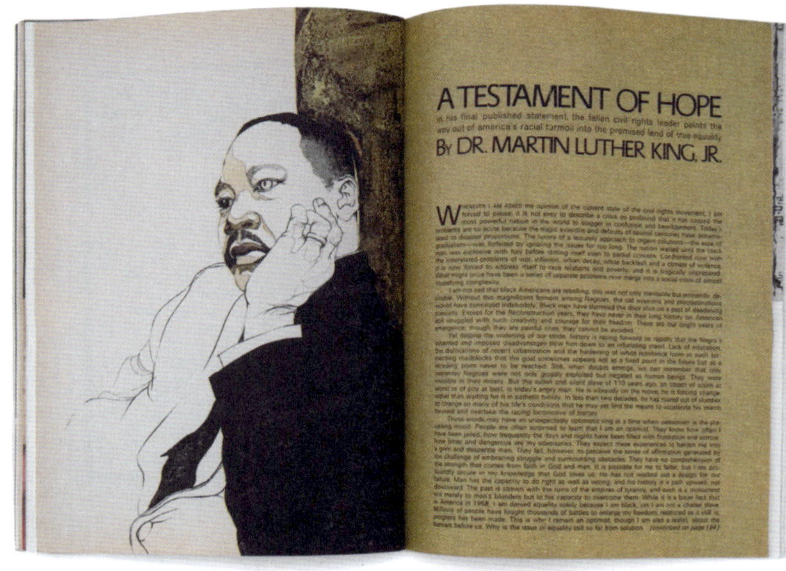

A TESTAMENT OF HOPE
By DR. MARTIN LUTHER KING, JR.

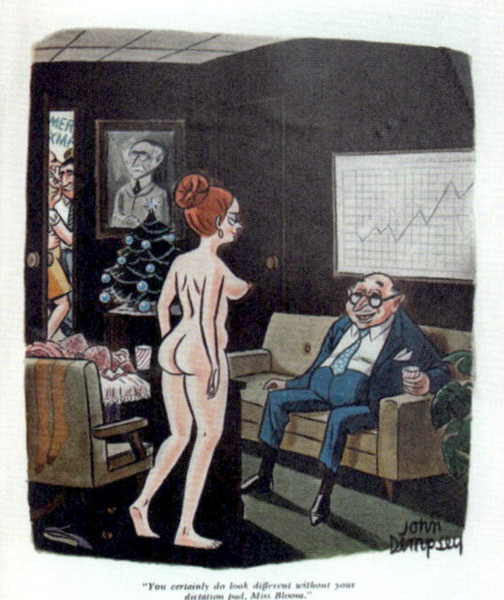

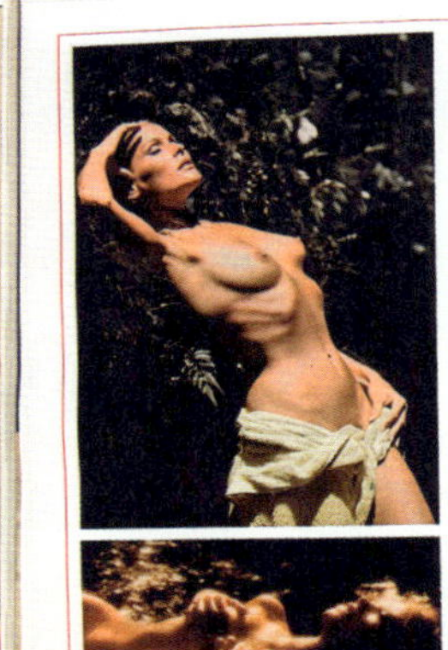

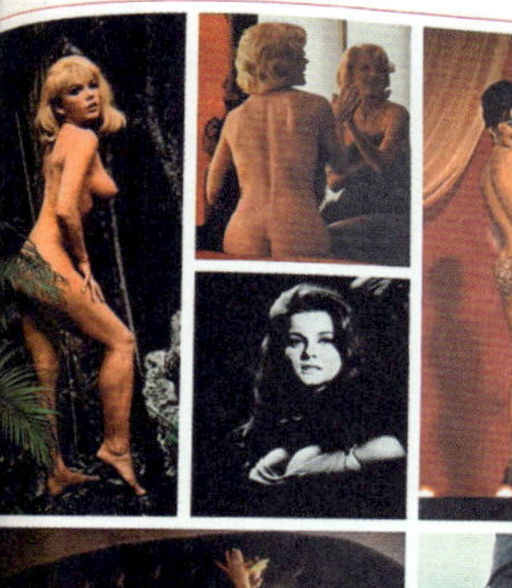

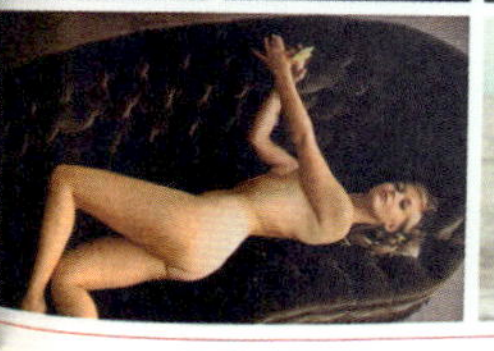

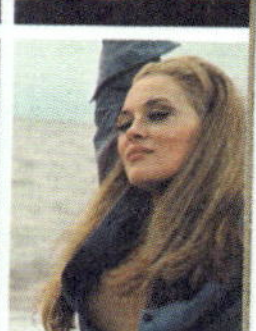

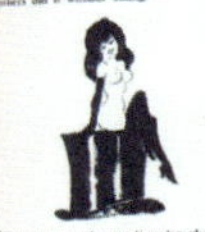

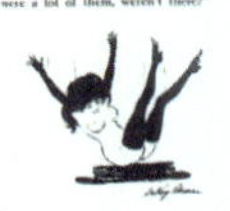

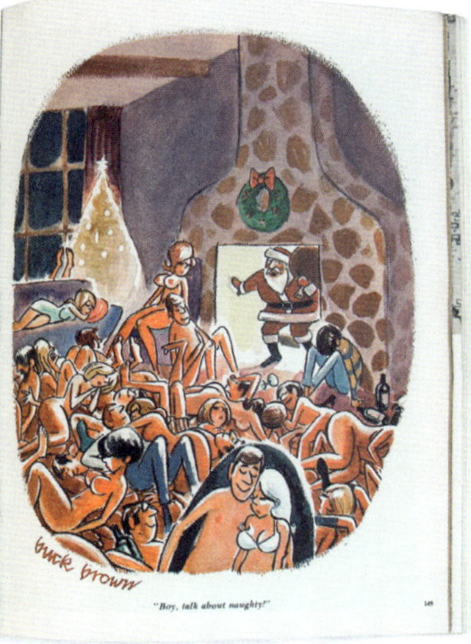

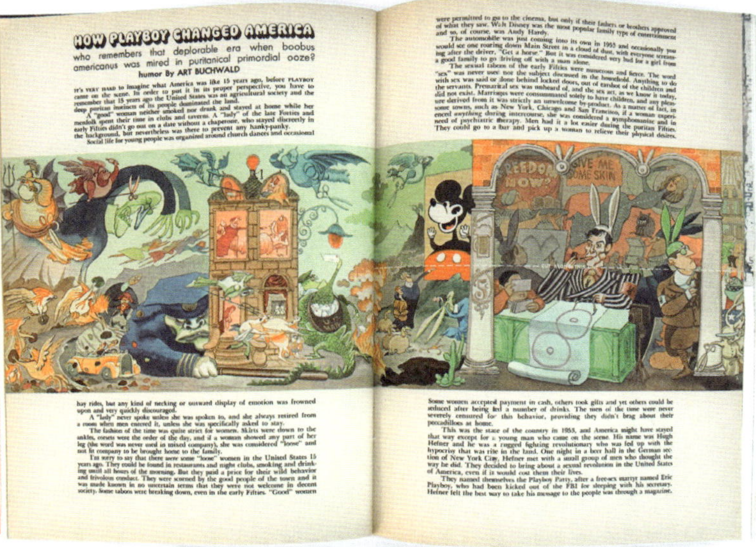

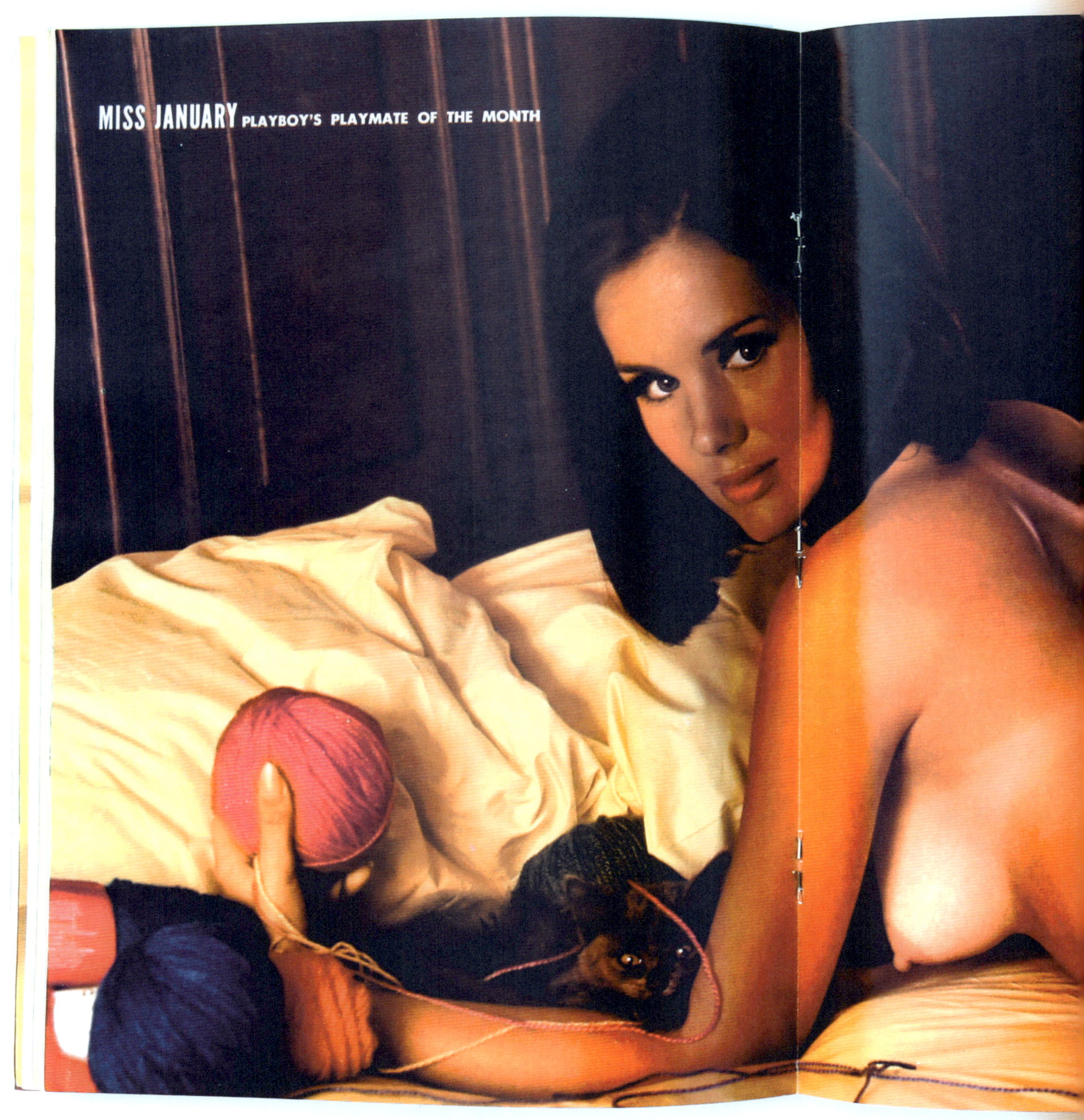

Playboy centrefold ,
January 1969, 15th bithday issue

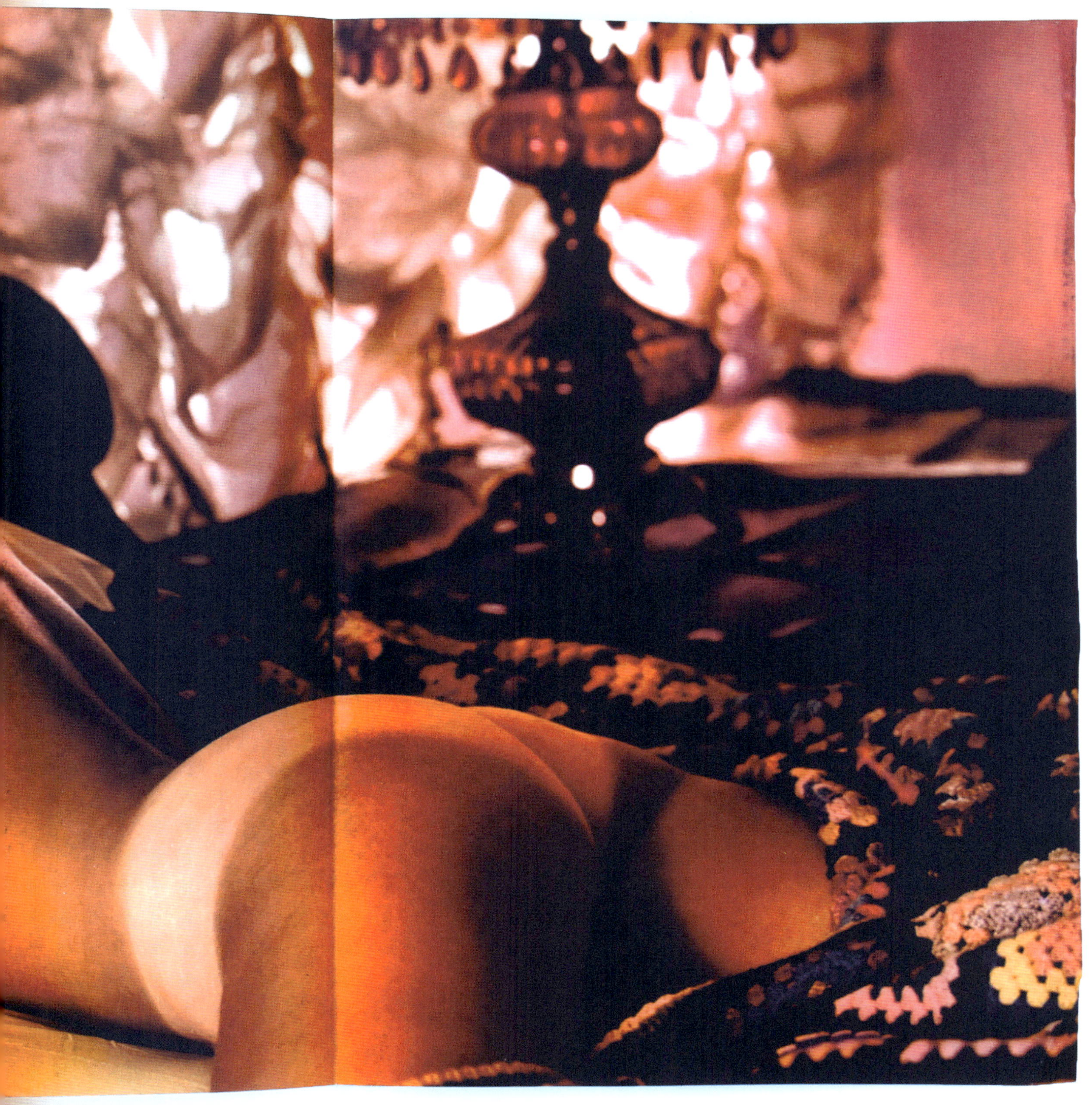

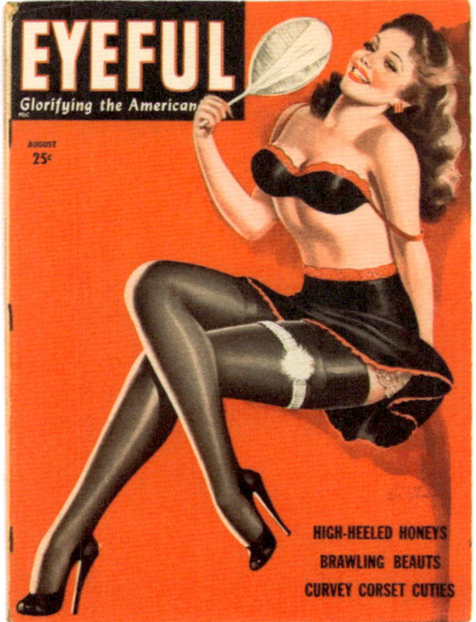

and has seen the error of their ways, now following in *Playboy*'s shoes by adopting a more sophisticated and softer image where their pictorial content is concerned.

In 1974, during the war between the P's, another infant pushed its way into the world, a little brother for the big boys that would soon make *Playboy* and *Penthouse* look like a children's magazine in comparison. *Hustler Magazine* burst into the nursery on the heels of the *Hustler Newsletter*, which was simply a cheap avenue of advertising for its owner's chain of strip clubs at the time. Larry Flynt was determined to break all the taboos with *Hustler*. His magazine showed much more explicit photos of the female genitalia, and depicted more hardcore themes like the utilization of sex toys, penetration and group sex. It was definitely more in-your-face than even *Penthouse*. In a 2011 bookstore signing, Flynt credited his casino in Gardena, California and his chain of bars and clubs with the bulk of his profits today, stating that less than five percent of his income comes from the print magazine. He also speculated that the print magazine would probably not be around in a couple of years. Whether due to his continued efforts to prove he is the biggest and baddest when it comes to raunch, or the simple fact that people are returning to a more leave-it-to-the-imagination mindset, his circulation in print has dropped from 3 million (*Hustler*'s peak) to just below 500,000. Definitely a telltale sign of something.

An honorable mention goes to *Screw Magazine* (first published in 1968), a weekly pornographic magazine that was printed in tabloid form, and was revamped by some former employees in 2005. And to *Club Magazine*, a spin-off publication of the United Kingdom's *Club International* and a monthly pornographic mag that leans heavily toward hardcore.

When the 80s came along, there was an explosion of sex magazines that began to dominate the ink-on-paper trade: *Juggs*, *Gent*, *Sucking Candy*, just to name a few and an almost endless supply of hardcore porn magazines where anything went; absolutely anything. Even the titles themselves left little to the imagination. Name any part of the human anatomy and there was a magazine for it, about it, or wearing its body part as the magazine's moniker. It was a decadent decade for men's printed entertainment.

The 90s rolled in and the new niche was specificity. Sex magazines for men became explicitly individualized. *Foreskin Quarterly*, *Booty*, *Finally Legal*, *Uncut*, *Teenz*; the list was long and lascivious. It seemed as though the industry was obsessed with covering every possible scenario the boudoir could conjure up, and every possible crack and crevice (pardon the intentional pun).

Then in 1997 a new venue for sex, drugs, and rock and roll booted onto the scene, or rebooted, depending on your connection back then; a little thing called the World Wide Web. And of the three bad seeds, sex

> page 125

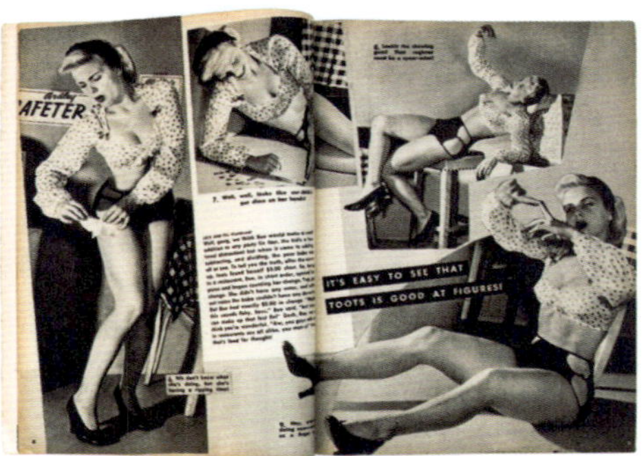

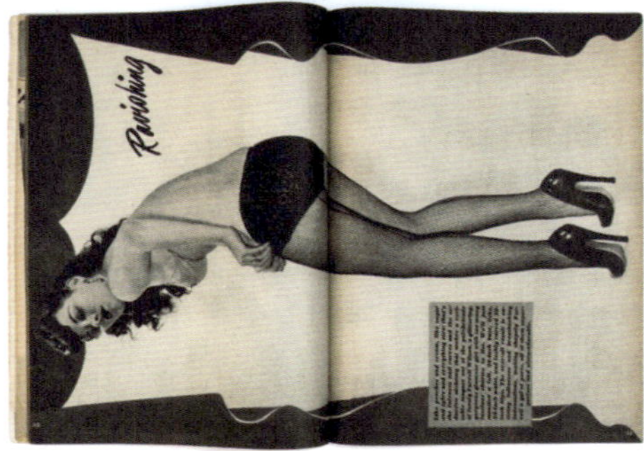

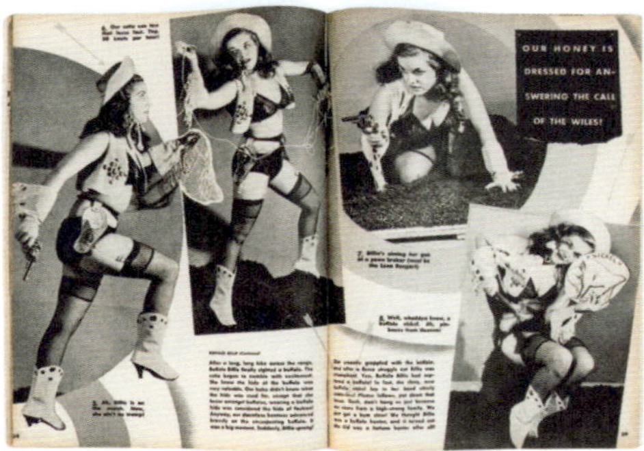

Eyeful Inside spreads ,
August 1948

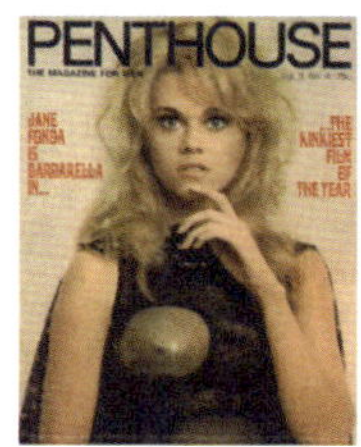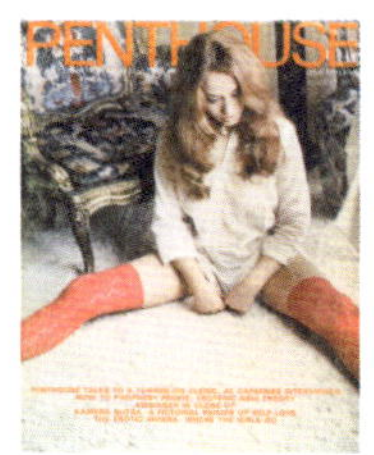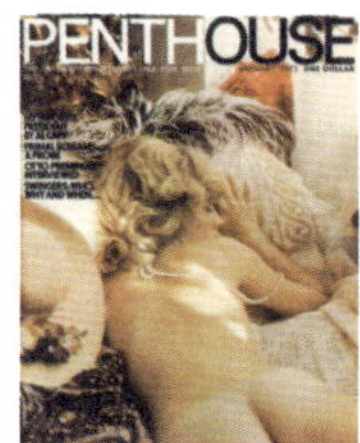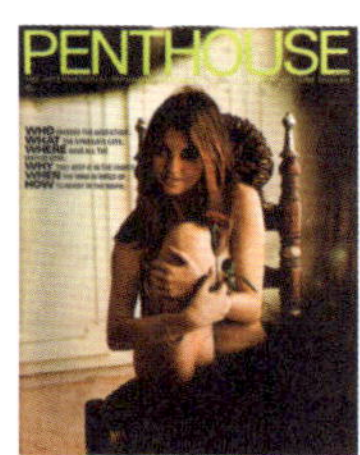

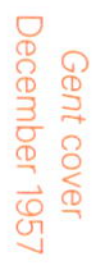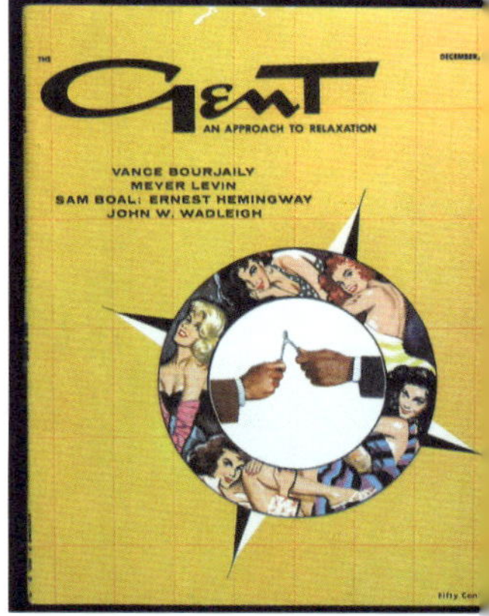

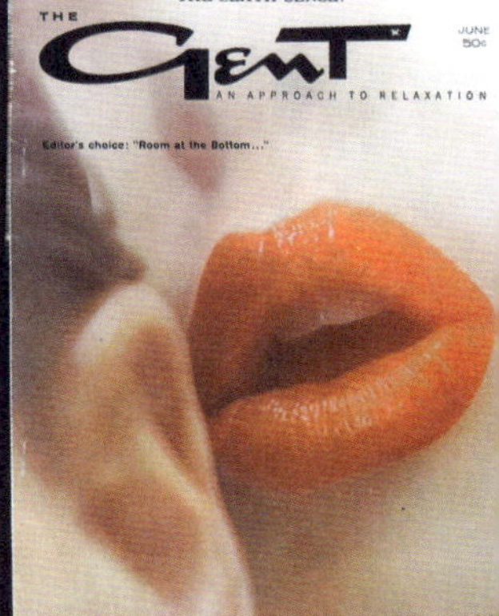

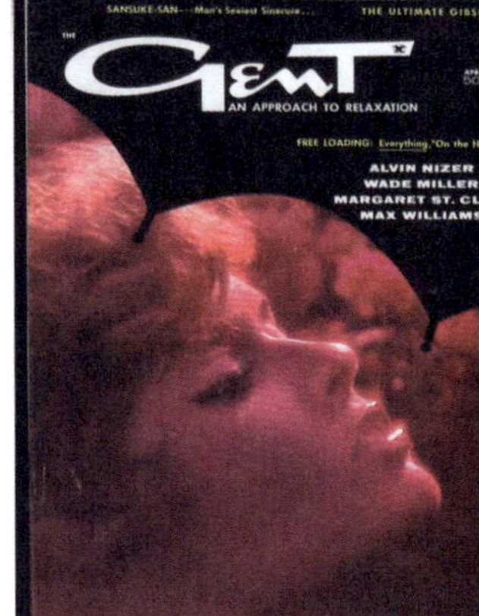

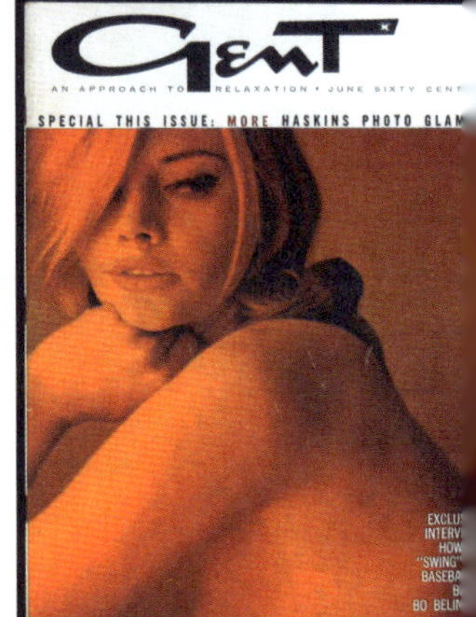

"IT HASN'T BEEN AN EASY ROAD FOR ANY OF THE MORE AFFLUENT MEN'S MAGAZINES"

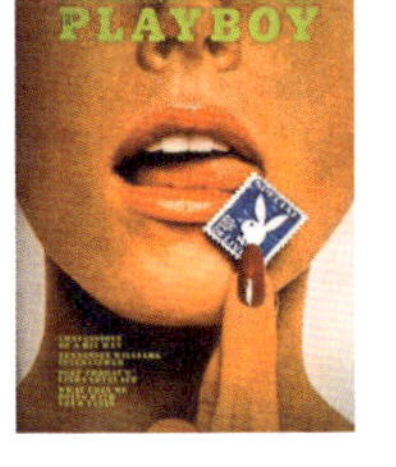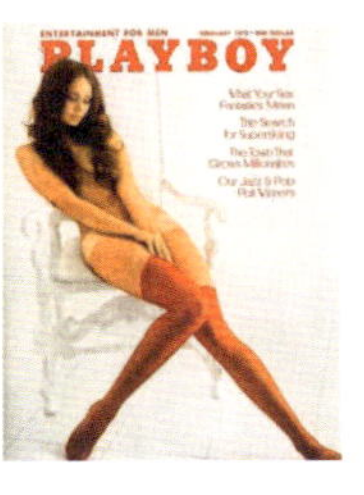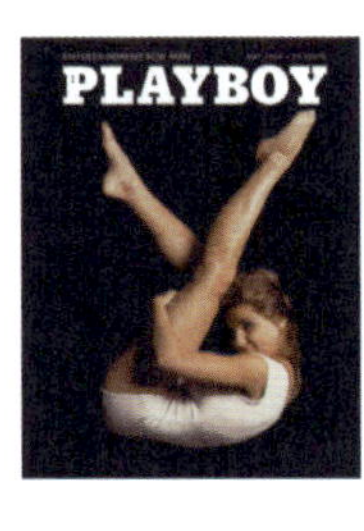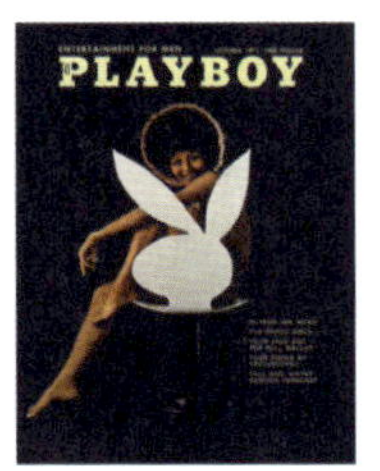

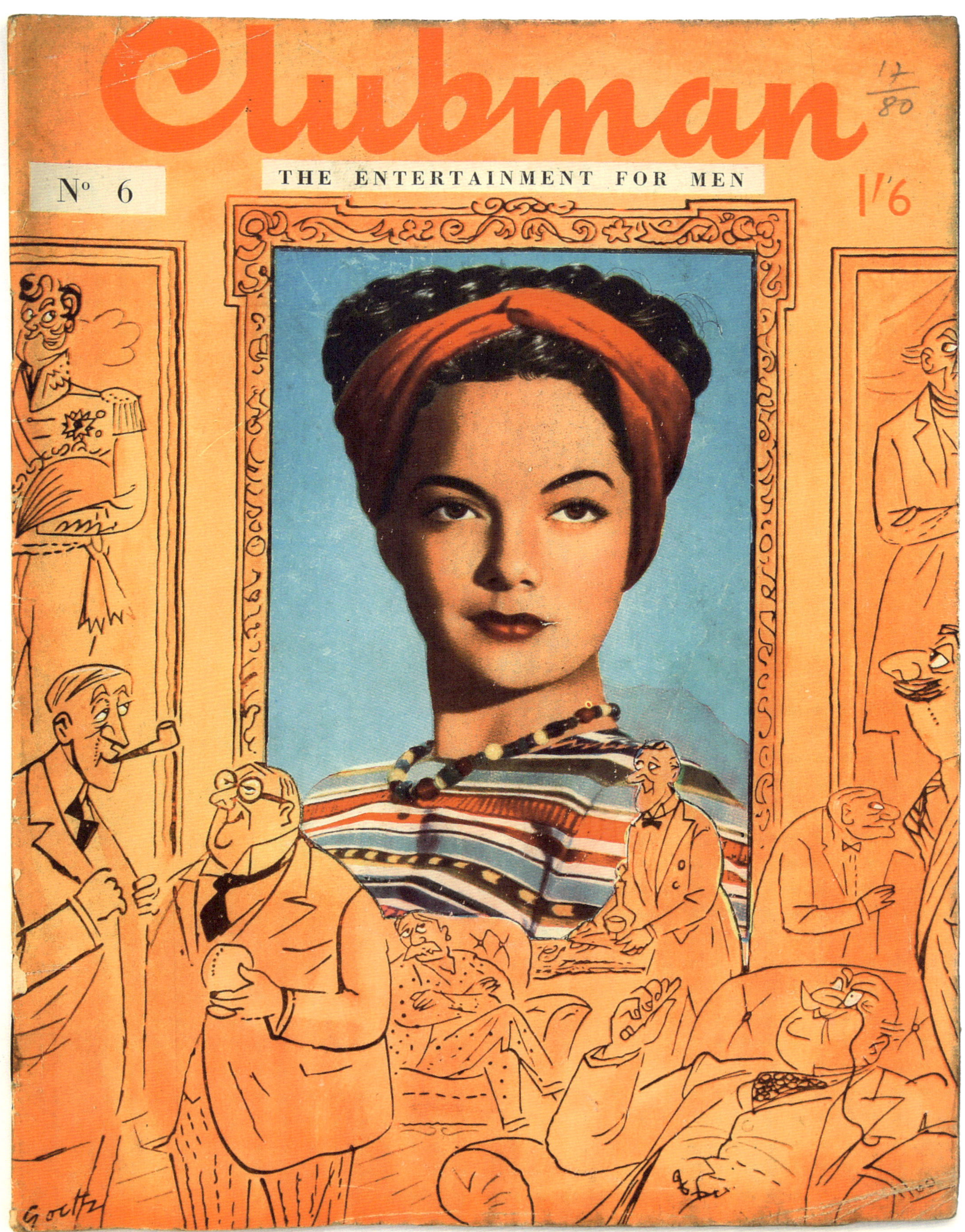

Clubman cover, February 1951

took the hardest hit. There were 110 new magazine launches in 1997, but they couldn't compete with all the free porn on the internet; sex magazine sales began to drop.

But even with declining circulation, men's magazines survived the 90s and the endless realms of cyberspace. With a new century came a new perspective, one that returned to a softer, gentler rendition of male/female relationships, like an early *Playboy*. Magazines like *Treats* and *Jacques* tried to depict the human form in a more artistic way, reminiscent of the early eras.

It hasn't been an easy road for any of the more affluent men's magazines. The American Family Association, a non-profit organization that promotes conservative Christian values, boycotted 7-Eleven convenience stores for two years until they stopped selling *Playboy* and *Penthouse*. In 1989 they boycotted WaldenBooks for the same reason, the selling of the two most popular men's erotic magazines in the United States. Consequently, WaldenBooks launched an ad campaign against censorship, asserting their first amendment rights. There was even the 2008 bill introduced to congress by Republican Congressman Paul Broun to ban the sale of *Playboy* and *Penthouse* at military bases, stating that consuming even soft porn incites men into committing sex crimes. These Puritan values and ideals that Americans treasured were in sharp contrast to the freer and more open attitudes of the Europeans. The United States had been founded upon Christian morals and values and these outspoken and motivated people threatened the men's magazines at every turn. It was a daily fight.

A genre that began to emerge from its mother's womb in the early 70s was one that would yet again shock certain groups of people: The gay and lesbian magazine. *The Advocate* was to the 70s and 80s what the app "Grinder" is to today's gay generation. The magazine was established in 1967 and is the oldest continuing LGBT publication in the United States. Before 1985, the magazine was tabloid-size and carried sexually explicit advertisements; then after owner David Goodstein's death, reduced down to a standard magazine format, sans the explicit ads. And of course, after *The Advocate*, in 1992, *Out Magazine* was founded and became the first general-interest magazine for gays and lesbians. Today with *Curve* (the nation's best-selling lesbian magazine), *FS Magazine* (a British mag about sex, relationships, drugs, HIV and many other things), the Australian magazines, *Blue* and *DNA* which features nude and semi-nude men taken by some of the world's top photographers, there appears to be a lucrative market out there for another little brother, or sister of the big boys.

The tendency toward toning down the more explicit, personal stuff and sticking strictly with the beauty of the human body seems to be a sign that we've come full circle. There is a fine line between erotica and pornography, the lead in the pencil so pale that sometimes you can't even detect it. Inherently we humans long for the beauty and wonder that the male/female body depicts. The baser, darker desires that throb deep in the heart of the creation surface on occasion, and eventually we shove them back into the aorta they seethed and erupted from; instead, reveling in the artistic, heavenly beauty that was intended. And as to whether men's magazines and their histories live up to that revelry, who knows. Not even the erotically born Mr. Magazine™ can answer that, no one can.

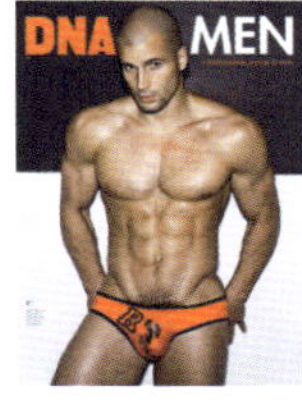

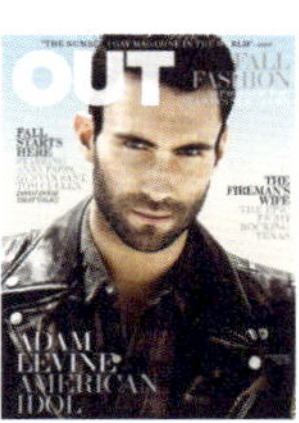

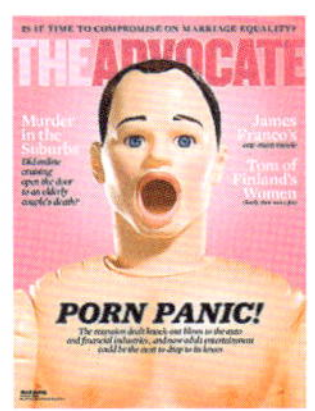

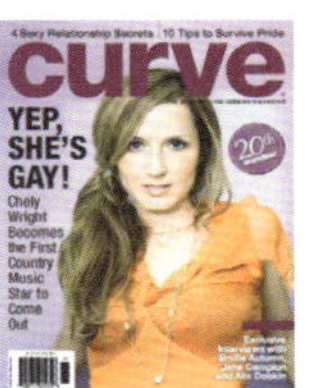

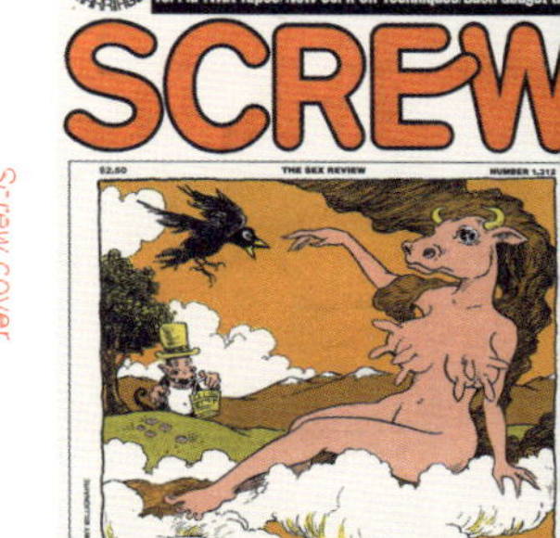

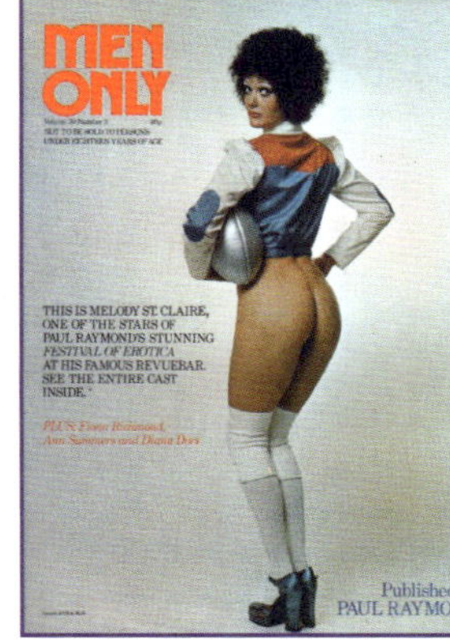

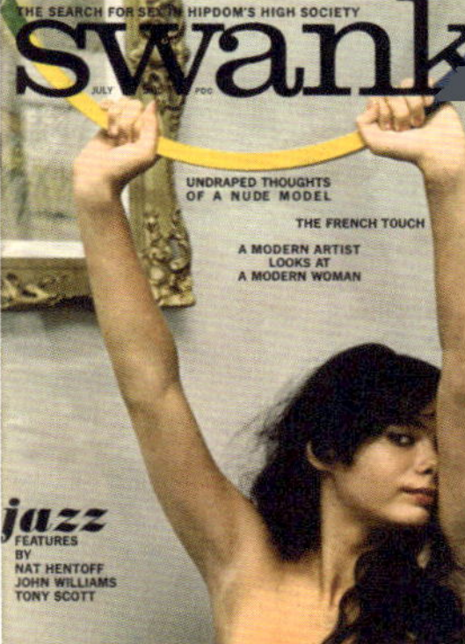

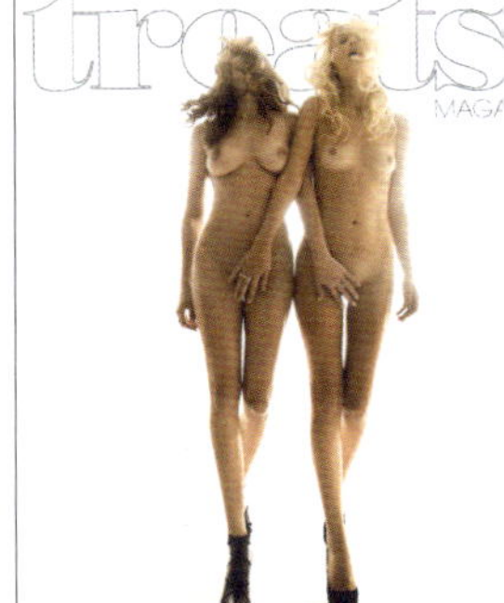

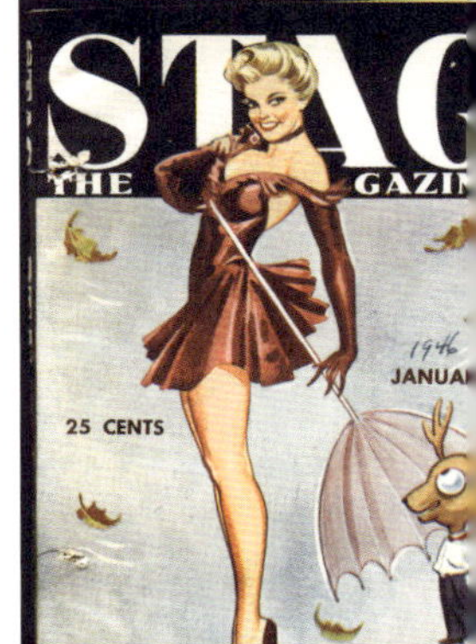

BERNARD BERT

Interview by Angelina A. Rafii

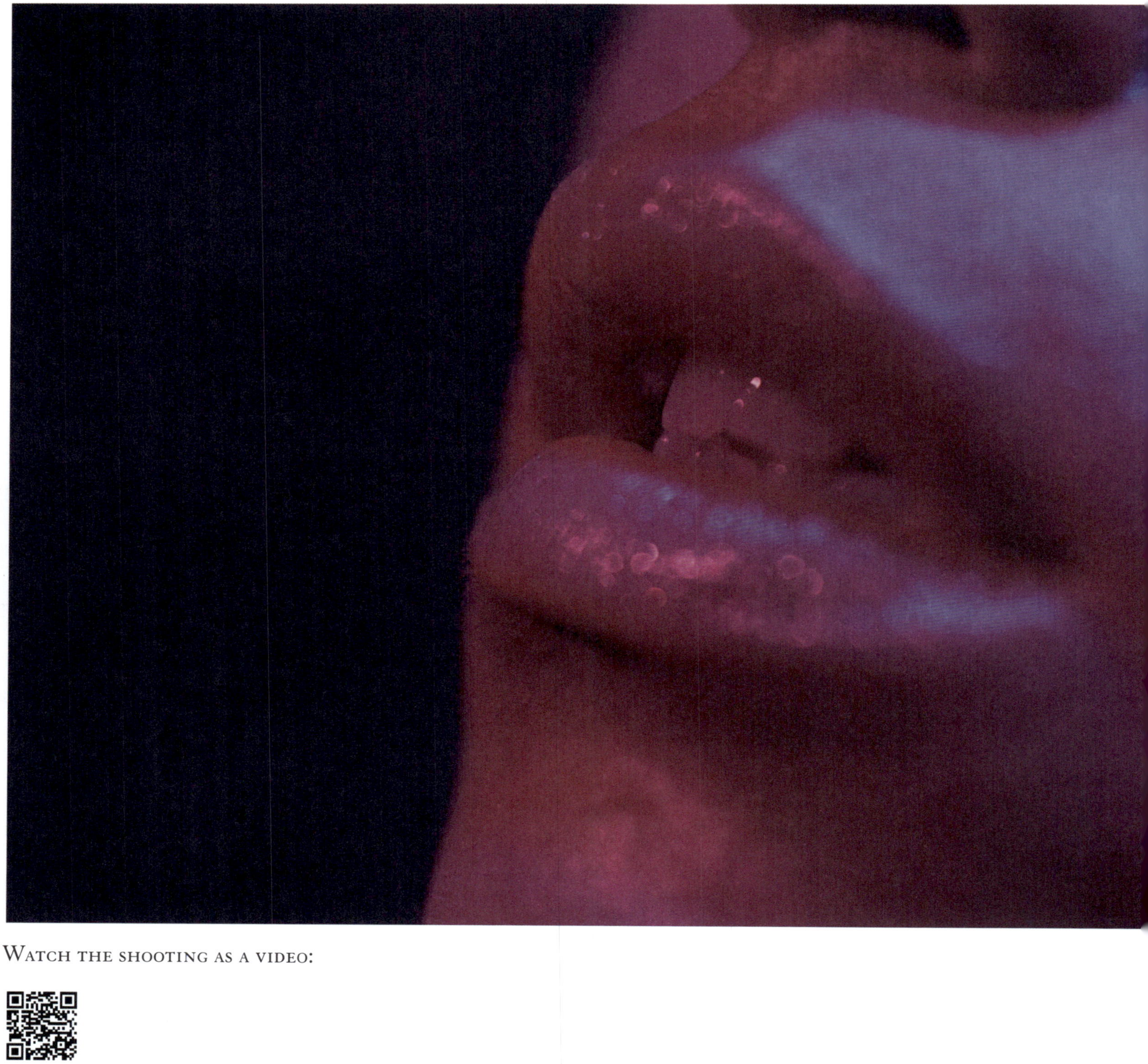

When you first moved to Paris you joined photographer Mondino's team. What was the most important lesson you learned and how has your photography evolved since?

Well, the first thing about those three years is that it was really challenging. Besides the fact that we worked with the best team whether it was hair, makeup, styling or models, the most precious lesson I learnt was to push the visual element to the limit inside the studio.

At that time we were not shooting digital but with film and Polaroïds. Mondino was always really demanding and many of the daily Polaroïds were actually the final shoot. Then we were shooting with film. The pictures were perfect. For Jean-Baptiste the idea was to do everything live, meaning that only what was not possible with live shots would be worked on during post-production. That was really magical. I still have so many Polaroïds from when I was there and they are so so close to the final picture that was seen around the world.

Do you find that there is a difference in approach when shooting erotic photography as compared to other forms and subjects?

Shooting erotic pictures does not sound different to me then shooting anything else. Photography or video are just ways of saying and sharing our own vision on a subject. When I was a kid my father was a photojournalist, there were many "photo magazines" at home. I was fascinated by the work of Helmut Newton, Lucien Clergue, Guy Bourdin etc... That was for me the first vision of erotic photography-mastering erotic photography. It was pretty impressive.

You also shoot video, what draws you to that medium in particular, what is the added advantage apart from the obvious?

The brand new available technology on video makes it now possible for anyone to do amazing video shoots. I mean technically at least. I always have been a fan of some amazing directors such as Ingmar Bergman and Vittorio de Sica for example. They were able to shoot "beauty" even in the most dramatic scene. Another reason I love doing video, now, is because most of my inspiration actually comes from music. Music brings the visual to another level. So much emotion can be added through it. Mixing images and music is what I love to do and it's such a powerful tool to tell a story.

In this particular series you showcase bondage and mirrors. It almost has a peepshow atmosphere, can you elaborate? What was the inspiration behind this particular work?

For this mirror shoot my idea was actually quite far from a peepshow inspiration even if I understand that it may look like it a bit. My idea was to use the mirrors and the girl looking at herself as a metaphor of us and our erotic and sexual needs. I wanted to show a strong and gorgeous woman in complete control of her own secret fantasy.

So the mirrors there are not viewers but represent her sexual and erotic maturity. The idea of the ropes and bondage came from Murielle from La fille d'O, she did all the lingerie that we shot that day and brought the idea of using ropes. In the end ropes and mirrors work together pretty nicely.

WWW.BERNARDBERTRAND.COM

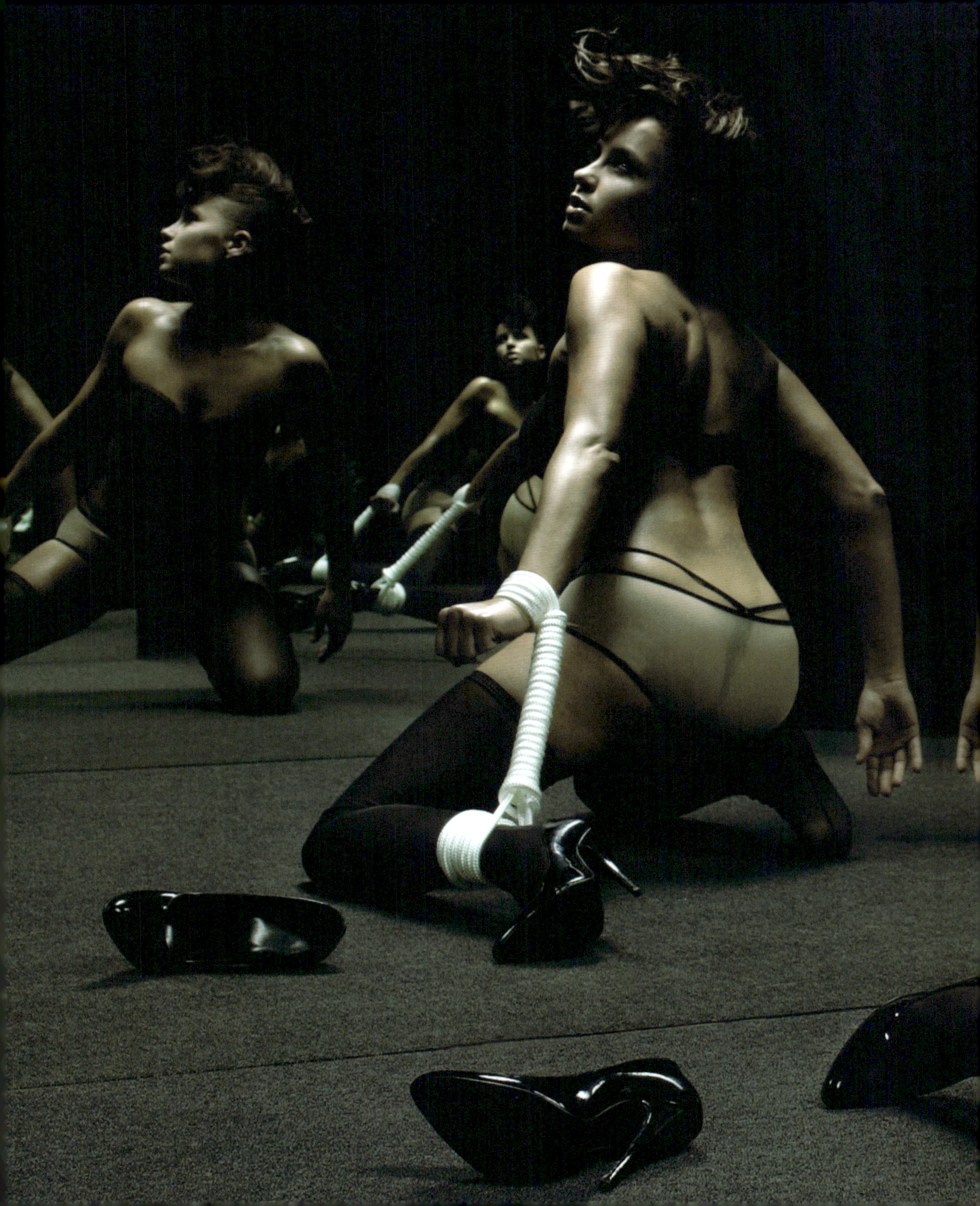

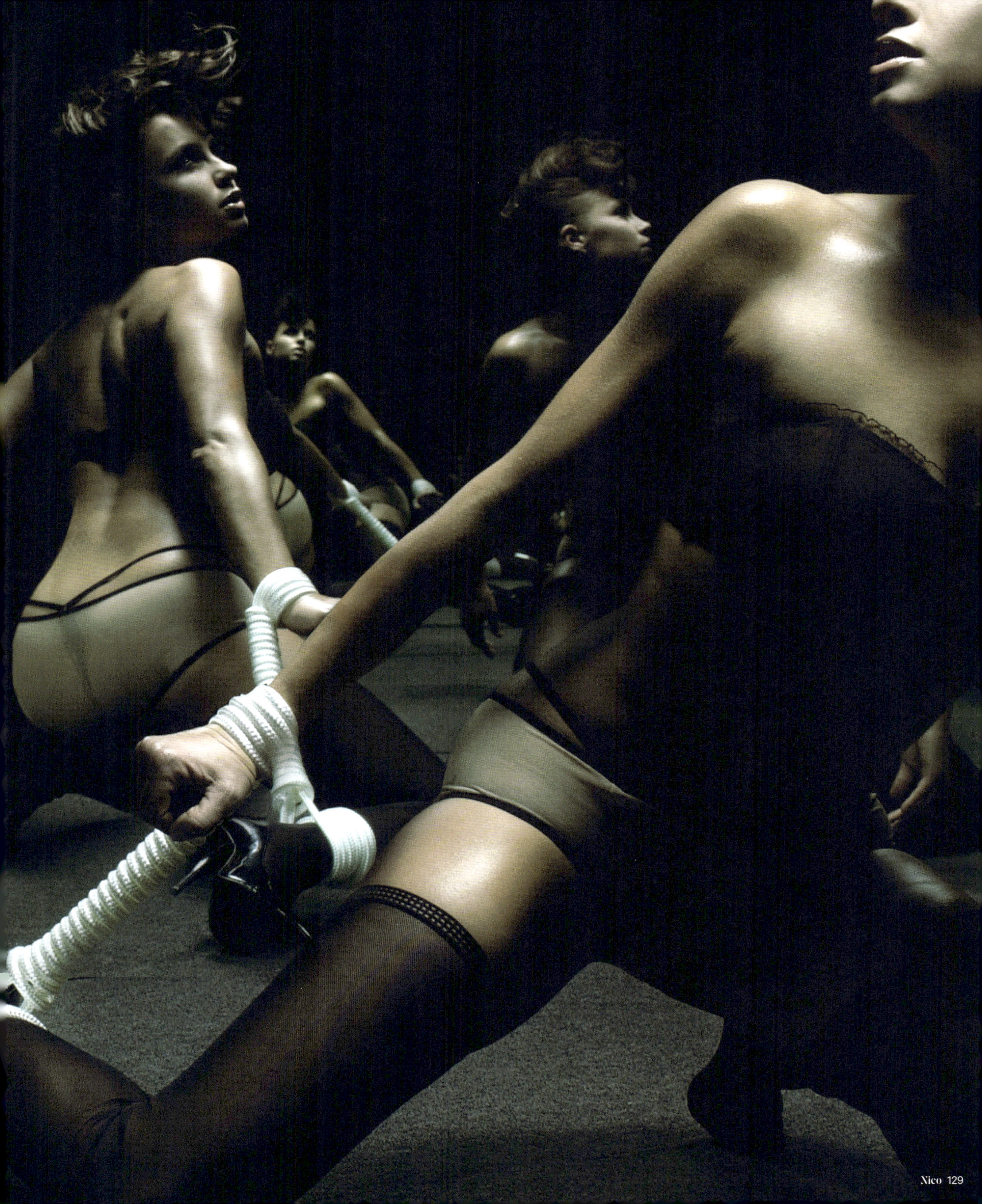

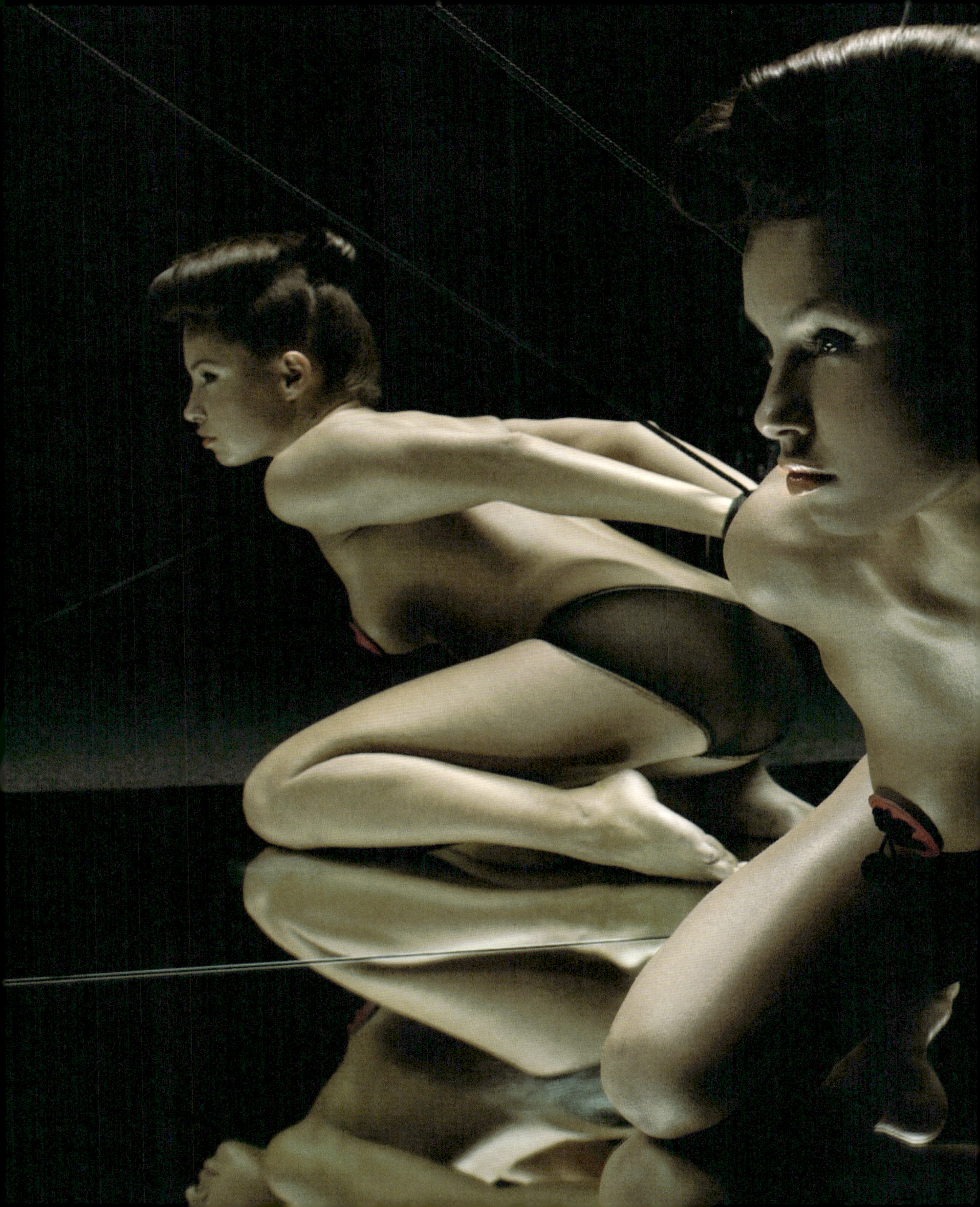

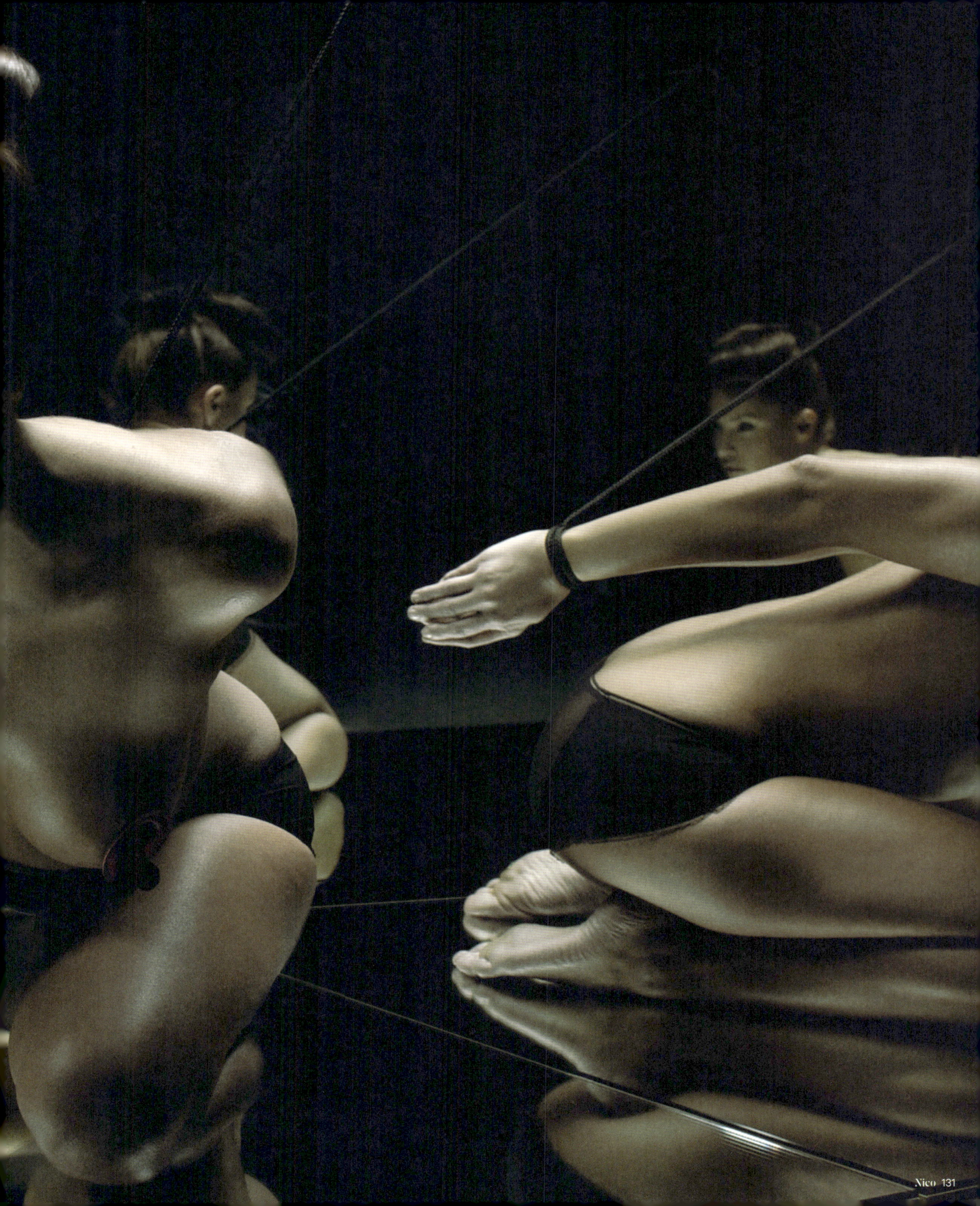

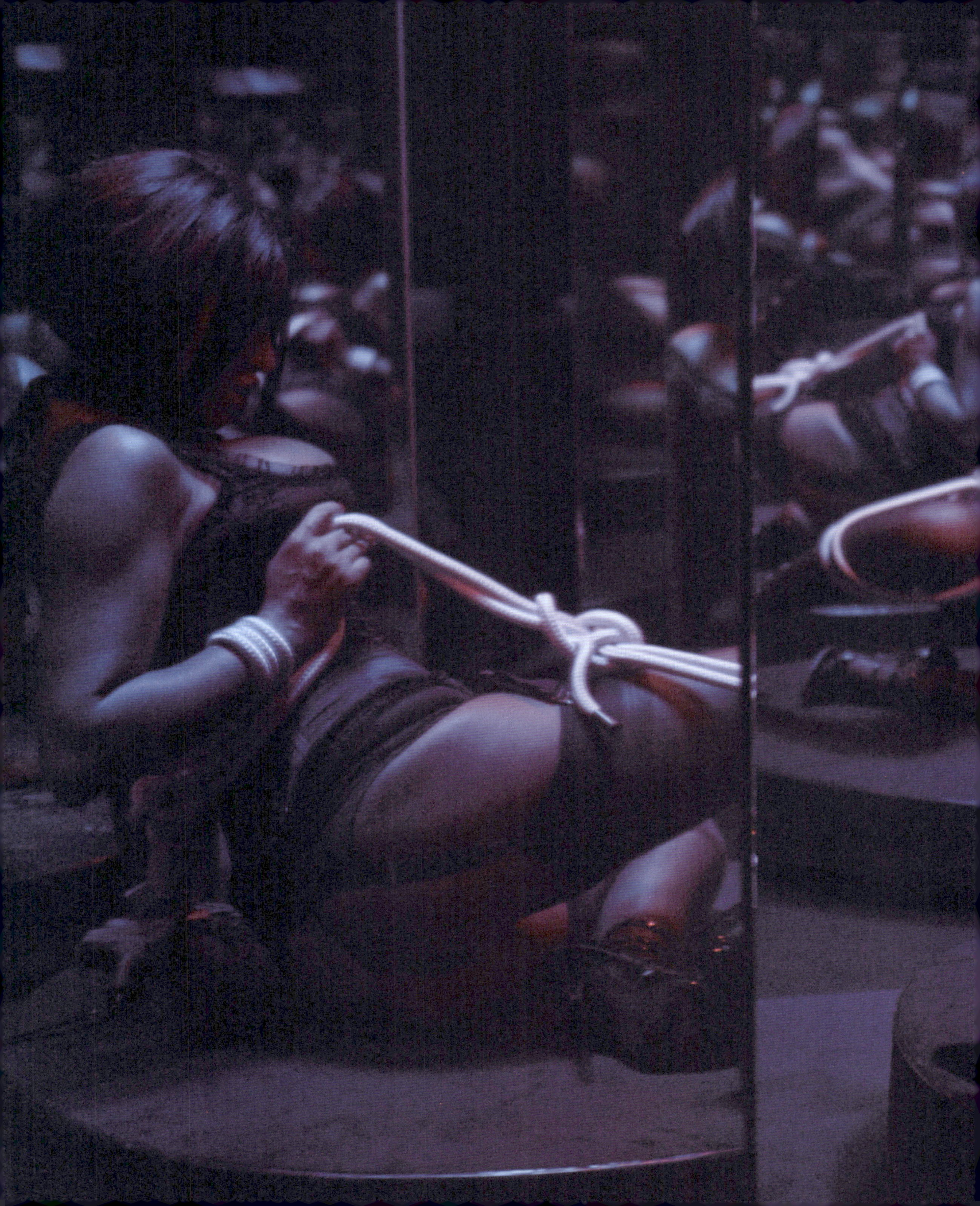

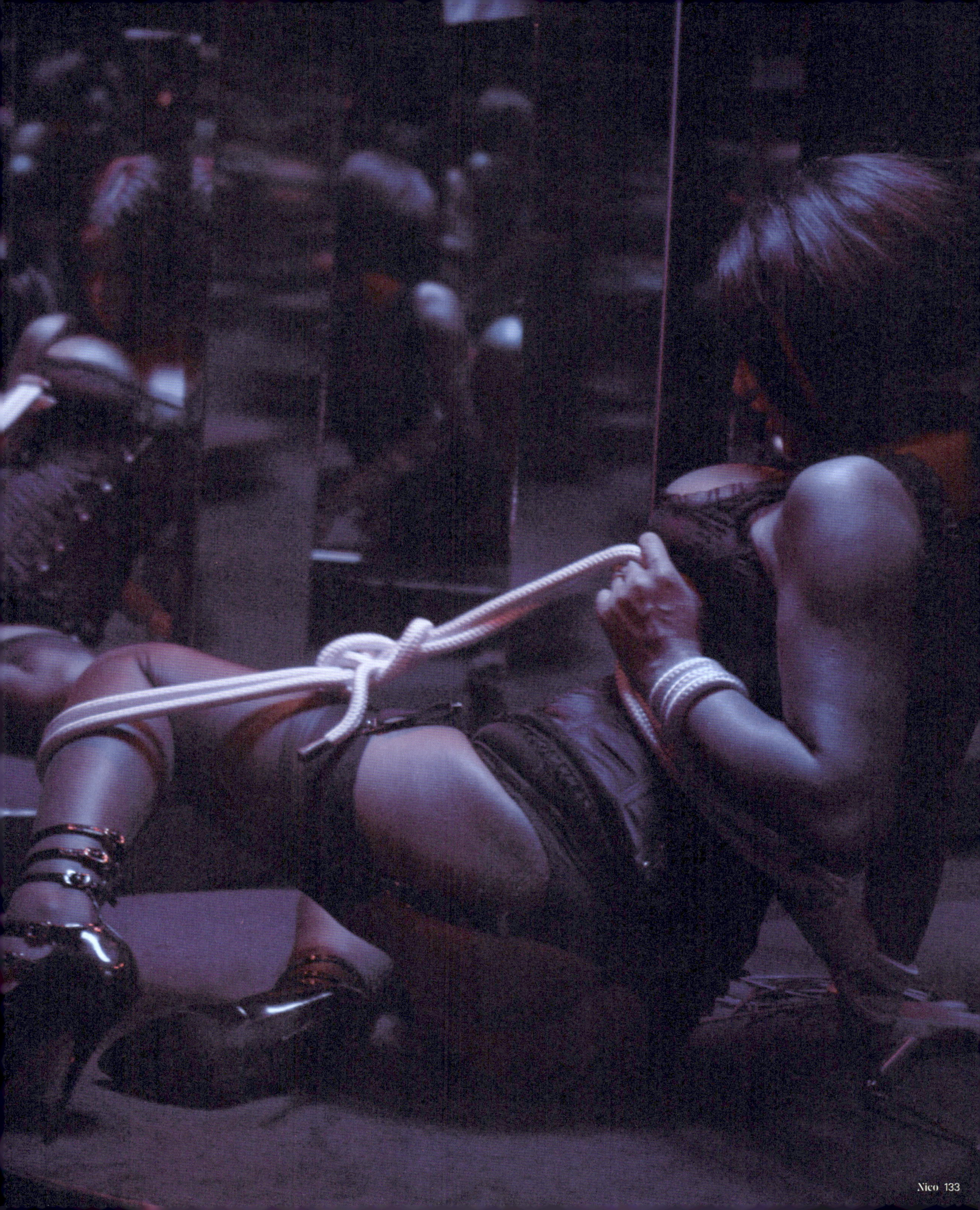

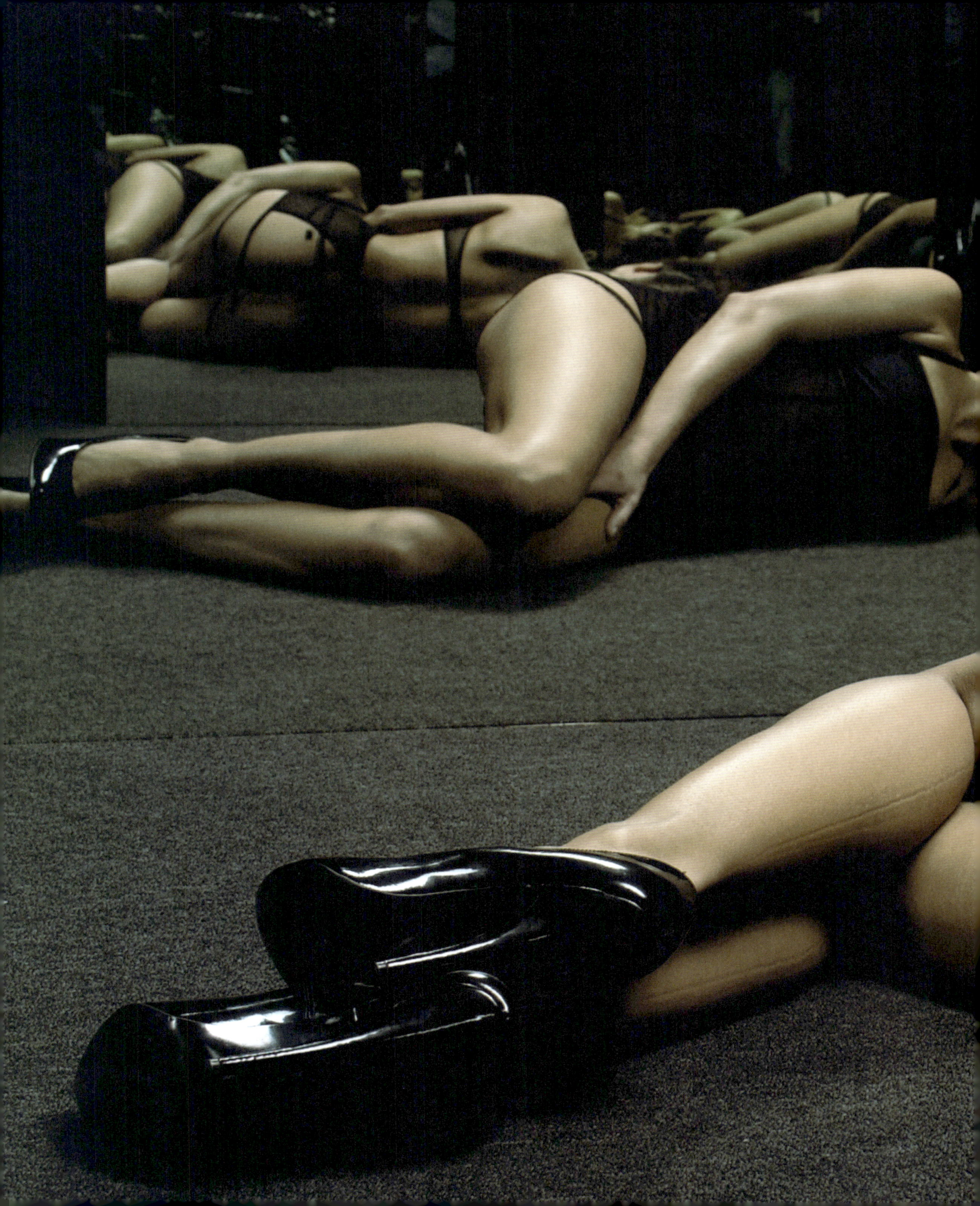

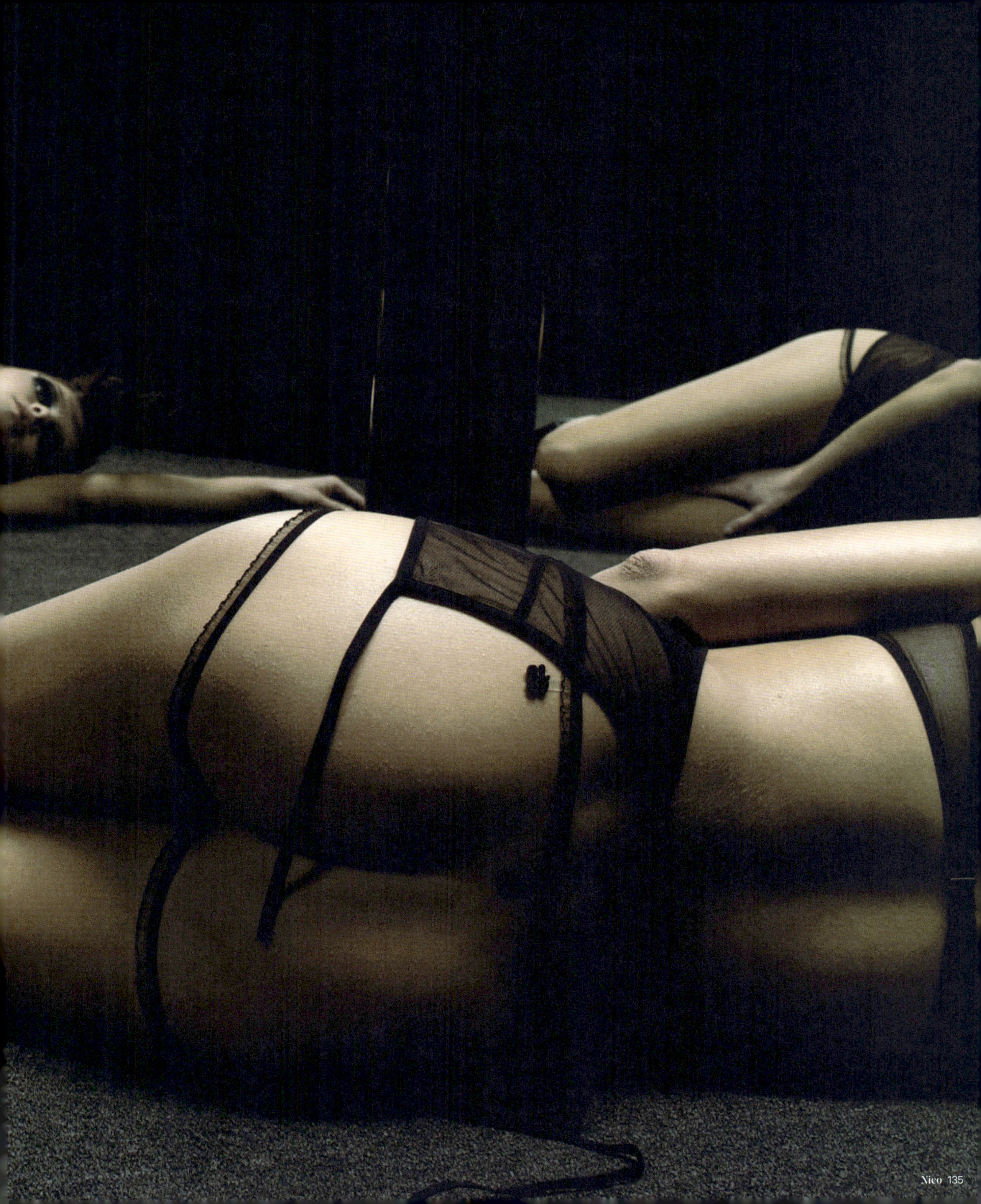

EDWIN TSE

Interview by Angelina A. Rafii

There seem to be quite a few recurring themes in your photography, apart from the lighting which is singular and beautiful. Can you talk to us about your obsessions and what's with the glasses? Do you have a teacher fetish?

I think glasses can transform a look so much, I suppose it's an accessory that you wear on your face. It's very noticeable unlike a bracelet, ring or necklace. There is just something about glasses that can give you a whole different personality. I think subconsciously I have a thing for cute nerdy girls, so maybe that has something to do with that too! There's something so irresistible about a smart woman!

A lot of the women you photograph have that "girl-next-door" quality. Do you exclusively work with models or are some shoots born out of random encounters?

I do like the girl-next-door look a lot. I shoot mostly with models, and sometimes with "regular people" as well. I do get asked by some girls randomly to take pictures with me because they like my work. I think there is something appealing and attractive about seeing the girl-next-door in the beautiful and sexy manner in which I try to portray them, as opposed to the sexy bombshell that is unattainable and more of a fantasy.

Sometimes, it is hard to tell when one thing begins and the other ends, so in your opinion what sets these concepts apart: eroticism, sensuality, nudes and pornography?

It's a good question, I suppose that it's really up to the viewer. More conservative views on sexuality can view everything as pornography. People with a more liberal view on that are a bit more open-minded and can see the difference. Someone's take on it can be totally different from mine, but I think the difference between eroticism/sensuality vs. pornography is that there is a real beauty in the former versus the latter. I think in pornography everything is all out there and it is what it is. The meaning is just about sex, something raw and straight to the point. I think with sensuality/eroticism it is often eluding to make you think more about it and it causes the viewer to see it and digest it and think about it more. There are often some underlying themes whereas pornography is just about sex and nothing else. Pornography also these days seems more fake and unrealistic. A lot of real women don't look like that- completely unreal proportions with no plastic surgery. With sensuality and eroticism I think both women and men can appreciate it. I often find that women really like a lot of my "sexier" work.

What do you think are some of the clichés linked to photography and eroticism and how do you avoid falling into them?

I don't really try to focus on what is going on out there, even if there are clichés. I try to really just focus on what I do and what feels right to me. I always photograph my subjects in a respectful and beautiful manner.

What is your ultimate fantasy?

Another good question! I suppose the best answer is to keep getting better and keep photographing the things I like and to be happy.

Melissa

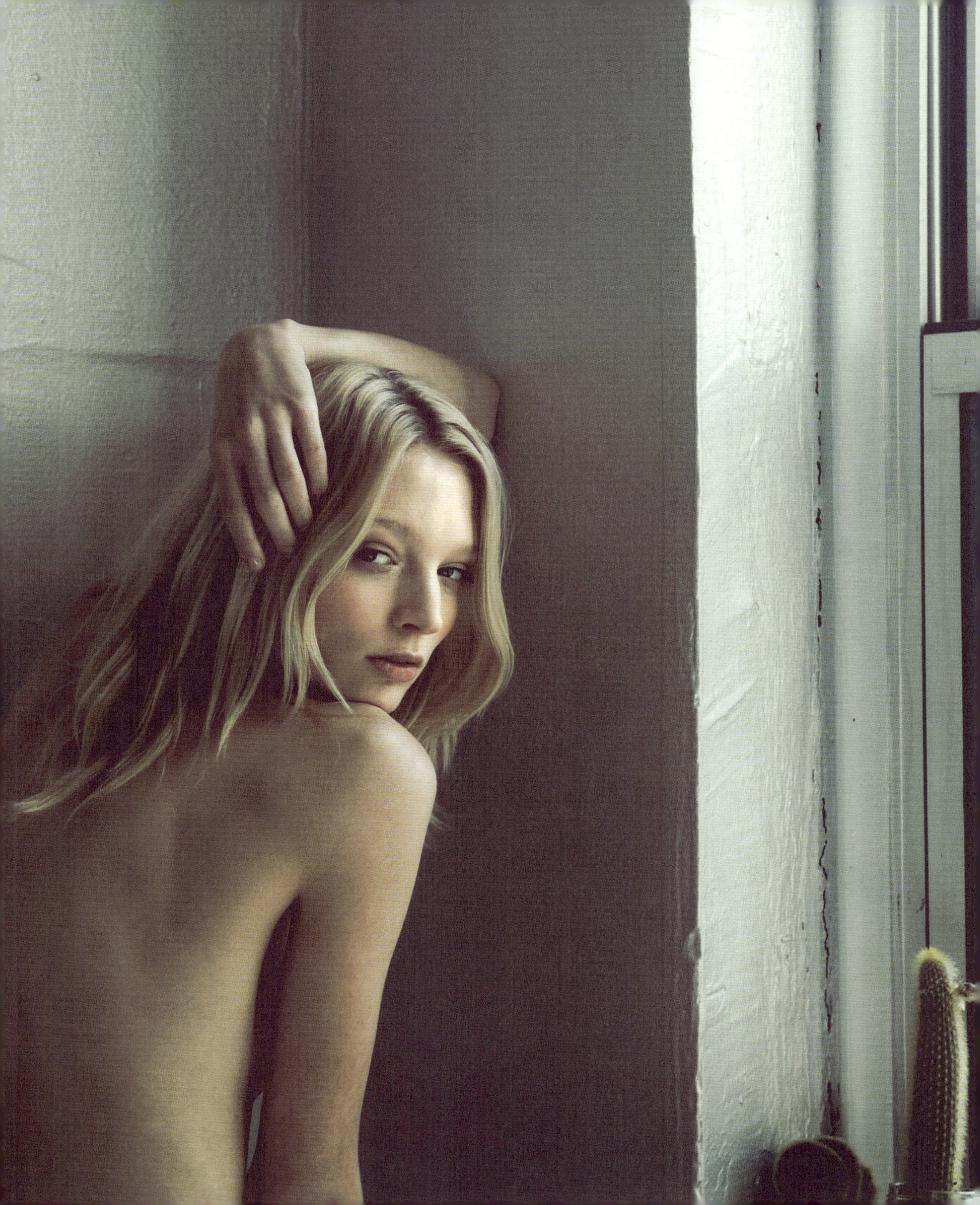

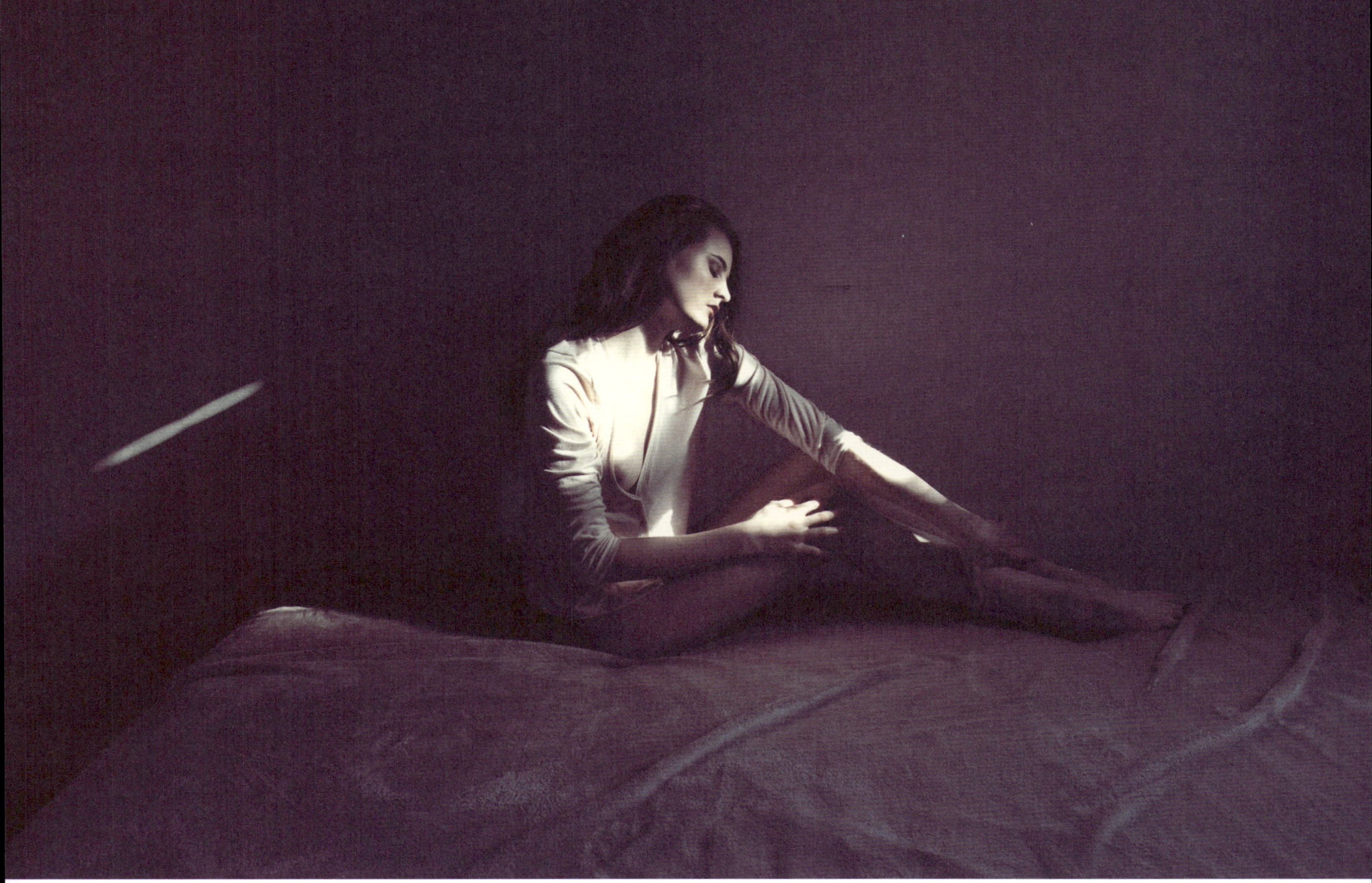

Siri

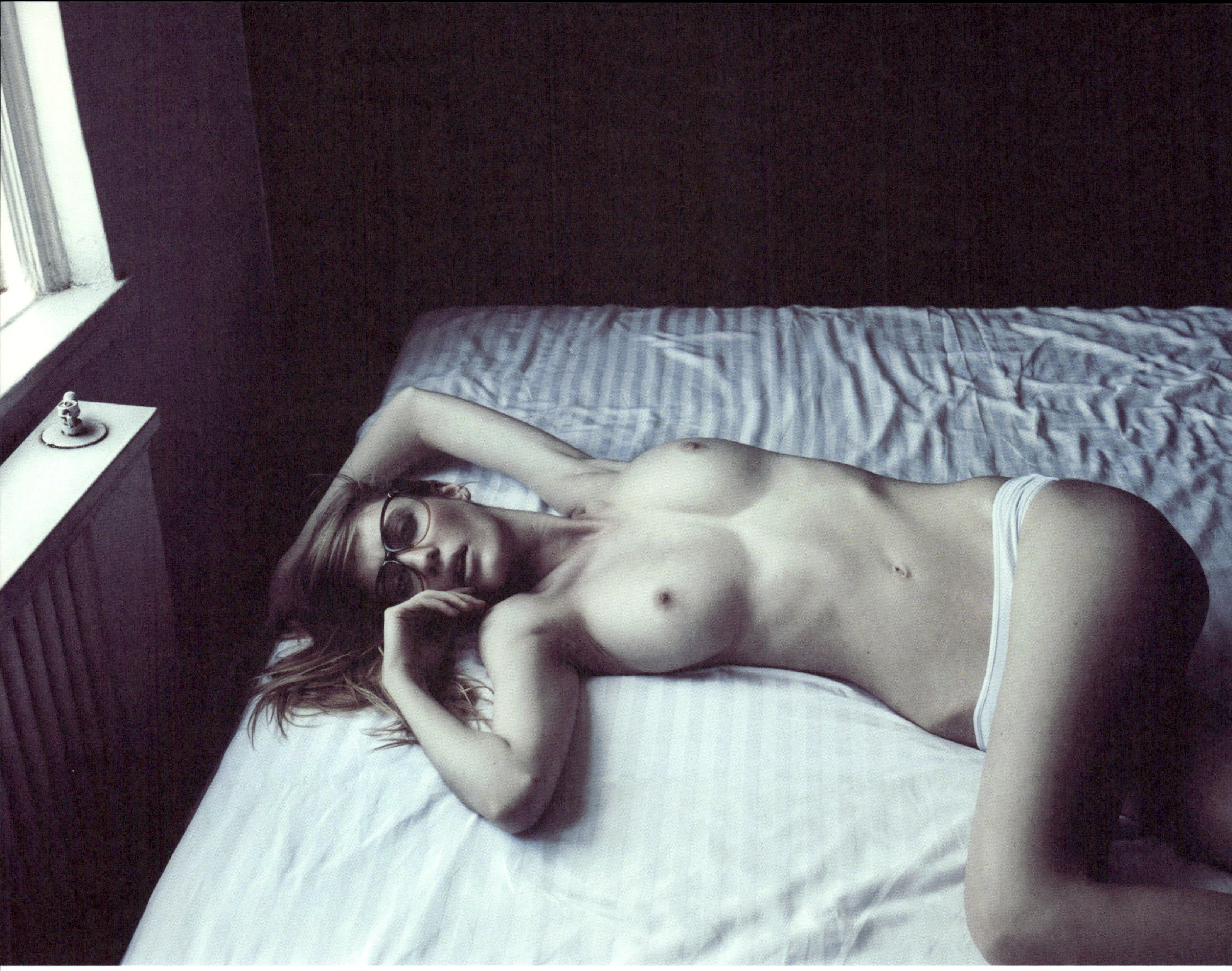

Enya

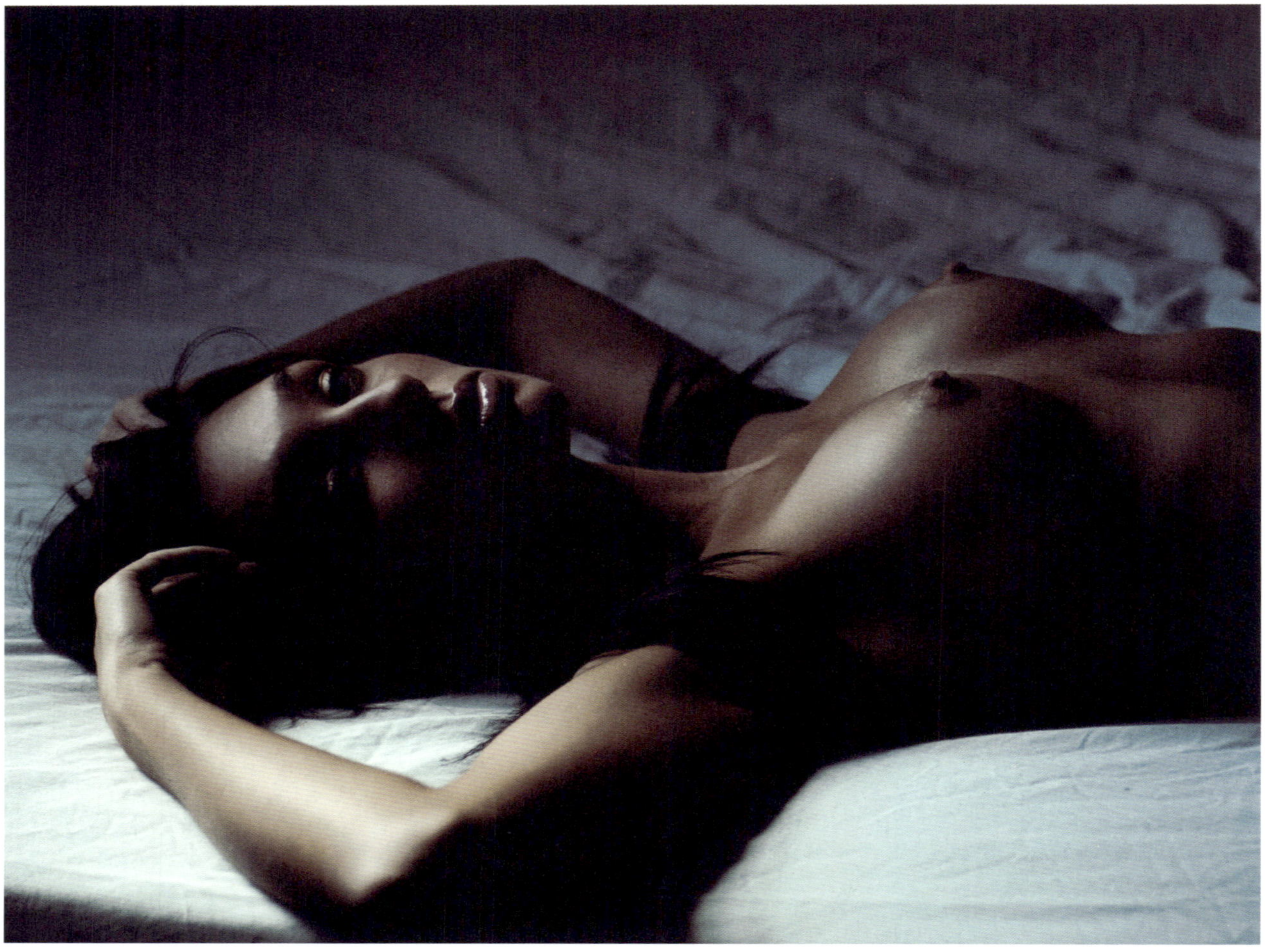

Erin

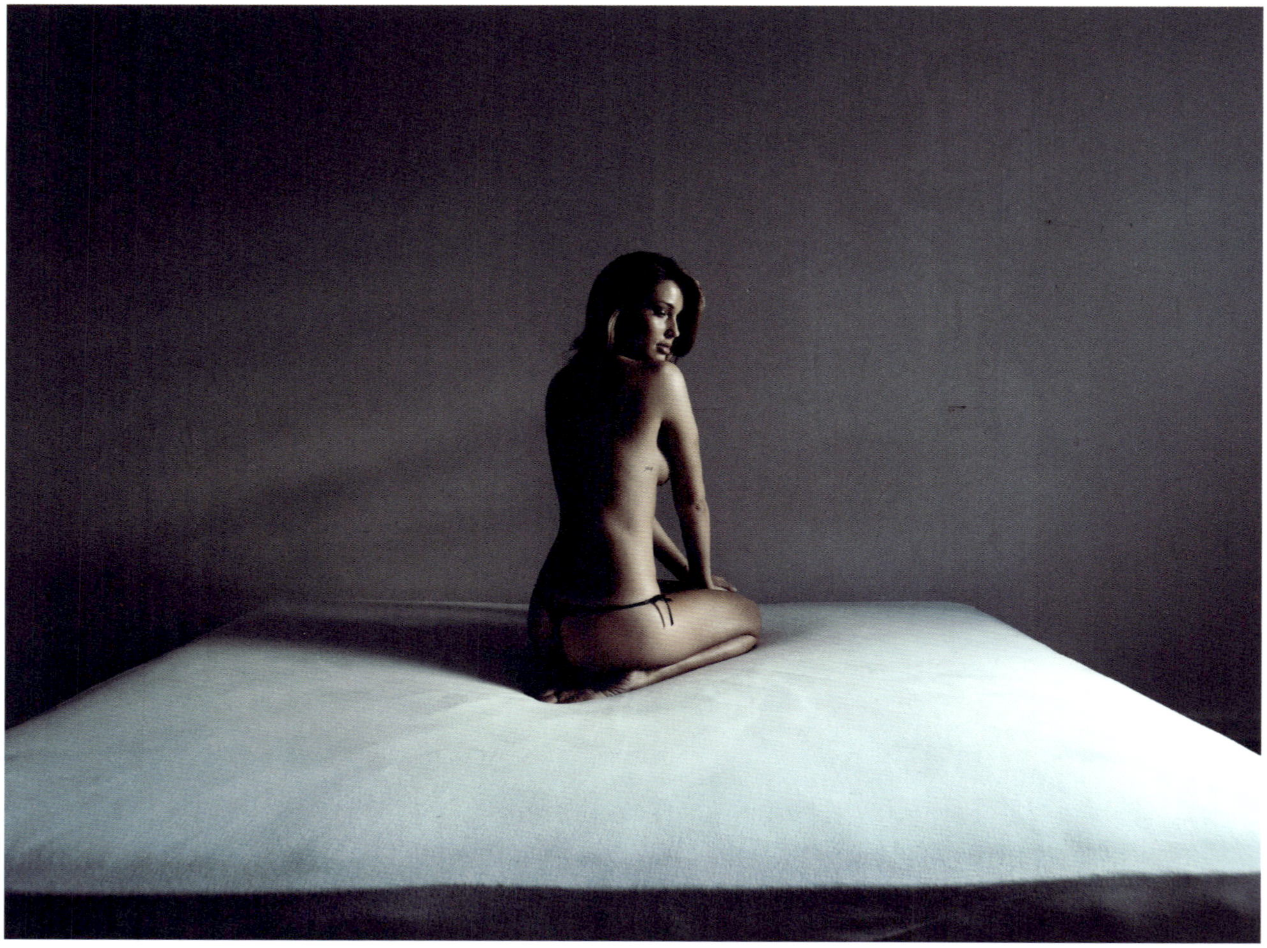

Simon

Juliet

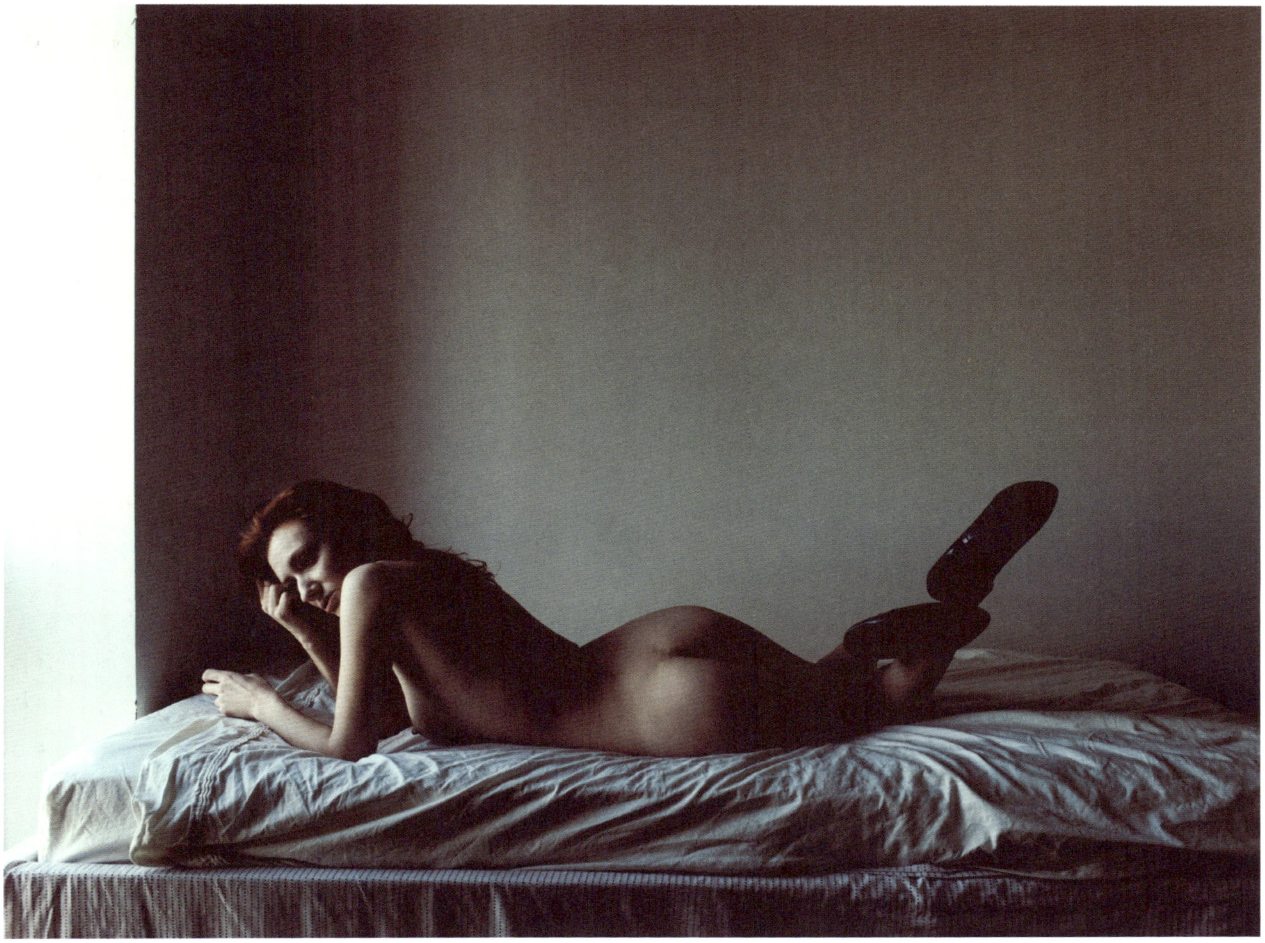

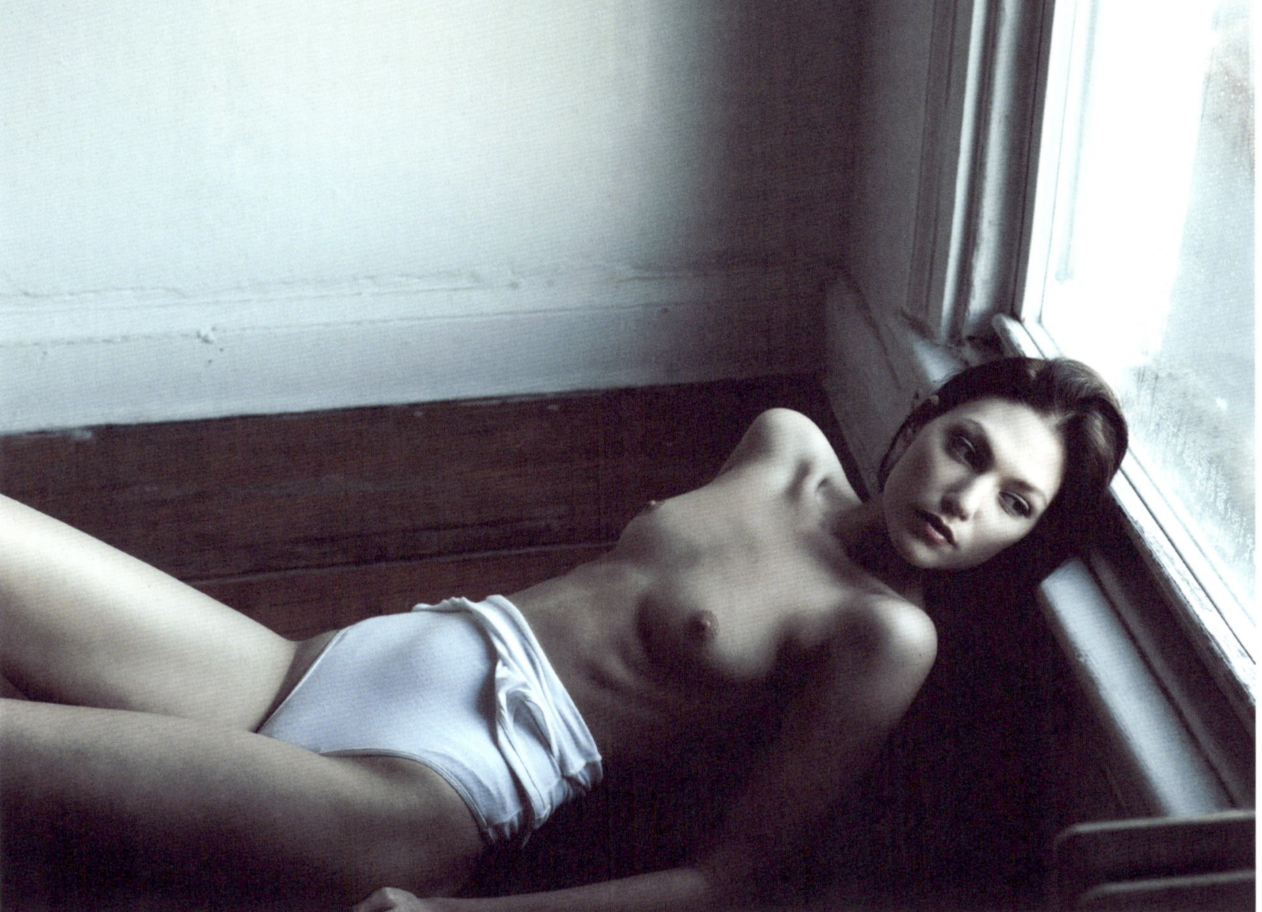

Mikaela

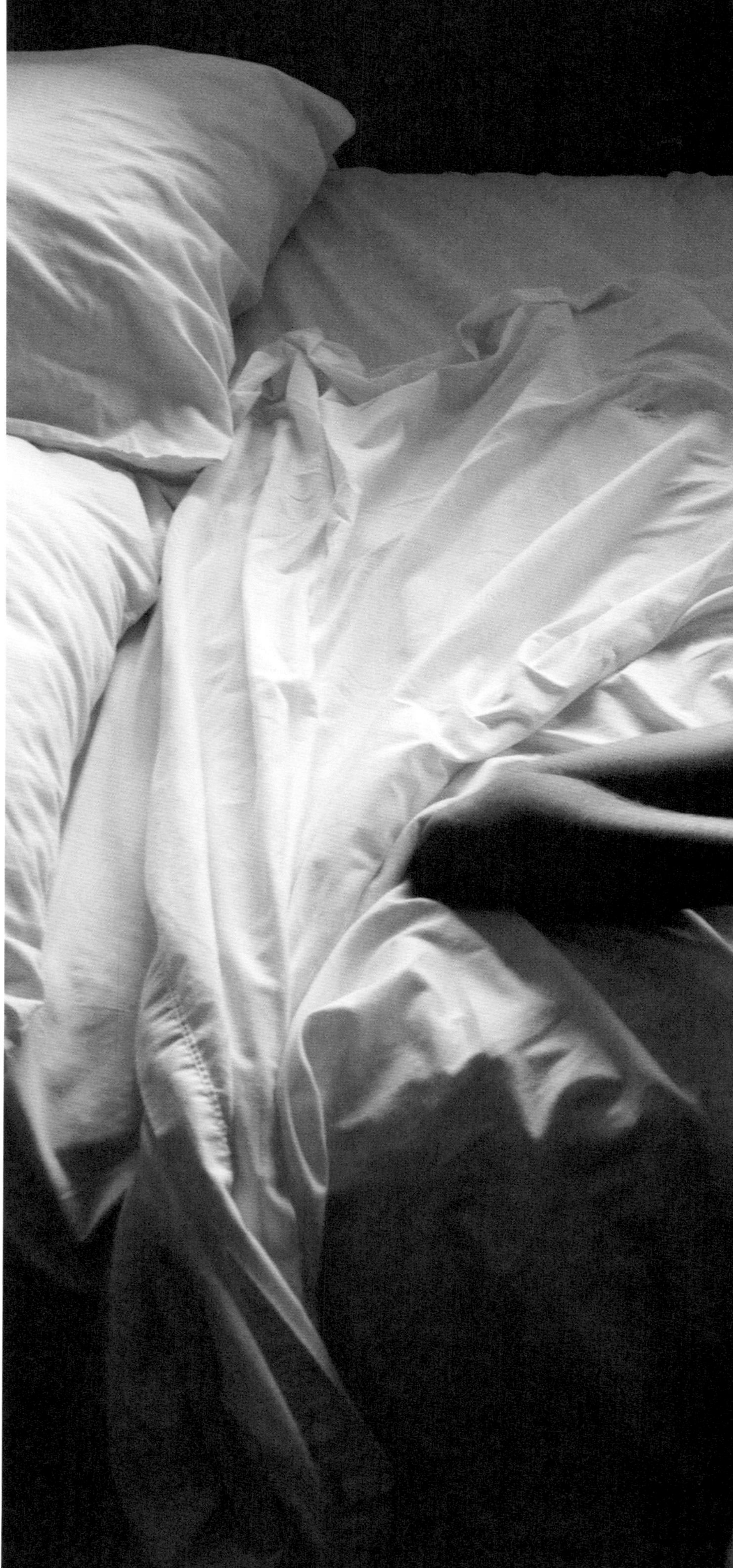

Barbara }

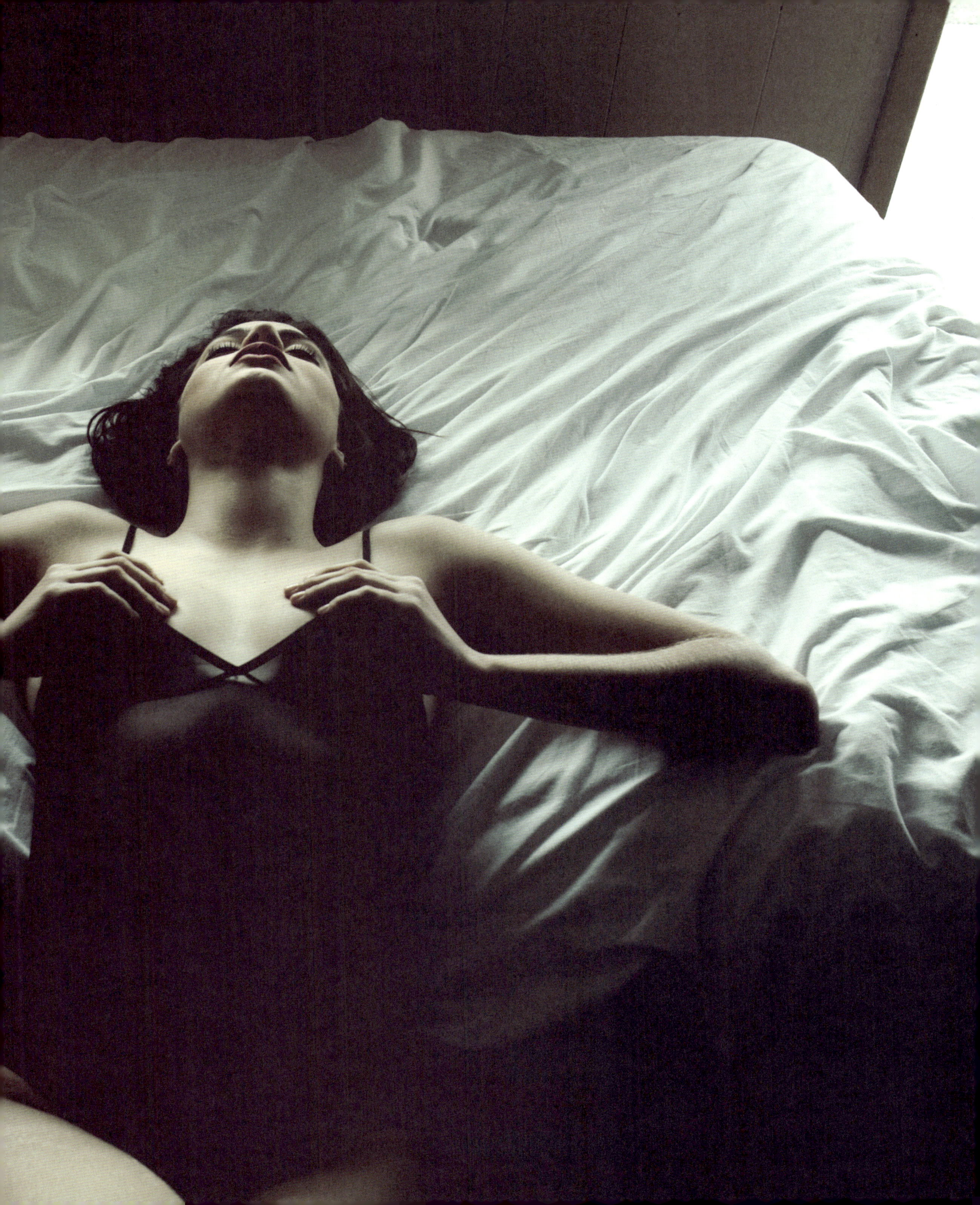

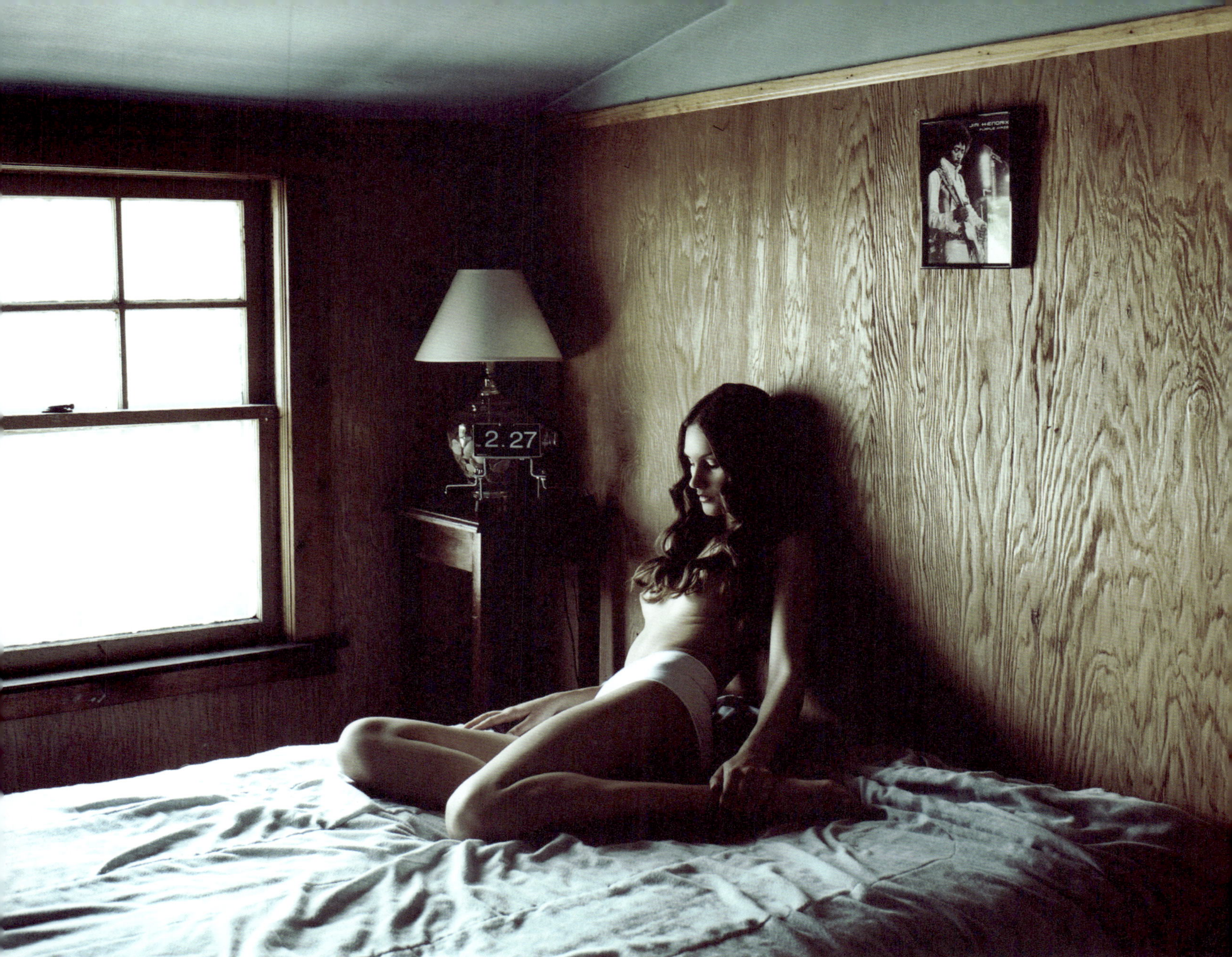
Ana

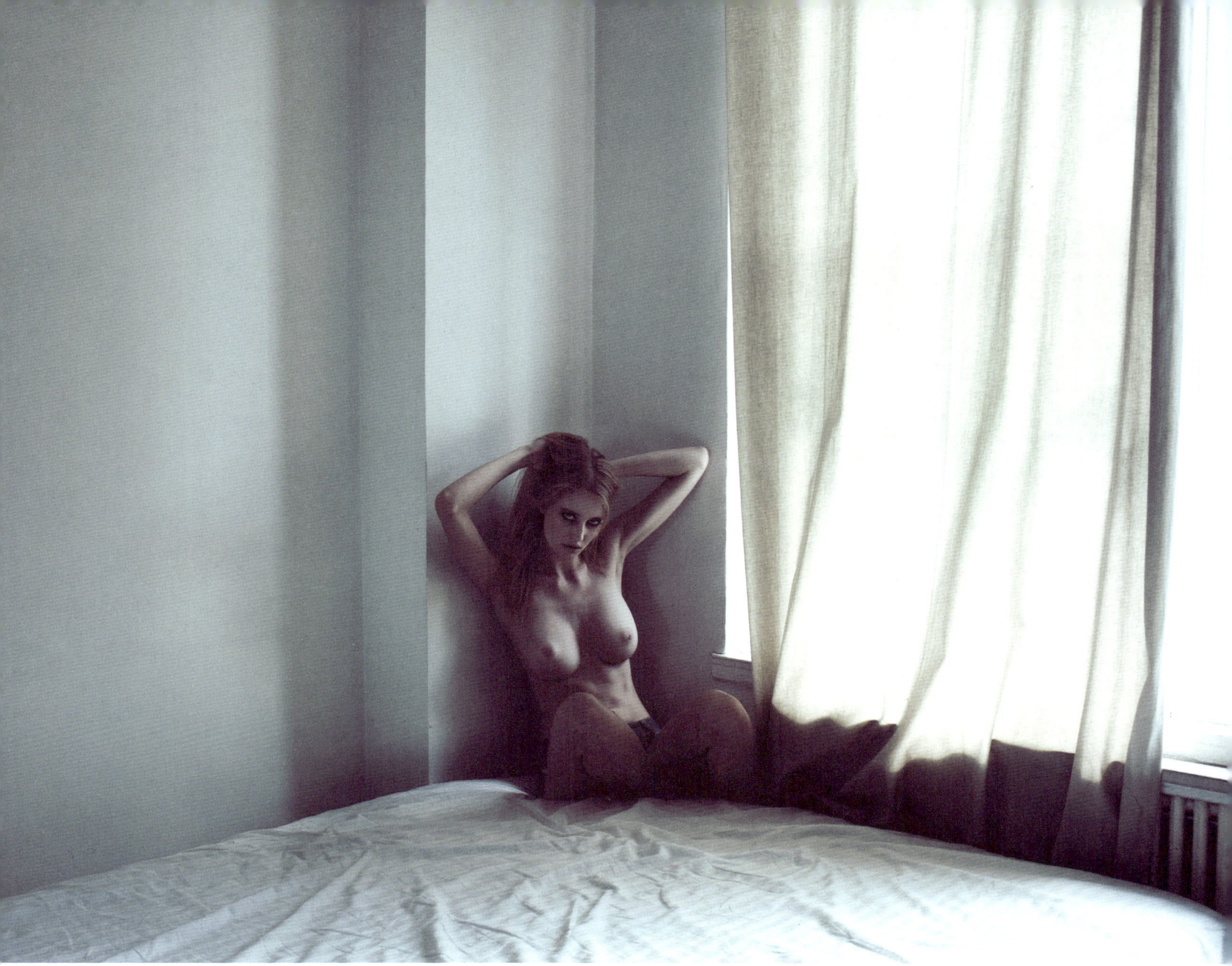

Enya

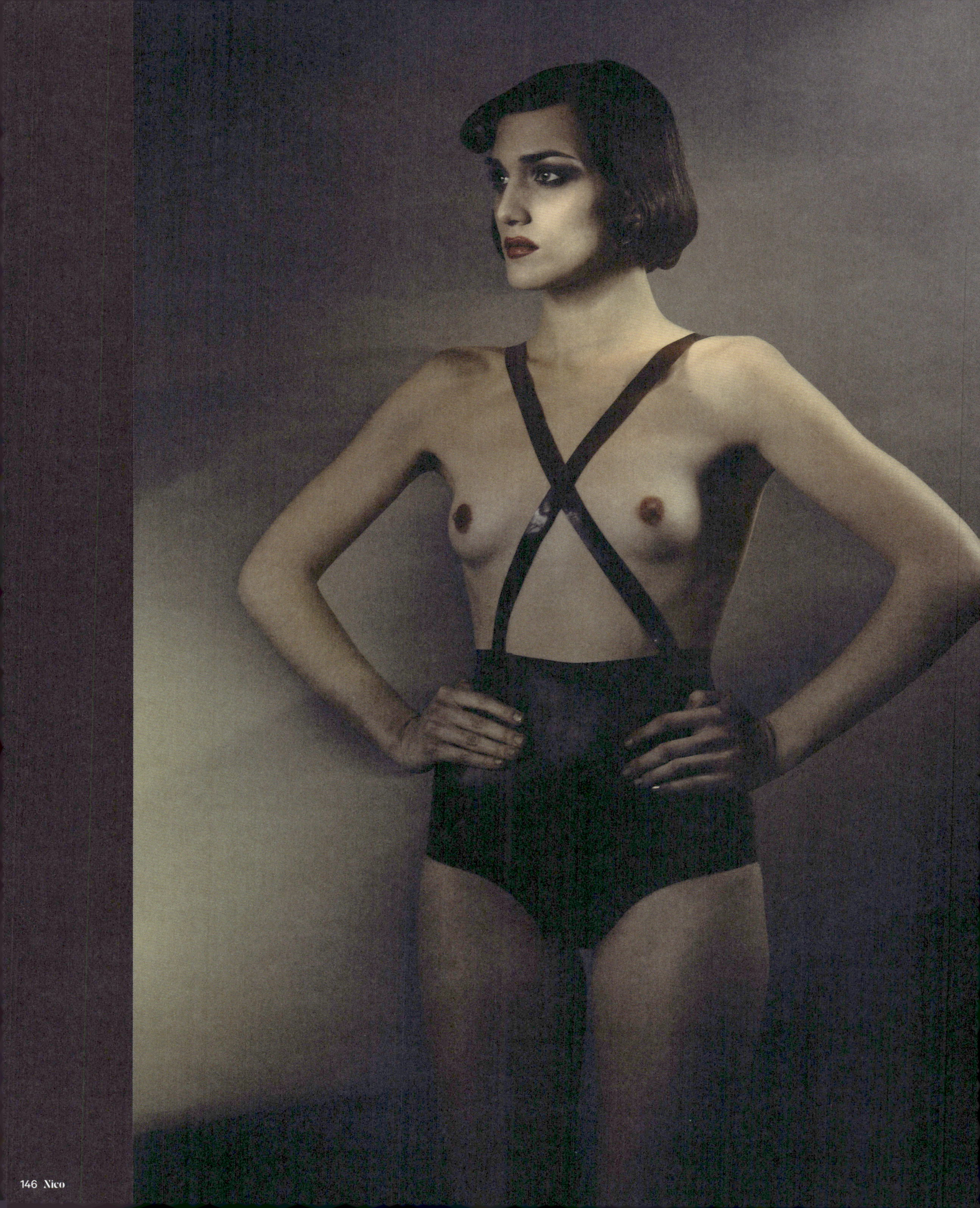

PHAEDRA BRODY

Interview by Angelina A. Rafii

Some photography is firmly grounded in reality. It is raw, sometimes ugly. When looking at your images, however, one has the impression of stepping right in the middle of a tale. The tone, the atmosphere, the mise-en-scène suggest something fantastical. What is it you are trying to share with the world around you and has your photography always been like this?

I started out photographing reality very much as it is, and even harsher at times. But then, as I explored lighting, and techniques, I moved towards a more personal, imaginary world, creating, rather than documenting reality. Offering to myself, and I suppose, to those who look at my photos, a refuge from actuality. Perhaps suffering from a form of Peter Panism, where I don't want to face the rawness of reality, and I wish tales were the truth!

Photographing nudes can be a slippery slope sometimes. It may just be a piece of exposed flesh; it may be highly sensual and playful, sometimes pornographic. What is it that makes the difference in your opinion?

Nudity for me is complete innocence. I feel a nude is not pornographic unless there is a very clear intention, to do pornography, i.e, an action from the part of the model (an expression, a gesture), or from the photographer, something "added" purposefully. However, I think pornography is in the eye of the beholder, so it is difficult to define. I believe what some could call pornography can at times be really strong and beautiful, especially if it conveys an emotion.

When looking at this particular work the women, on the one hand exude empowerment and sensuality, while on the other they seem both vulnerable and sensual. What story are you trying to tell here and what is the process. Does it start with the girl or with an idea/mood?

I like to think every woman holds those two women within herself (with all the millions of variations in between), and in her intimacy, depending on her mood, the circumstance, what she is wearing or not wearing, and even the time of the month, she lets one or the other manifest itself. When I create an image, it starts off with my own mood, which transforms into an idea for a shoot, and I usually look for the girl who suits what I want to do. Being based in Paris, and having model agencies around me, makes this achievable. But at times, I have let myself be inspired by a woman, to do a particular style of shoot, and more often, during the shoot, I try to stay open to unexpected aspects of the model's personality, and to adapt to these, and take advantage of them, letting myself be inspired and stimulated, rather than imposing my initial vision.

What do you find most challenging in your work and what are some of the challenges you have set for yourself that you would like to achieve in the short-term?

When I work in fashion, I find it challenging to show clothes, convey emotion, and please a client all at once. On a more personal level, and more interestingly, I find it challenging to do a photo session, knowing that probably the best images will be accidents. And so to find oneself 'directing' a shoot, and at the same time, creating an accident-prone situation, at times even trying consciously to make something happen, it could be a lighting accident, or the model doing something spontaneous and unplanned, or showing an unexpected emotion, it could even be anger, that could make a shot more special than one had hoped.

Any upcoming projects?

To continue exploring, mostly. But also, more concretely, a series of portraits of Scottish characterful men in kilts, that will take me back to my roots, and temporarily, back to realism.

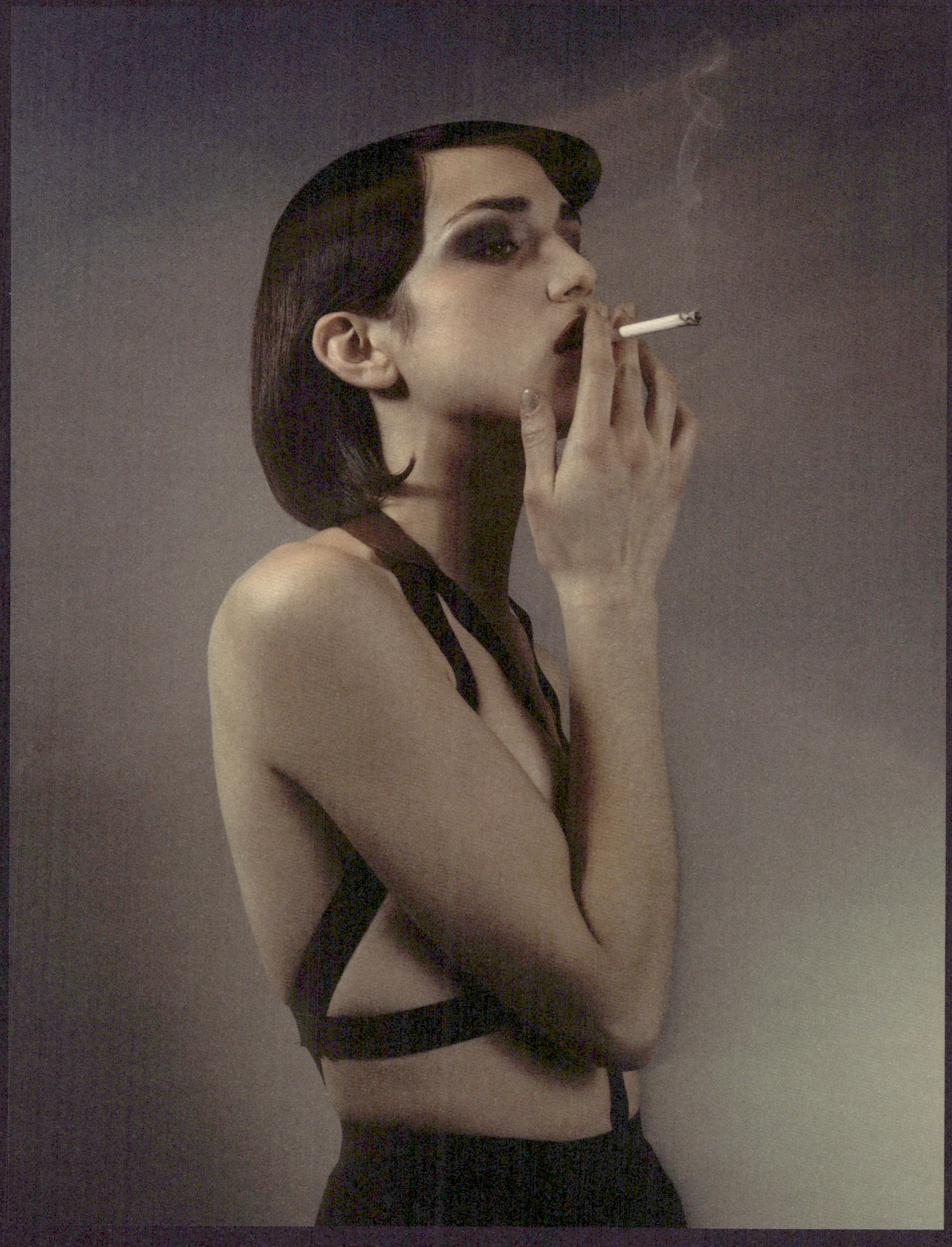

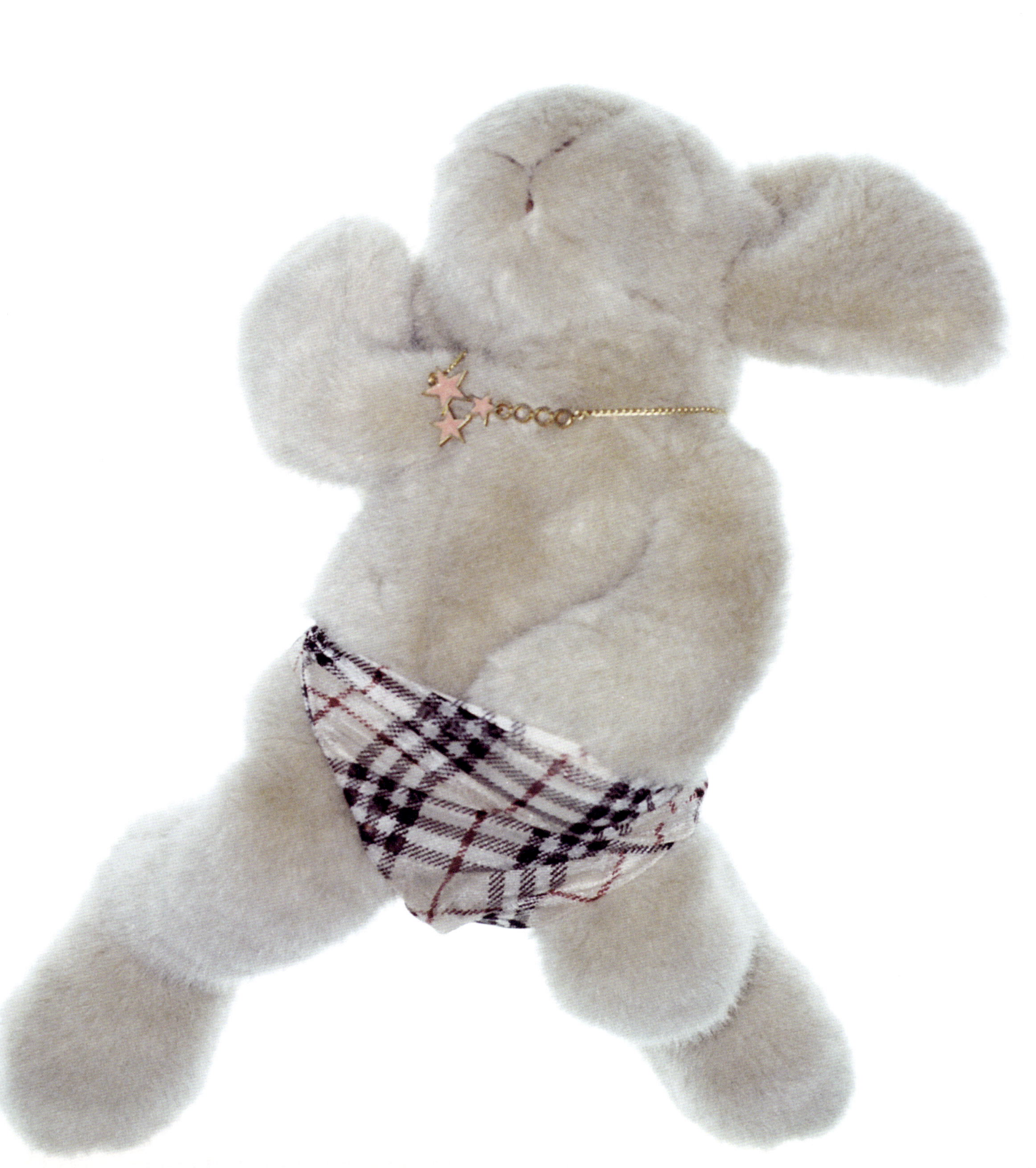

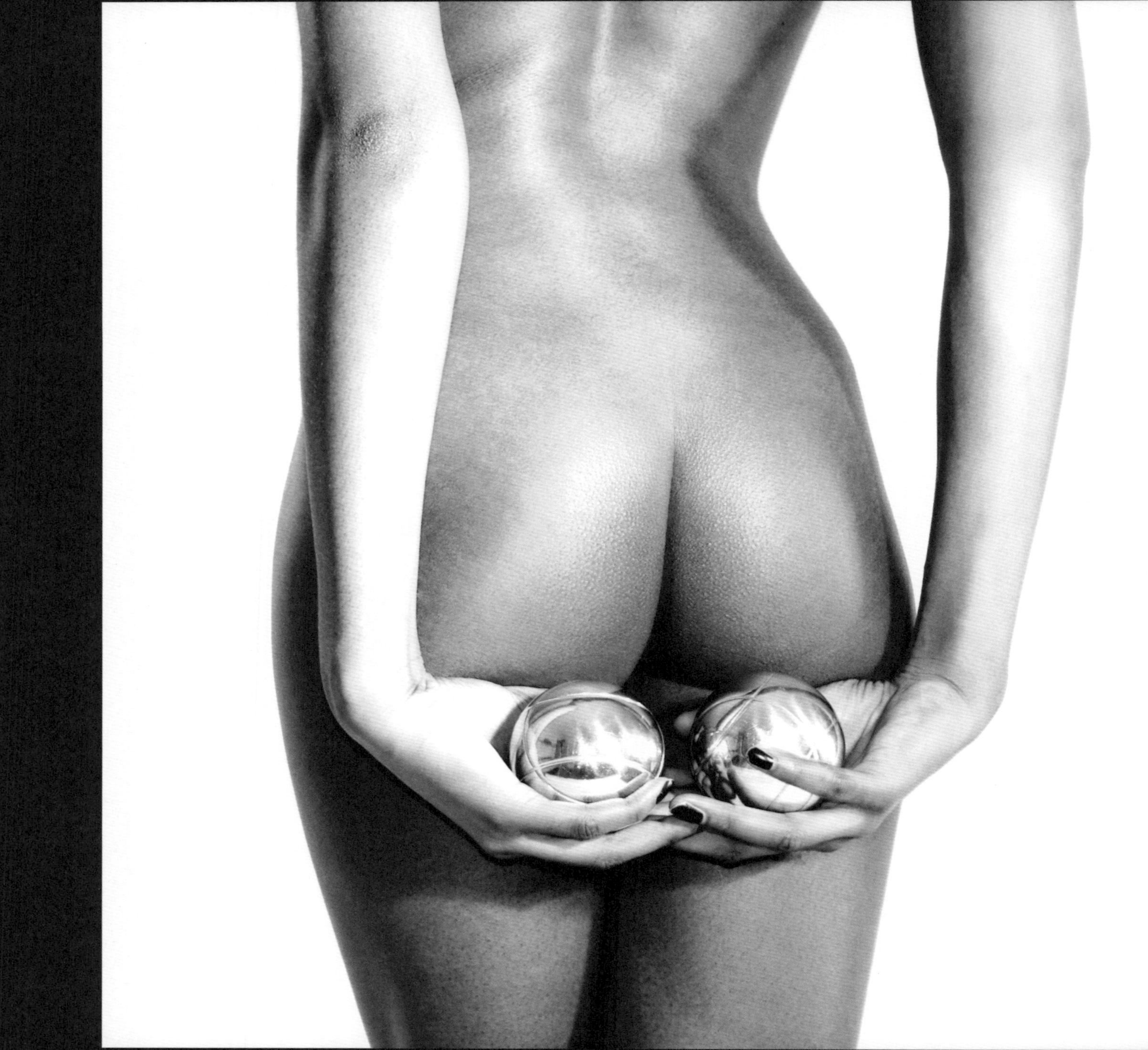

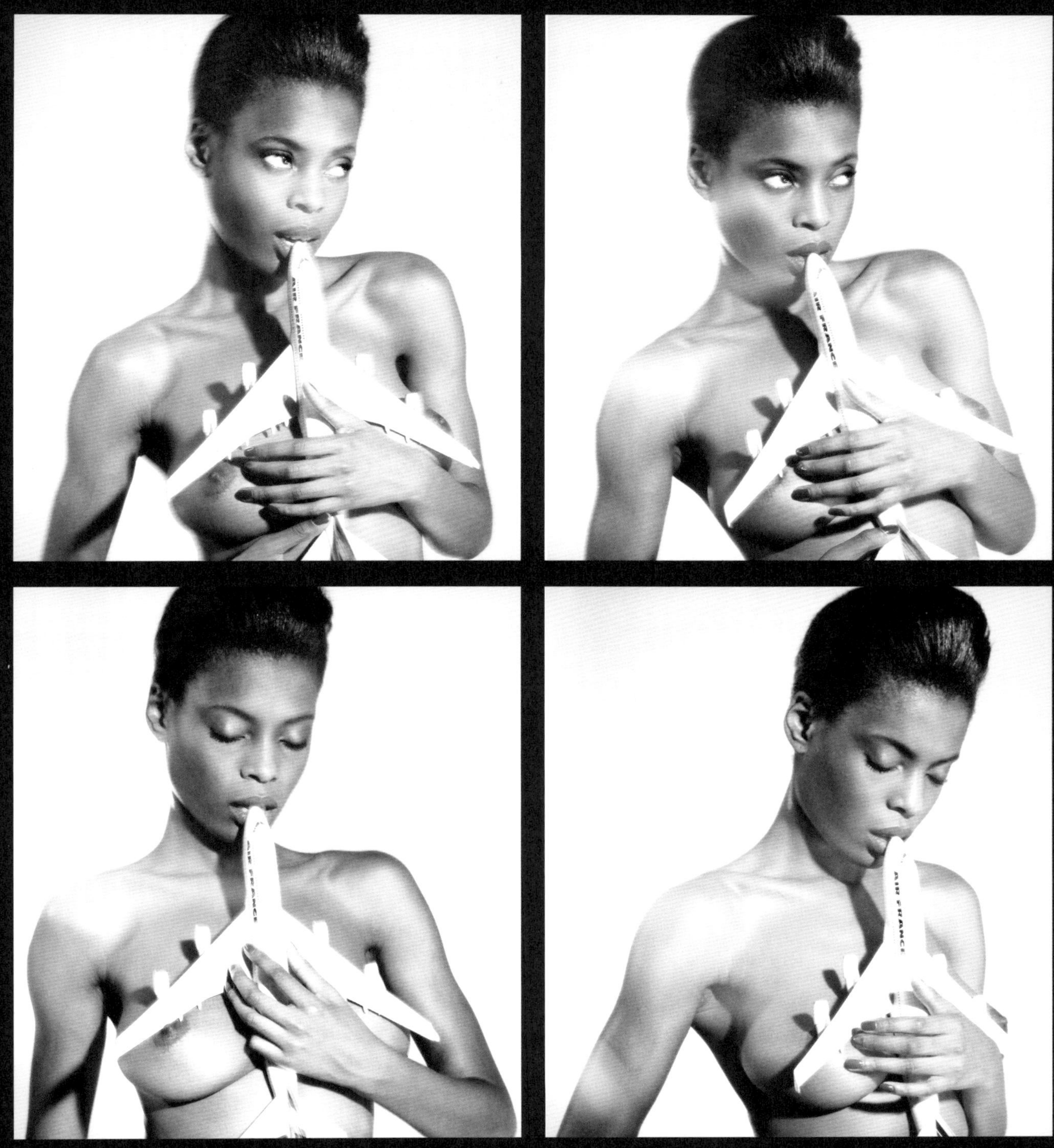

Nic

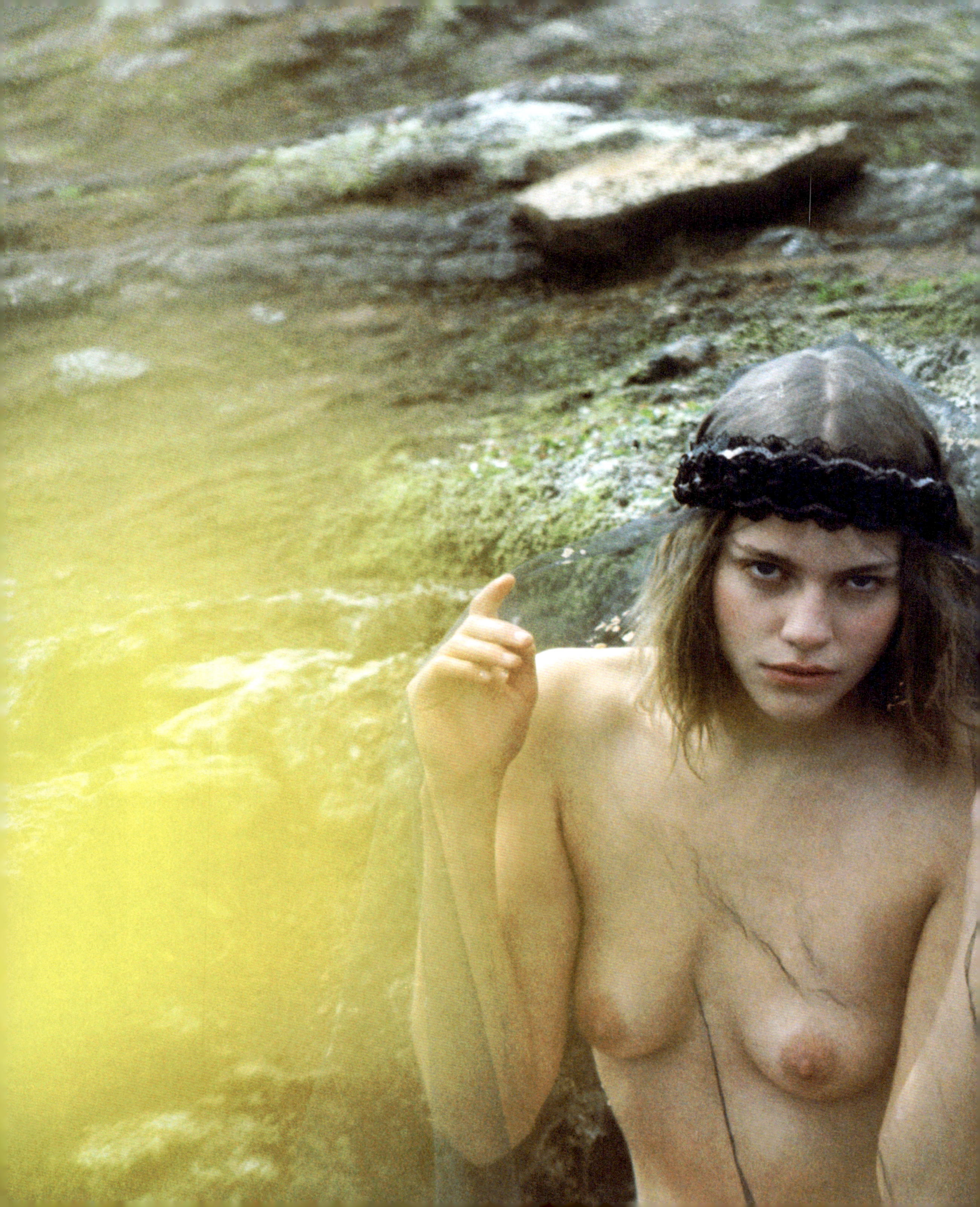

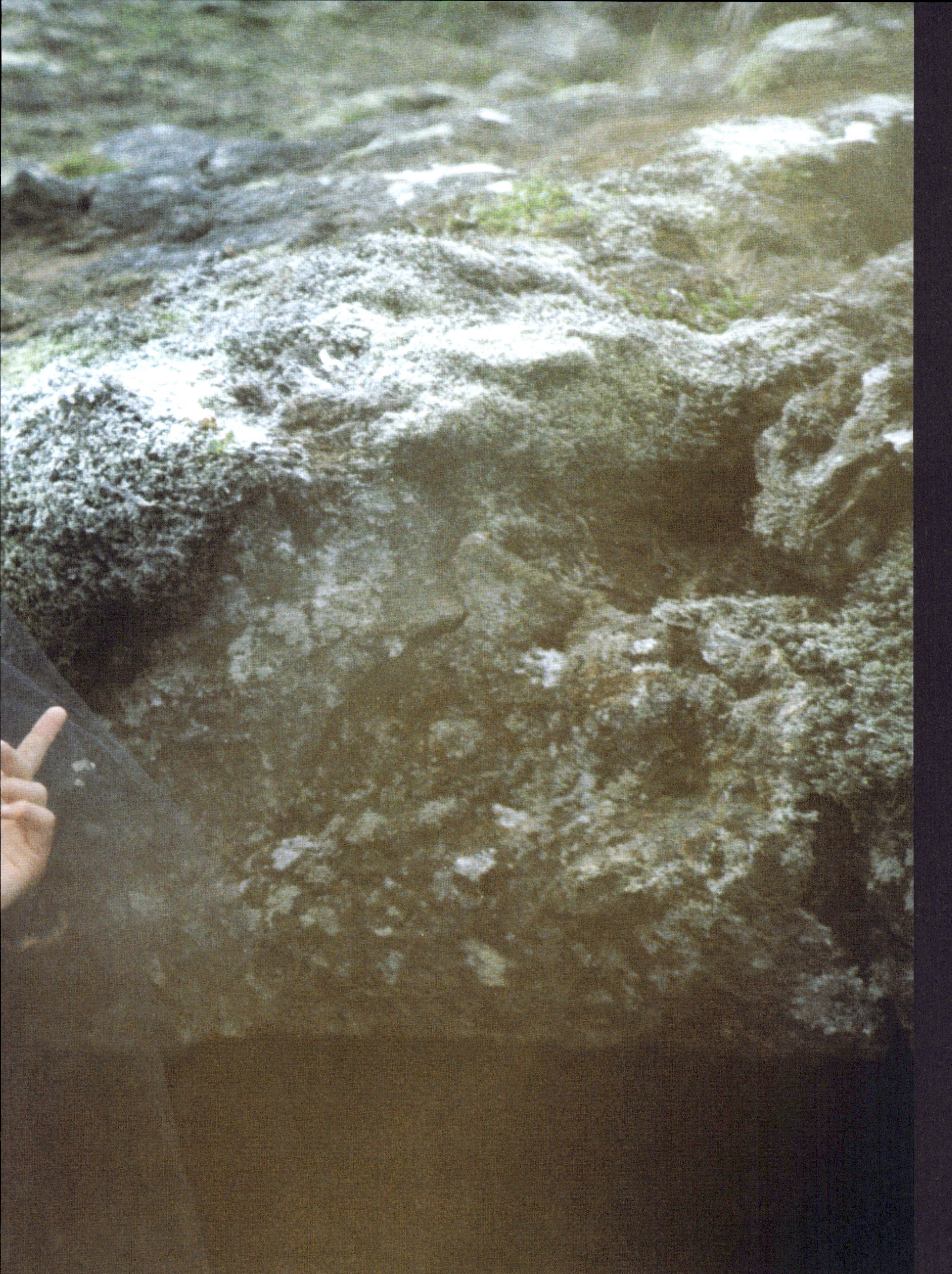

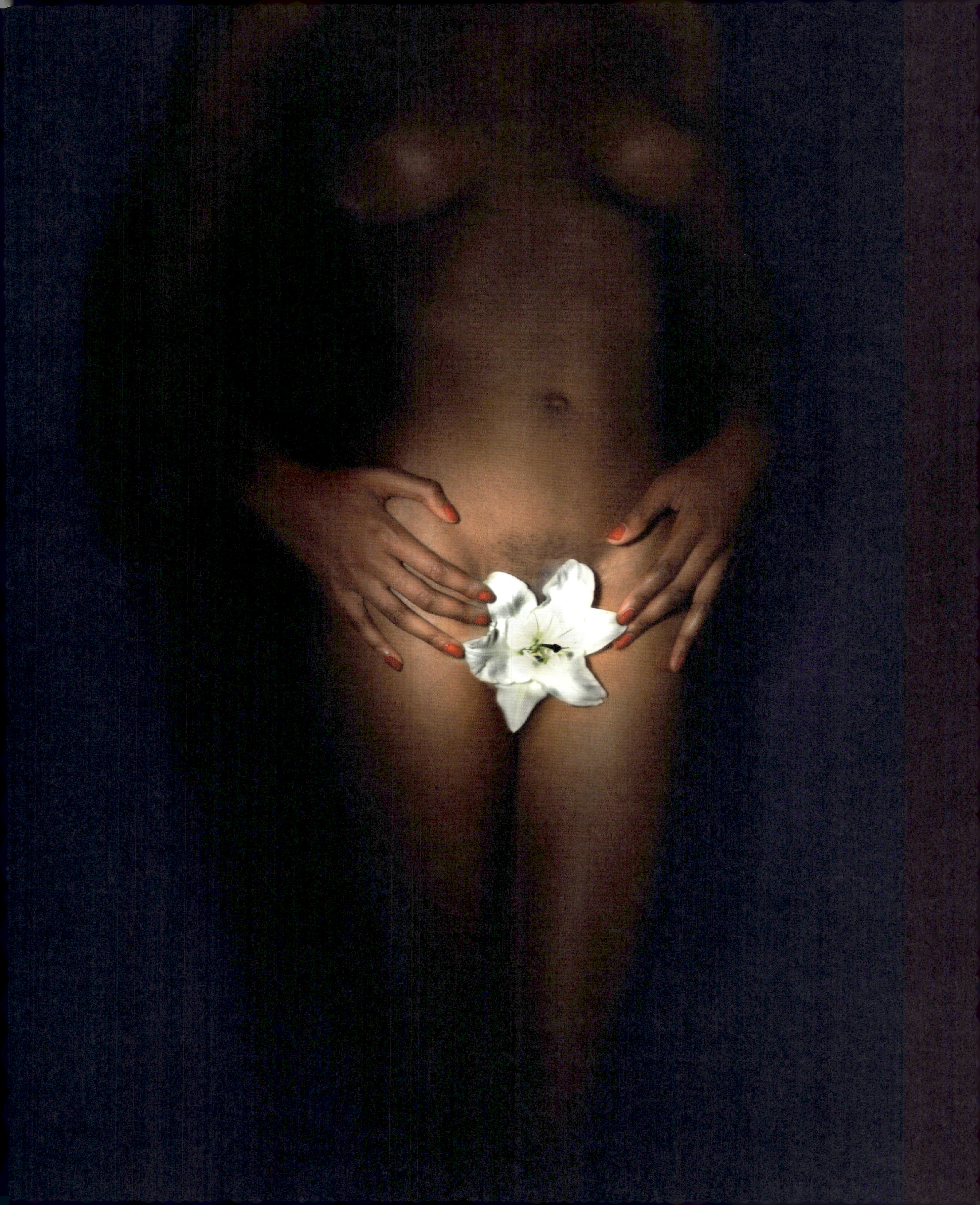

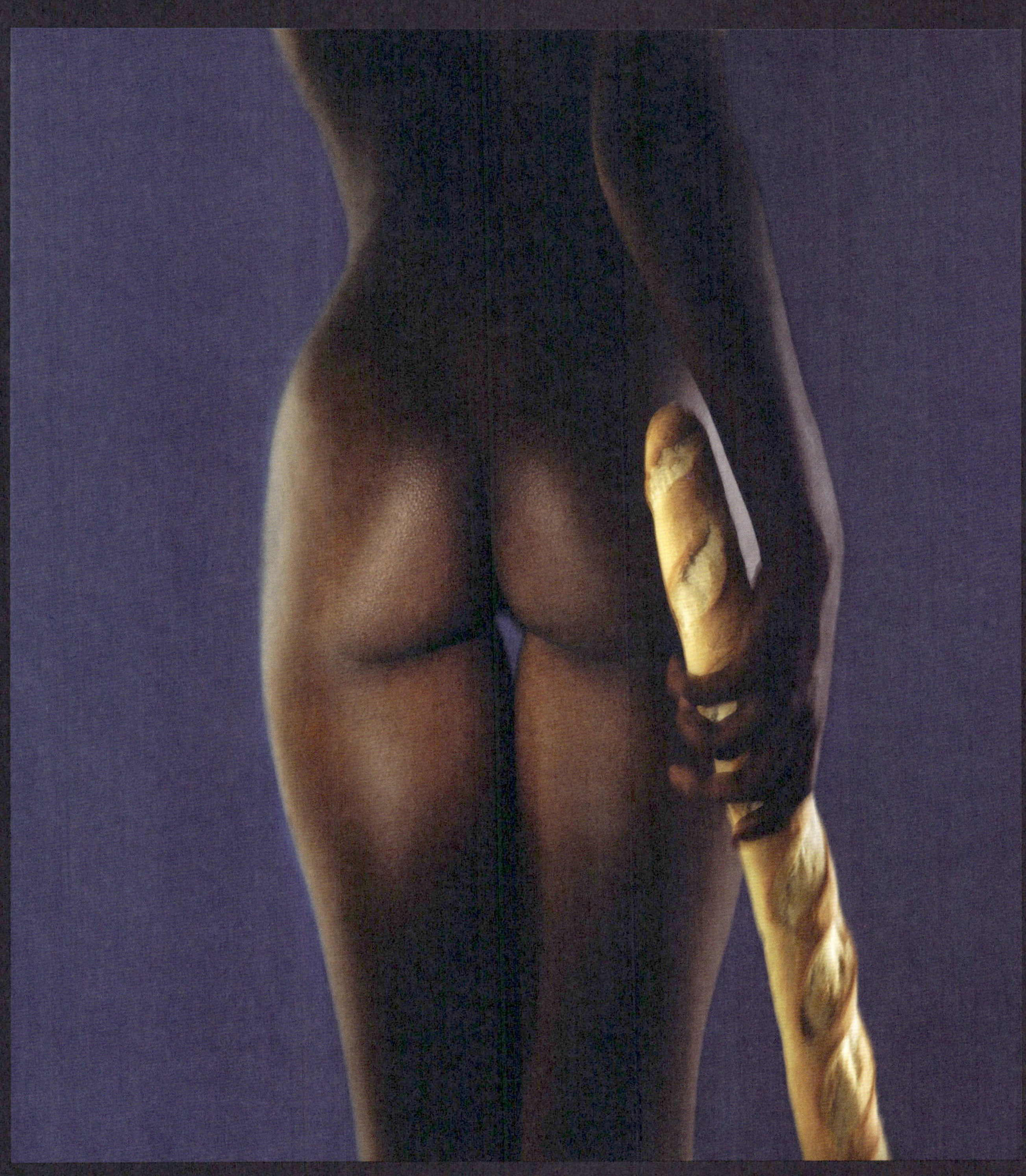

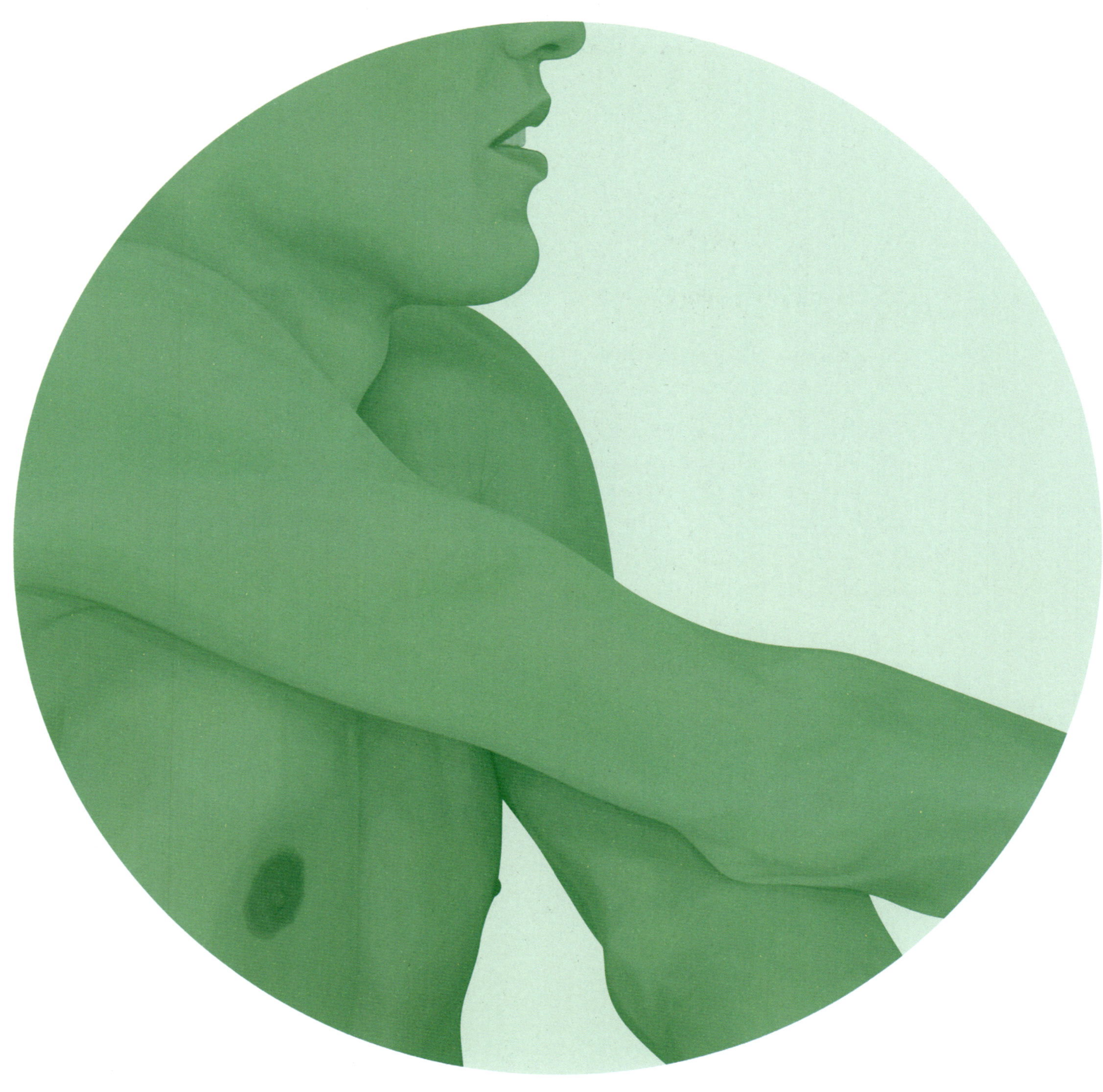

JULES JULIEN

Interview by Angelina A. Rafii

What inspired you to do this work? There is almost a voyeuristic element to it, as if someone was looking through a keyhole or a pulled curtain, was this deliberate?

This series was actually commissioned by *les Inrocks* magazine in France. Every month they create a CD with a compilation of the latest musical releases. The art director asked me to illustrate covers for a whole year, so it came to 11 CDs. His brief asked for erotic elements with some skin and as a reference The Ohio Players. I wanted to work on naked body fragments that would leave out the rest of the scene, somewhere between frustration and imagination.

Do you think that the playful aspect of eroticism lies in leaving part of it to the imagination and not revealing too much?

Eroticism is the poetry surrounding sex. An ear or a neck, a hand or a thigh… those elements alone tell a story, and that story implies in itself the rest of the body. Desire is intense, strong and fragile at the same time, like a vision that captivates the mind.

These illustrations differ from the work you usually do, can you explain.

When I work on commission I like to push the idea of a "meeting" to the limit, in the sense that my work is at the meeting point between myself-and everything that represents-and the client. It's a mutual discovery of some sorts that allows me to broaden my horizon and try new things. In the end, what I really enjoy in my work is experiencing the unknown.

What are some of your future projects?

I just finished illustrating *'L'histoire de l'œil'* a book by Georges Bataille, which will be published shortly in England. I am also preparing a solo exhibition, which will take place in Berlin at the Rise gallery in December.

JULESJULIEN.COM

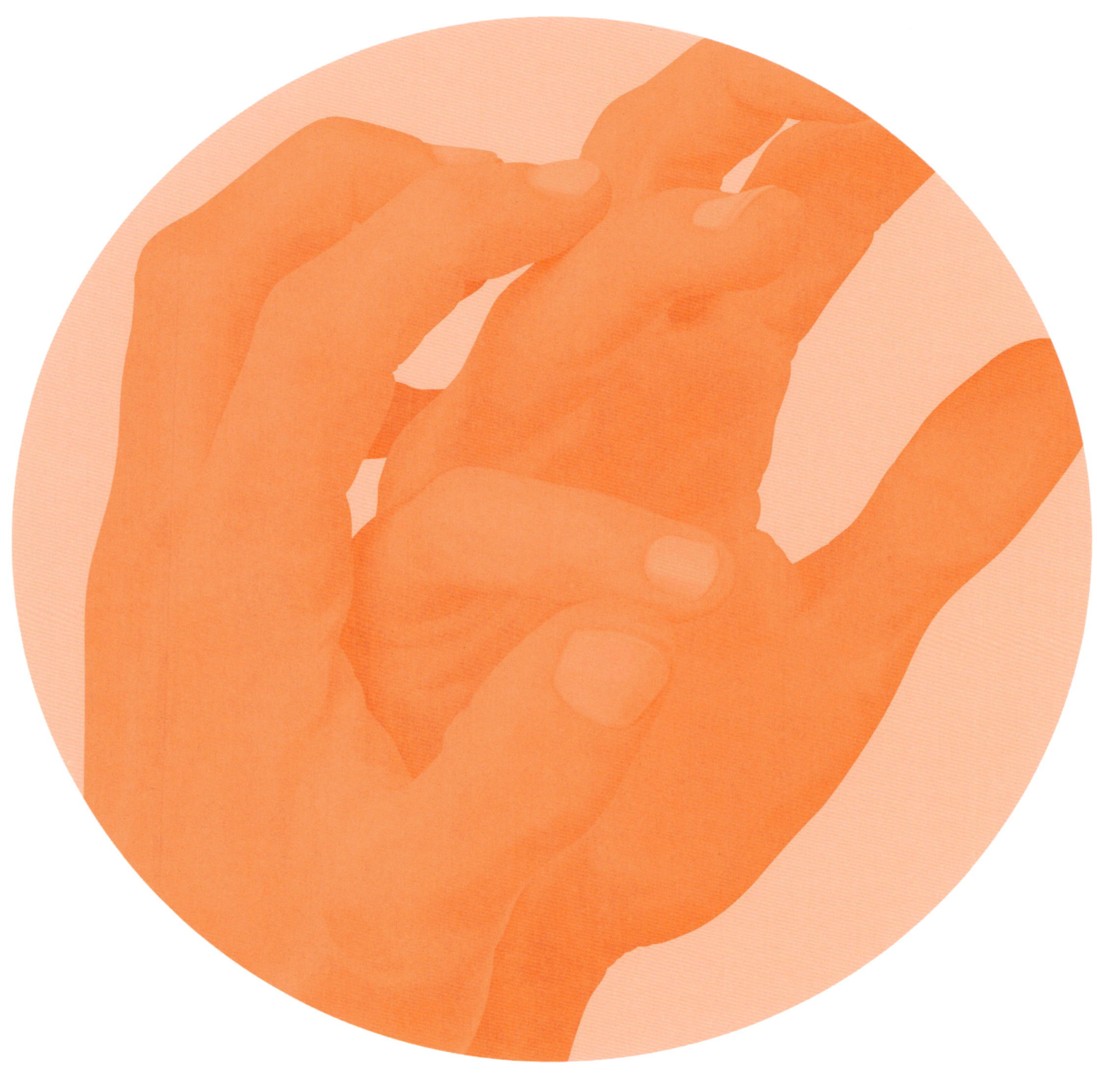

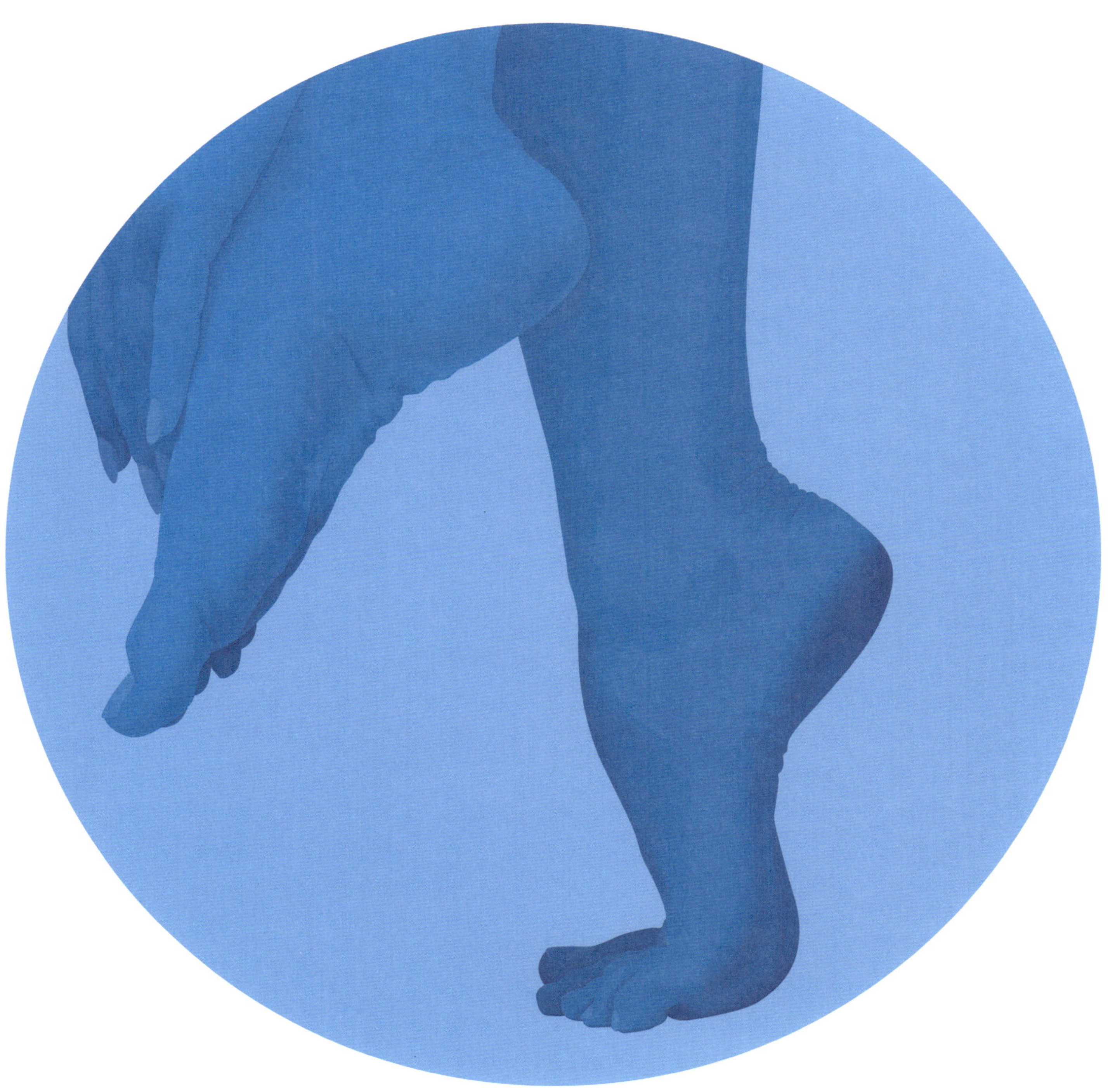

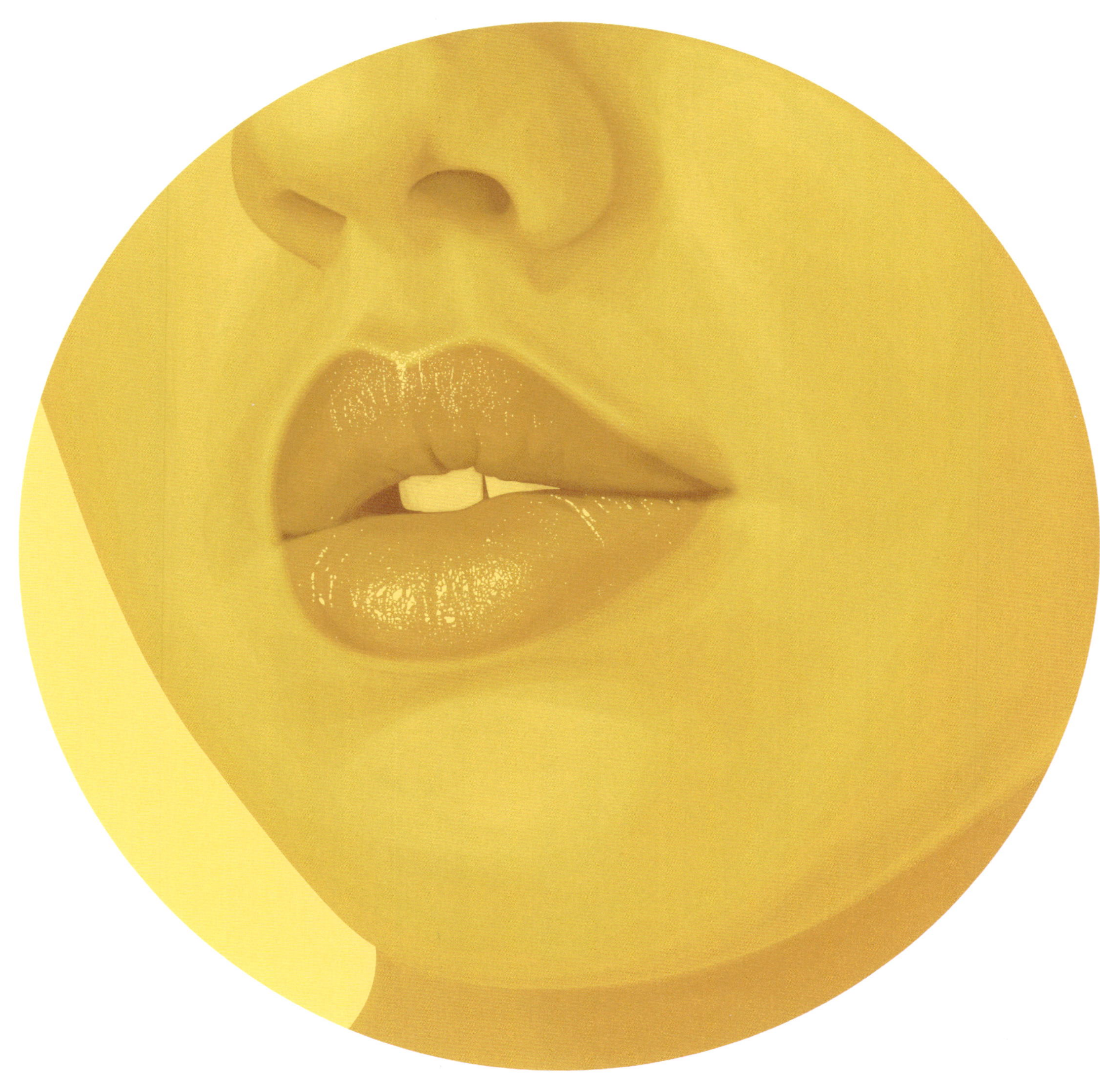

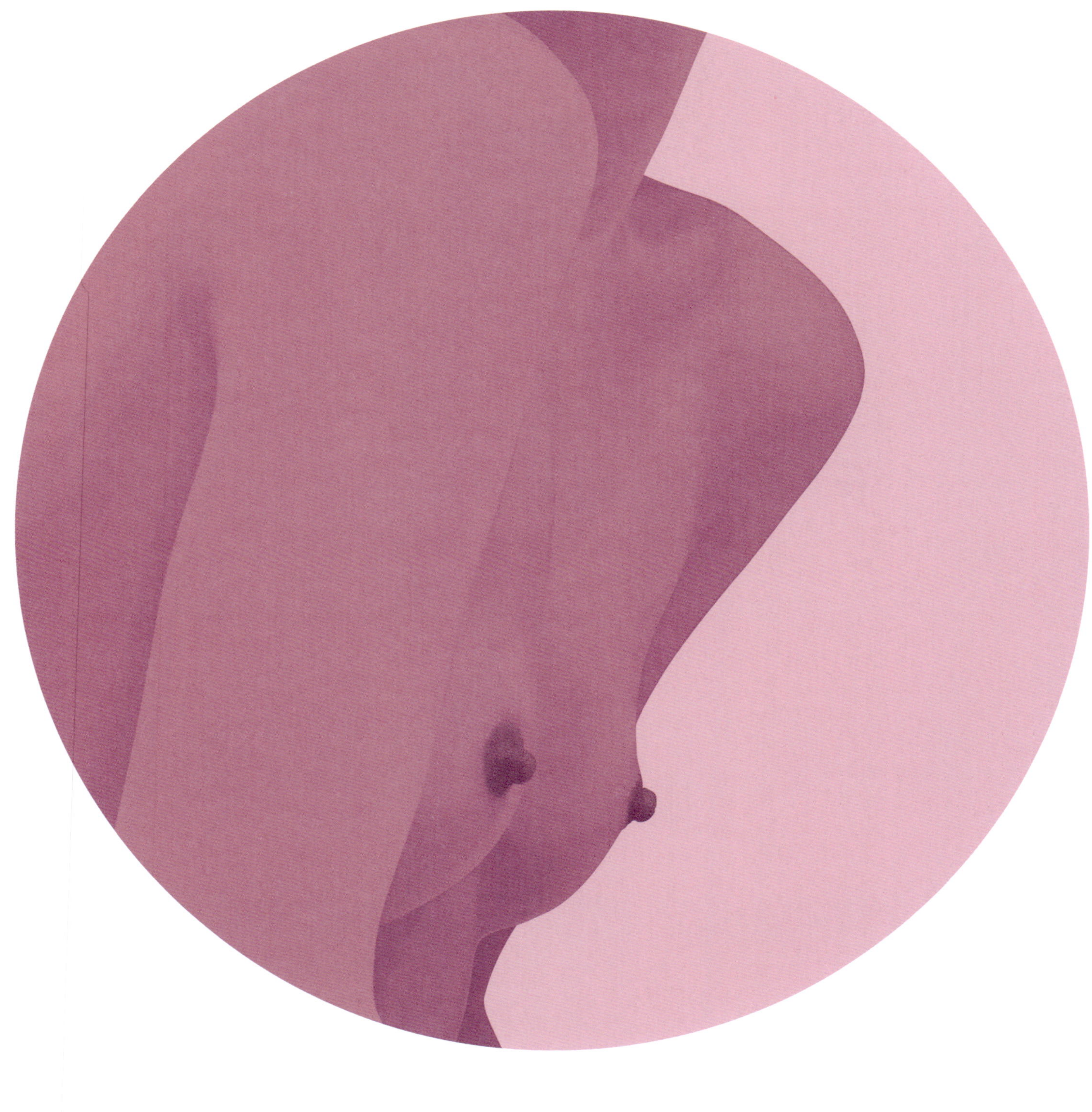

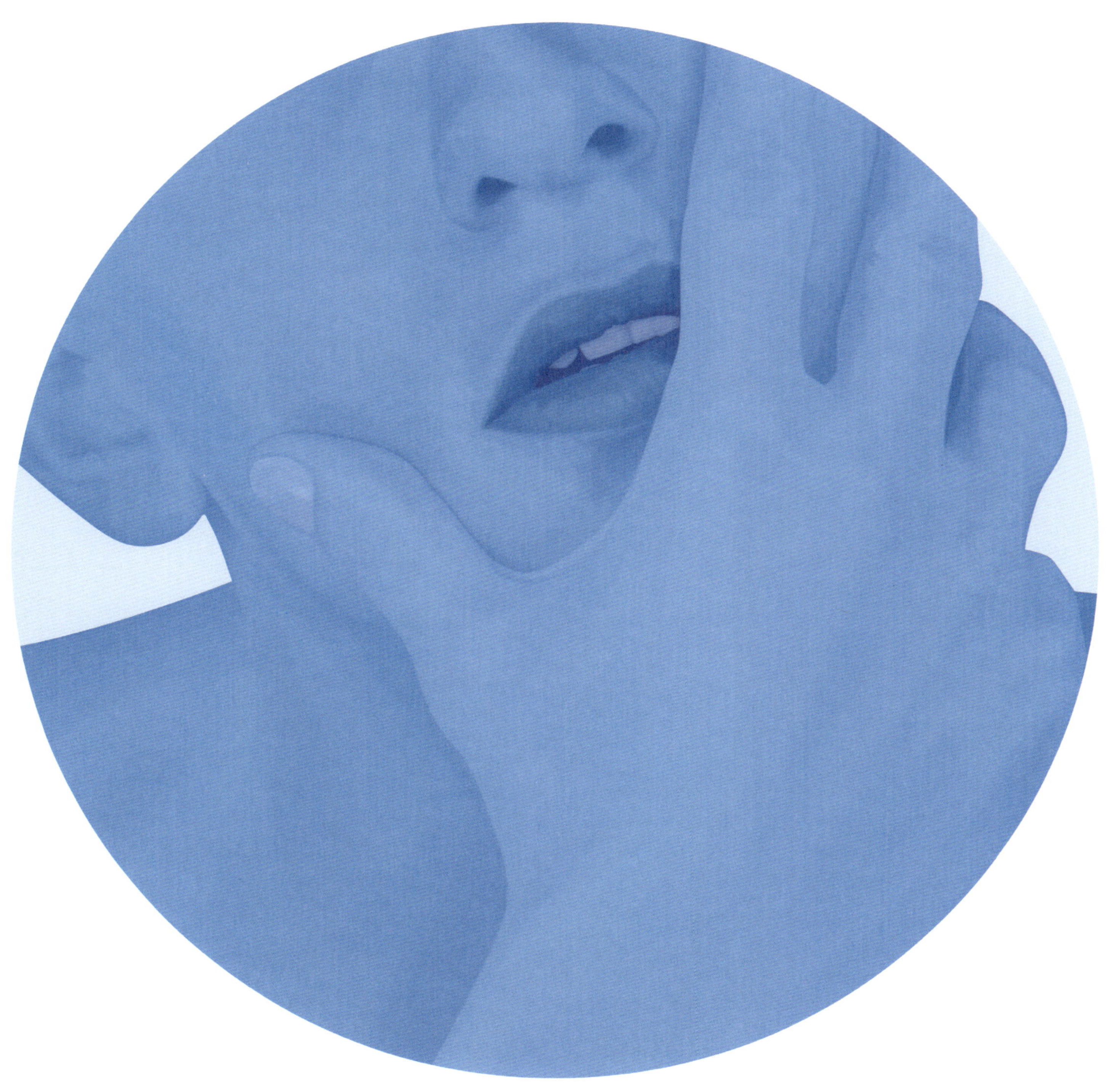

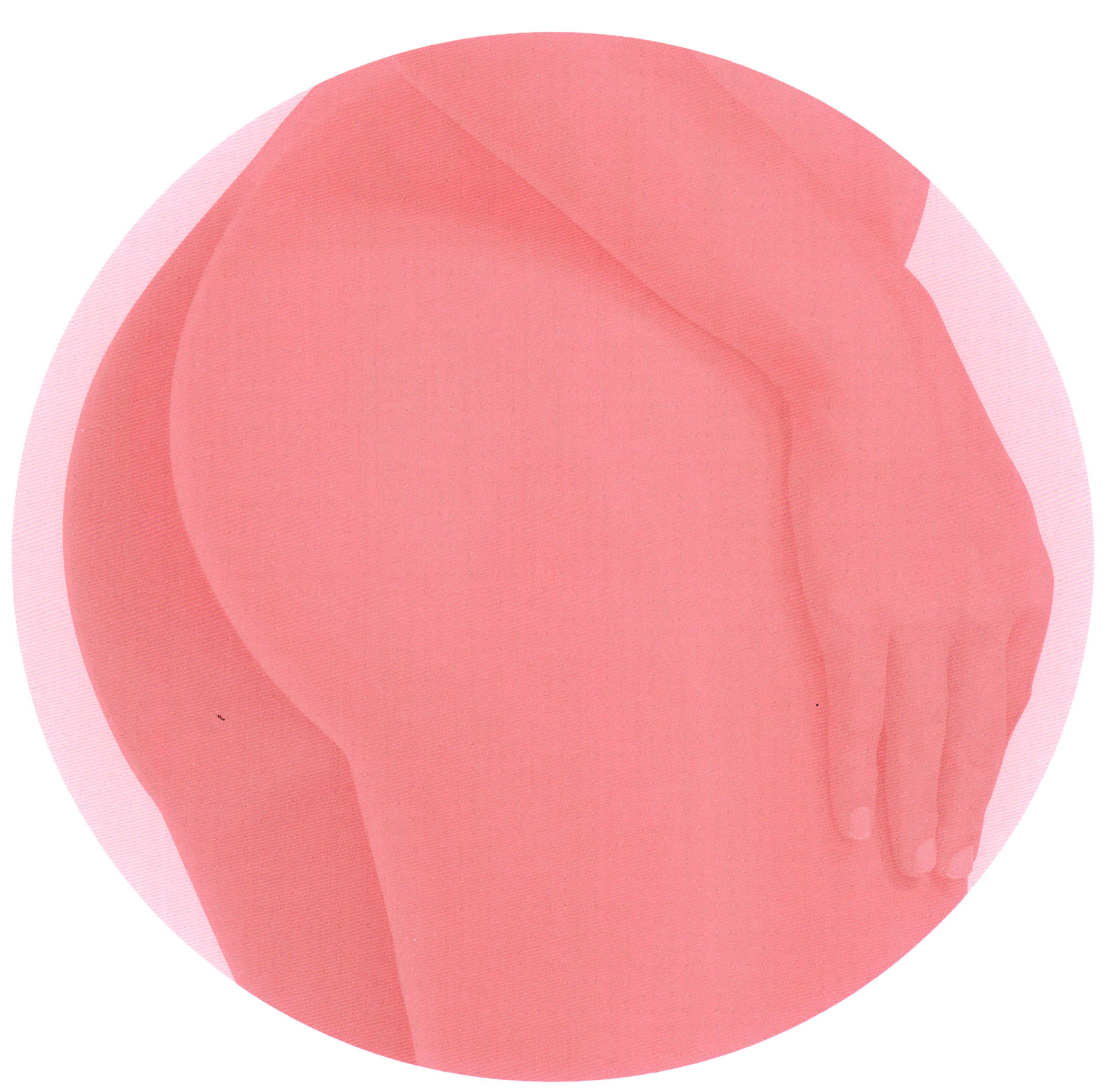

HANNA PUTZ

Interview by Angelina A. Rafii

Your background is in modelling, so how did you find yourself behind the camera? What are the major differences for someone who has been on both sides? Are there things that you find go amiss when you are being photographed and which you try to remedy in your own photography?

It was never really about wanting to become a photographer, I just wanted to create images and found the camera to be an easy "tool" for that.

I would say I'm influenced by my former profession as a model in the sense that I felt I wanted to photograph my friends, a lot of them models at the time, but I didn't want to take photographs of models, meaning of someone producing him-or herself "for" a photograph.

If you work as a model you are obviously very aware of how you come across in a photograph, you're very present "in the moment", since posing for a photograph is essentially your job. That's what I'm interested in: Can there ever be a moment of "not posing" whenever there is a camera involved (without talking about a moment where someone isn't aware of being photographed)?! Is that even possible? And, which kind of an image (of self) or moment do you want the viewer to believe in? I question the means of identity within my work through the notion of posing and, generally, what Identity means, within the medium of photography. That interest might partly come from working as a model myself, so yes, modelling did influence my concerns within my work but I wouldn't say it influenced my way of working with someone.

It might help that I know how it feels to stand in front of a camera, but I generally treat everyone with respect when I photograph them and I'm very thankful if someone dedicates their time and energy and allows me to photograph them-but I think that it would be the same even if I had not worked as a model myself.

You often are in a privileged position to photograph your friends, who are major names in the modelling business. In front of your camera they are stripped of any artifice and are often captured in their most natural state. Can you talk to us about that-the exchange and the process?

Those girls are my friends, most of them I have known for years, so there's not much difference for me if I photograph someone with a major name as opposed to someone who is not well-known. If there is a difference, then it depends on how well I know someone when I photograph them. Besides, I find every one is very different in front of a camera, especially models.

Who are some of the other people who fascinate you, photographically speaking?

I admire Roni Horn's work immensely and have more recently become very infatuated with artists such as Elad Lassry, Annette Kelm or Roe Ethridge, as I find their approach to photography very interesting. Other than that I also adore Rineke Djikstra's or Taryn Simon's work.

There is often a sense of solitude and isolation in your images, is that deliberate? Can you explain?

I enjoy it when people look like they have been left undisturbed. I don't necessarily like it when images look like someone is doing something "for" the camera or for an image. In a time where there's overflow of stimuli and images, I simply don't feel the need to be very loud or spectacular in my images. It seems to me that in our time people feel an immense need to be pushing everything "out there", presenting themselves to the world on a very high scale, even their most intimate, private situations at times. It seems to be important to put yourself out for the world to see; whether it's facebook, YouTube, casting shows, talk shows or all the reality shows out there. A lot of it is about presenting yourself to the world, wanting to become famous, wanting to be seen/heard or listened to by everyone. I guess that's one of the main reasons I like my images to be of people being alone with themselves and for themselves rather than presenting themselves for anything or anyone. It is about solitude, but not in a negative or lonely way at all. It's more about being oblivious of everything that's around and being close to ones self.

Is your approach different when photographing nudes?

Not really. Nudity itself is not so much of a concern in my work; it's mainly about leaving clothes outside of the image as a means of self-representation.

What defines eroticism and sensuality for you? Are there examples of other people's works you admire, if so why?

My work doesn't really deal with eroticism or sensuality especially when I photograph someone naked as I already said, however, if it comes to sensual images, I really like Lina Scheynius' work. Her work is very sensual to me, and I feel you can always tell that it comes from a female point of view, which I enjoy very much.

You are participating in the Hyères Photography Festival how did that come about?

After visiting the Festival last year and really enjoying it, I wanted to participate this year myself, and since it's open entry I sent my portfolio in. I'm very happy and honoured to be part of it, as it really is a great festival and it's an honour for me to be selected as one of 10 finalists out of over 800. I'm very much looking forward to being able to showcase my work there.

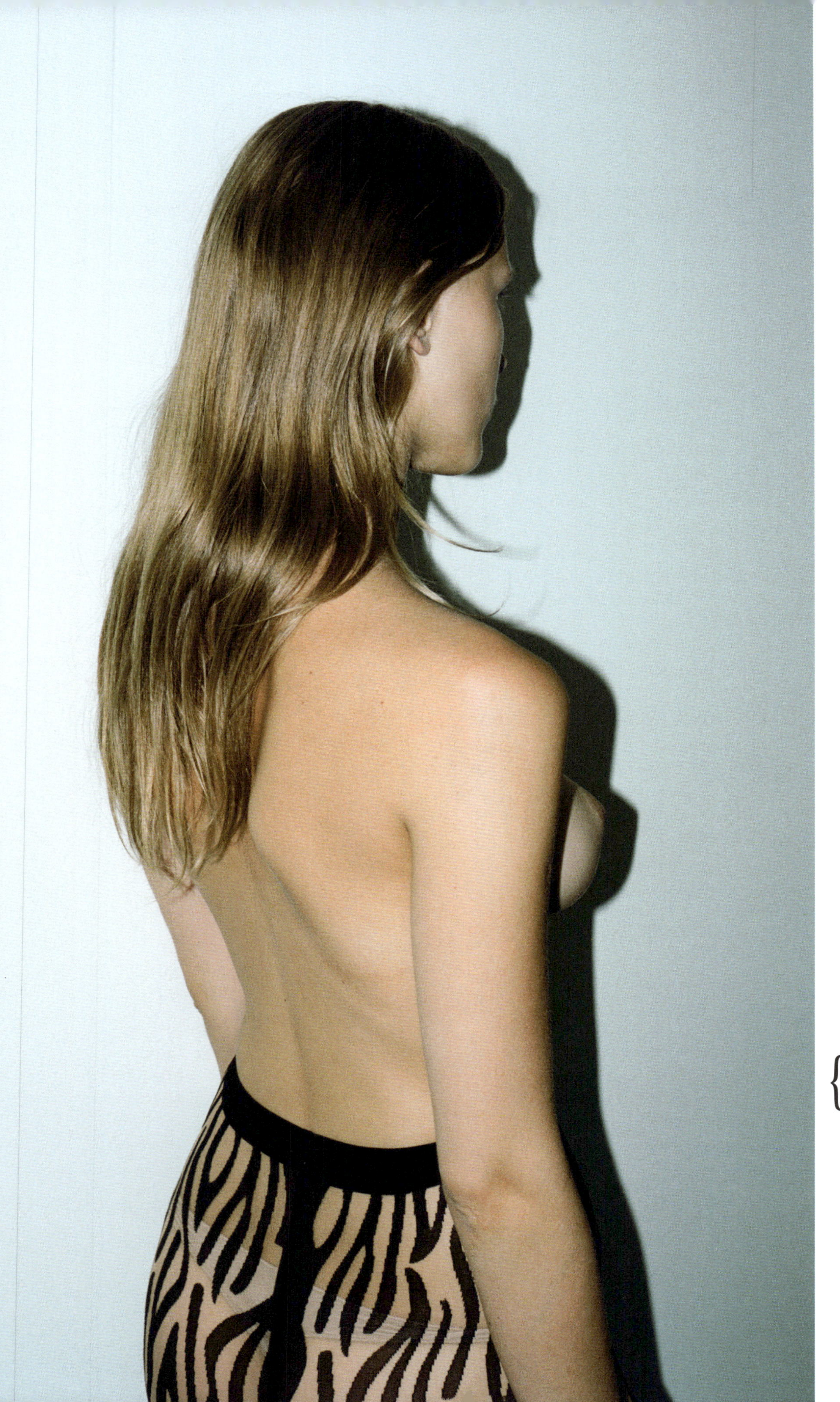

Untitled (A.K 1) 2011
58 x 80 cm
Color Photograph
Edition: 6 + 3 A.P.

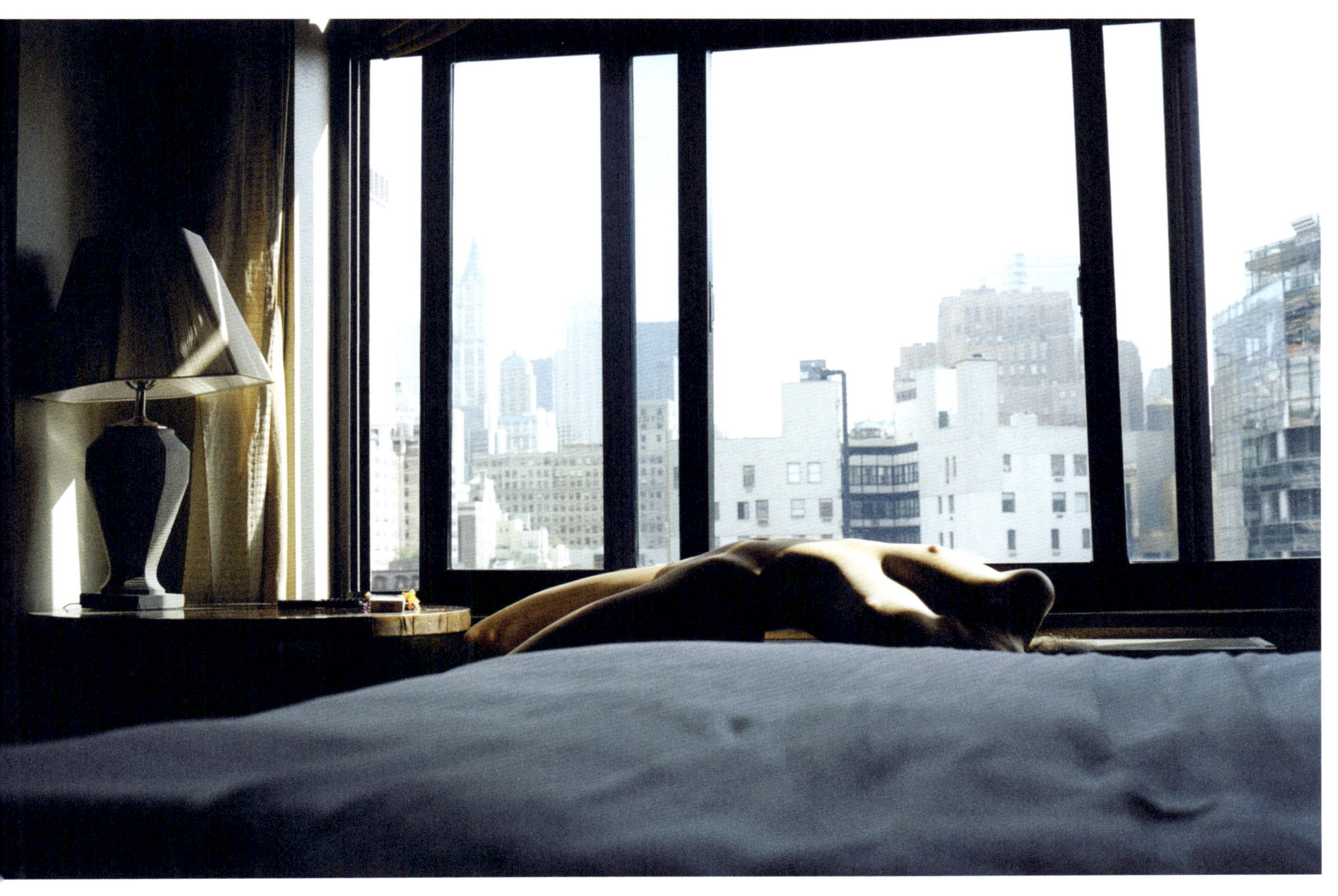

Ich habe keine Zeit , 2009
80 x 110 cm
Color photograph
Edition: 6 + 3. A.P.

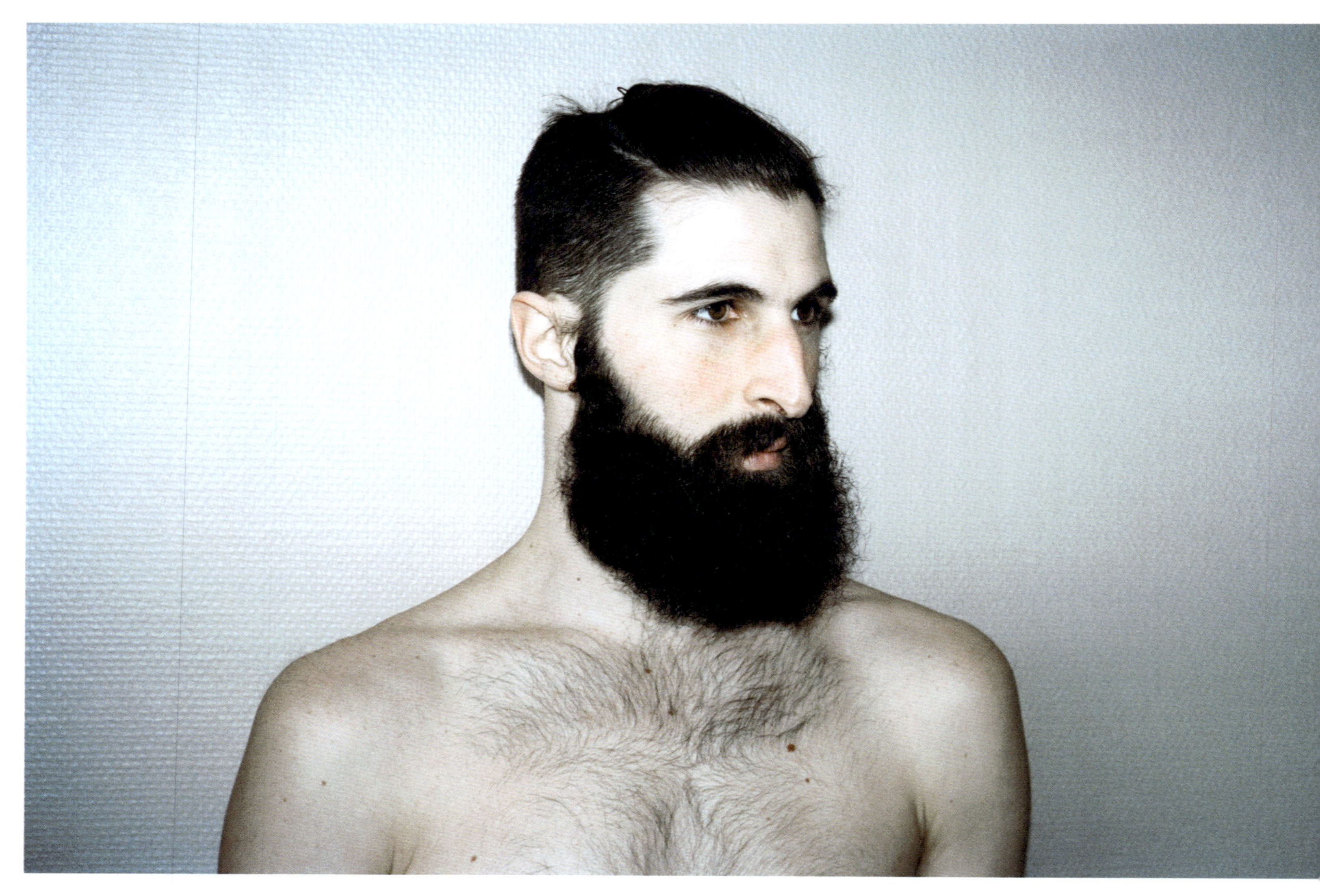

Untitled (B. Dukhan 1), 2011
80×110 cm
Color Photograph
Edition : 6 + 3 A.P.

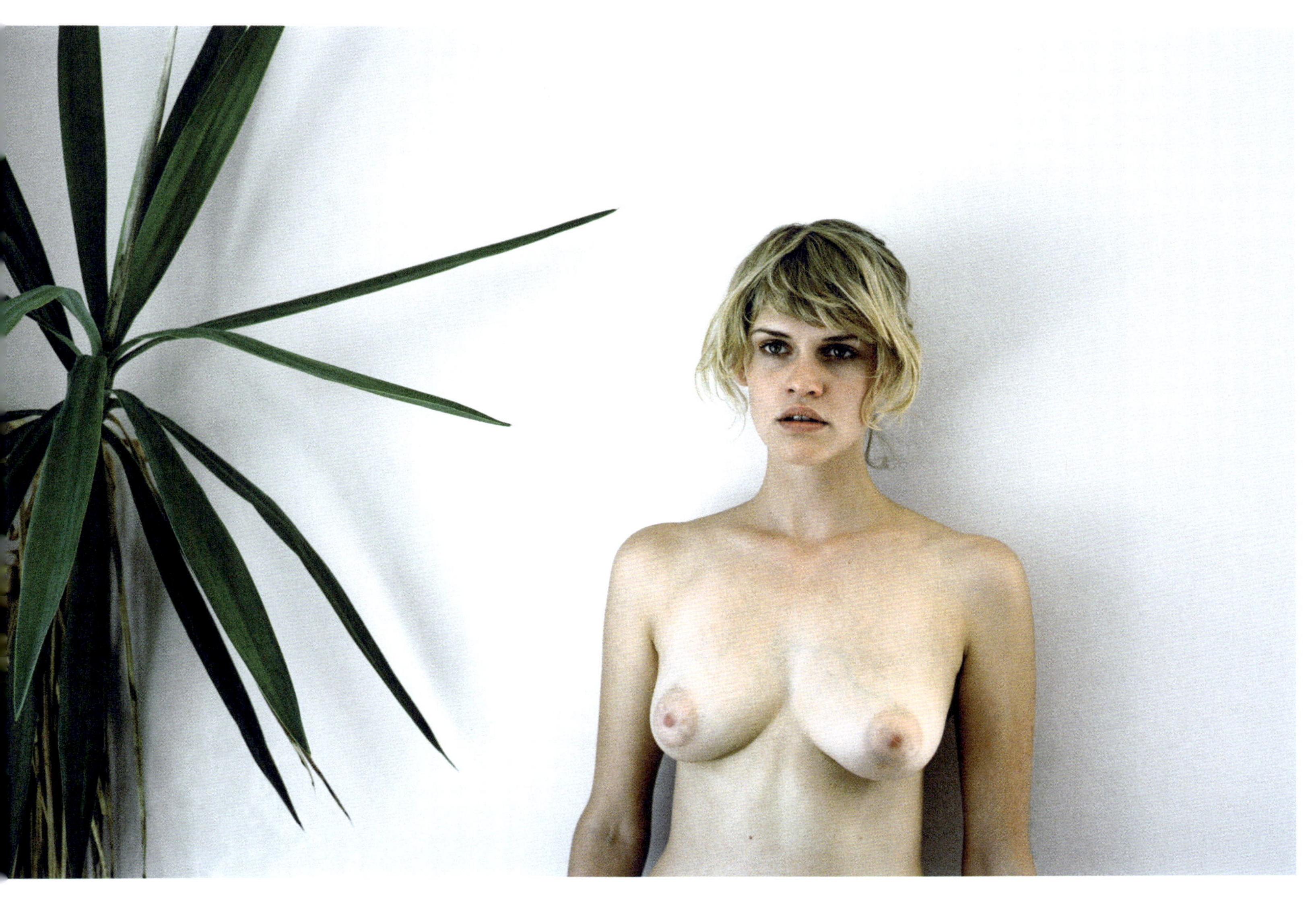

Untitled (Mignonne 2) 2011
80 x 110 cm
Color photograph
Edition: 6 + 3. A.P.

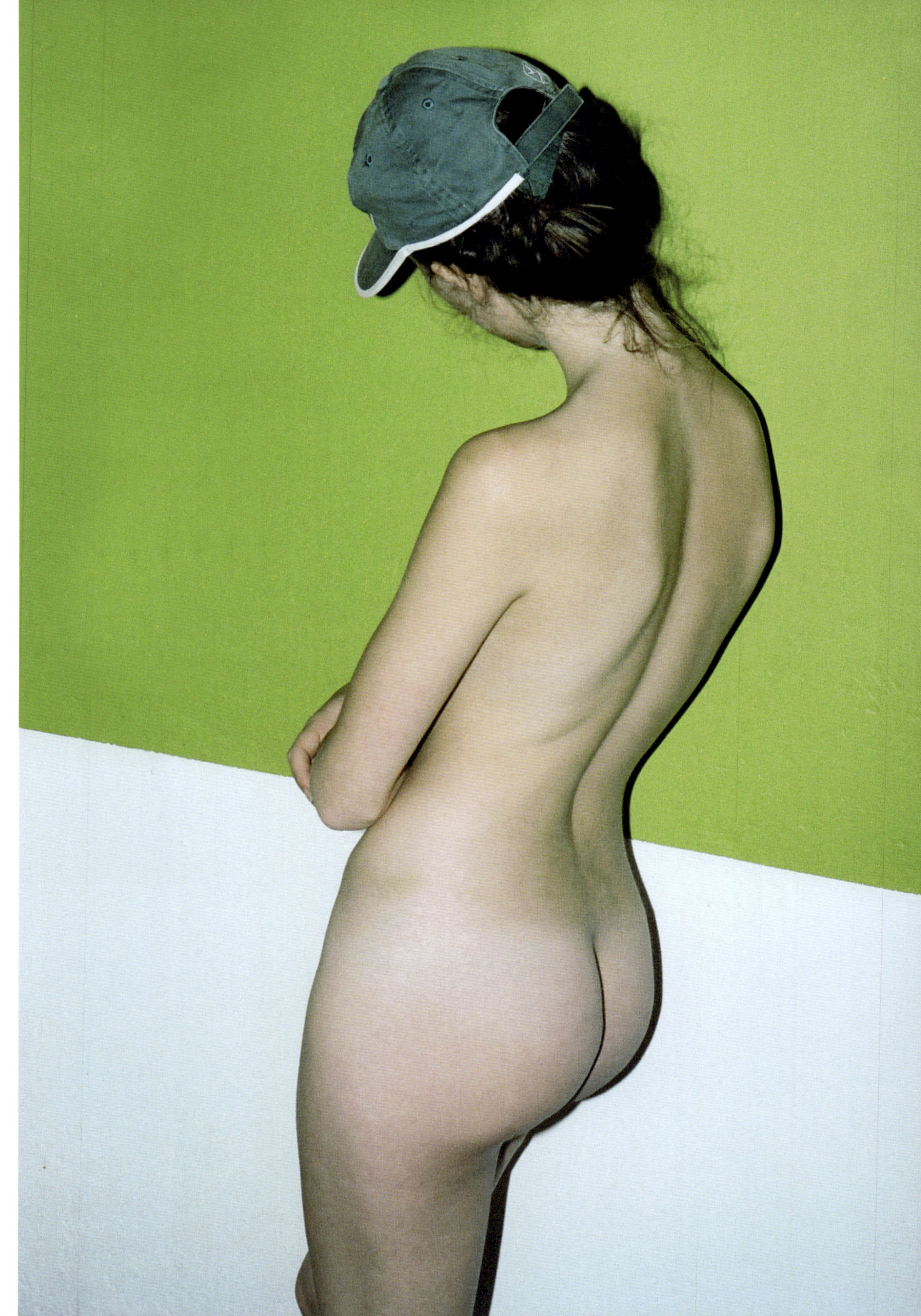

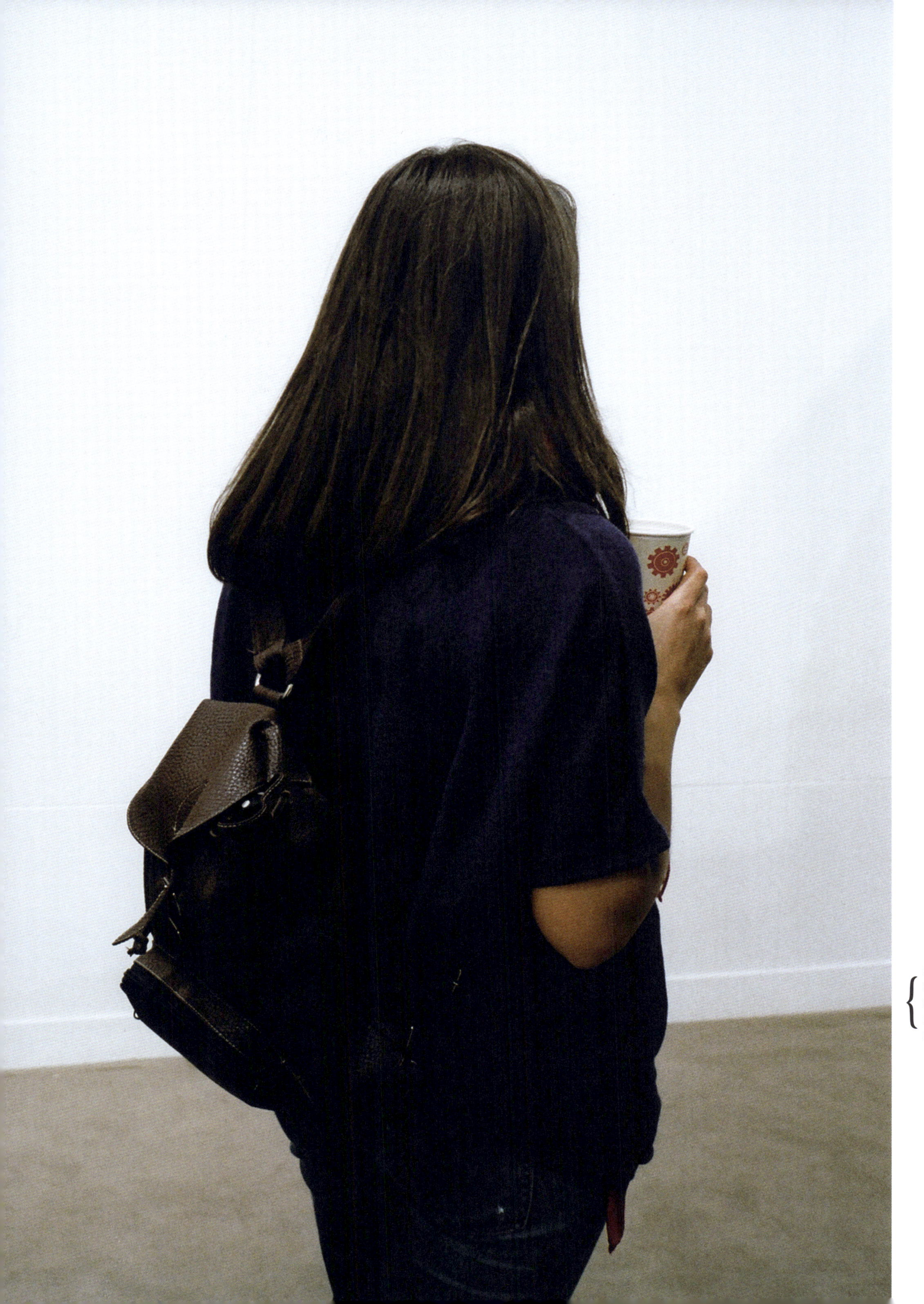

Untitled (Tiss 1) 2011
80 x 110 cm
Color photograph
Diptychon
Edition: 6 + 3.A.P.

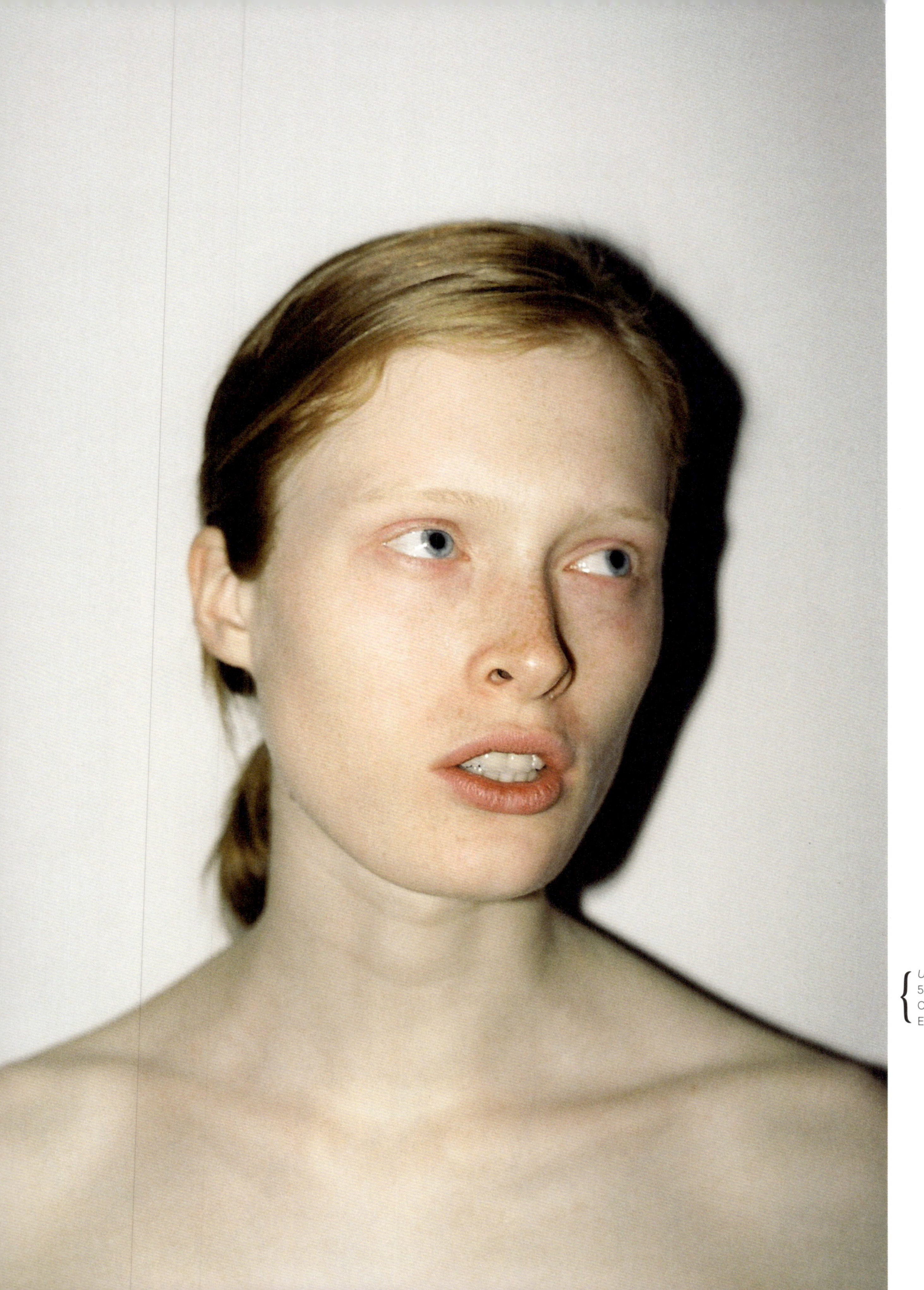

{ *Untitled (Ilva H. 1)* 2011
58 x 80 cm
Color Photograph
Edition: 6 + 3 A.P.

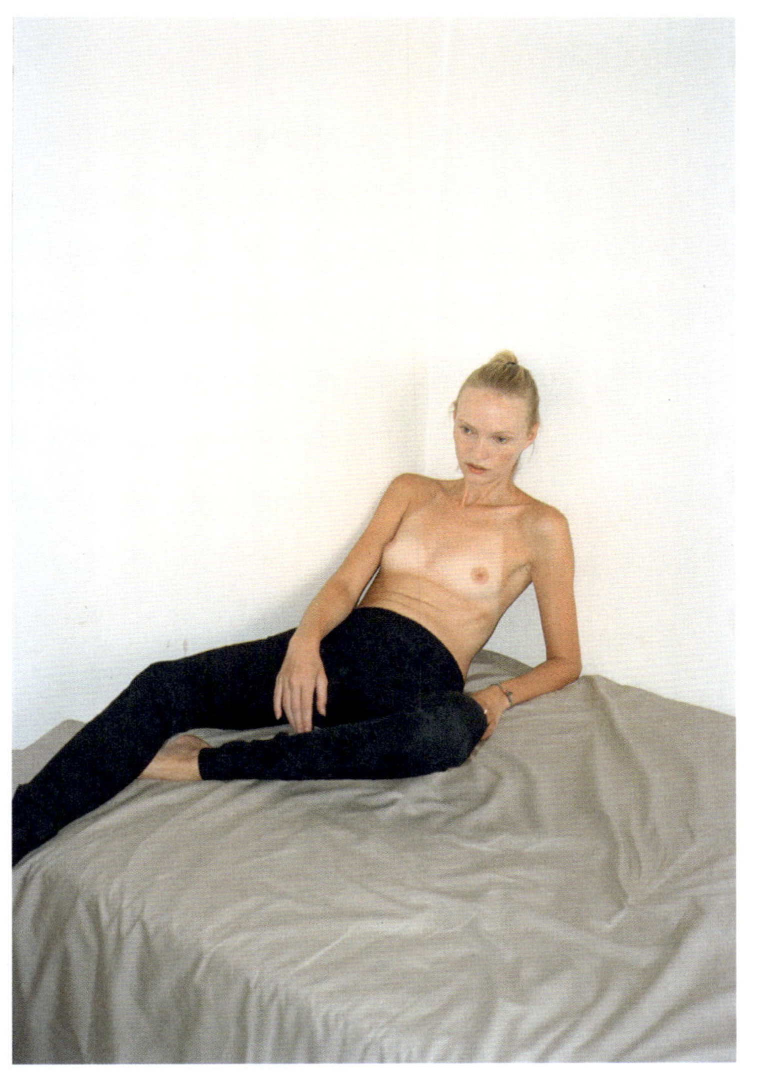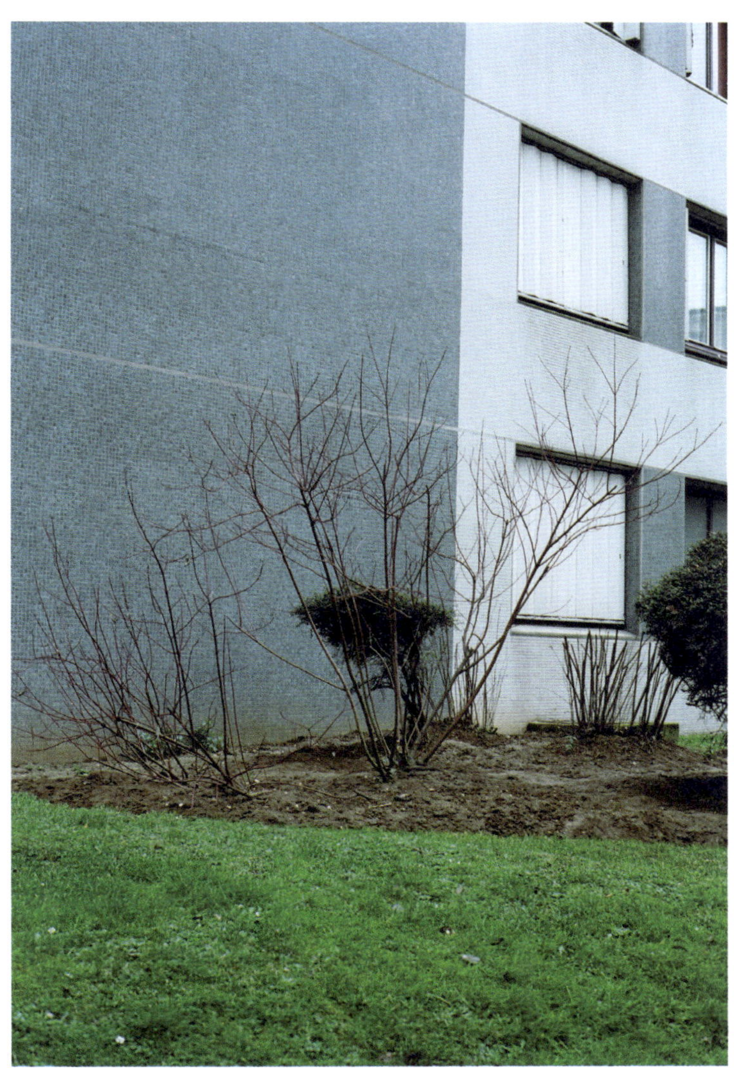

Untitled (Z. 24) , 2011
80 x 110 cm
Color photograph
Diptychon
Edition: 6 + 3.A.P.

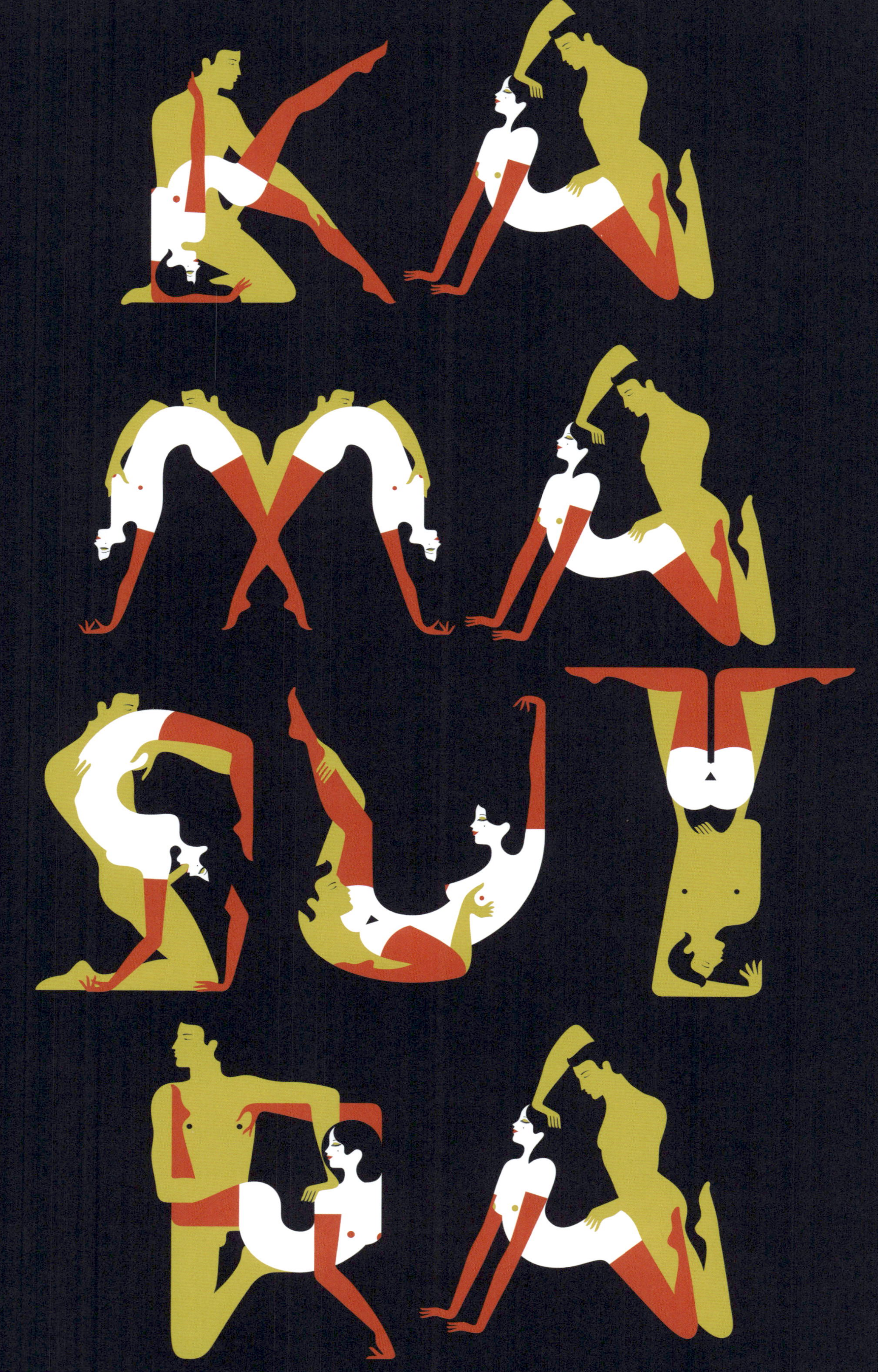

MALIKA FAVRE

Interview by Angelina A. Rafii

You started drawing at a very young age and then went to art school. You also have a very distinctive style. How has it evolved over the years from when you started as a little girl? And what made you stick with this particular technique?

I drew pretty much every day as a child and mainly drew girls: princesses and fairies as a child, amazones and fashionistas as a teenager and mostly realistic drawings when I was in art school. My mum taught me to first draw the body and then dress it up so that is how I learned proportions and how to draw the female form. When I went to art school at 18, life drawing taught me to let my illustrations breathe and suggest lines that are not on the page. But at that stage, my style was very "graphic novel"-like: it was almost automatic after so many years of drawing every day and I wasn't able to distance myself from it and do something else. It was only a couple of years ago, that I decided to experiment with vector drawings. I loved the sharpness of the lines and the almost logotype approach that was coming out of my drawings. I finally found a way to use all that I had learned and pare it down to its essence. Now that I know where each line is, I can suggest it, play with the negative space around it etc.
I strongly believe that you can ruin an illustration by adding to it. I try and remove any unnecessary element until I reach that line between figuration and abstraction.

Penguin and *Wallpaper* asked you to create an alphabet for them around the theme of eroticism, and you also have other work that portrays the sensual. Is that something you particularly are drawn to and enjoy?

I love the cheekiness of erotic drawings and I think both clients were attracted to that playfulness. My approach is a very feminine one, I think: I think sex is a fun and playful thing and I am not interested in shocking anyone. I am just drawing what makes me smile and what I think is sexy. I loved doing both projects: drawing letters is a challenge every time and pushes you to come up with the most unexpected positions. It is a bit like a jigsaw puzzle. And it seems to make other people smile too. When you look at both those alphabets, I am barely showing anything. Most things are suggested and for the viewer to imagine. I like that interaction.

For some you felt like you needed to fight your inner inhibitions. What does a conversation you have with yourself in that instance sound like and how do you end up convincing yourself? Do you use any of your personal fantasies to draw these erotic figures?

Ahaha, I might disappoint here but these girls I draw are not me, far from it. For one, I am not flexible enough! I think the playfulness and fun of those projects is very much like me but I am more prude than the girls I draw.
The Kama Sutra project was very challenging because I had to get very close to that line where sexy and naughty becomes vulgar and crude. Also the fact that I never did an alphabet with men before was challenging: You can abstract girls much more easily than men so it was a bit of a struggle to find that balance between showing enough not to be called a prude and not giving everything away. And finally, I had 20 years of drawing women behind me so I knew exactly how to play with the curves and body shapes. With the man, I had to find my feet and figure out what I wanted to draw or leave out. I had many conversations with myself, which I will keep secret for now. Not giving too much away.

What would be going too far for you? Or is there no limit, particularly when using illustration?

Everyone has their own boundaries depending on their upbringing, taste and surroundings. I am very open so I think you can draw almost anything tastefully, but it has to be done in an interesting way. An illustration can actually be more violent than real life so I think there are definitely limits. I have mine, you have yours and they are probably different. At the end of the day I think taste and craftsmanship are the most important things: I am sure, I could get offended by a very badly drawn apple, more than a beautiful erotic position.

WWW.MALIKAFAVRE.COM

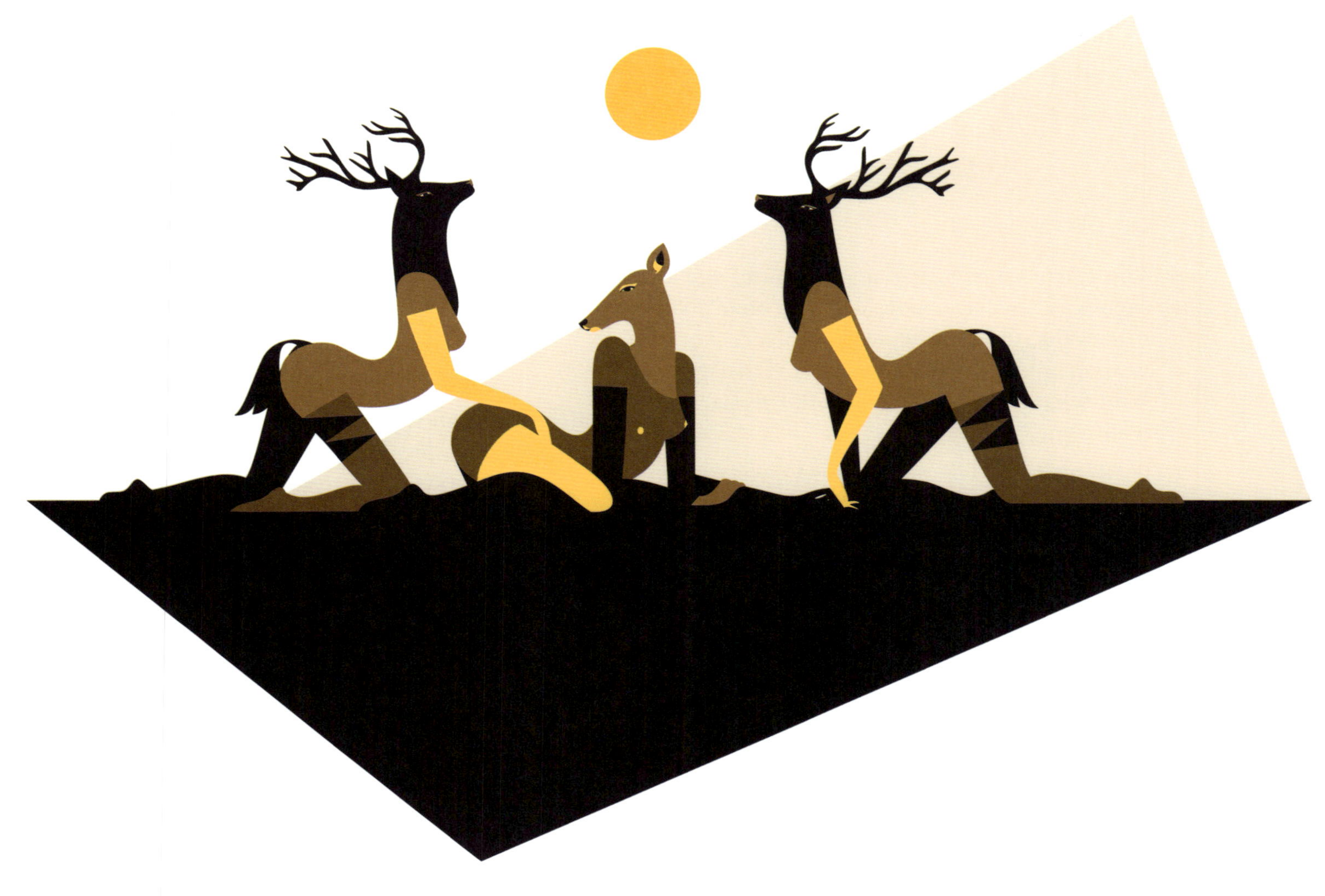

Lust Triangle deers

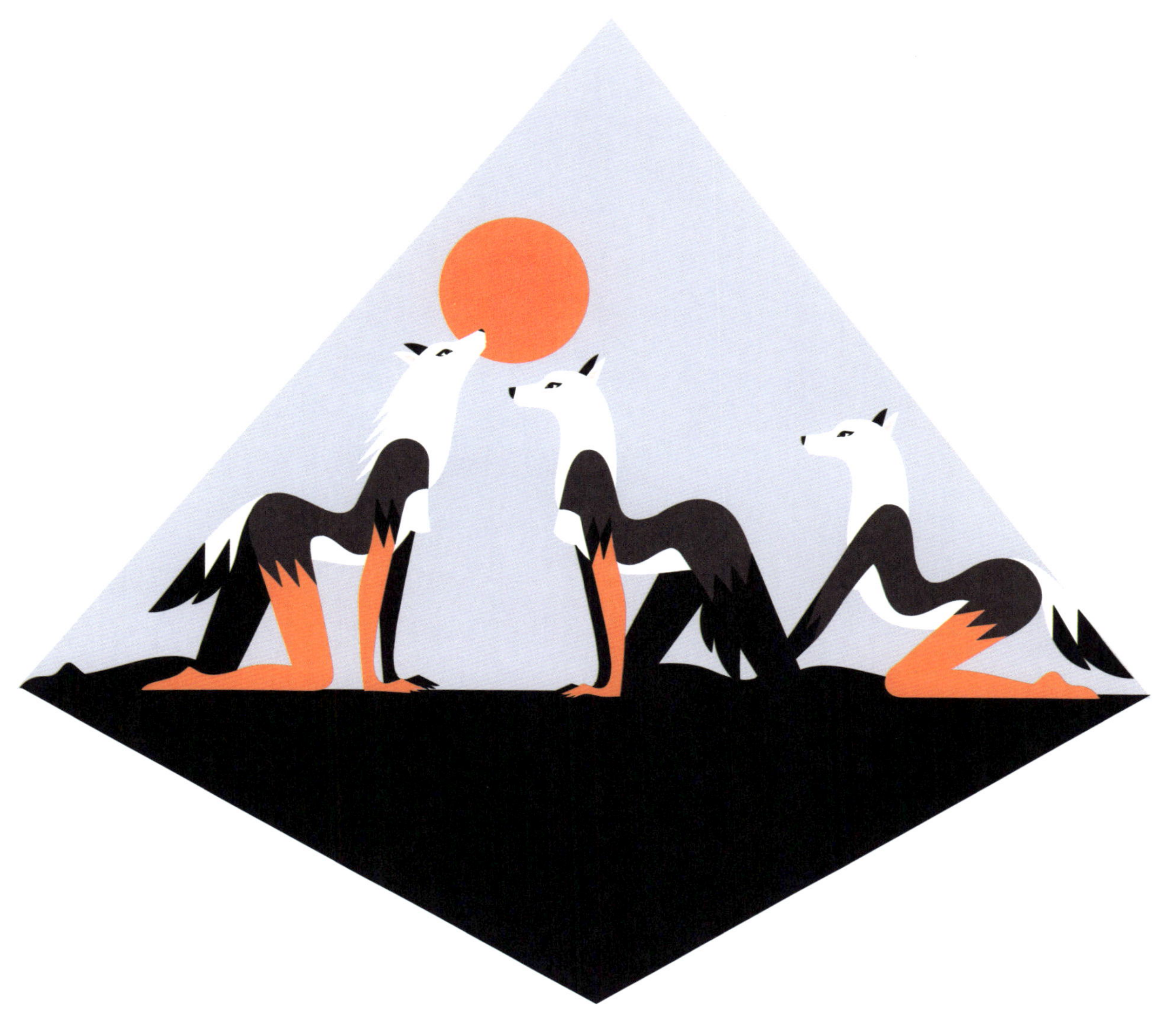

Lust Triangle wolves

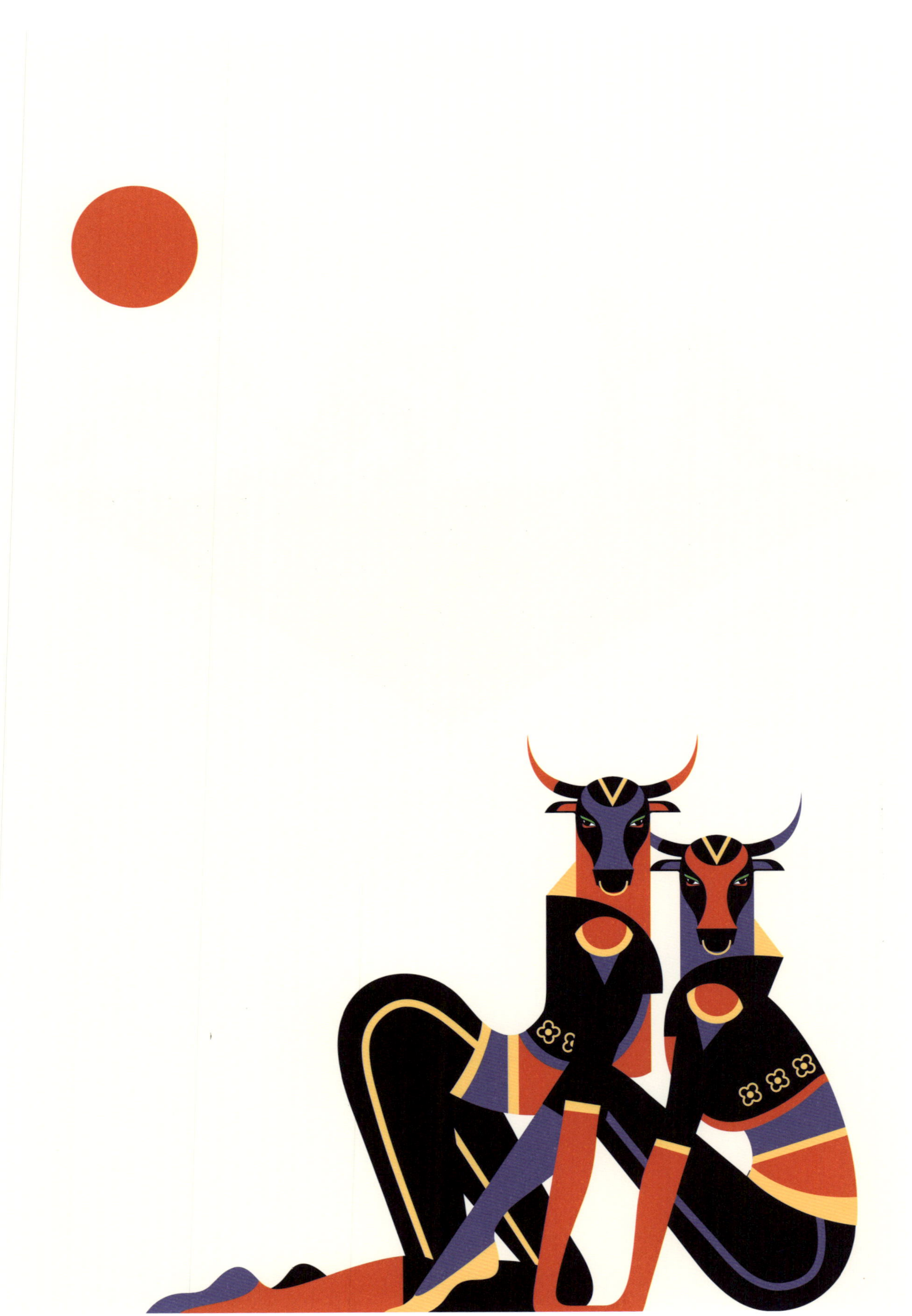

{ Code

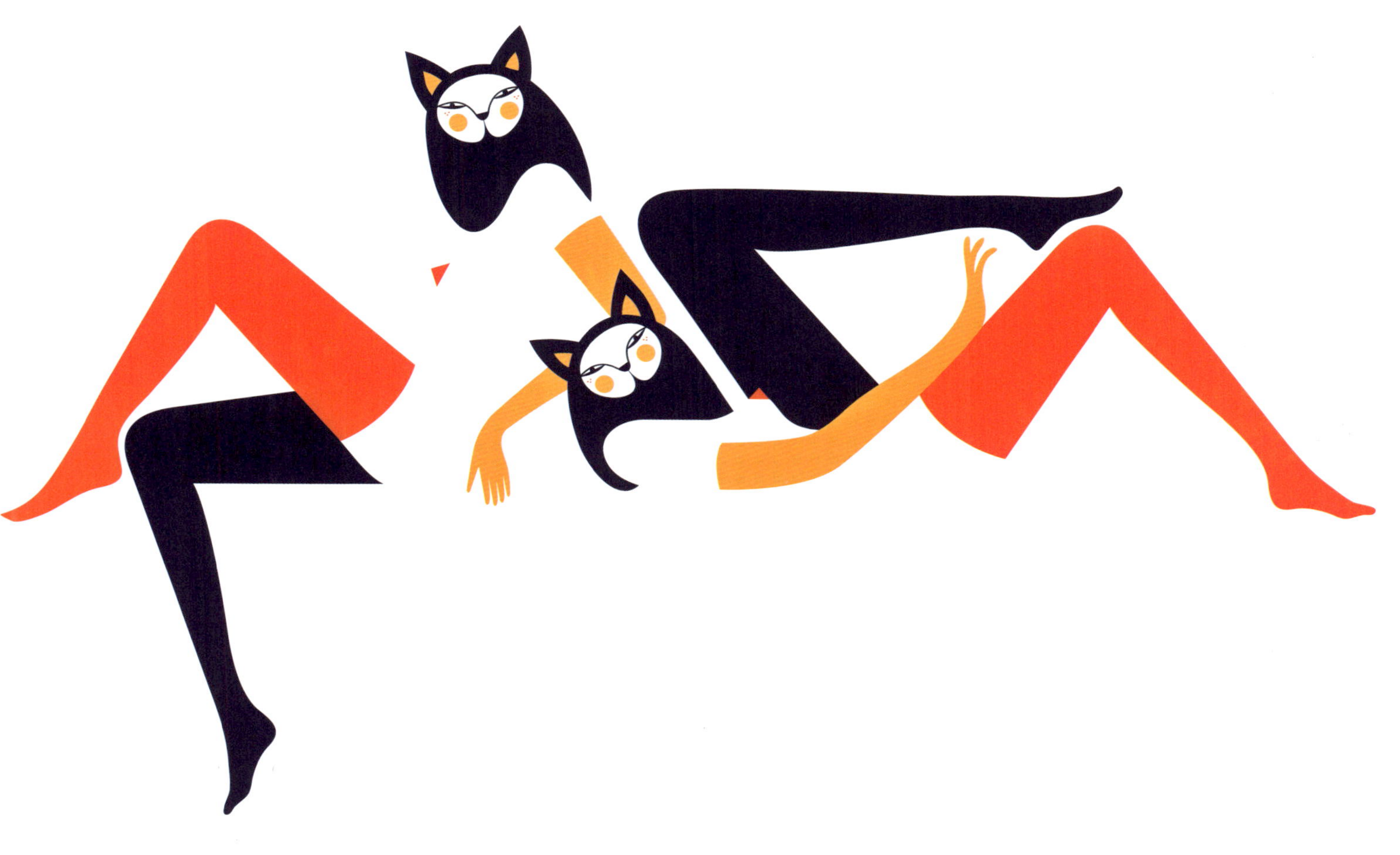

Hybrids

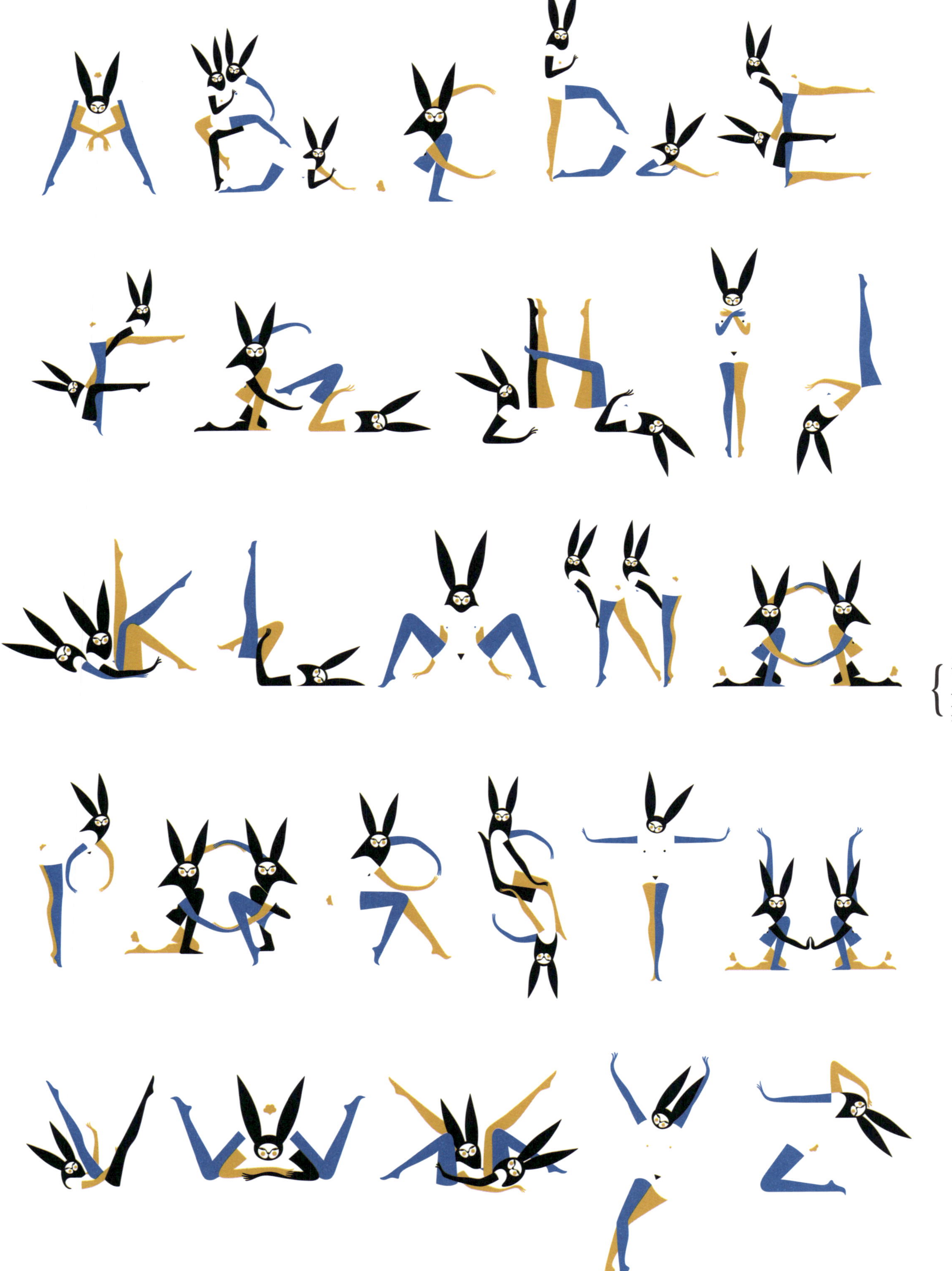
Alphabunnies

Alphabet commissioned by Wallpaper magazine for their Sex & Art issue, 2009

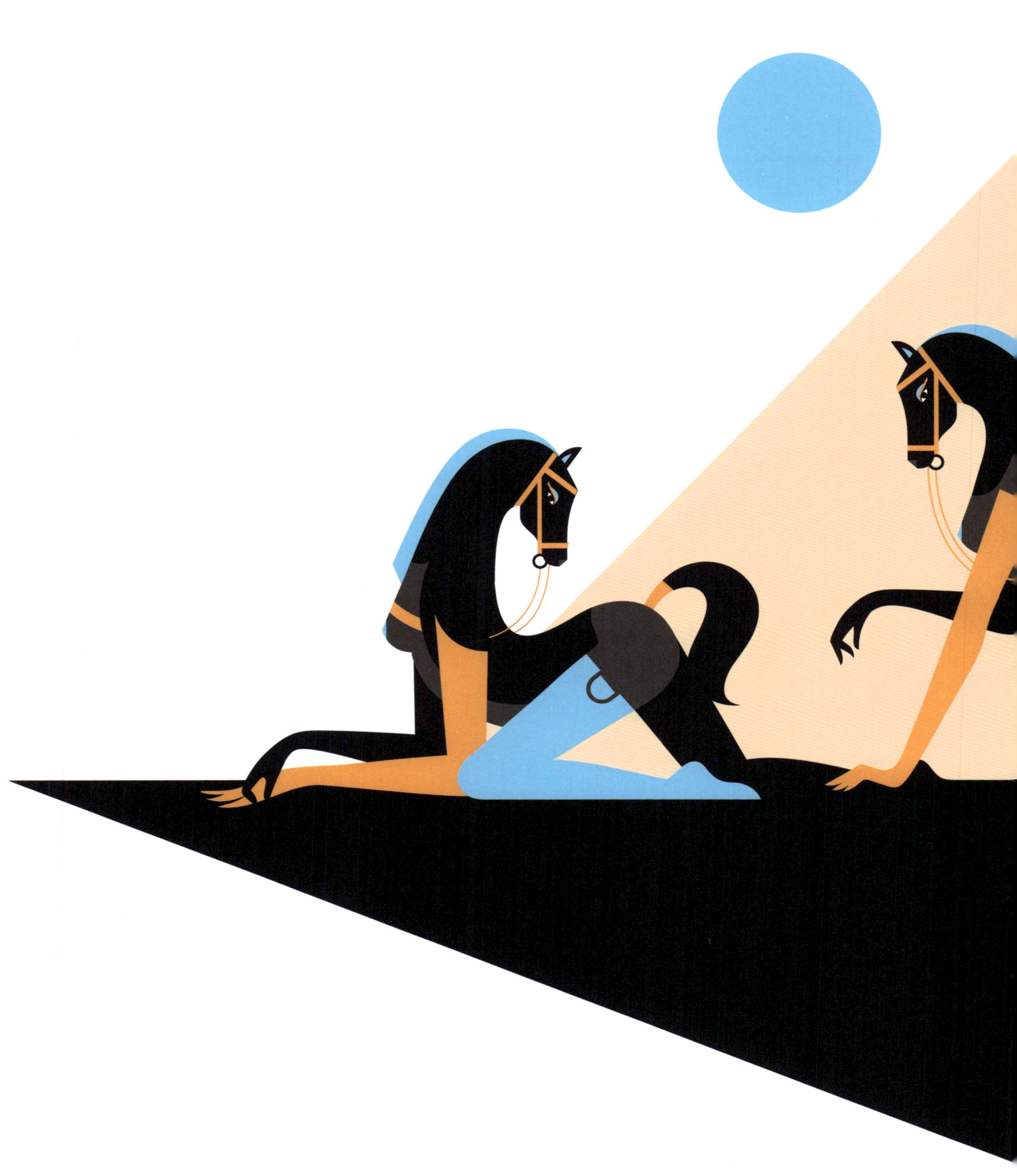

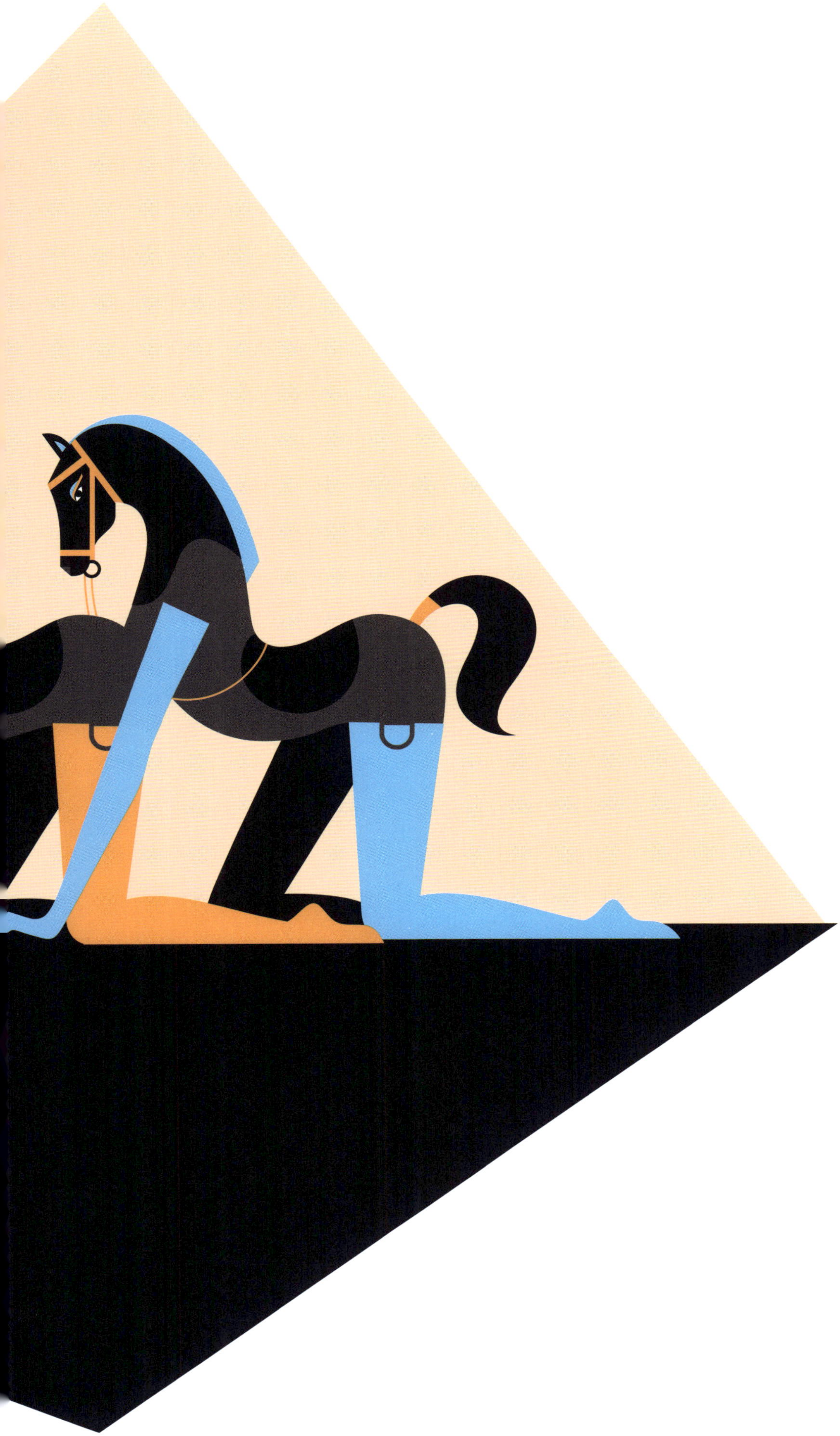

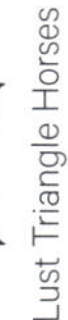

Lust Triangle Horses

AUTUMN SONNICHSEN

Interview by Angelina A. Rafii

You call yourself the accidental pornographer. When and how did this happy accident occur?

I don't really call myself that. It was kind of a joke at one point, because I was documenting and making portraits of a lot of women that are involved in the porn industry a few years back, and it became the name of a blog that I had for some time.

Your photography seems to be a celebration of both women and light (even when it is nighttime there is always a flicker somewhere). What is it you are looking for?

I think that what I'm looking for varies from shoot to shoot. What I look for in one model is not necessarily the same thing that I will expect from another. But in general, I'm interested in the experience of looking, of seeing what each girl can bring me and watching the way she opens herself up to me and the camera. The light is a way of paying attention. But what happens in the shadows is important too.

What is it about the female body that fascinates you?

The body as a working tool and display piece simultaneously.

There are images that are playful and carefree, others that are sensual and still others that are provocative. Does it depend on your mood? Are there places you won't go or do say f taboos?**

It depends on my mood, depends on the job, and most of all it depends on the model. But there aren't many places I won't go; I'm not particularly interested in boundaries.

Models or "girl-next-door", especially in the context of erotic photography-what are your thoughts?

I'm open to all kinds of girls. But, if you want to make an erotic image the most important thing is that the girl has to be pretty enthusiastic about whatever she's doing.

Are there challenges in your professional life that you have set as a benchmark for success? If so what are they?

I'm working on my first book, a collection of all of my favorite girls. I'll be pretty excited when it's done.

WWW.AUTUMNSONNICHSEN.COM

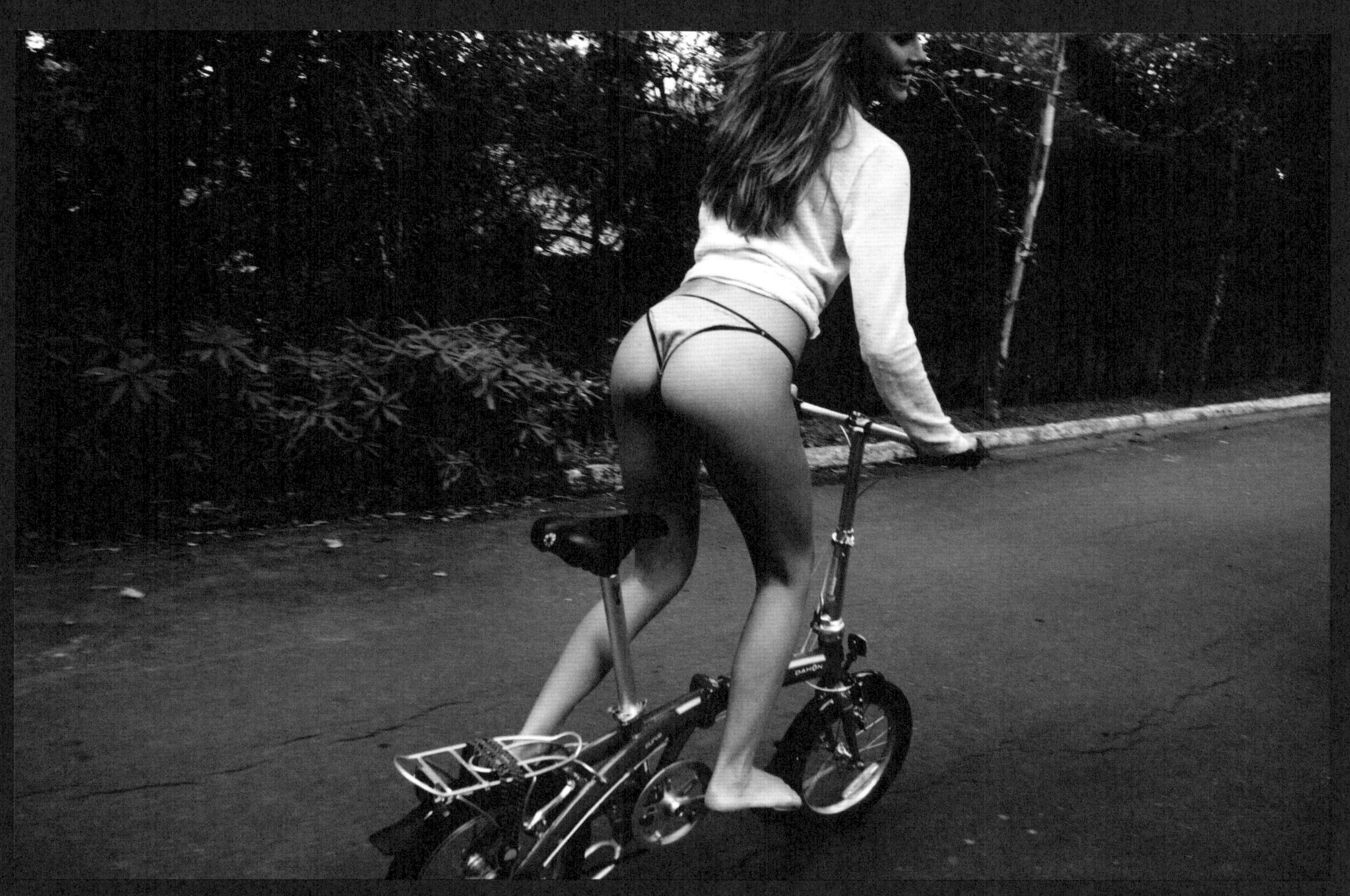

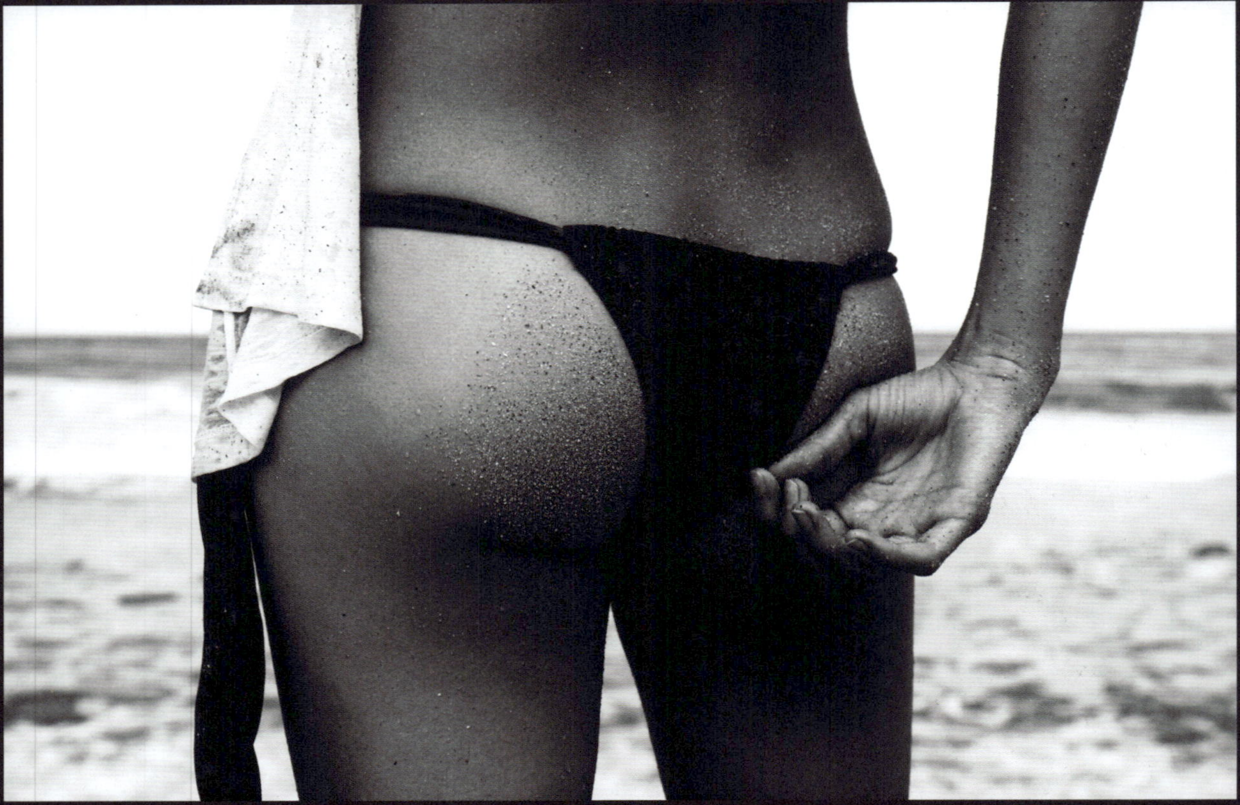

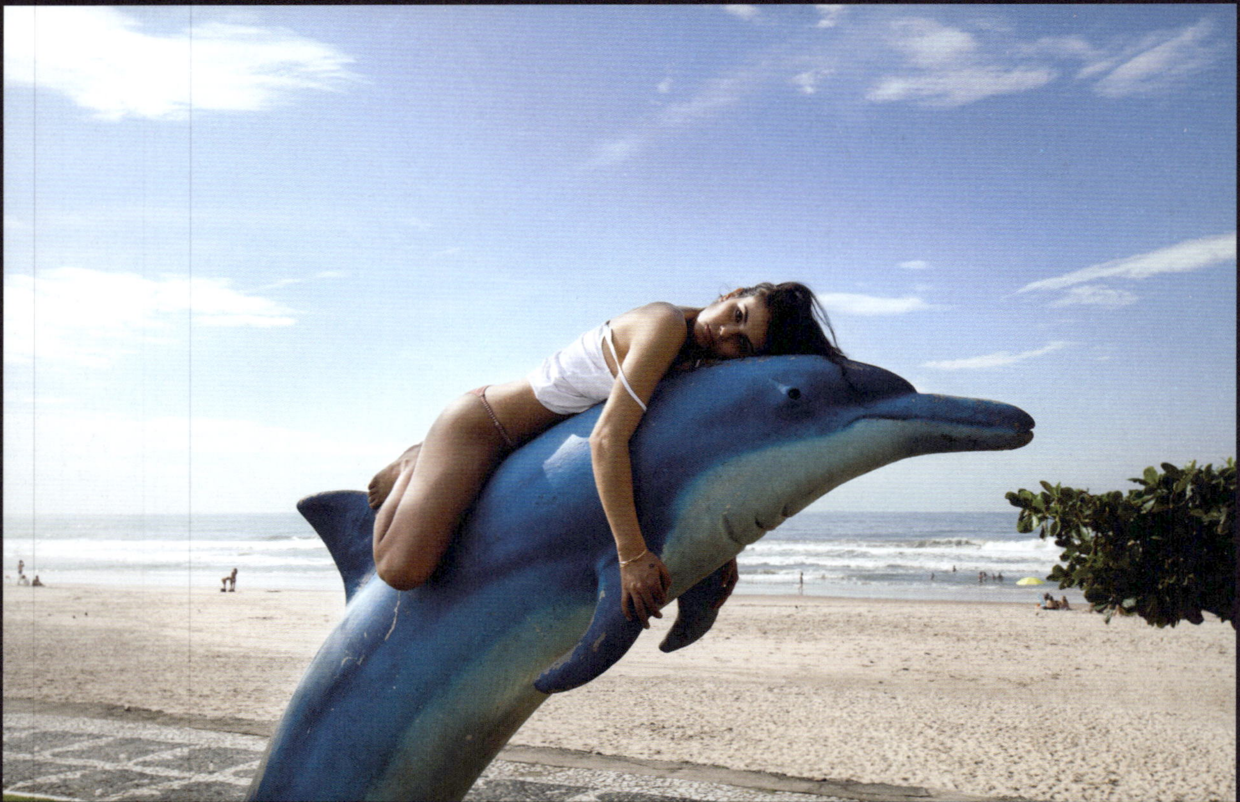

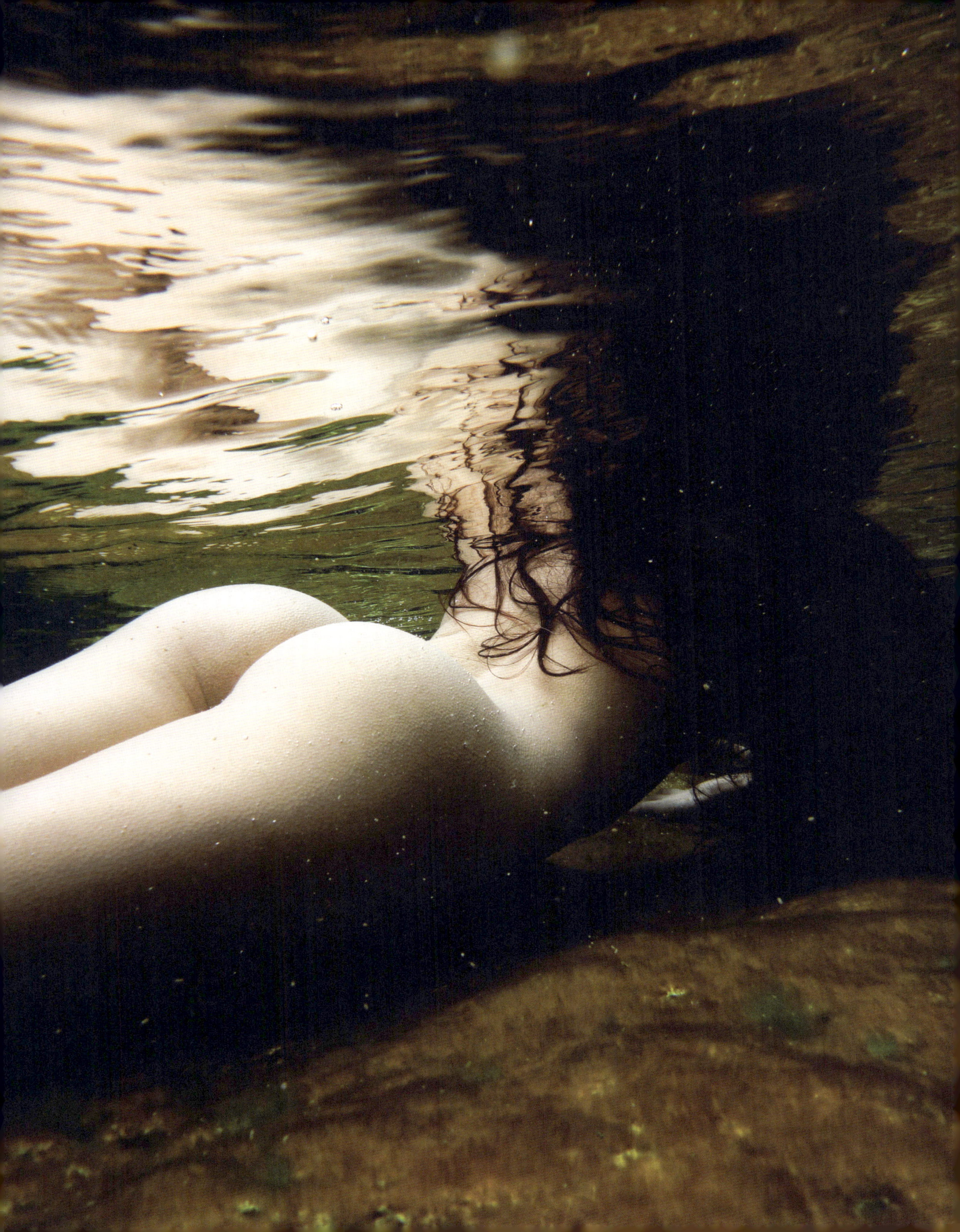

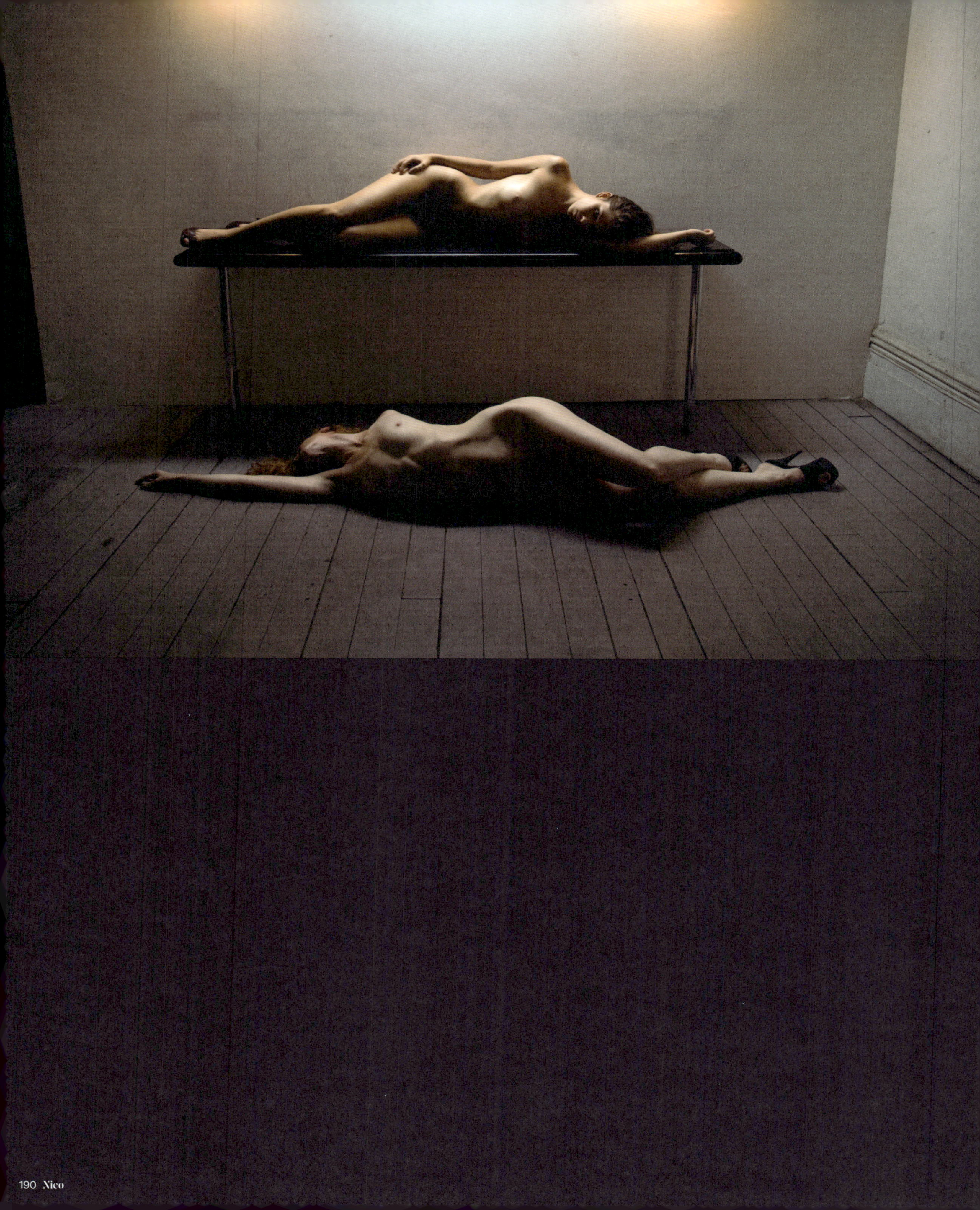

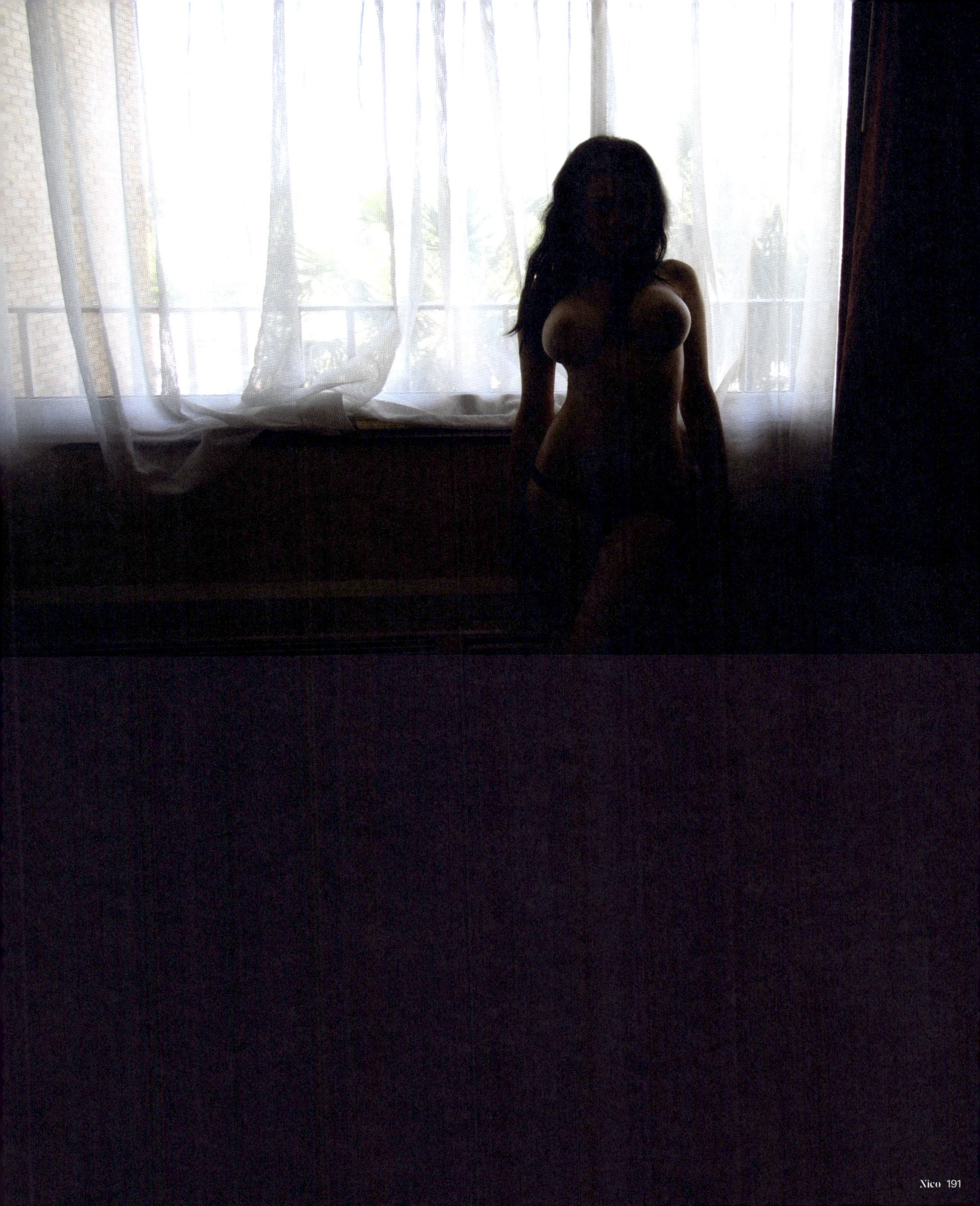

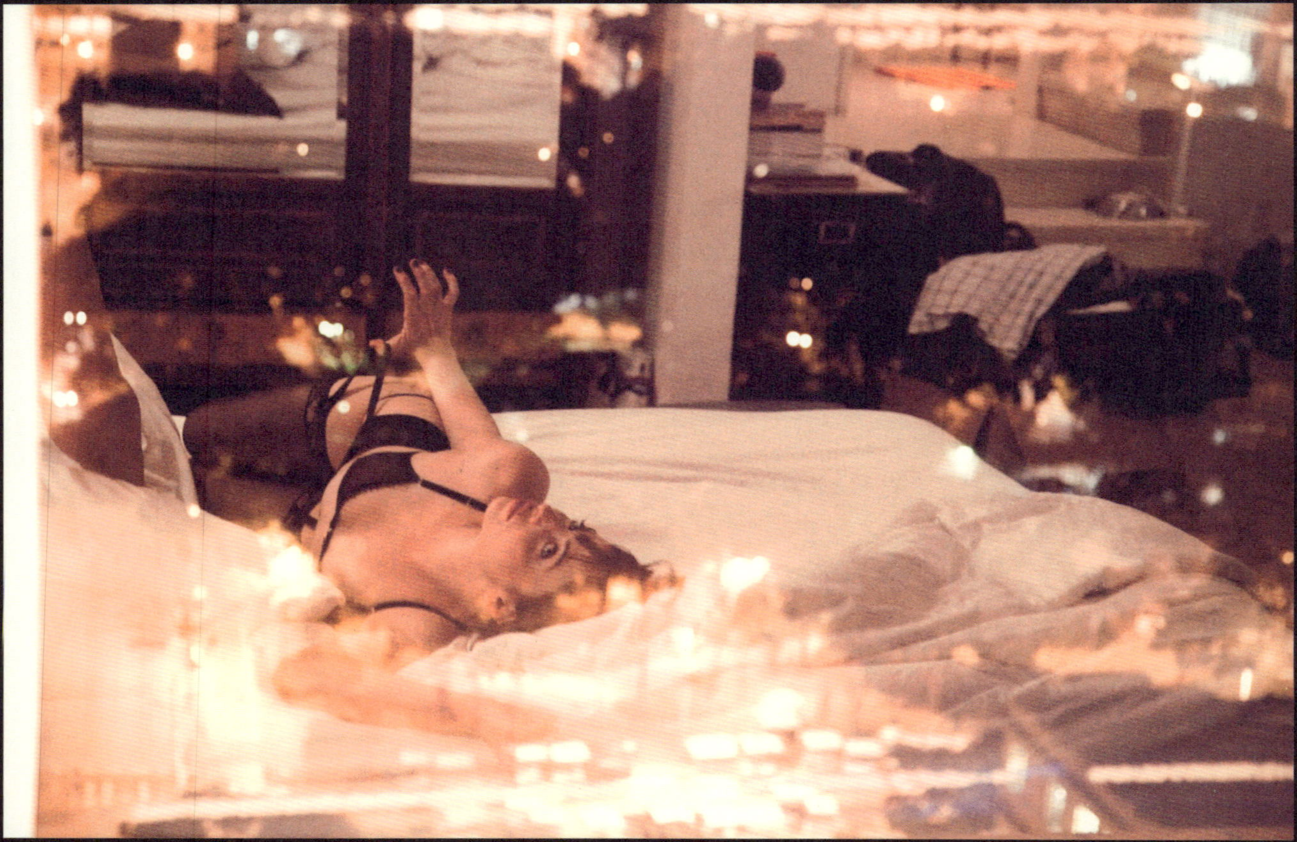

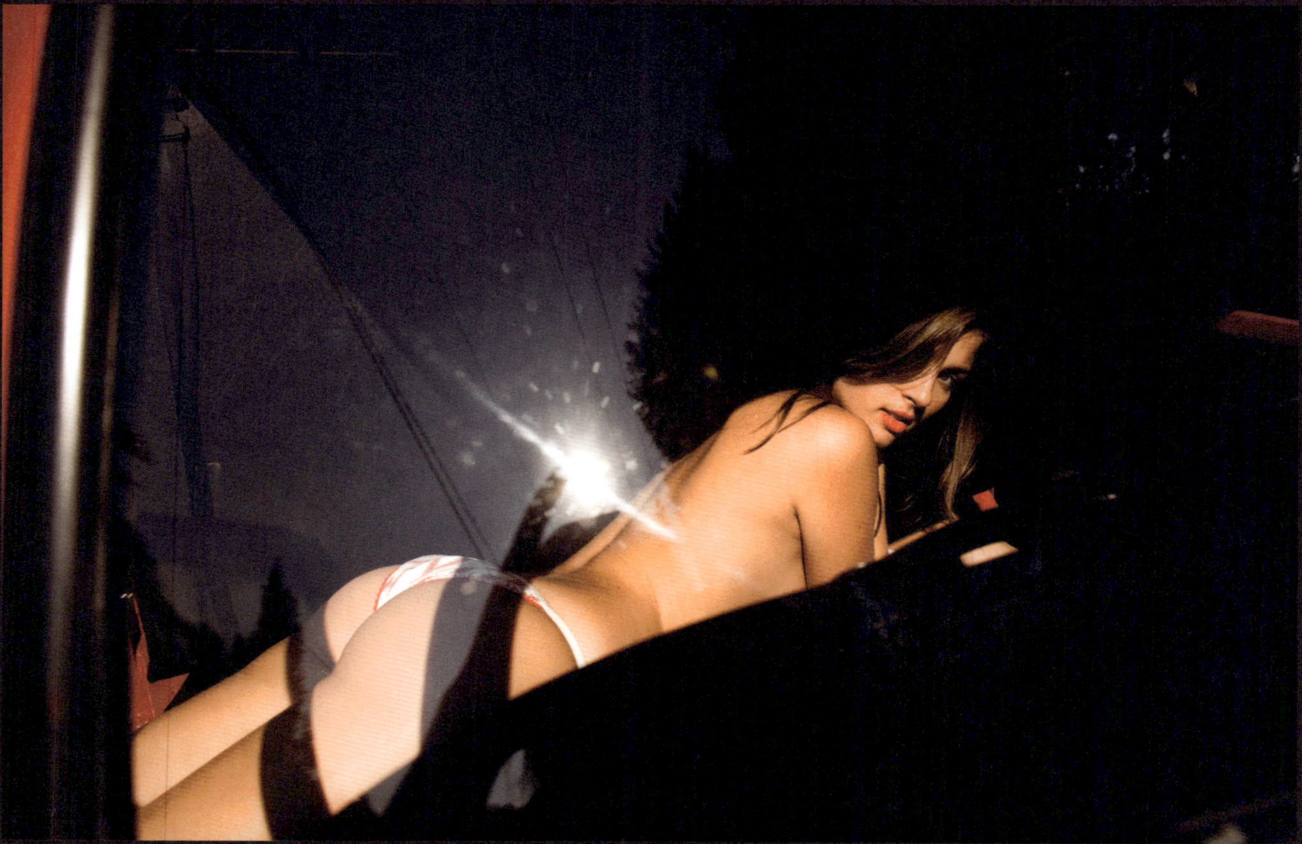

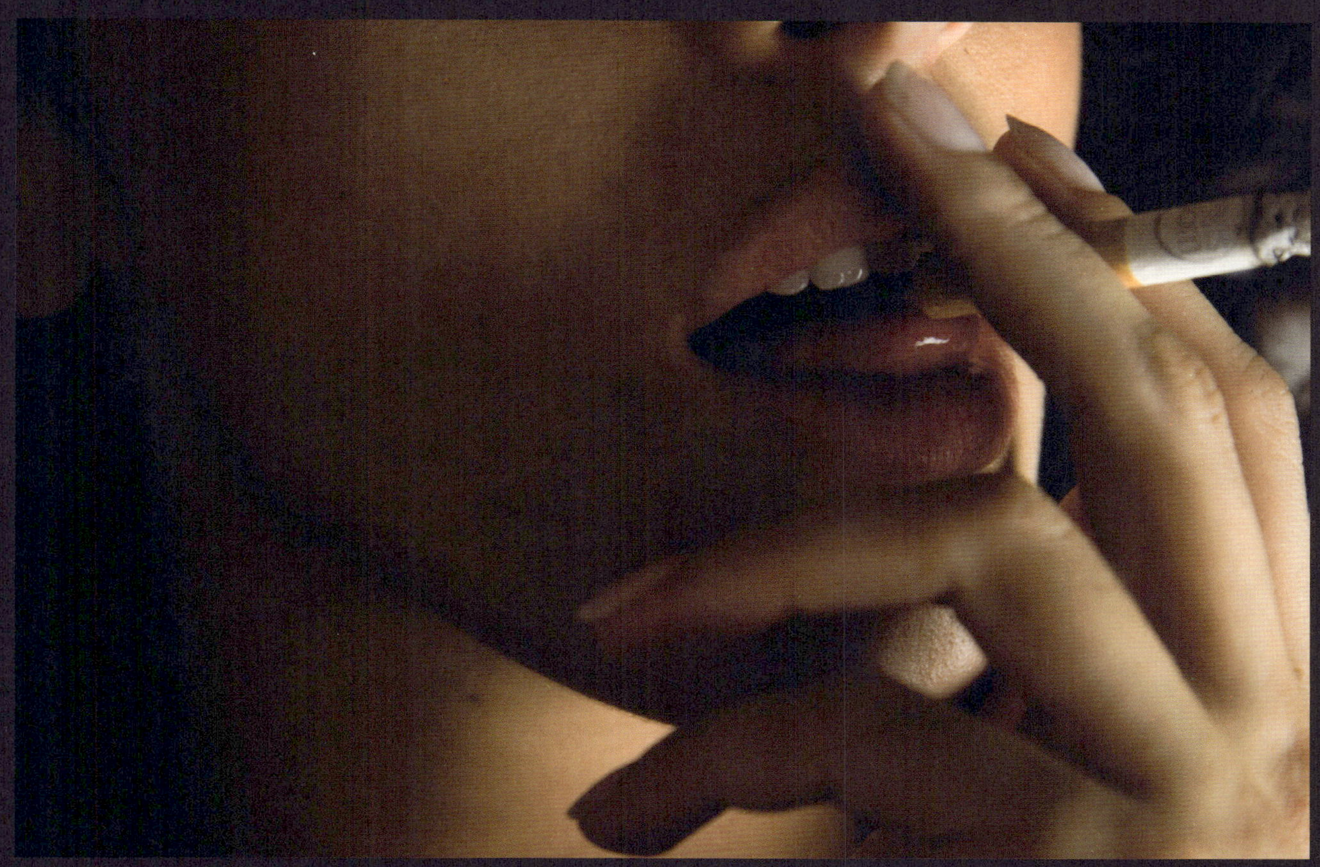

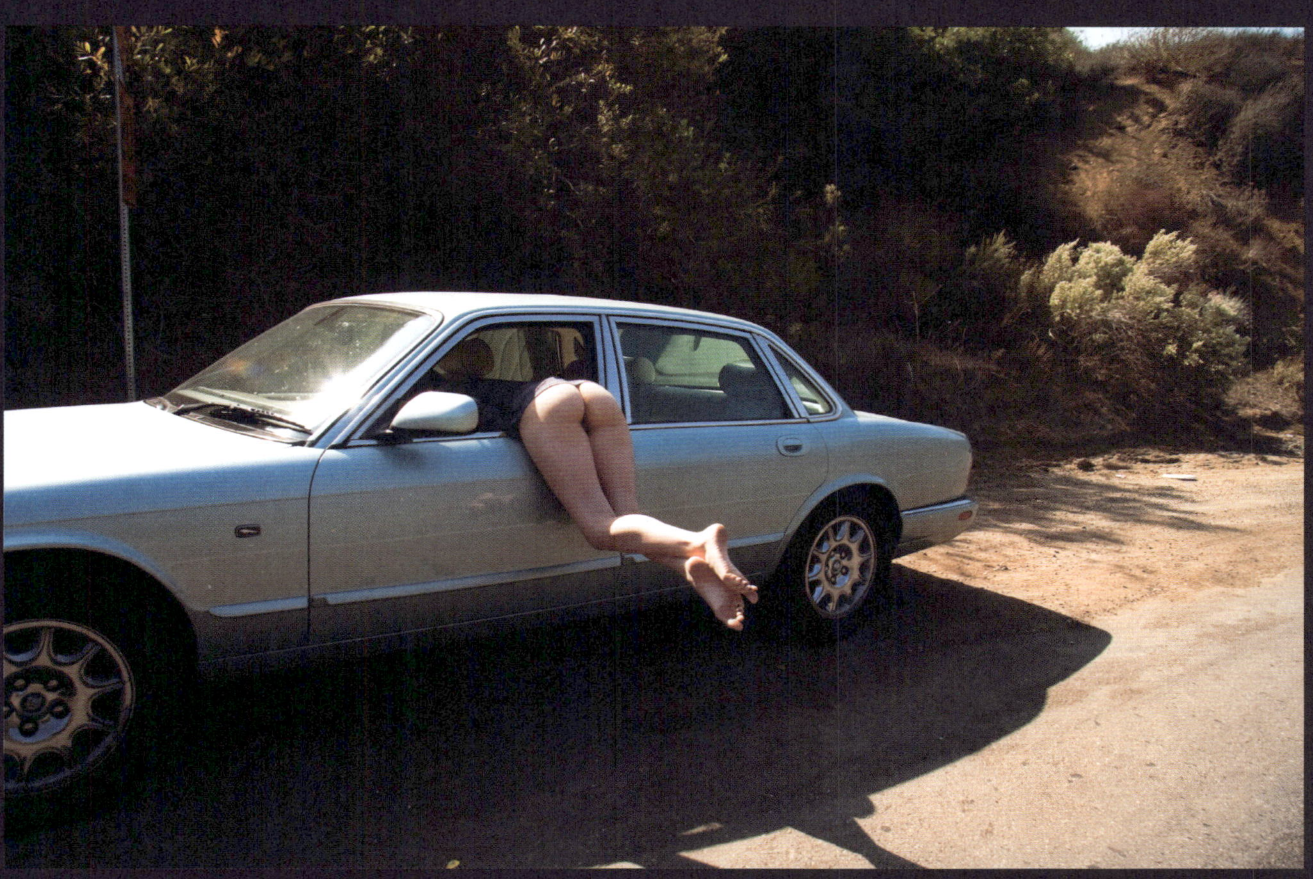

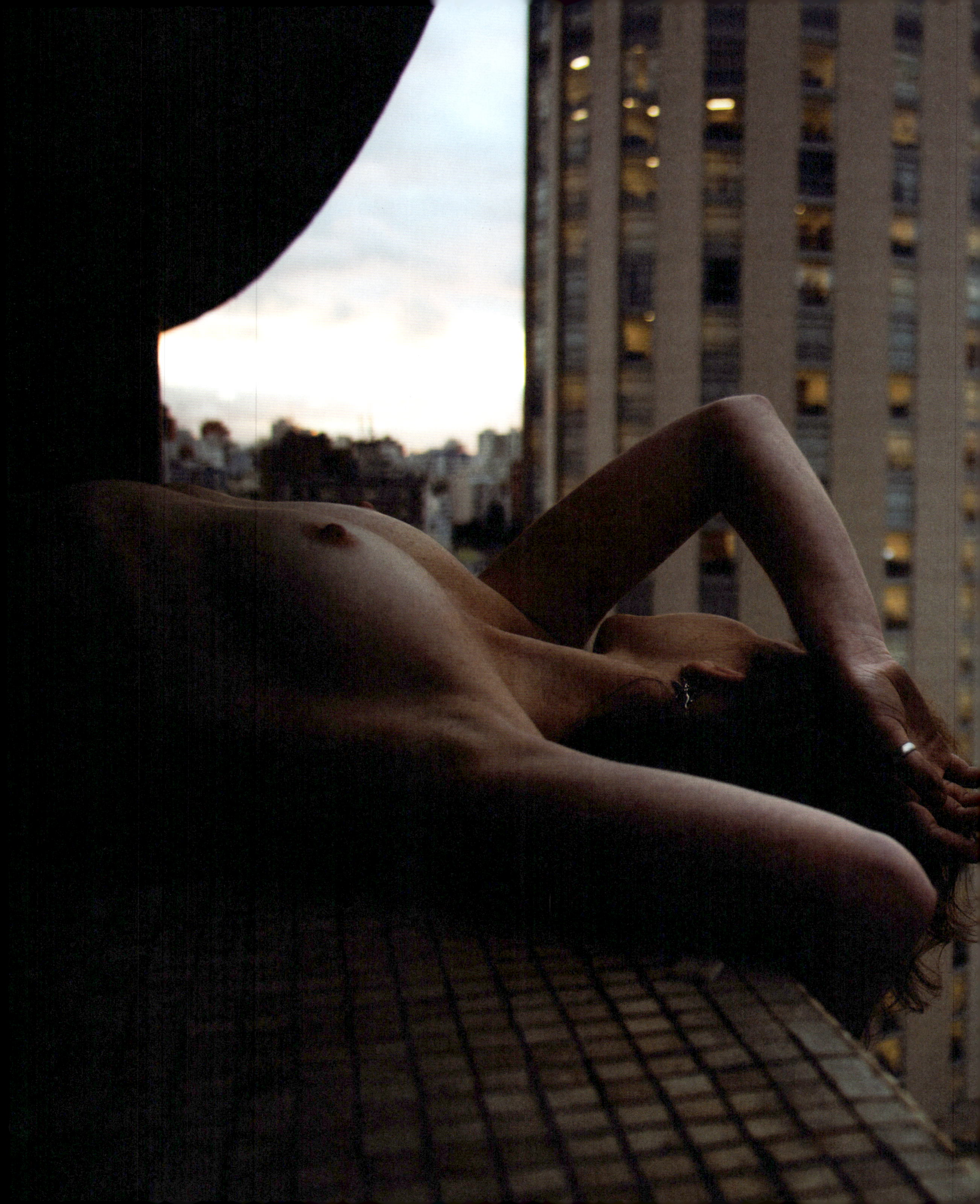

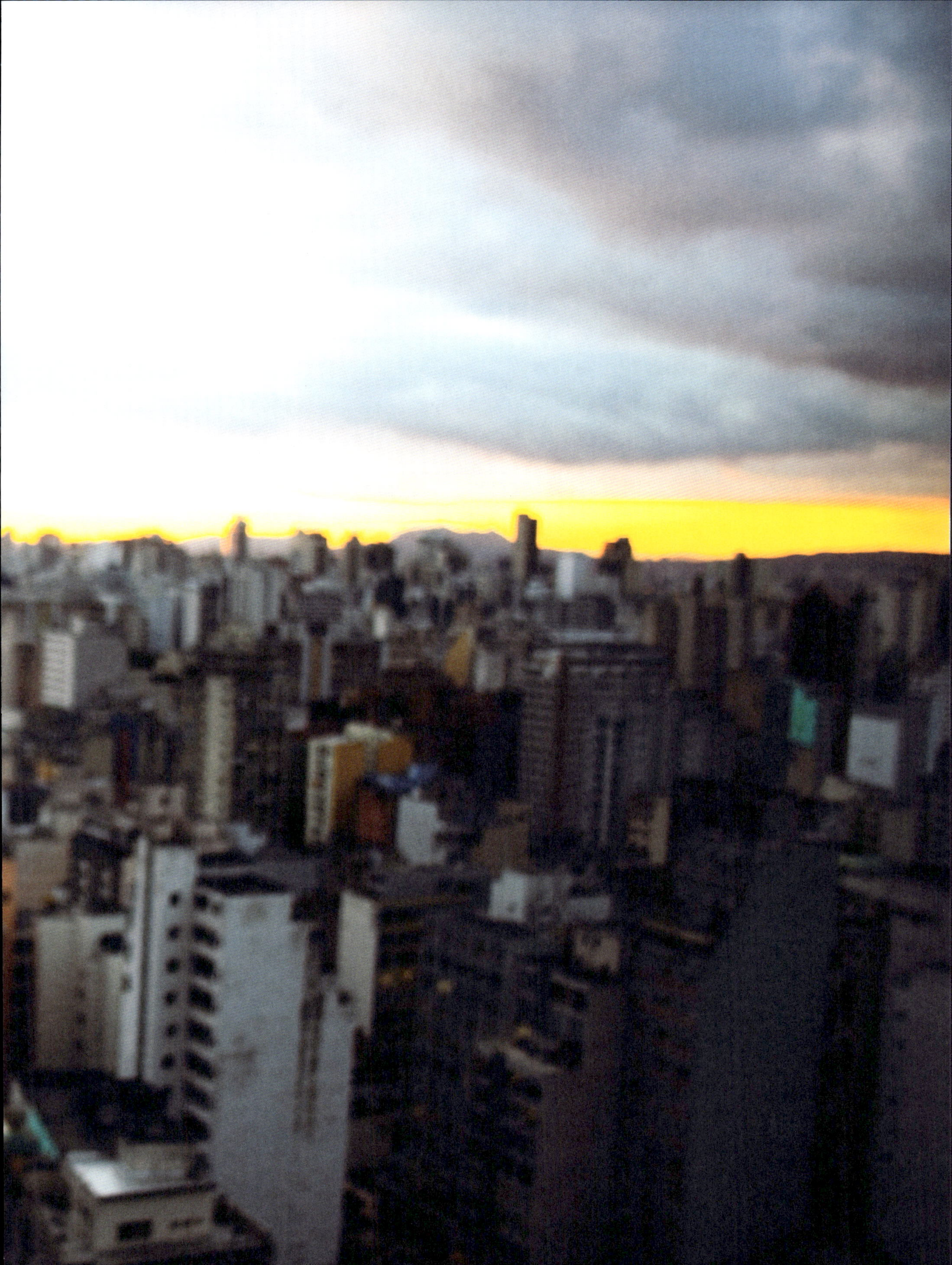

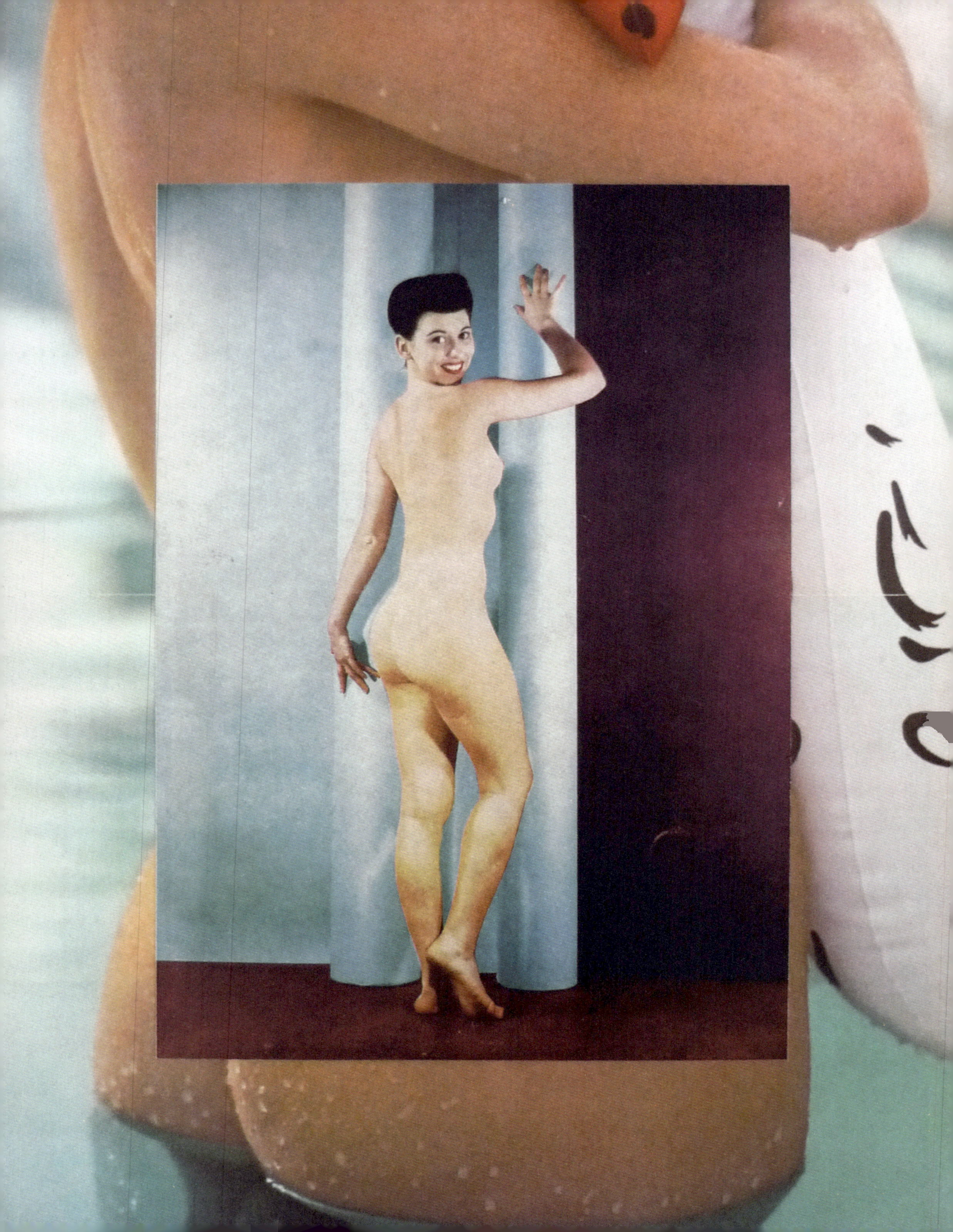

JUSTIN MORIN

Interview by Angelina A. Rafii

What inspired you to do this work? Do you find that the eroticism that is considered retro differs very much from what we see today and why did you chose to oppose the two in your work?

These collages were created for a solo show named Teaser, which took place last summer in Galerie Jeanroch Dard in Paris. I've realized that my work, which is quite minimal, doesn't really reflect the sensuality of doing sculpture. It's a quite common thing to say, but it's a very physical process. The whole body is engaged: the contractions of the muscles, the effort, the sweat So everything was about this erotic energy. The collages are entitled 'shapes and forms: display'. They are the addition of two pictures, but I clearly see three elements in them: the two female protagonists and the prop. On each black and white picture, there's an element that looks like a sculpture: a cube, a plinth, a column These objects of display act like bridges between the two universes and become invested with a sexual connotation. Of course,

there is a lot of difference between the black and white pictures (which come from magazines from the fifties), and the colour ones (which come from the seventies). They are more naïve and leave more space for imagination.

Is it something that you wish to explore further?
Definitely. I'm already working on new pieces, mainly sculptures, exploring these notions.

These collages differ from the work you usually do, can you explain.

Well, they may seem less complex than the previous ones, but I've worked the same way. All the pictures came from vintage magazines that I bought on Internet. It was quite a challenge to find them because I had a very precise idea about the images I was looking for. I wanted the compositions to be simple, with no variations, so in a way, there's this minimalist sensitivity that define my productions.

MEDICA-MENTEUSE.COM

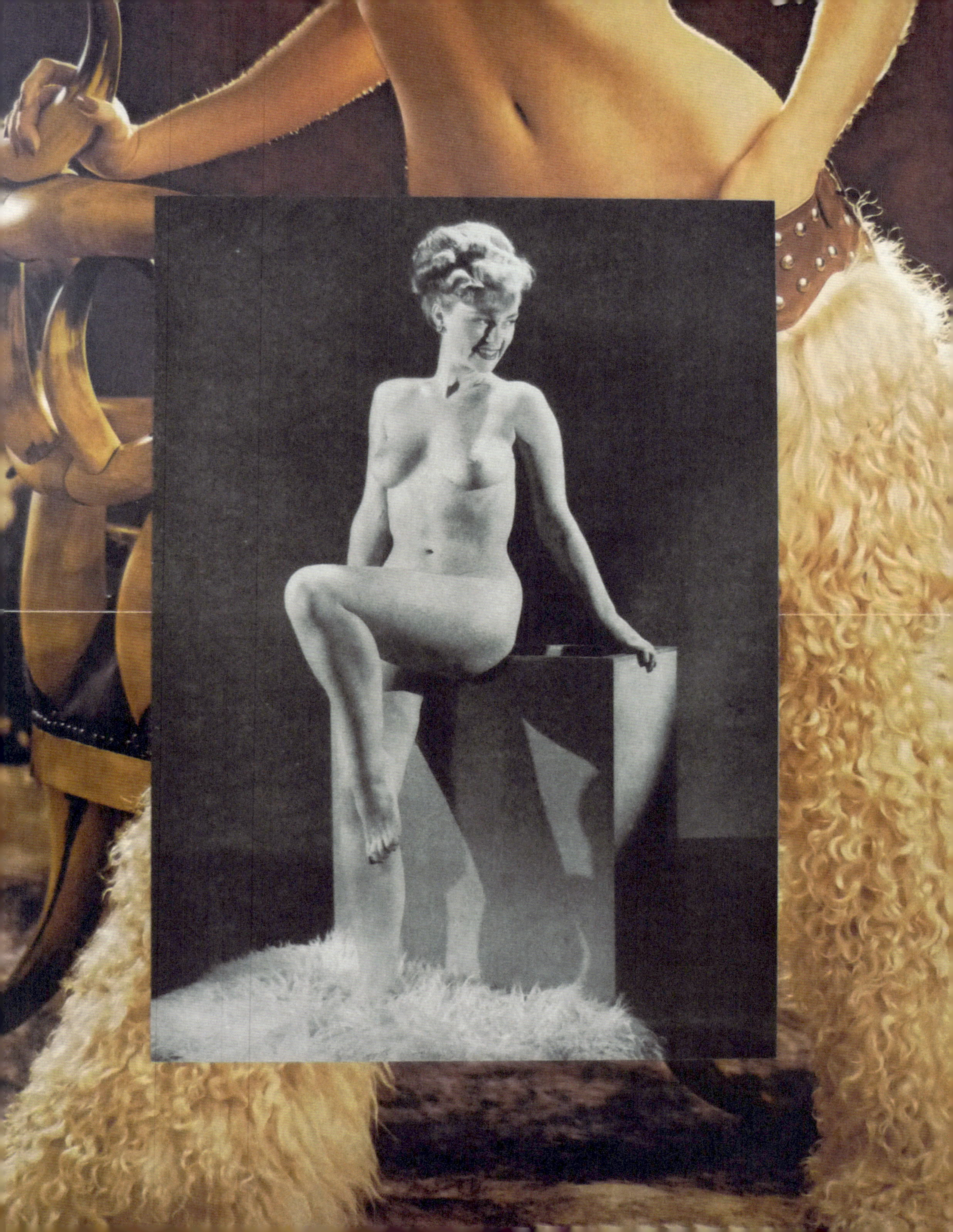

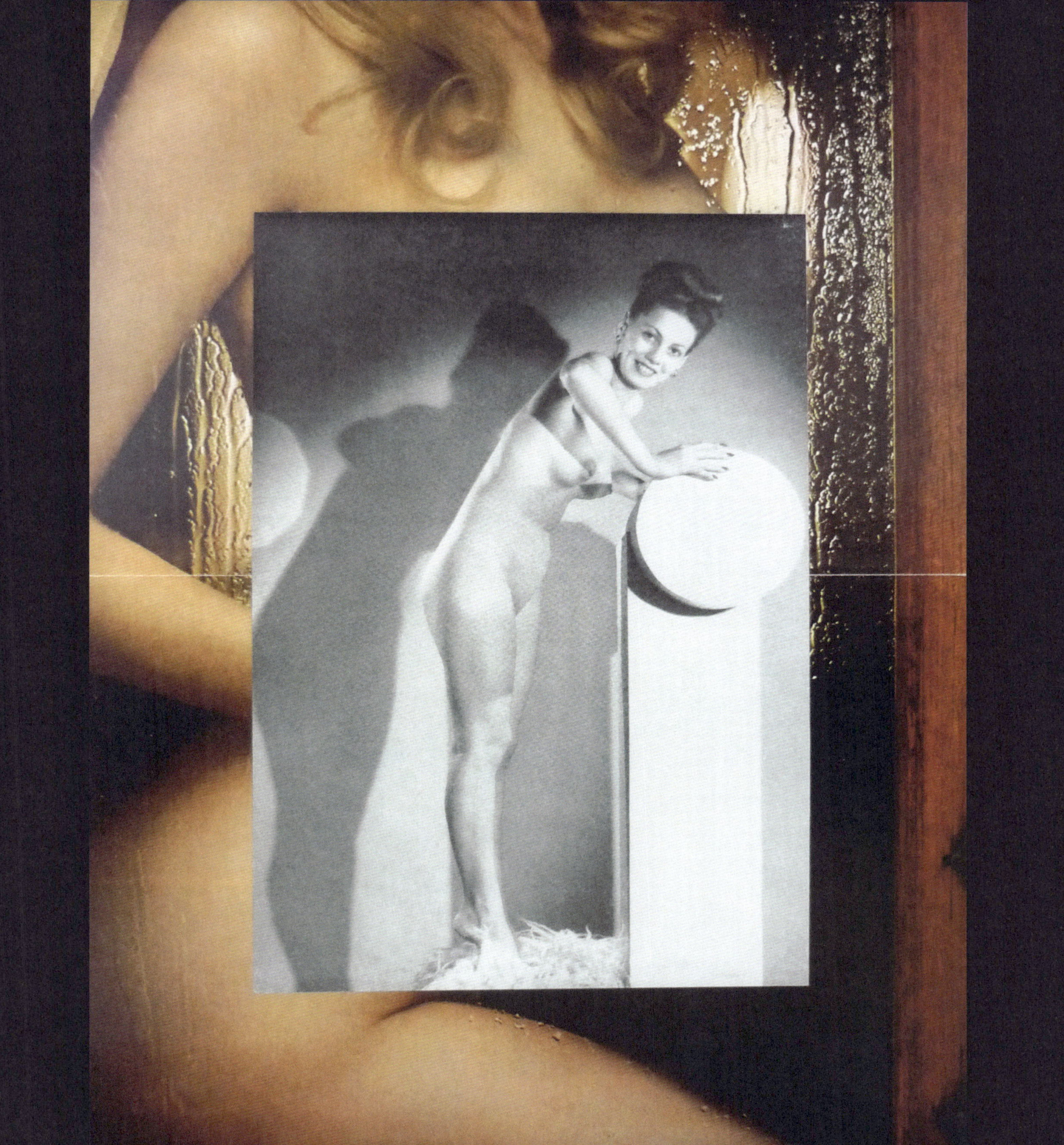

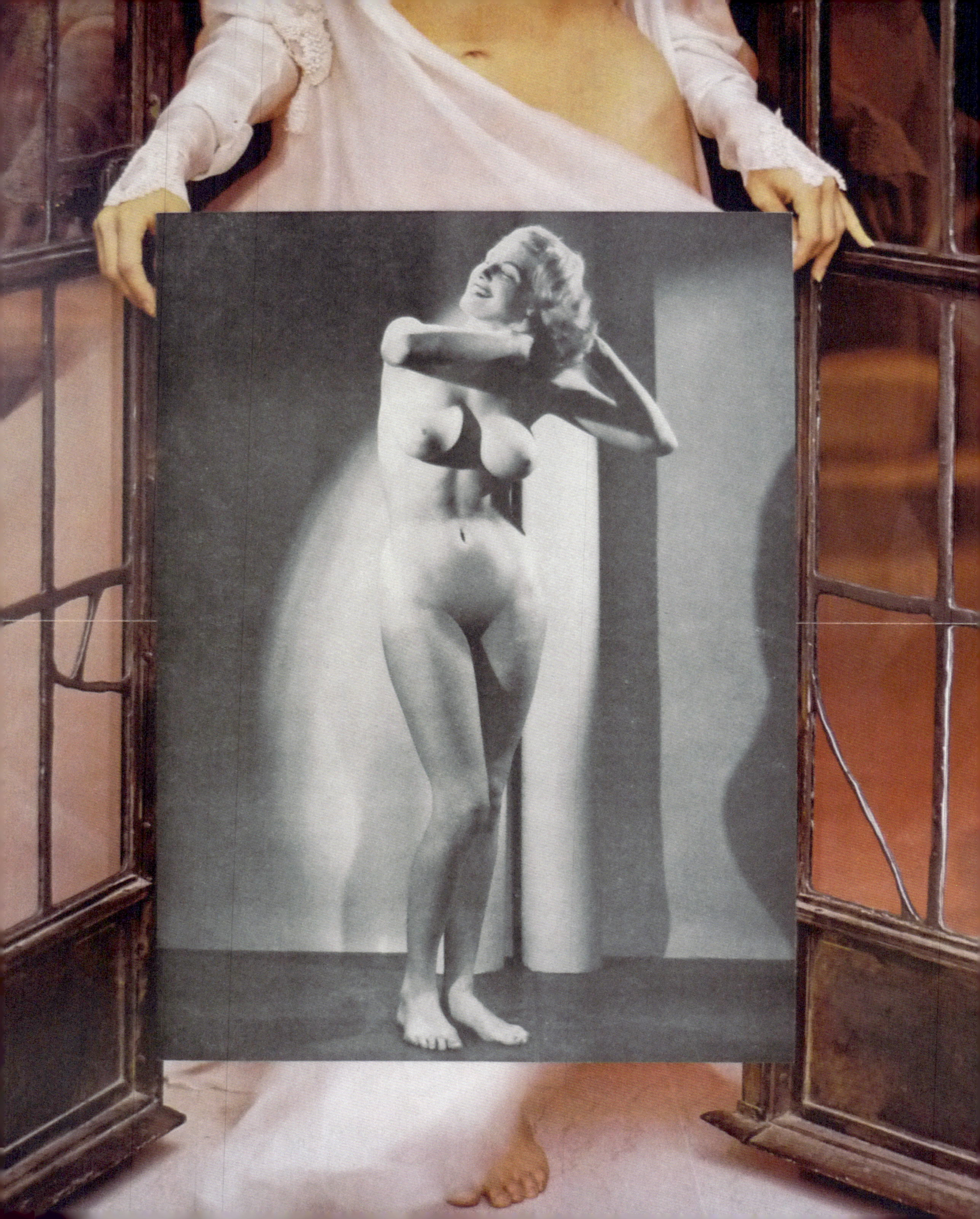

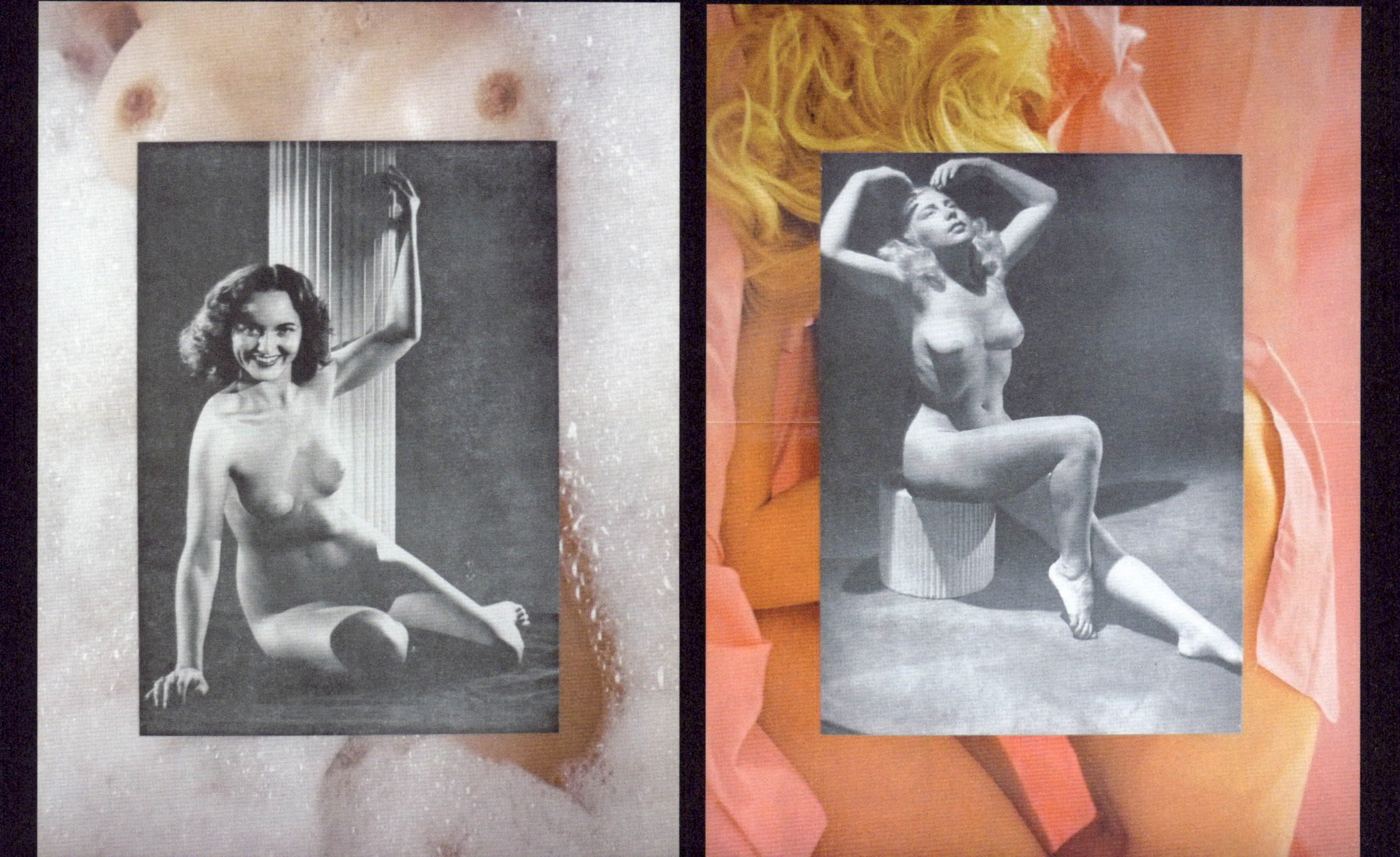

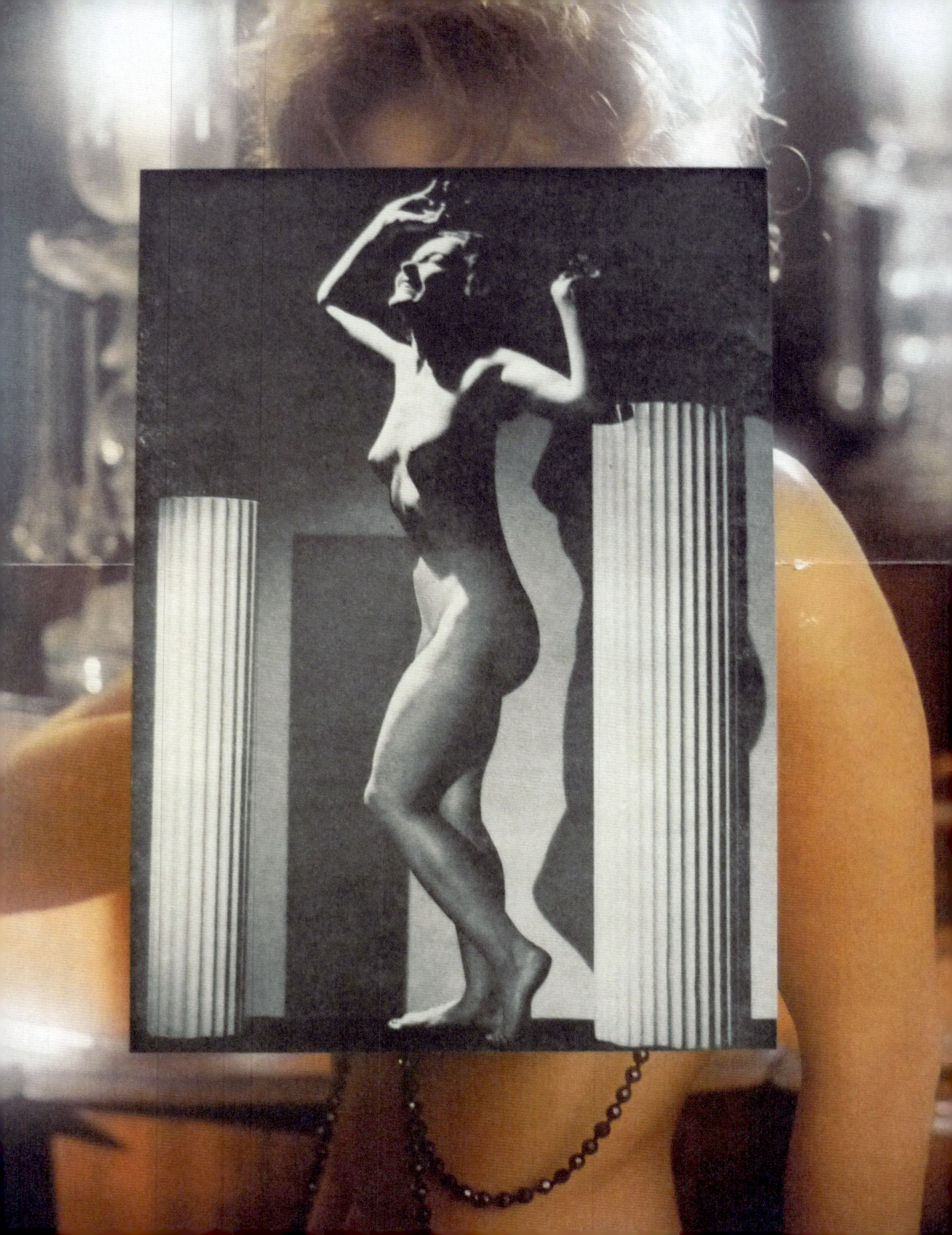

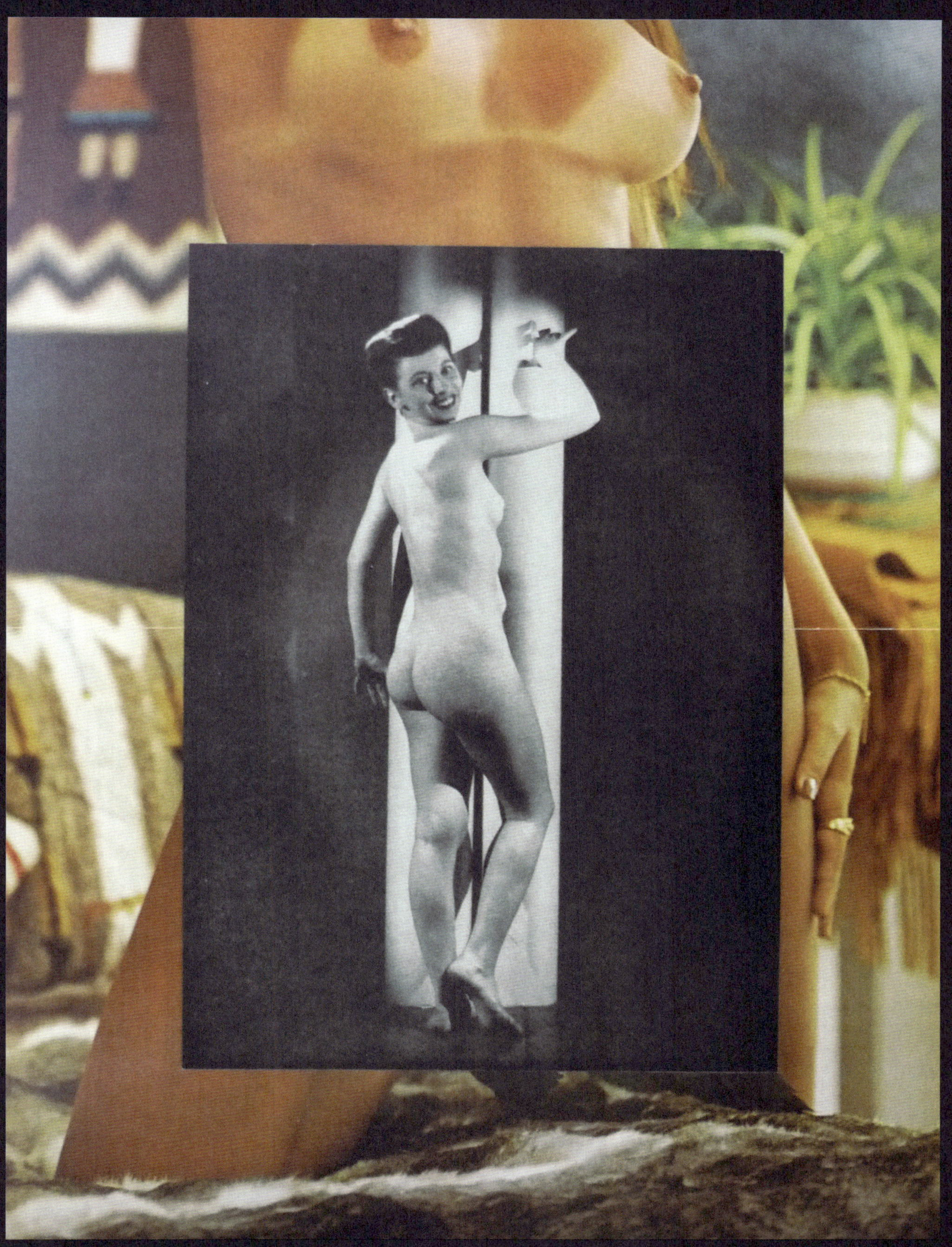

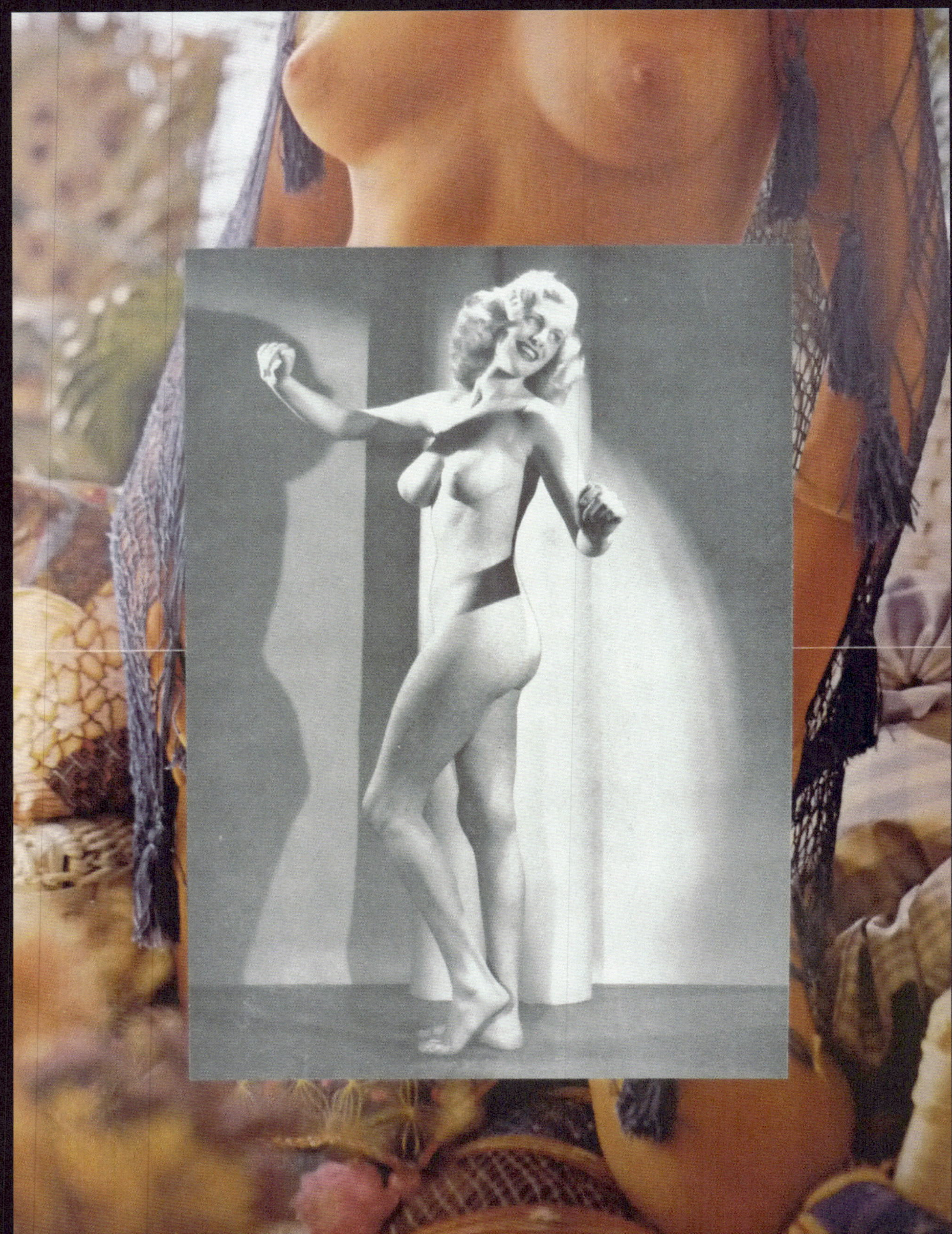

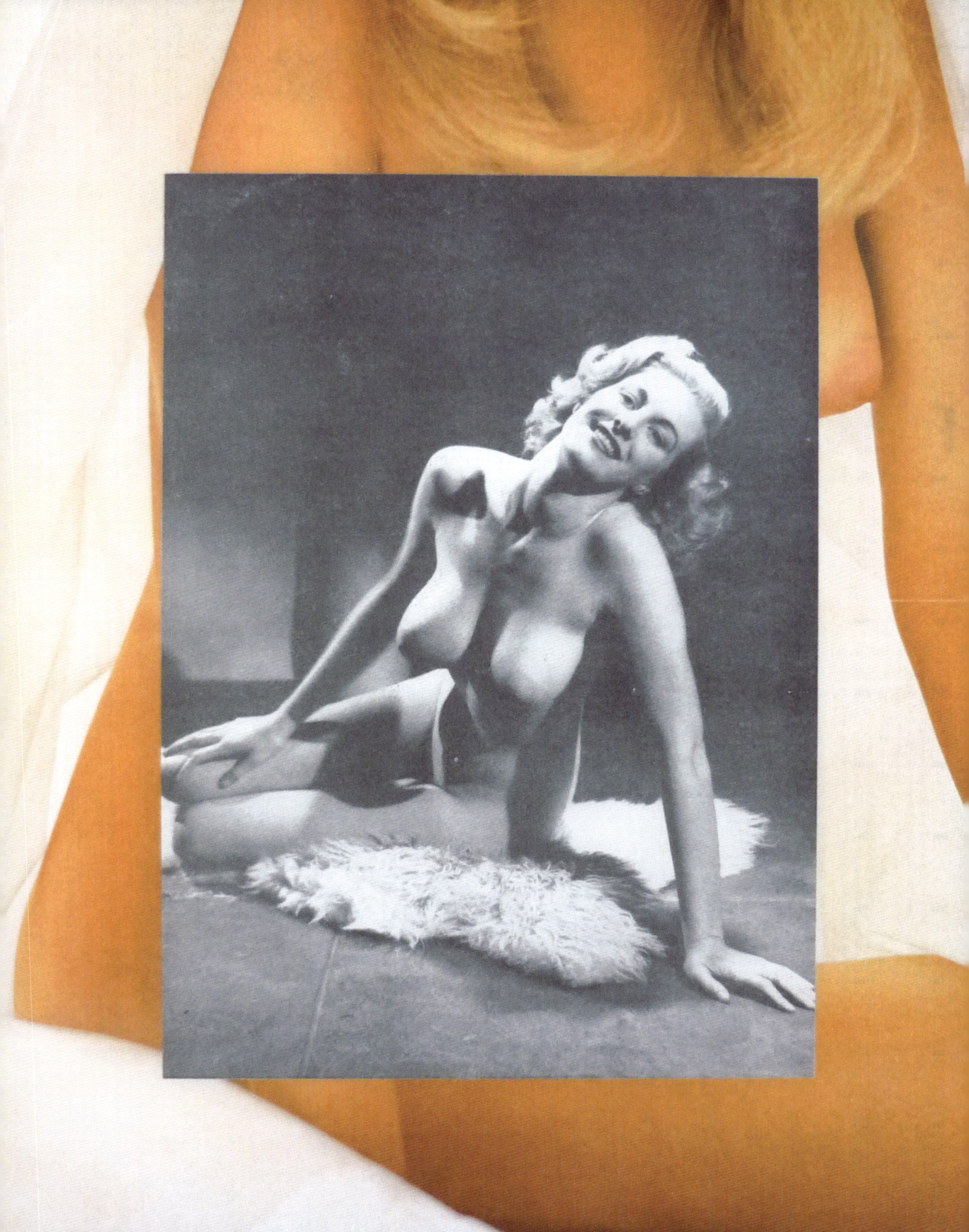

HANNES CASPAR

Interview by Angelina A. Rafii

Can you tell us a bit about your background and your inspirations?

In former times I spent much time listening to music and watching movies. I was generally interested in creative things, but didn't know exactly, what my profession could be someday. So I tried some different things, did some awful jobs until I got a digital SRL as a present. At first I was primarily taking shots of abstract and graphic things but after a while I was bored so I decided to take pictures of friends and models. Since then, it has become a kind of obsession. It's great fun to meet strangers, get to know each other and take shots. My inspiration is daily life, but of course also pictures from the Internet and magazines.

How is working with nudes different from your other work?

Actually there is no big difference. Basically even my nude works are portraits. The only difference is that the human body is involved and that means that I have many more possibilities.

Your work is very aesthetic and beautiful, do you have a specific idea in mind or is the whole process spontaneous? Do you set boundaries for yourself when photographing nudes? What do you consider to be vulgar or too much?

I rarely have concrete ideas in my mind. I mostly get inspired when I see fresh faces. So the whole work process is very intuitive and spontaneous. Actually I don't set any boundaries but of course there are some things I don't like, but I don't have to think about it… I just focus on doing my job. That said, I don't like nude pictures of women posing in a very sexual way. To me, that's poor and stupid.

I find that there are three major themes in your nudes: shadow play, water and "acrobatics". Can you explain?

(Laughs)…yes, indeed. These things are always exciting. My work is very simple and reduced. Sometimes little details tell the story.

WWW.HANNESCASPAR.COM

VIDEO

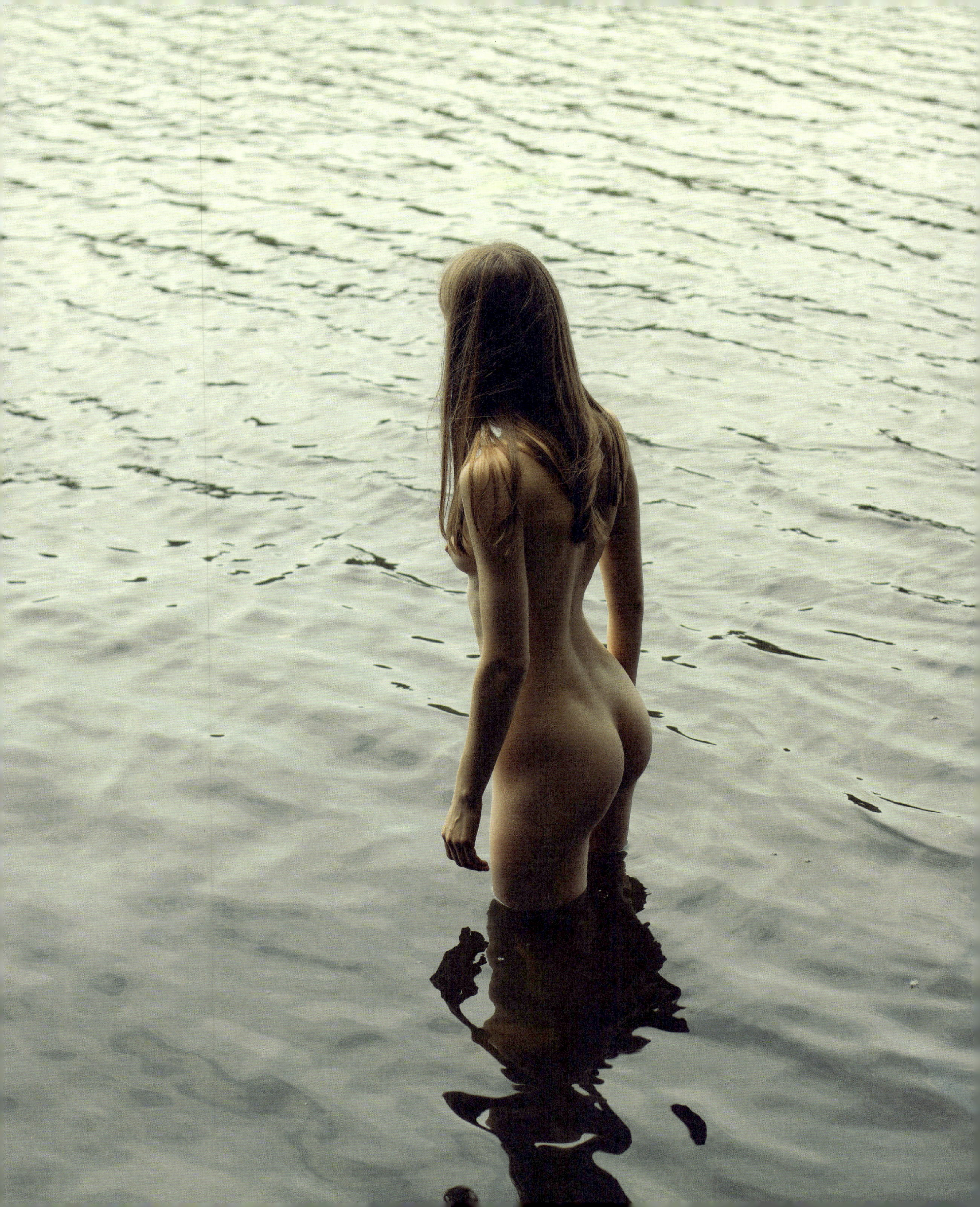

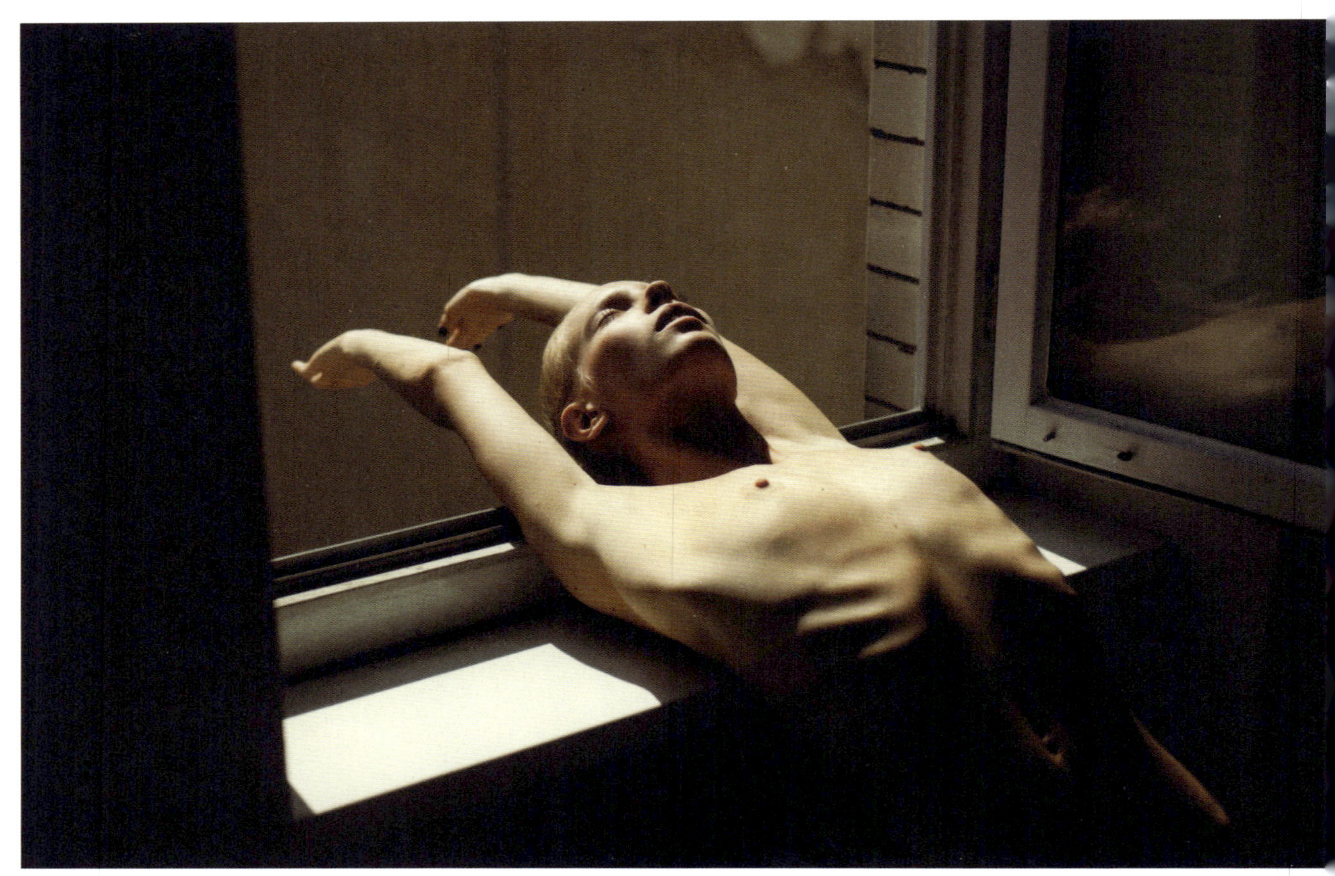

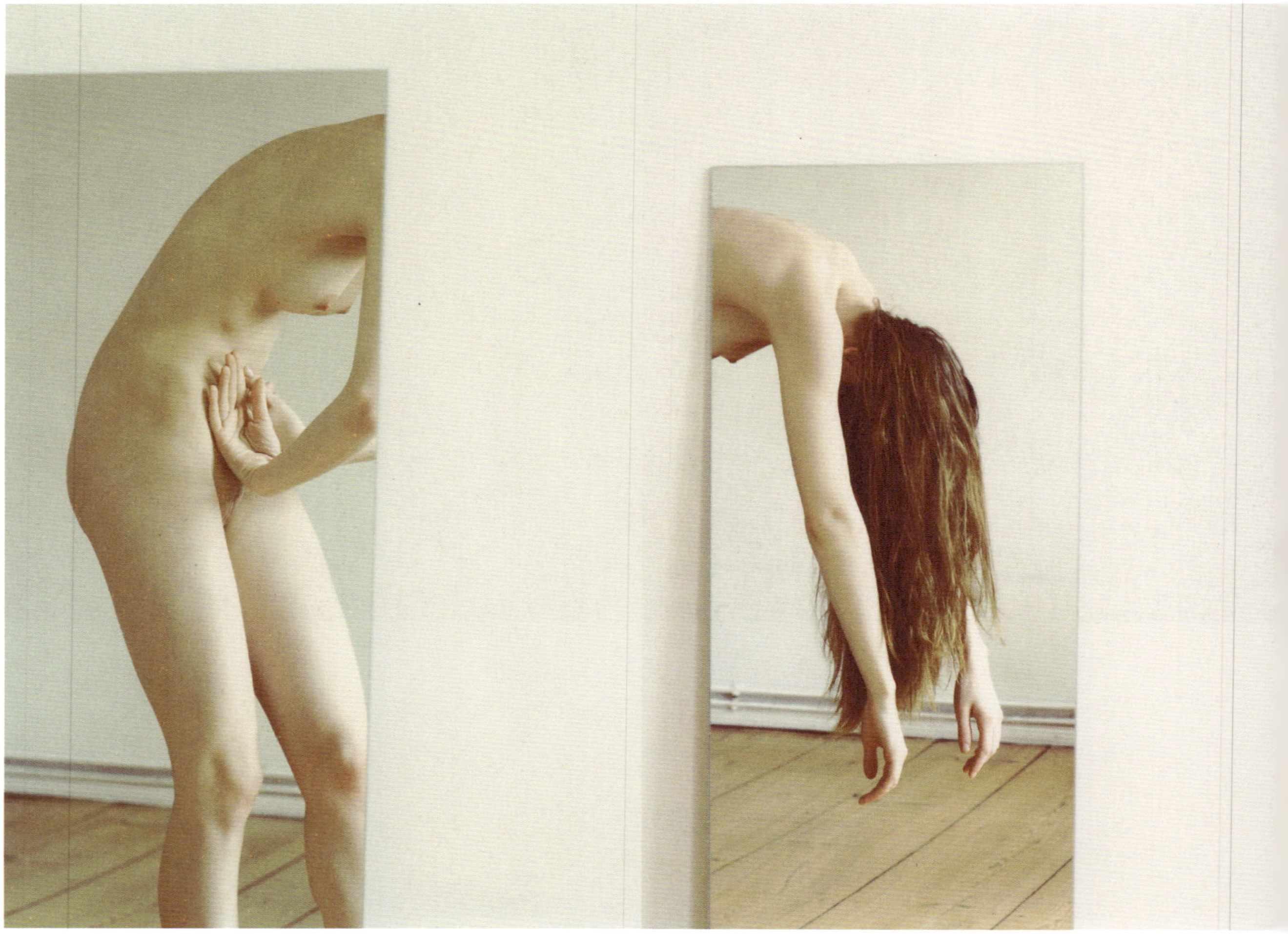

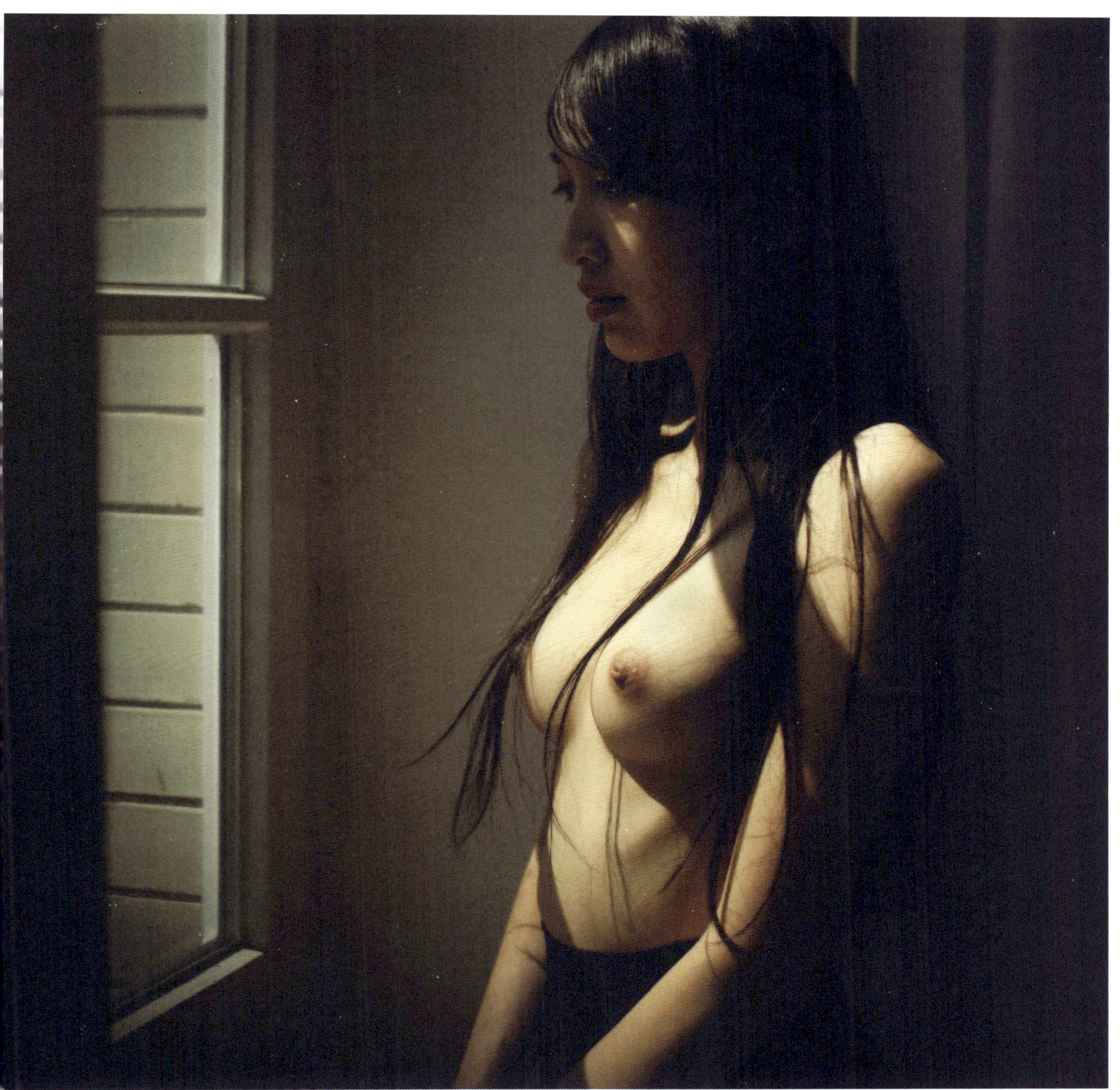

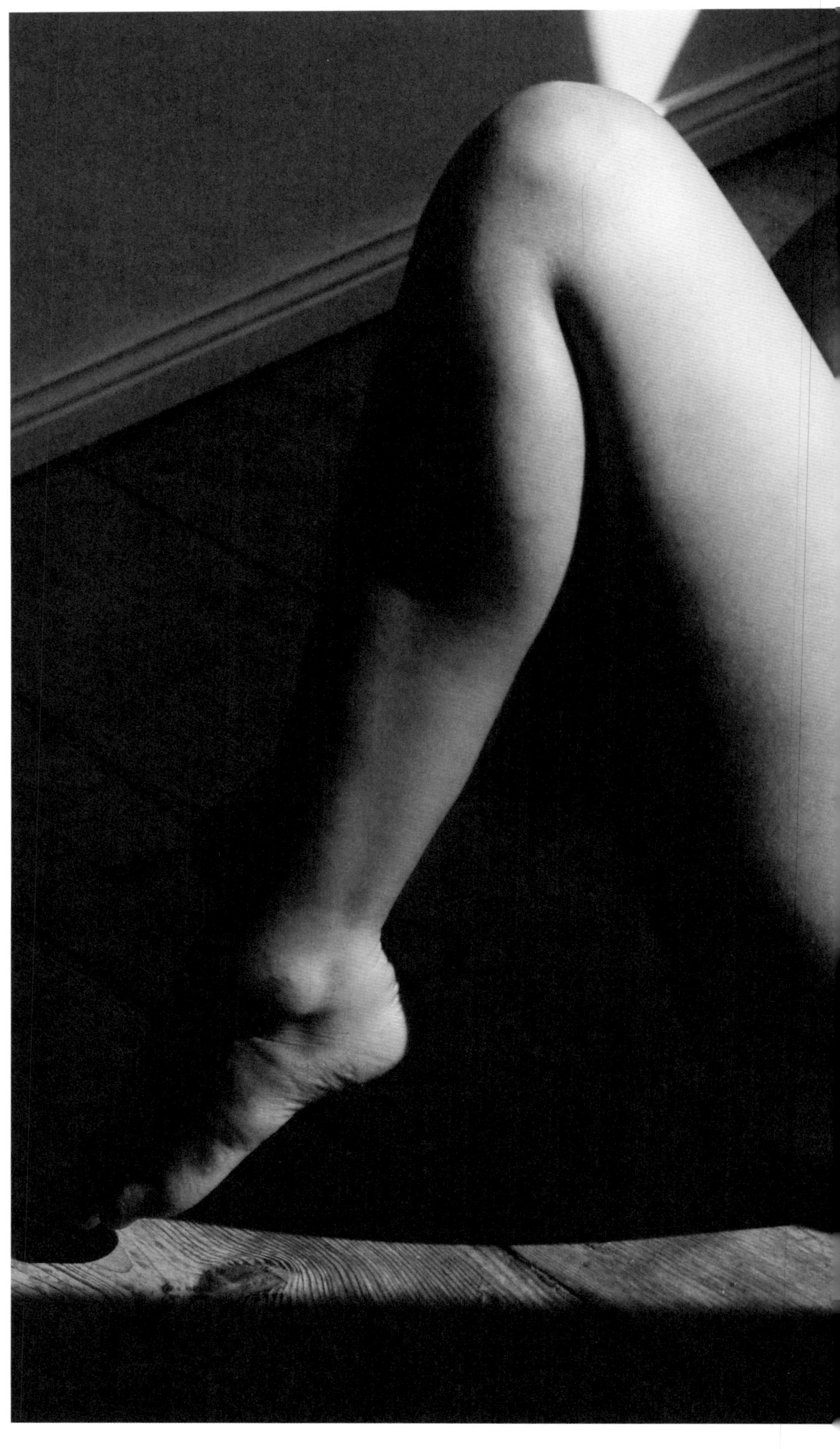

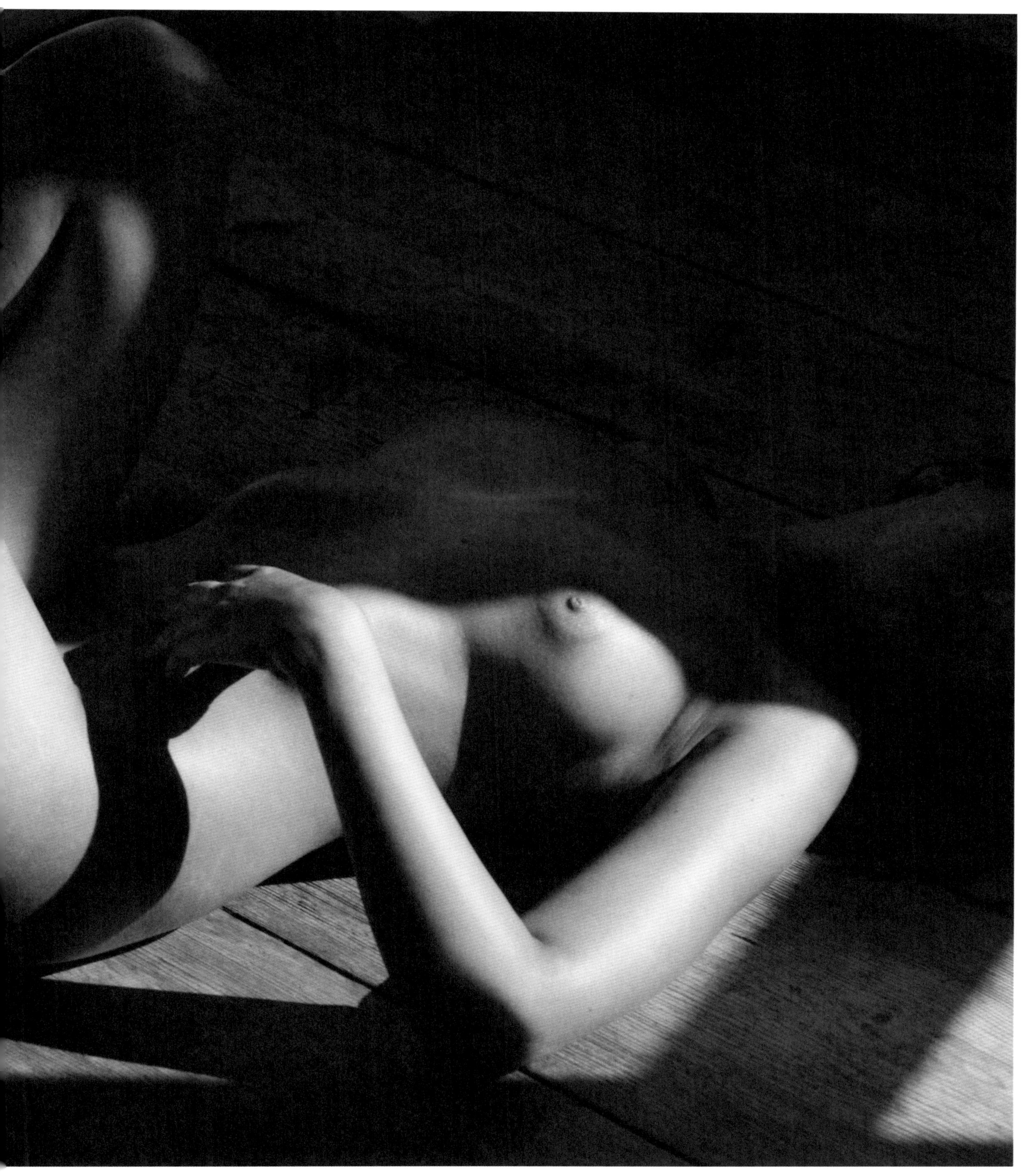

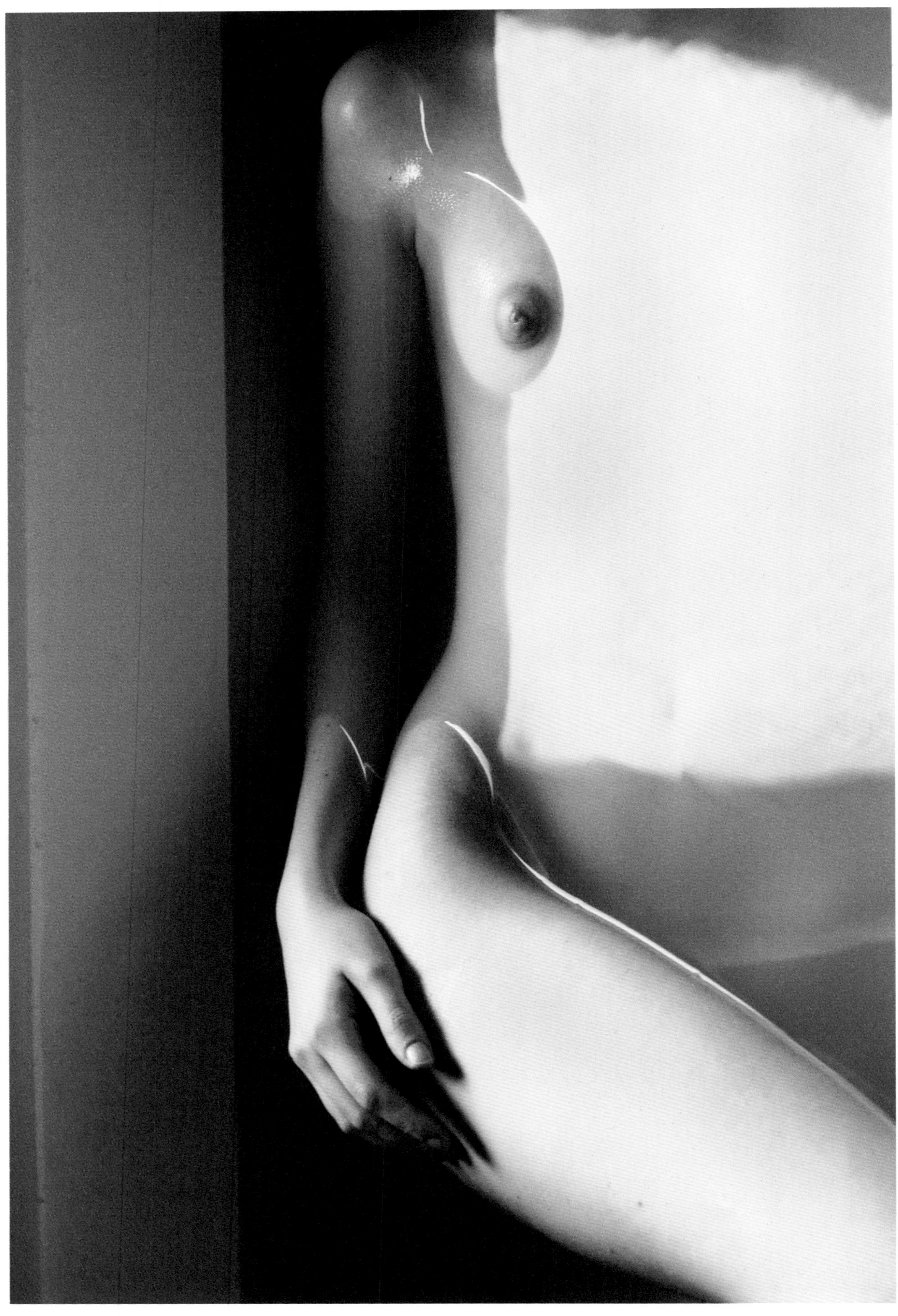

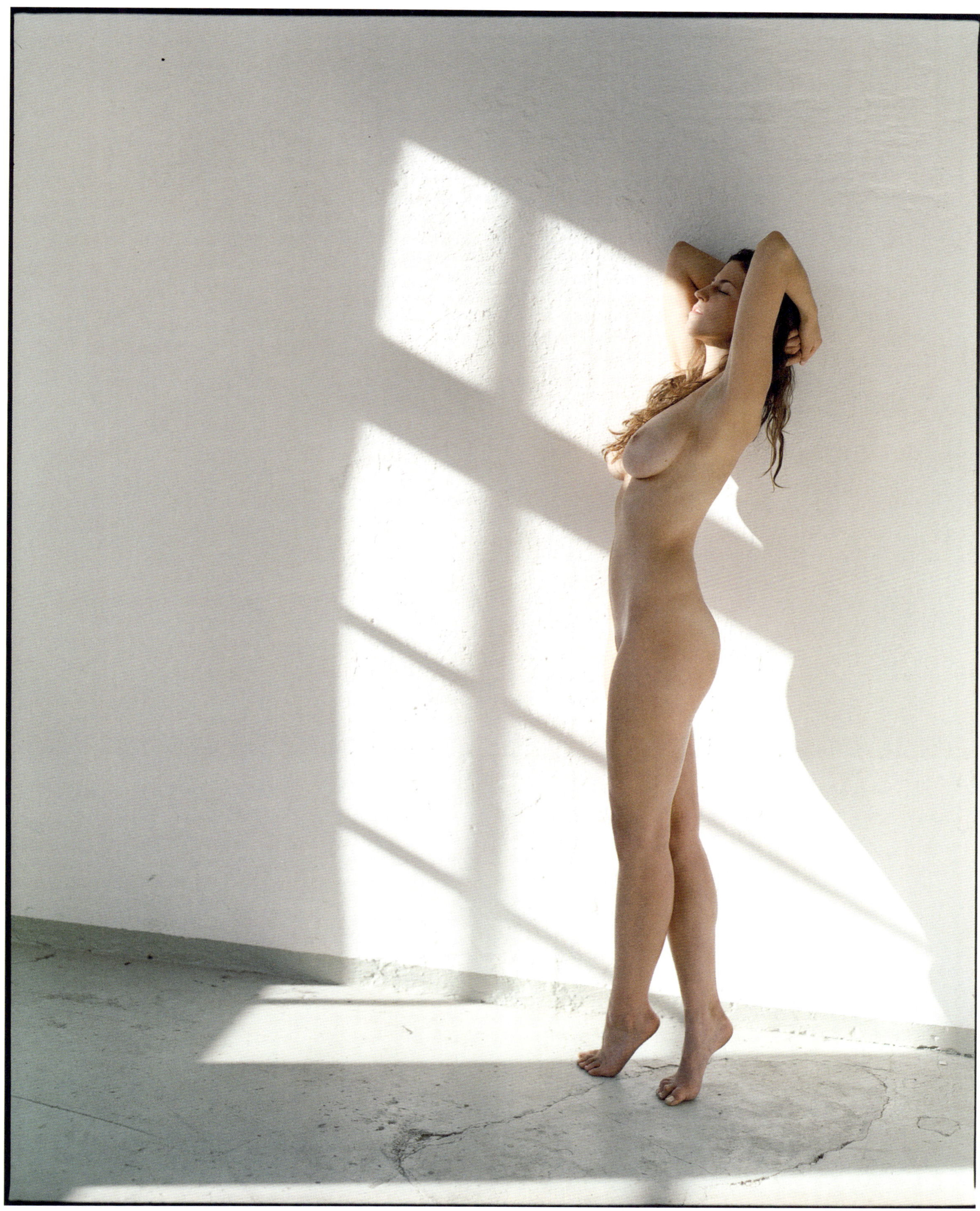

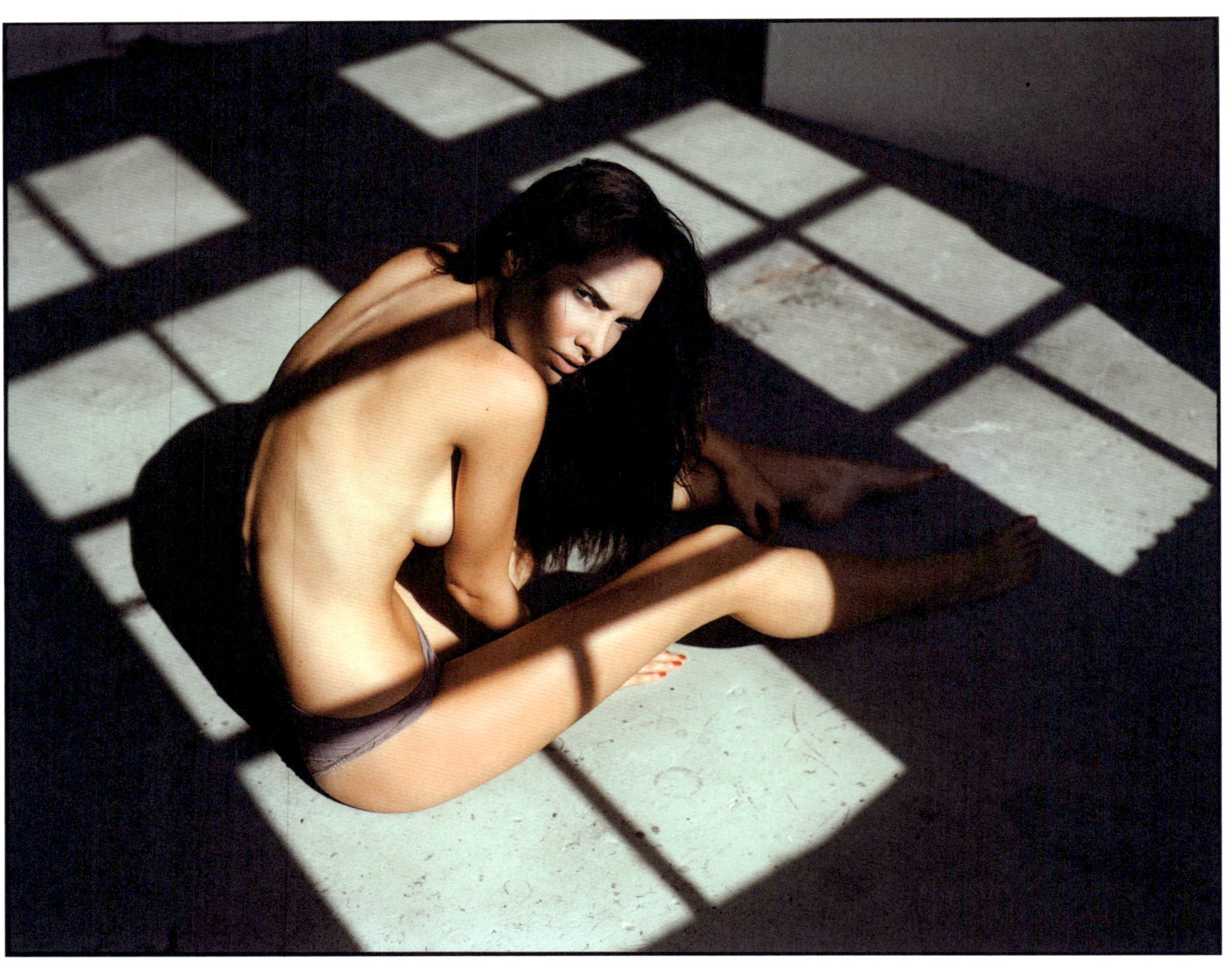

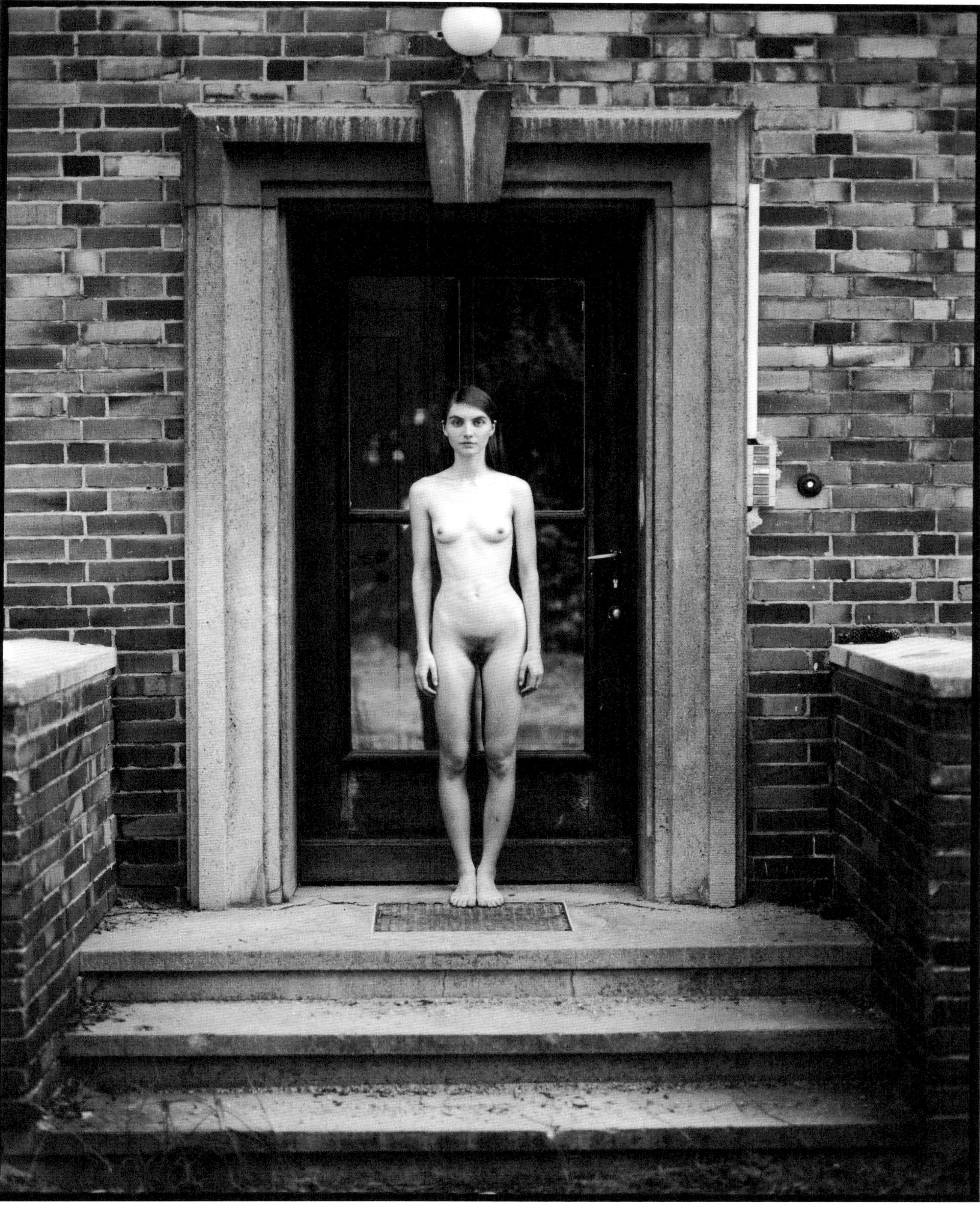

YULIA GORODINSKI

Interview by Angelina A. Rafii

Where do you take your inspiration, what influences your work?

Most of my images are shot spontaneously, so I am often inspired by a particular location or unexpected surroundings. Many times I find I come up with an idea for a photo on the spot. I am also inspired by the inherent aesthetics of common objects and how their juxtaposition within a particular setting can create an unusual visual dynamic. Sometimes it's simply a play of light that starts me thinking, but I am also influenced by the tone created in certain art-house films or music.

You have said that you do not show your nude photographs to your mother. Does that mean you still attach an aura of modesty around nudity? It is exposed yet remains private somehow?

My mother eventually discovered my nude photographs a year ago, when a courier arrived at our door to deliver a magazine where my images had been published. She told me how inappropriate it was and asked me not to do any nude photos in the future. Since then I have only done two nude images, neither of which she knows about. And yes, I do attach an aura of modesty around nudity, there are areas that I would never expose and I do try to avoid my images looking vulgar; I think my photos themed around melancholy exemplify this the best. There are some nude photographs that I have done in the past that I would never do now, so my approach has certainly changed over the last few years.

When did you first decide to explore nudity in your photographs and why?

There is no particular reason that I started taking nude photos. I got into photography in 2007 and I started taking nude photos in 2008. I remember I was in my room taking a photo against the wall and I decided to shoot semi nude. I liked the result and ever since continued shooting nudes. But I think the instigator was that I saw some nude photography online and was impressed by how, when it was of a high artistic quality, it surpassed mere pornography or eroticism, to become something that was naturally beautiful.

There is a sense of longing in a lot of your photographs. Can you explain?

At the time in which some of the images were taken I was longing for love and care, as well as greatly missing a particular special person. I was lonely and felt hurt and wasn't surprised to see this seep into my work. I think art often displays a sense of longing, of what was or might have been, but it is not always easy to find ways of expressing that. Sometimes the simplest compositions take the longest time to arrive at.

YULIAGORODINSKI.COM

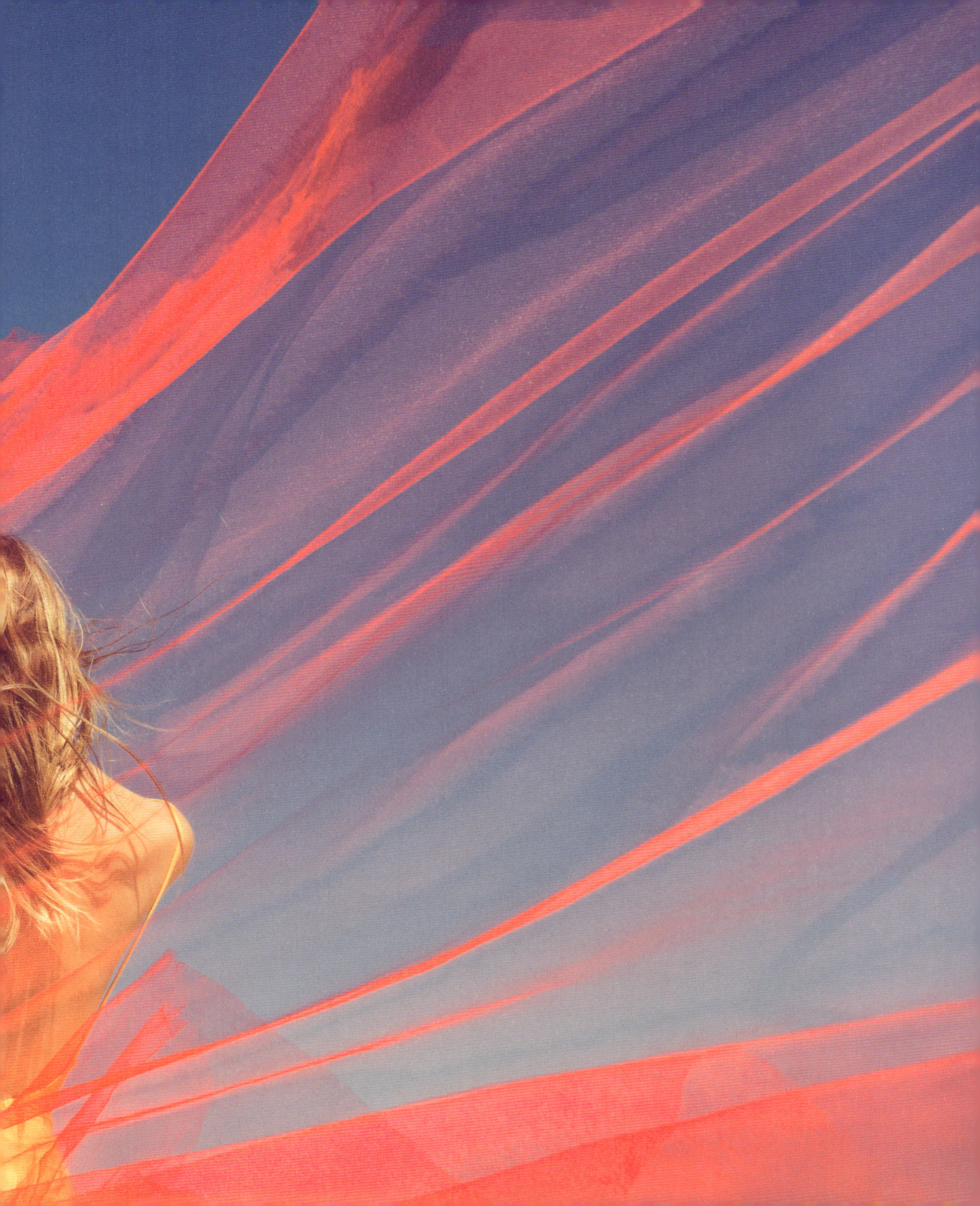

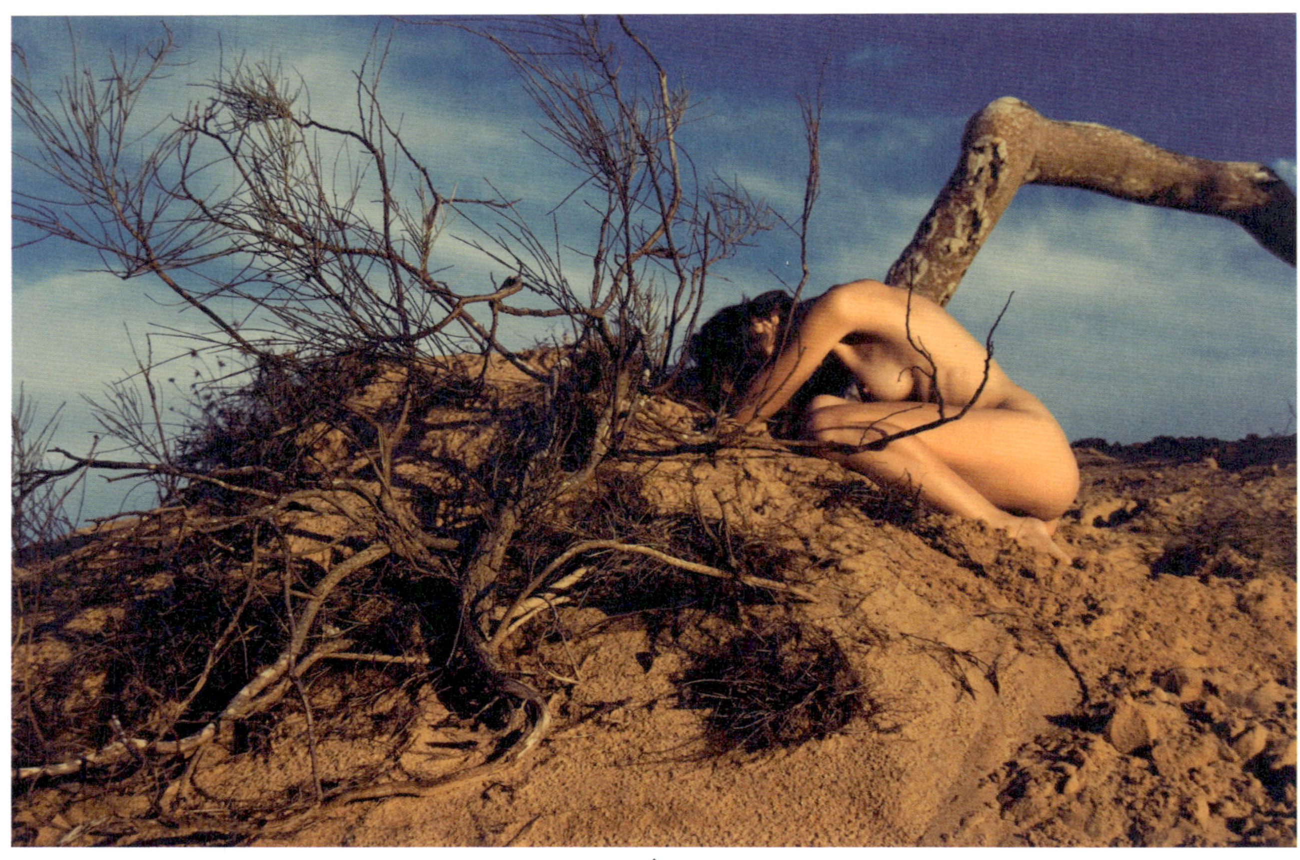

Exquisite pain

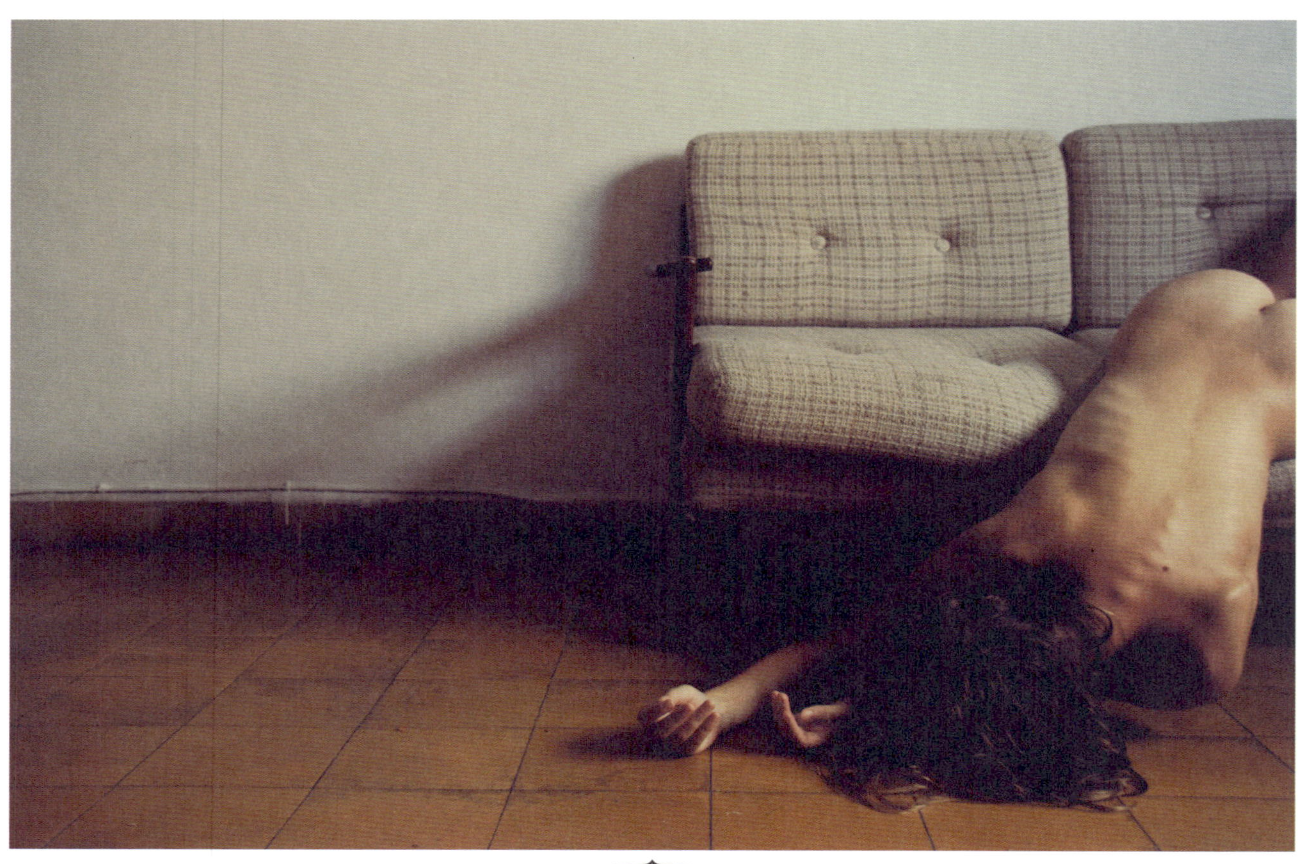

September 30th

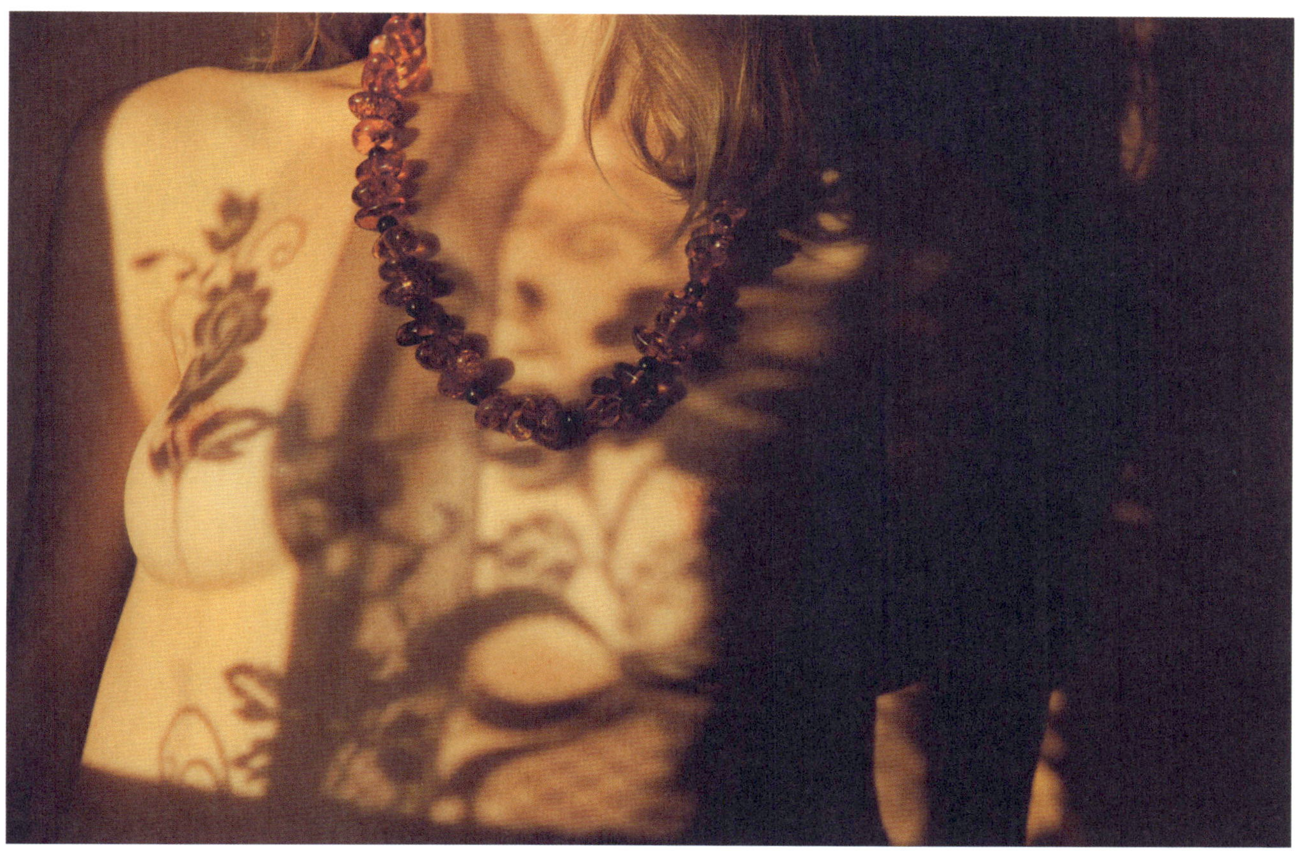

November 1st

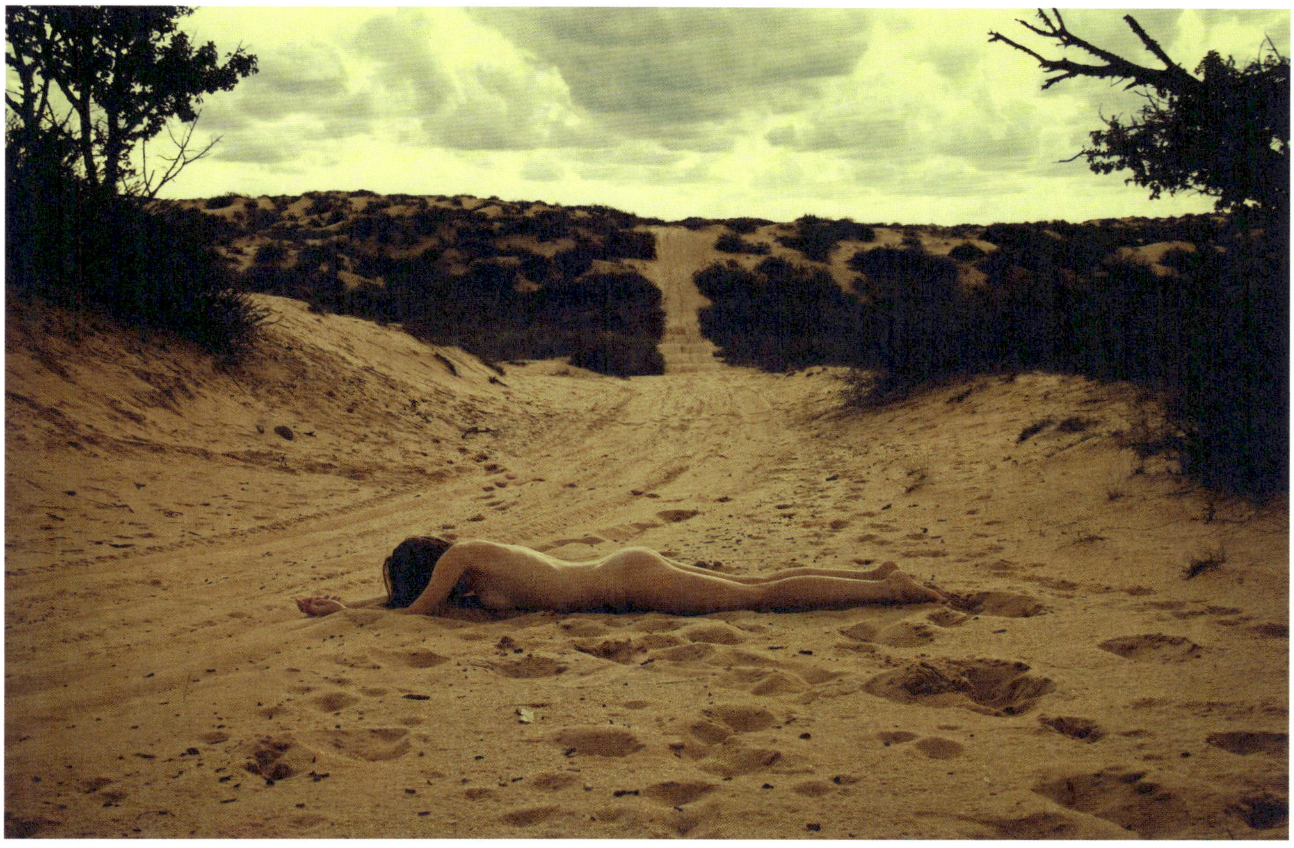

Abandoned

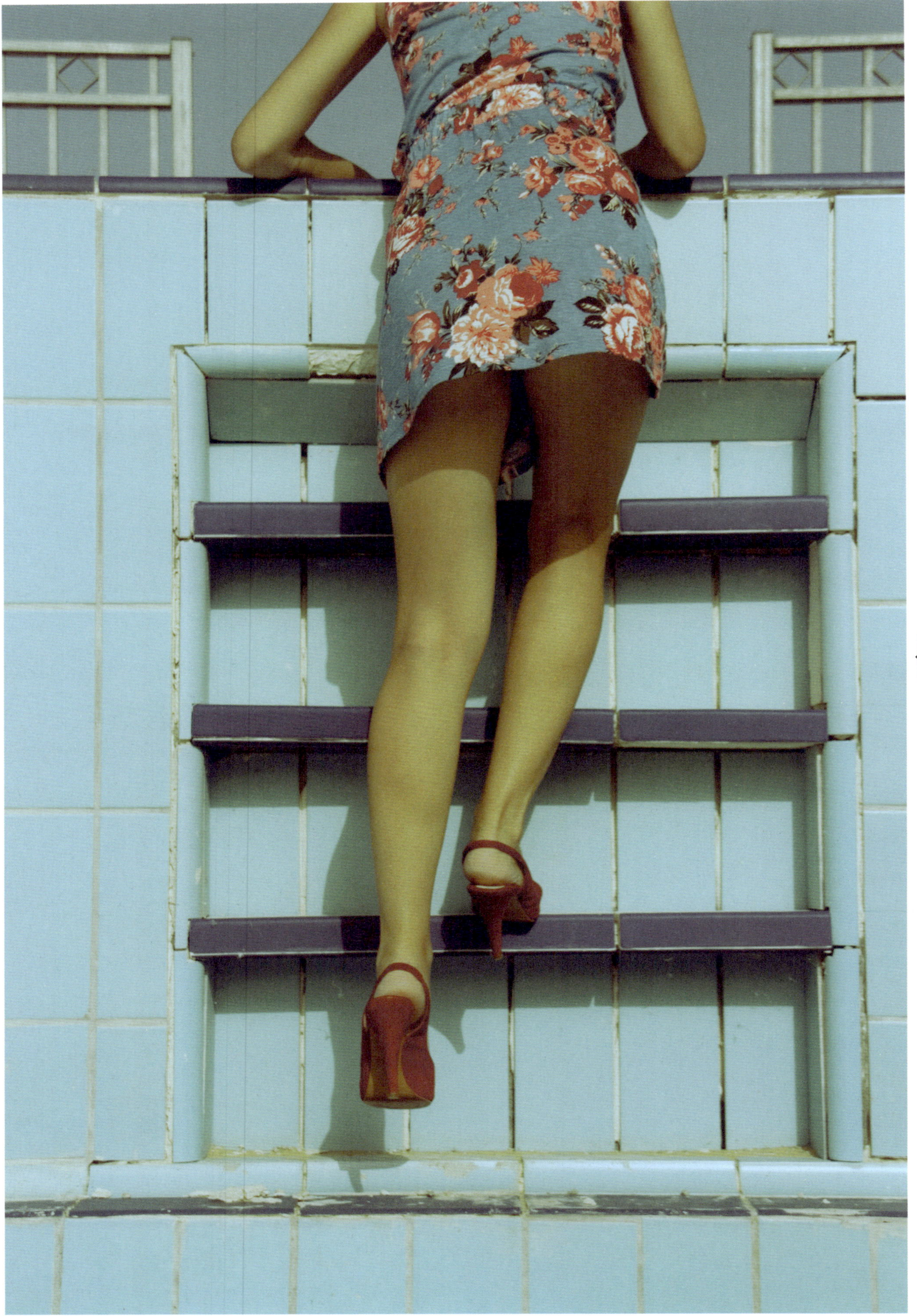

{ Escaping

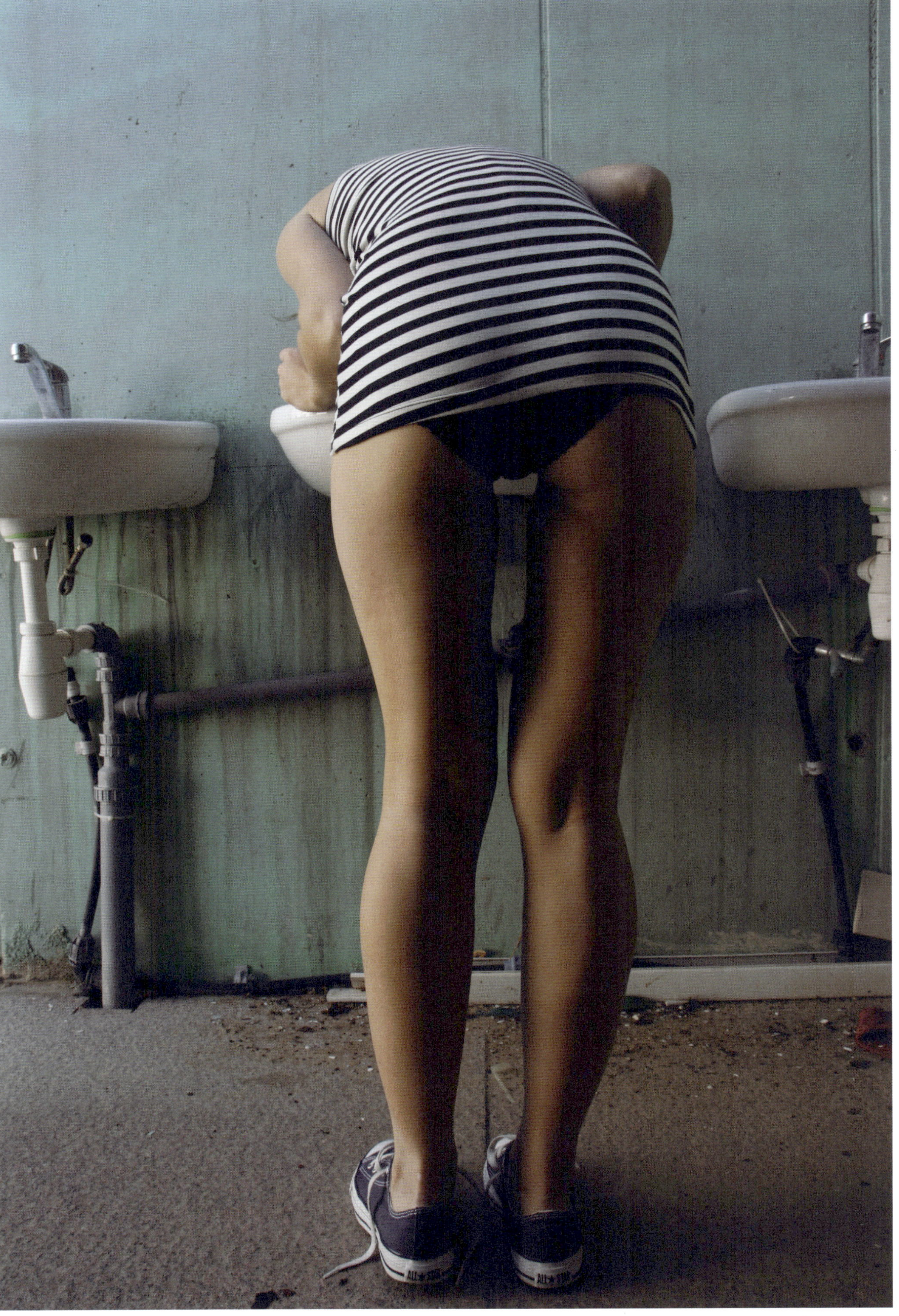

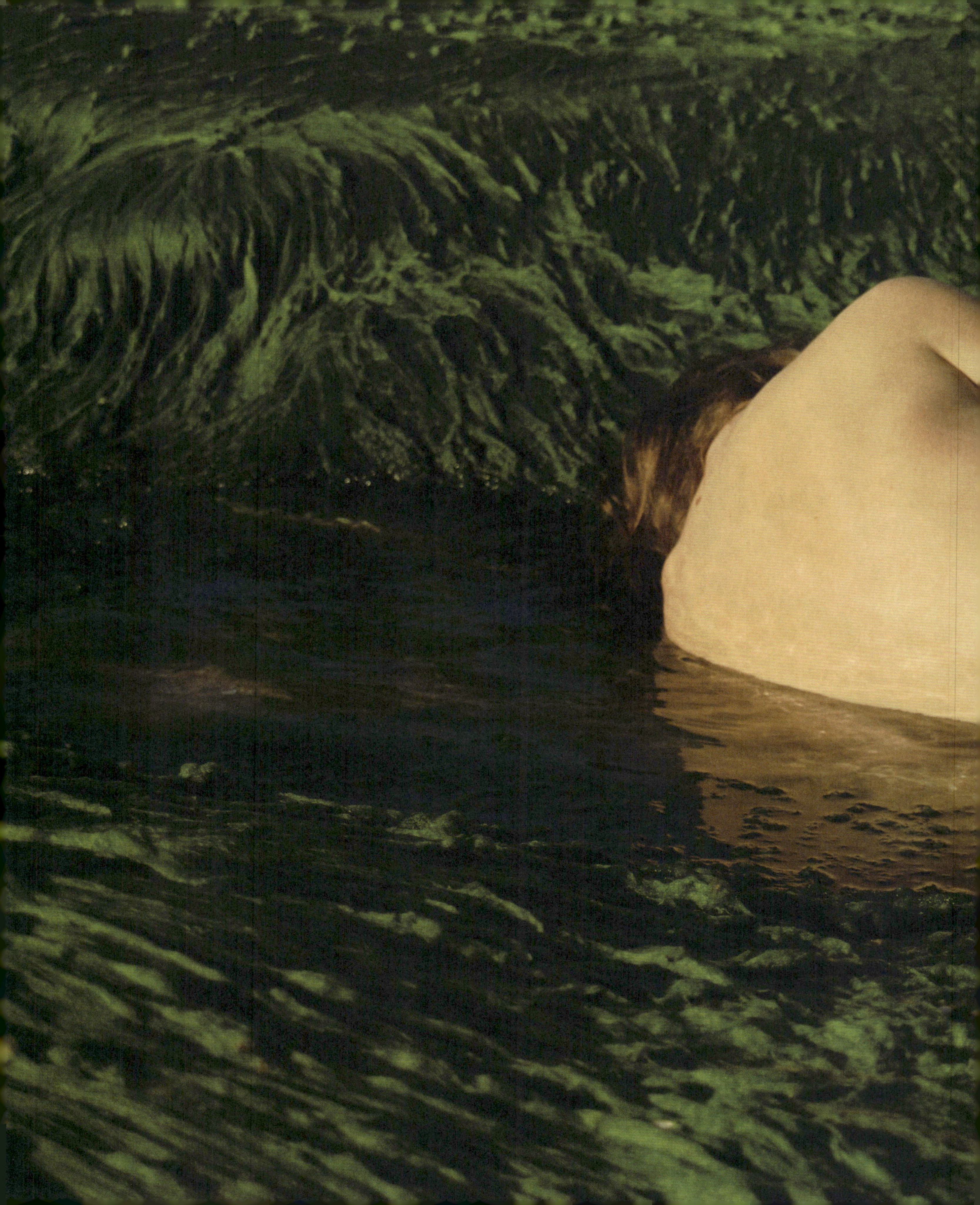

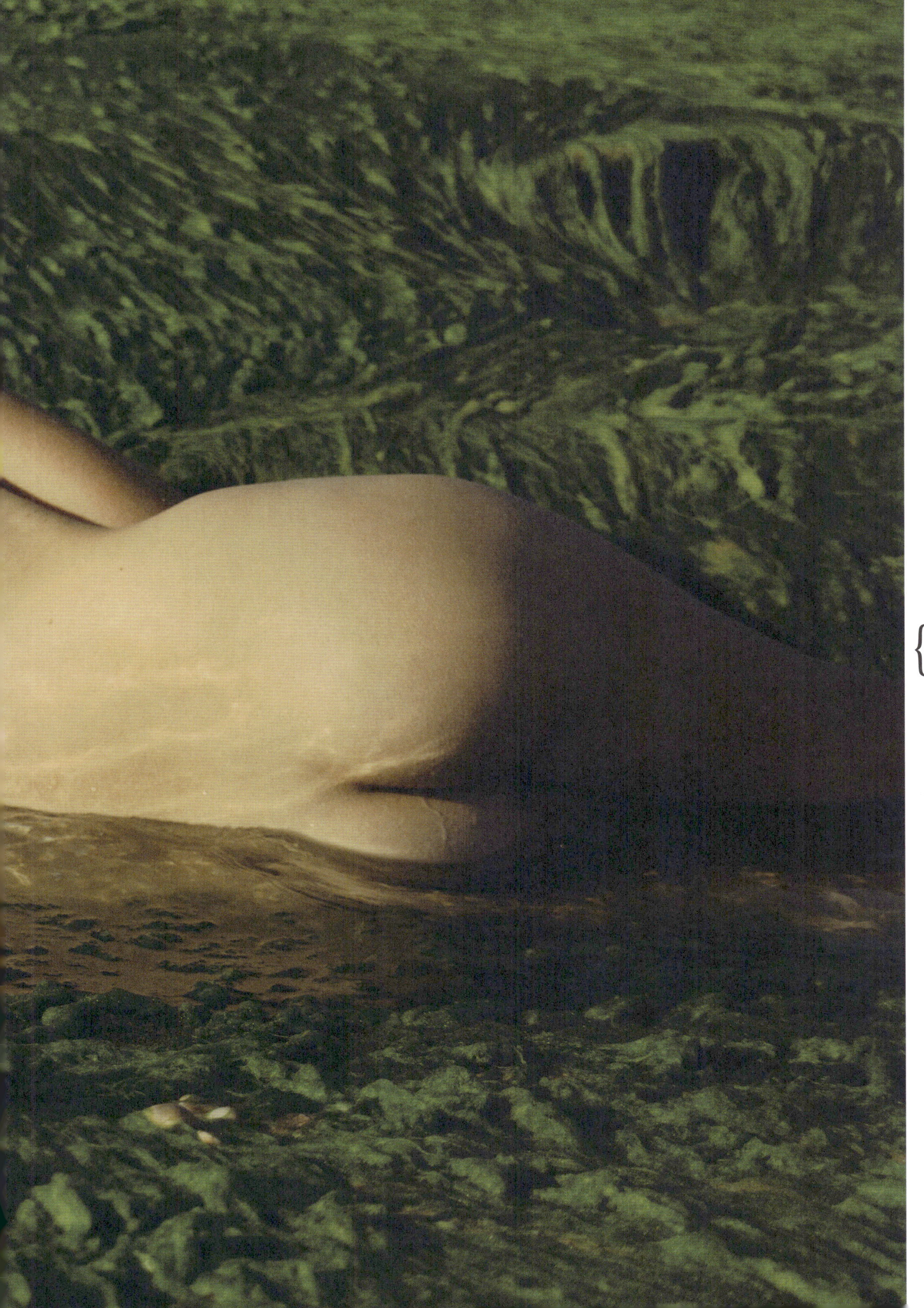

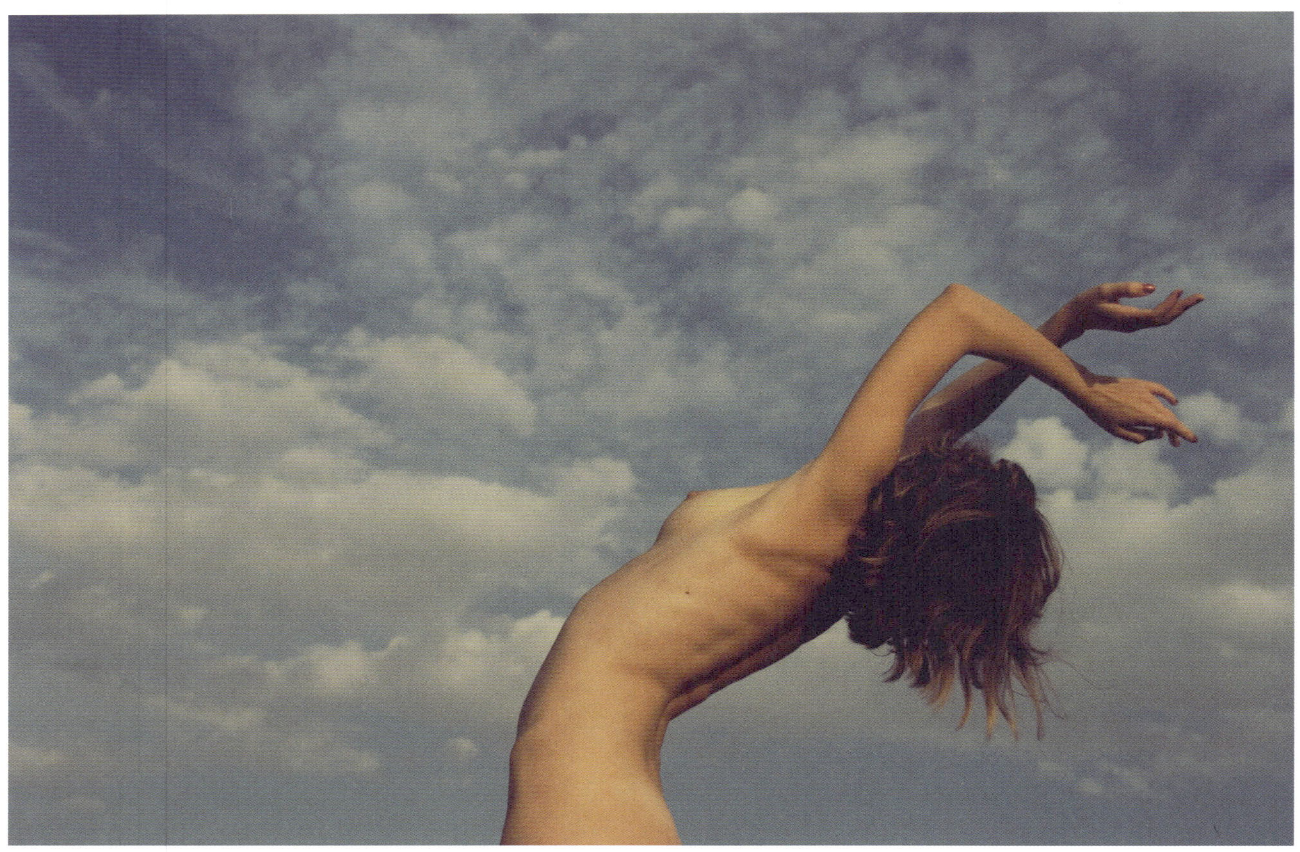

I to sky

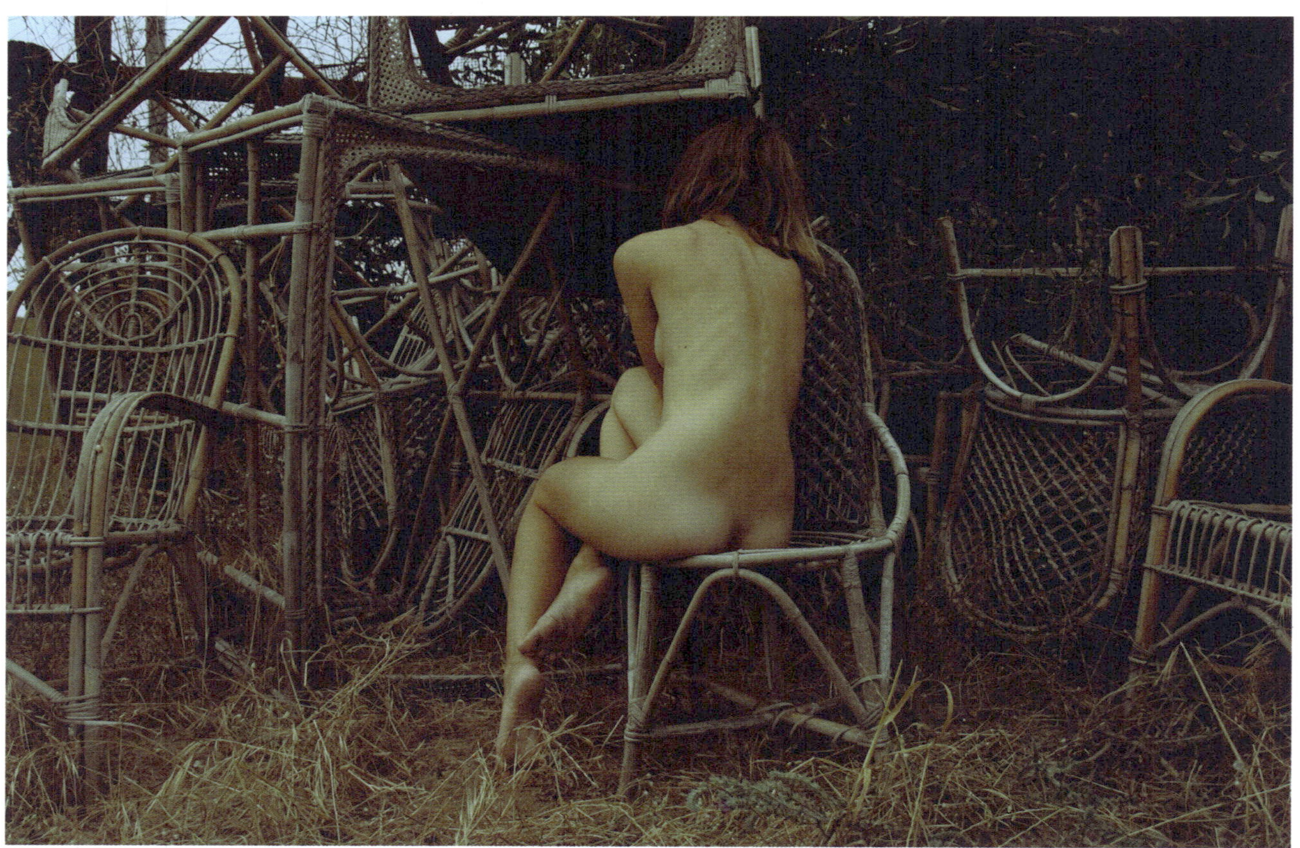

Solitude

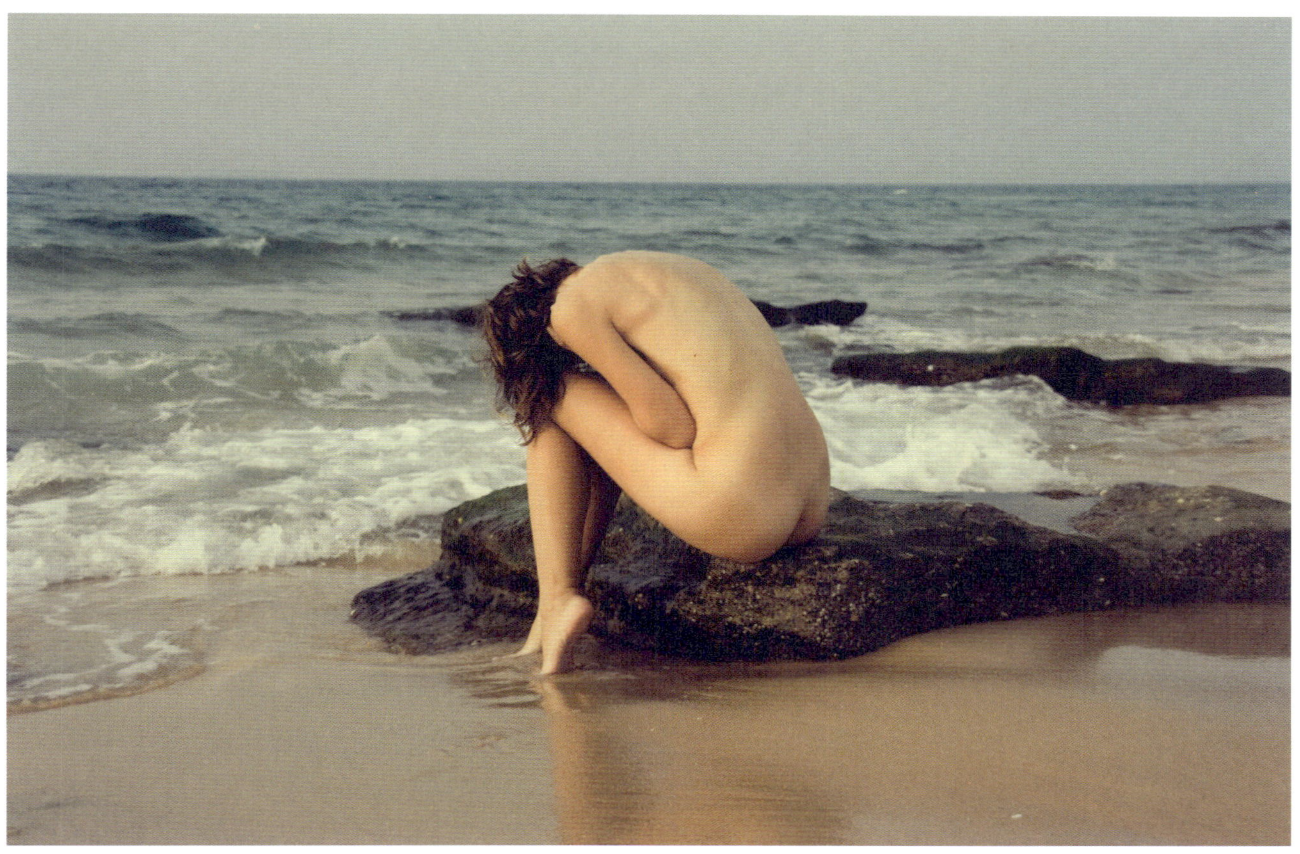

Drowning in loneliness

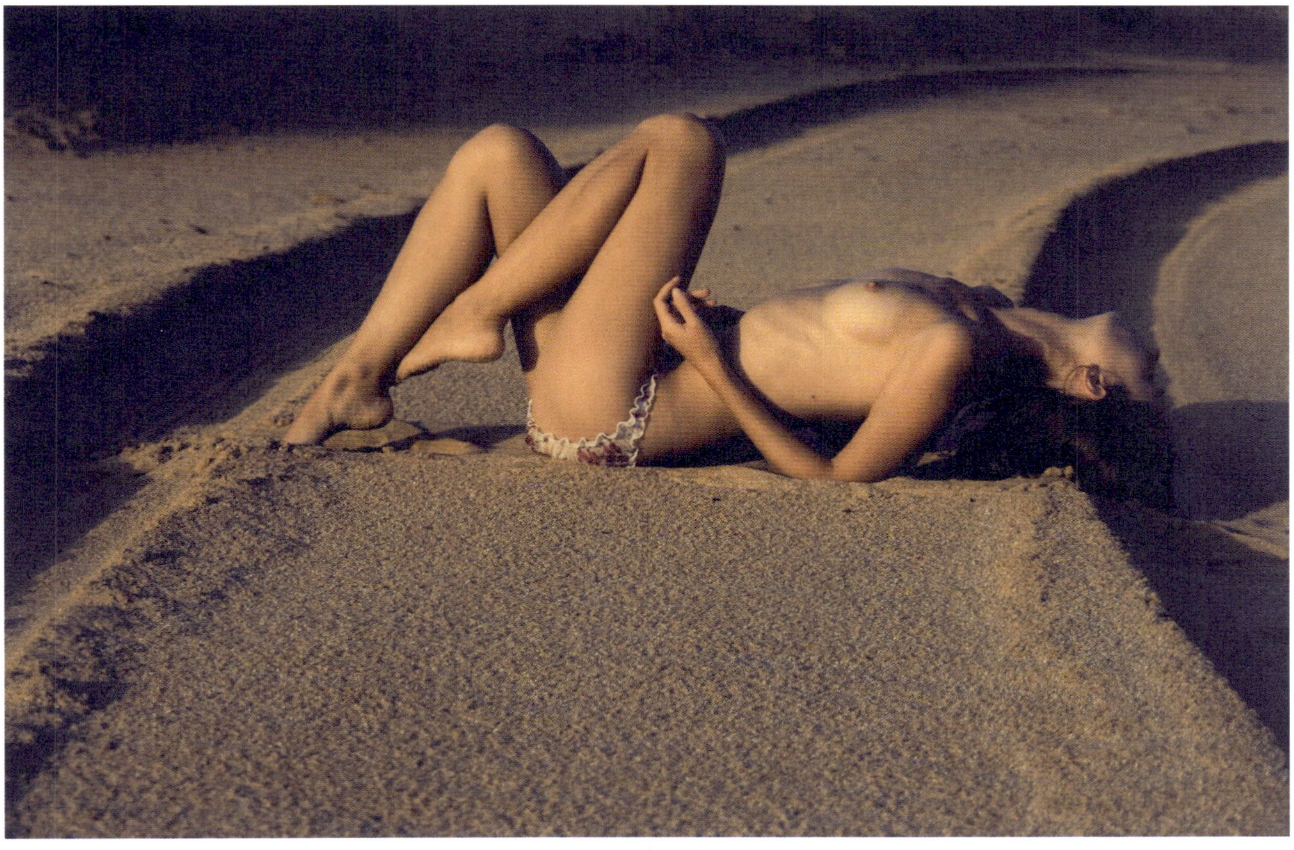

Suicidal tendencies

Call for entries

For the next issue we will continue our foray into the fascinating world of eroticism in media. Help us make it memorable by submitting ideas for erotic magazines and/or photographers, illustrators and artists who have delved into the subject matter.

Visit our website:
www.nicomagazine.com
or simply drop us an email:
office@maisonmoderne.lu